Seeking Legitimacy

Aili Mari Tripp explains why autocratic leaders in Morocco, Tunisia, and Algeria have embraced more extensive legal reforms of women's rights than their Middle Eastern counterparts. The study challenges existing accounts that rely primarily on religiosity to explain the adoption of women's rights in Muslim-majority countries.

Based on extensive fieldwork in Morocco, Algeria, and Tunisia and an original database of gender-based reforms in the Middle East and North Africa, this accessible study analyzes how women's rights are used both instrumentally and symbolically to advance the political goals of authoritarian regimes as leverage in attempts to sideline religious extremists. It shows how Islamist political parties in the Maghreb have been forced to dramatically change their positions on women's rights to ensure political survival. In an original contribution to the study of women's rights in the Middle East and North Africa, Tripp reveals how women's rights movements have capitalized on moments of political turmoil to defend and advance their cause.

AILI MARI TRIPP is Wangari Maathai Professor of Political Science and Gender & Women's Studies at the University of Wisconsin-Madison. She is author of several award-winning books, including *Women and Politics in Uganda* (2000), *Museveni's Uganda: Paradoxes of Power in a Hybrid Regime* (2010), and *Women and Power in Postconflict Africa* (2015).

Seeking Legitimacy

Why Arab Autocracies Adopt Women's Rights

AILI MARI TRIPP
University of Wisconsin, Madison

CAMBRIDGE
UNIVERSITY PRESS

CAMBRIDGE
UNIVERSITY PRESS

University Printing House, Cambridge CB2 8BS, United Kingdom

One Liberty Plaza, 20th Floor, New York, NY 10006, USA

477 Williamstown Road, Port Melbourne, VIC 3207, Australia

314–321, 3rd Floor, Plot 3, Splendor Forum, Jasola District Centre, New Delhi – 110025, India

79 Anson Road, #06–04/06, Singapore 079906

Cambridge University Press is part of the University of Cambridge.

It furthers the University's mission by disseminating knowledge in the pursuit of education, learning, and research at the highest international levels of excellence.

www.cambridge.org
Information on this title: www.cambridge.org/9781108425643
DOI: 10.1017/9781108348621

First published 2019

Printed in the United Kingdom by TJ International Ltd, Padstow Cornwall

A catalogue record for this publication is available from the British Library.

Library of Congress Cataloging-in-Publication Data
Names: Tripp, Aili Mari, author.
Title: Seeking legitimacy : why Arab autocracies adopt women's rights / Aili Mari Tripp.
Description: Cambridge, United Kingdom : Cambridge University Press, 2019. | Includes bibliographical references and index.
Identifiers: LCCN 2019010898| ISBN 9781108425643 (hardback : alk. paper) | ISBN 9781108442848 (paperback)
Subjects: LCSH: Women's rights – Africa, North. | Women's rights – Middle East.
Classification: LCC HQ1236.5.A355 T75 2019 | DDC 323.3/40961–dc23
LC record available at https://lccn.loc.gov/2019010898

ISBN 978-1-108-42564-3 Hardback
ISBN 978-1-108-44284-8 Paperback

To my fabulous, energetic, and artistic sisters
Eva Swantz and Lea Swantz

Contents

Figures

Maps

Tables

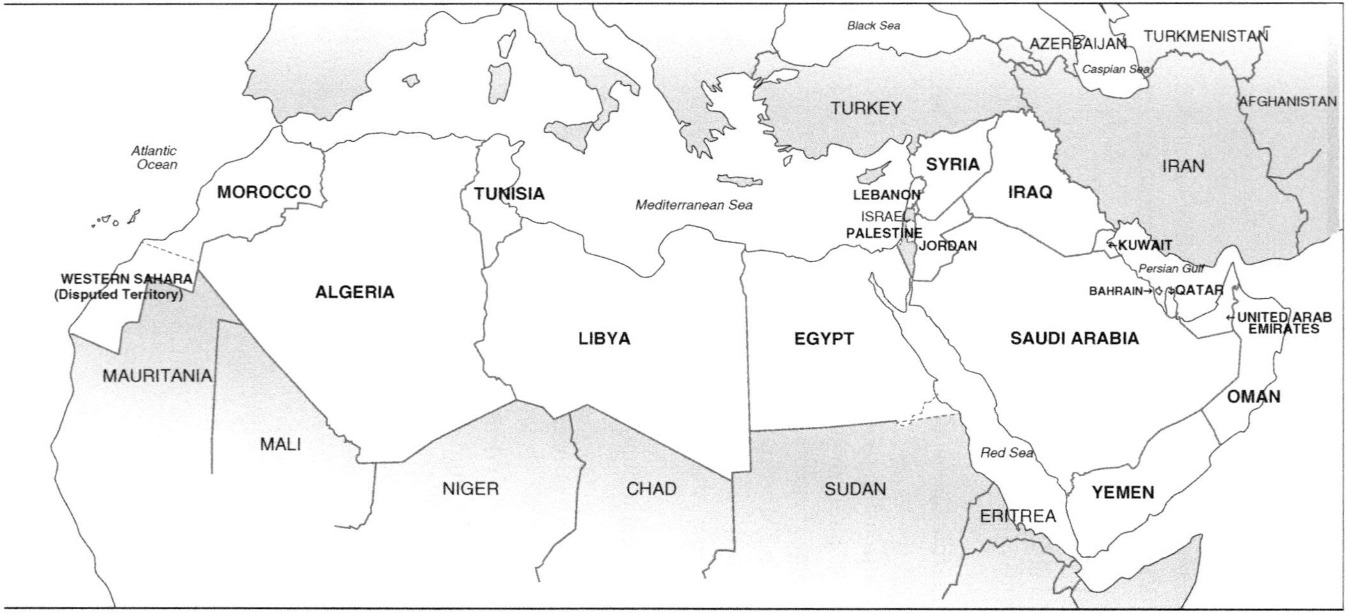

Map 0.1 Map of Arab Middle East and Maghreb
Credit: Eva Swantz

Acknowledgments

My first interaction with Moroccan women activists was in 1989 when I met Fatima Mernissi in Helsinki, Finland, at the United Nations University World Institute for Development Economics Research (WIDER), where I was conducting research. There she had organized a meeting of anti-fundamentalist activists from Algeria, Morocco, and Tunisia, and several of us at WIDER met with her and other conference participants who were to form the Collectif Maghreb-Égalité 95 in 1992. The group became a network that inspired many of the gender reforms described in this book. I remember being totally in awe of this tall brilliant woman in a long red dress, so poised and confident, with such depth of knowledge and insight. Later I read her books, including *Beyond the Veil* (1975) and *Islam and Democracy* (1992), and felt drawn to Morocco and the sense that there was something special about the country and its people. I wanted to know more. I embarked on a twenty-five-year detour and went on to research and write about women's movements in East and West Africa, but I always knew I would somehow find my way to the Maghreb (Algeria, Morocco, and Tunisia), having focused my graduate studies on the Middle East and North Africa. My instincts were right. Little did I know how much my scholarship and life would be affected by this encounter with Mernissi.

Writing this book has been an incredible personal and professional journey for me: sometimes challenging, but definitely more rewarding than I ever imagined when I first embarked on this project. I cannot even begin to express how grateful I am to all the people who helped me along the way. The generosity and warmth of people in the Maghreb was overwhelming at times.

This book could not have been written without the help of my amazing research assistants, including Sawsene Najjar, who was so much more than a research assistant and became like a second daughter to me. She helped me see Morocco through the eyes of a young woman. She accompanied me on our adventures, interviewing countless members of parliament, government officials, women's rights activists, and many others in a research project that took us as far as Dakhla and Laâyoune. Her diligence, dedication, kindness, and support were unsurpassed. Another big thank you goes to Nourredine Bessadi, who met me at the airport in Algiers with a bottle of water, a SIM card, money, and a taxi, knowing that everything would be closed on a Friday. This was the beginning of what turned out to be an enormously fruitful collaboration and one in which I learned so much, not just about Algeria, but also about Amazigh culture. One could not ask for a more supportive colleague. I am also enormously grateful to Raied Yahya and Kaden Paulson-Smith, who worked on a major database of legislative and constitutional reforms, and to Morgan Matthews, who proofread the manuscript. Yasmine Morchadi and Rim Touzzelti also provided invaluable research assistance.

I am so grateful to all the wonderful people who helped me navigate life in Morocco, especially colleagues at Al Akhawayn University in Ifrane, including Doris Gray, Michael Painter, Katja Žvan Elliott, Derek Elliott, Rabha El-Mahdi, Zaynab El Bernoussi, Lisa Schade Eckert, Kenza Oumlil, and Nizar Messari. I enjoyed the company of many other visiting scholars I met at Al Akhawayn, like Susan S. Davis, Michael Willis, Bozena Welborne, Jonathan Wyrtzen, and the many fascinating people who came through Ifrane to give talks. I cannot think of a better place to have been affiliated in Morocco than the Hillary Rodham Clinton Center for Women's Empowerment at Al Akhawayn University. Doris Gray, who directed the center, went way beyond the call of duty in offering me not only intellectual and logistical support, but hikes, dinners, and, above all, friendship. The conversations with this kindred spirit continued in Ouarzazate (Morocco), Berlin, and all the way to my home in Madison in the United States. And, of course, there is the Fulbright community who also sustained me in Morocco: many thanks to Jim Miller, Rosemary Peters, Anna Boots, Amelia Burke, and many others.

Special thanks go to my dear friend and Arabic and Darija teacher, Abdelghani El Kharroufi, who has been incredibly generous, patient, and kind. He makes me laugh like no one else can. I have learned so much more than Arabic from our weekly discussions, which still continue over Skype, as we discuss the news from Morocco and the region, Moroccan culture, our families, and life.

Thanks to those who gave me my start in Morocco, including the people at the Arabic Language Institute in Fez as well as Sanaa and Youssef Aït Ahmed and their daughter Hassna, the family I lived with in the old walled part of Rabat, known as the *medina*, during the summer of 2015. That summer I had so much fun with fellow *medina* dweller Salma Reghay, who spent hours with me walking the streets of Rabat and sitting in parks and coffee shops, chatting about everything under the sun. I will always treasure my friendship with Suzanne Baazet, who miraculously managed on occasion to escape her three little boys at home and busy work schedule to share stories about life in Morocco with me. Thanks for all the laughs, which I desperately needed!

Naima Korchi took me to the Saharan provinces of the disputed territory, Western Sahara, not once, but twice. It was a mind-blowing experience for me because of the extraordinary warmth and generosity of the Saharawi people I met and learning about the unique status of women in this society. I would never have had the access I had if she had not accompanied me and shared her contacts and knowledge of this challenging region. I cannot even begin to repay her for her generosity of time and spirit.

Many people helped me along the way and for that I am incredibly appreciative. They read my work, provided useful feedback, and helped me in so many other ways. These include Mohammed Masbah, Fatima Sadiqi, Souad Eddaouda, Zakia Salime, Rachid Toutouh, Hanane Darhour, Naima Benlarabi, Raja Rhouni, Achraf Guaad, Isabelle Werenfels, Najia Hichmine, and Mohammed Oubaha from Ouarzazate, Morocco, who "adopted" my husband and I as his parents. In the United States, I received assistance from Marwa Shalaby, Nevine El Nossery, Alice Kang, Nadav Shelef, Kathryn Hendley, Michael Schatzberg, Myra Marx Ferree, Amaney Jamal, Asifa Quraishi, Gretchen Bauer, Crawford Young, and many others. I know there are so many people I have not mentioned here, but I am no less grateful.

In Algeria, Robert Parks at the Centre d'études maghrébines en Algérie provided an institutional home and invaluable assistance, as did the Centre d'études diocésain Les Glycines. Thank you to all the people who enriched my stay in Algeria of whom I can only mention a few: Houda Ben Younes, Tahir Kilavuz, Jean-Baptiste Meyer, Elizabeth Perego, Alexandra Gueydan-Turek, and, of course,

Souryana Yassine and her colleagues, who so warmly welcomed me to Tizi Ouzou.

I must mention the American Academy in Berlin, where I spent the spring of 2017. There I was nourished not only by the wonderful food at the academy, but also by the beautiful surroundings and most of all by a brilliant community of scholars, including Jane Newman, Pamela Foa, Paul Guyer, Mark Pottinger, Kate Brown, Marjoleine Kars, and Sasha Bamford-Brown. There were many others I could equally thank. It was also lovely being so near my dear friend of fifty years, Ulrike Anderssen-Reuster, with whom I could reconnect.

Last but not least I have my family to thank. My sister Eva Swantz drew the beautiful maps in the book, as she has done for all my books, and for this I am enormously grateful. My husband Warren Tripp and son Lloyd Tripp visited me in Morocco and, together with other dear family members, cheered me on from afar. Lloyd, much to my delight, cooked wonderful plant-based meals for me as I was finalizing the manuscript and ran errands. It is this unconditional family love and support that one depends on the most and for which one is most grateful. The birth of our beautiful grandson, Nico (to my daughter Leila and Jason Bunge), during the process of writing the book was the highlight of this time period for our family.

Funding for this project came from multiple sources in addition to the American Academy in Berlin. I was also supported by the Fulbright Program, the Feminist Scholars Fellowship from the Center for Research on Gender and Women at the University of Wisconsin-Madison, by the College of Letters & Science and the Graduate School at UW-Madison, and by the Carnegie Corporation of New York. For all this support I am immeasurably grateful.

Thank you from the bottom of my heart to all who were part of my fantastic Maghrebian adventure! Until we meet again, شكرا جزيلا!

Abbreviations

AAMU	Association of Algerian Muslim Ulema
ADFM	Association démocratique des femmes du Maroc (Moroccan Women's Democratic Association)
AFEPEC	Association féministe pour l'épanouissement de la personne et l'exercice de la citoyenneté (Association for the Development of the Person and the Exercise of Citizenship)
AFTURD	Association des femmes tunisiennes pour la recherche sur le développement
APC	Assemblée populaire communale
APN	Assemblée populaire nationale (Algerian People's National Assembly)
ATFD	Association tunisienne des femmes démocrates
AU	African Union
AWI	al-ʿAdl wal-Ihsane
CEDAW	Convention on the Elimination of All Forms of Discrimination Against Women
CEWLA	Center for Egyptian Women's Legal Assistance
CIDDEF	Centre d'information et de documentation sur les droits de l'enfant et de la femme
FARD	Femmes algériennes revendiquant leurs droits
FGM	female genital mutilation
FIDH	Fédération internationale des droits de l'homme
FIS	The Front for Islamic Salvation
FLDDF	Fédération de la ligue démocratique des droits des femmes
FLN	Front de libération nationale (National Liberation Front)
IAF	Islamic Action Front
ICRAM	Initiative concertée pour le renforcement des acquis des marocaines (Government Plan for Equality)
LTDH	Ligue tunisienne de défense des droits de l'homme
MENA	Middle East and North Africa
MPDC	Mouvement populaire démocratique et constitutionnel

MSP	Movement of Society for Peace
MTI	Islamic Tendency Movement
NCW	National Council of Women
ODA	Overseas Development Assistance
PANIFD	Plan d'action national pour l'intégration de la femme au développement (Action Plan for the Integration of Women in Development)
PJD	Party of Justice and Development
PPS	Parti du progrès et du socialisme (Party of Progress and Socialism)
PSC	Personal Status Code
SCAF	Supreme Council of the Armed Forces
SIGI	Social Institutions and Gender Index
UAF	Union de l'action féminine
UNDP	United Nations Development Programme
UNFPA	United Nations Population Fund
UNFT	Union nationale de femmes tunisiennes (National Women's Union of Tunisia)
USFP	Union socialiste des forces populaires (Socialist Union of Popular Forces)
WLUML	Women Living under Muslim Laws

Introduction

The Moroccan king Mohammed VI announced in 2018 that, in his capacity as the commander of the faithful, he was allowing women to become an *'adoul* (notary), a position which previously had been the domain solely of men. The *'adoul* draws up marriage contracts, divorce settlements, and other certificates; approves wills; and adjudicates inheritance. The Supreme Scientific Council, the highest religious authority in Morocco, said that the decision was based on legal provisions allowed by the Maliki School of Islamic jurisprudence, which is dominant in Morocco. Women and women's rights activists welcomed this reform in a country where women already serve as judges, lawyers, and expert witnesses in large numbers. Nevertheless, a spirited debate ensued in social media and the traditional media, with some opposing the decision, citing women's natural forgetfulness and other mental deficiencies, their fragility, and temperament. Others cited the Qur'an to argue that women's testimony has half the value of men's and for this reason they could not serve in such a capacity.

Debates about women's abilities were revived and for one commentator, Ihsane Elidrissi Elhassani, this brought back a sense of déjà vu over the debates regarding the Personal Status Code (PSC) reforms, the first woman member of parliament, the first woman minister, and the first women in the police force. She argued that in all these cases, women were being put on trial with the sole aim of trying to prove their inferiority. "Forgetfulness is debated as if we were still stuck in the oral tradition, and the agreement of the parties cannot be recorded in writing." One noted scholar in a TV appearance tried to explain that men had a gland in their brain which was absent in women, allowing men to be able to speak, listen, and remember information all at the same time. When questioned, the male scholar was forced to admit, without even a hint of irony, that he had forgotten the name of the gland (Elhassani 2018).

Policy reforms, like allowing women to become *ʿadoul*s, serve as carefully choreographed symbolic enactments by the authorities to signal a particular stance on gender equality, modernization, and religious authority. The message is not lost on those for whom it is intended. However, each audience receives the same message differently, some as a sign of expanding women's rights, while for others the latter are seen as a challenge to an older order and way of life.

In the Middle East and North Africa, women, their bodies, and women's rights often proxy for key positions on religion, politics, morality, and modernity. They are a line in the sand or a litmus test for rulers in Arab countries, pitting conservative Islamists of various stripes against secularists and feminists, and juxtaposing modernizers against those who wish to preserve the status quo or even take society back to the time of the Prophet Mohammed. It is a shifting line as Islamists of various orientations, particularly those represented in parliament, have come to defend certain women's rights in more recent years in countries like Morocco, where they control the government (*Aujourd'hui Le Maroc* 2017). Islamists traditionally have been associated with attitudes that support an Islamic state, the implementation of *shariʿa* (Islamic) law, preferences for religious over secular political parties, support for clerical involvement in politics, and the view that piety should be a characteristic of politicians (Gorman 2017).

Few issues are as potent as women's rights or have drawn such large crowds into the streets in the Maghreb (Morocco, Tunisia, and Algeria), both for and against. Half a million members of Islamist groups demonstrated in 2000 against the proposed PSC reforms in Morocco. In Algeria, the issue of women's rights and the Arabization of education were the two issues that galvanized the Islamists in the 1990s. Women were among the most prominent targets of violent attacks by Islamist extremists during Algeria's Black Decade of conflict (1991–2002): these were women who taught in schools, who drove cars, who worked, or who refused to veil. During the debates over a new constitution in Tunisia in 2014, thousands of Tunisian men and women protested the Islamic Ennahda party's vision of gender equality rooted in complementarity (separate but equal roles for men and women), demanding parity instead. These are but a few examples of the ways in which women's rights have taken center stage in the Maghreb and have been key to the major political and societal conflicts of the day.

One indication of the centrality of women's rights is the intense interest shown by men in discussing these topics. I myself was curious why, in North Africa, conferences and workshops on women's rights consistently involved large numbers of men of all ages, sometimes even half of the participants. Men were as engaged as women in these topics, and their discourses were earnest, probing, and thoughtful. This is very different than what one finds in the United States, where such conferences have primarily been the domain of women, especially academic events. Perhaps this difference can be explained by the intense interest women's rights holds for both women and men alike in the Maghreb. The symbolism they hold extends well beyond the actual rights themselves and they proxy for a range of ideas from modernity to progress, nationalism, democracy, and secularism.

For societies in which women have been historically excluded from public space by being enclosed in their homes and courtyards, by being veiled, or by being excluded from certain occupations, sports, and leisure activities, the advancement of women's rights can be dramatic, explosive, and transformative at so many levels. Women's rights reflect the contours of key debates in the Maghreb today about the political future of the region. As much as these are issues that pit people against one another, they are also points of convergence, of curiosity, and of dialogue. And that is what makes the subject of women's rights in North Africa so critical to understanding politics in the region, especially at a time when these rights are gaining ground.

Women's rights are also sometimes linked to a growing trend of Amazigh (Berber) activism in the Maghreb that is pushing back against conservative and especially extremist elements, in what some are calling a post-Islamist era in the Maghreb (Charef 2017). Because of the negative connotations associated with the term "Berber" in the Maghreb, I use the terms Amazigh (singular) and Imazighen (plural) as well as Tamazight (the language grouping) associated with the people, who encompass many diverse tribes and peoples. Post-Islamist sentiment seeks to combine religion with rights, liberty, and dogmatism. It recognizes pluralism of thought and secular approaches or what some call Islamic liberalism. Perhaps one might consider it a form of pragmatism (El Haitami 2012).

Central Questions

The expansion of democracy and women's rights has historically been linked, as evident in cross-national studies (Inglehart and Norris 2003, Htun and Weldon 2018, Tripp 2013). However, many of the dynamics that hold globally become less salient when regional factors are taken into account and when one looks at a variety of women's rights measures. For example, democracy falls out of the models when one looks at the factors that have advanced female legislative representation in Africa (Hughes and Tripp 2015, Tripp and Kang 2008). In Africa, democratic countries are as likely as nondemocratic countries to adopt gender quotas, and they are as likely to have higher rates of women in parliament. In the Middle East and North Africa (MENA) region, various women's rights have been adopted in some authoritarian countries and less so in others. This book examines why this is the case by comparing the Maghreb with the Middle East.

The adoption of women's rights provisions in nondemocratic countries, when looked at from a regional perspective, challenges numerous assumptions developed with respect to Western countries about how and why women's rights are adopted. This is because the mechanisms that explain women's representation in terms of labor force participation and the expansion of the welfare state, which are linked to the spread of democracy and cultural change in Europe, simply are not as important in countries where women are primarily engaged in agricultural production, in the informal economy, or working in the home. Instead, the role of women's movements and top-down institutional reforms driven by the political elite feature as more significant factors in shaping policy in parts of the world like the Maghreb.

Scholars sometimes dismiss such reforms in authoritarian or nondemocratic countries, perhaps regarding them as window dressing, or as carrots to appease women's rights activists, adopted by autocrats who do not have any intention or capacity to enforce women's rights legal reforms. To be sure, these policies often arise out of such cynical motivations. But often there are other considerations involved. If they were of no import, there would be little debate over them. Yet, one finds some of the fiercest struggles over the content of such reforms. This study takes a closer look at the motivations of authoritarian leaders in making these legal reforms.

These observations lead us to some key questions explored in this book: Why do authoritarian or semi-authoritarian states adopt women's rights policies, even when there may not be popular pressures to do so? Which laws are they more likely to adopt? Why are political and economic laws relating to women easier to reform than family law? Why do leaders adopt women's rights legislation when it would be easier to ignore it? What are the consequences for feminists and women's rights activists when authoritarian states take the initiative to advance women's rights? Does it help or hurt activists' causes, especially when women's own interests are not reflected as central to the policy change? What are the consequences for women's rights and for women themselves? When does the advancement of women's rights represent genuine change in authoritarian contexts and when does it serve to perpetuate and legitimize existing authoritarian regimes? Why do some Arab and Muslim societies adopt more women's rights legal reforms than others?

This book explores some of the possible reasons women's rights policies have been adopted in the Maghreb and Middle East: the intention of improving the quality of life for women and men and children; as a means of strengthening the economy and modernizing society; as a way to promote an image of their societies to the world as modernizing, while maintaining Islamic values; as a way of distinguishing themselves from the Islamist opposition, particularly extremists; as a way of garnering the political support and votes of women; as a response to popular pressures from women's rights and civil society activists; to keep up with the requirements of international treaties like the Convention on the Elimination of All Forms of Discrimination Against Women (CEDAW); and sometimes to appease donors. In some autocratic countries, leaders have sought to promote women's rights as a way of extending patronage to women to foster loyalty and in some leftist-led countries they have promoted women's rights as an expression of ideological commitment to egalitarianism.

This book looks at the consequences of the adoption of policies under authoritarian rule. Are they, for example, deployed to divert attention from other undemocratic goals? After the 1994 genocide in Rwanda, the country's president, Paul Kagame, encouraged women to enter public office. Women also fought hard for their rights. The number of female legislators jumped from 4 percent in November of 1994 to 61 percent in 2018. Numerous pro-women's rights laws were passed and other measures were taken to advance the status of women. However, these and other policies allowed the Kagame regime to hide behind the smokescreen of women's rights to win positive international acclaim and visibility at a time when their human rights violations and the politicization of ethnicity were increasingly being called into question.

Sometimes, if women's rights are implemented in an authoritarian manner by decree and without a mandate of popular support, they may not be sustained or they may become a part of a ping-pong game, adopted and rejected as part of a tussle between successive leaders. This happened in Egypt under Nasser, Sadat, Mubarak, and Sisi. Women's rights activists may find their reputations tarnished if they are seen to ally themselves too closely with an autocratic regime, even when they themselves have suffered as targets of the regime, as was the case under Ben Ali's rule in Tunisia. Leaders may respond to competing pressures, as the Algerian leaders did in 1984 when they adopted a regressive Family Code to appease the Islamists. This devastated women's rights leaders, who had been pressing for a more progressive code. Authorities use women's rights for their own purposes, but that does not mean women's rights activists have no influence; nor does it mean that women cannot benefit from these rights, even in limited ways. This book shows how there are multiple and often competing agendas involved in the struggles over women's rights.

There are some ways in which the adoption of women's rights appears to be similar in democratic and nondemocratic contexts. As in democracies, the laws in autocratic countries can be the product of societal pressure and negotiations between various societal coalitions (Kang 2015). The adoption of women's rights can serve utilitarian purposes that have little to do with women themselves in both contexts. The policies in democracies and autocracies may be adopted without much societal pressure, or they may be products of massive protest movements. As one finds in democracies, policies in autocracies are uneven, with progress in some areas and not in others. There can also be huge inconsistencies between the constitution and laws, between laws themselves, between areas of legislation and between laws and their enforcement. Within both types of regime, conservative parties may adopt women's rights as it becomes a useful way to gain votes.

Women's rights can also serve nationalist goals in democracies to promote a nation as an exemplar to others. Improving the conditions under which women work – through better day care, parental leave, women's training, and other such provisions – makes it possible to expand the workforce to "narrow future age dependency rates and reduce associated financial pressures" (Esping-Anderson et al. 2002, 24). According to such utilitarian arguments, the employment of women taps into the talent of a useful and educated workforce and helps curb social exclusion and poverty.

In Europe today, far-right extremist parties, like Marine Le Pen's National Rally, are increasingly attacking liberals for not being sufficiently concerned about women's rights. Le Pen argues they have ignored the patriarchal spread of Islam by supporting immigrants. She claims: "I am scared that the migrant crisis signals the beginning of the end of women's rights" (Sengupta 2017). The European far right has long seized on the *hijab* (head covering) as a symbol of patriarchy. More recently, many of them have said that attacks on gays and women in Muslim enclaves in Europe are evidence of the Islamic threat to European values. In a book focusing on contemporary France, Italy, and the Netherlands, Sara R. Farris (2017) labels this exploitation and co-optation of feminist themes by anti-Islamic and xenophobic campaigns as "femonationalism." She shows how right-wing nationalist parties use gender equality to justify their racism by characterizing Muslim men as dangerous to Western societies and as oppressors of women. Thus, even within democracies, women's rights are used for diverse political and policy purposes that extend beyond women's rights themselves.

This book explores the overarching question of why authoritarian regimes adopt women's rights with the recognition that both the question and the answer can only be context-specific. To that end, I ask why Morocco, Tunisia, and Algeria have converged in their adoption of women's rights legal reforms? Why do they differ from most of their neighbors in the Arab Middle East, with whom they share a religion, language, and historical rulers, adopting more women's rights reforms earlier and at a faster pace? The book hypothesizes that authoritarian leaders in the Maghreb have used women's rights to push back against the expansion of Salafi and other religious conservative tendencies internally. They also have used women's rights to serve other instrumental purposes, such as creating a modernizing image of their societies. At certain critical junctures of changes in power or social upheaval, women's movements have been able to push for reform or resist backsliding and thus they have been able to effect change. To understand how this happened and why women's rights have been so central to the major developments in the region, I argue that one has to also take into consideration not only the events that occurred, regional dynamics, but also the symbolic dimensions of politics, which is the battlefield upon which many of the struggles were enacted.

Region Matters

To date, most studies in the Maghreb, with some important exceptions, have primarily looked at developments within individual countries around specific gender-related issues. They have tended not to ask broad comparative questions relating to women's rights. Important individual-country studies have dealt with various aspects of the themes touched on in this book. They have, for example, focused on the adoption of quotas in Morocco (Darhour and Dahlerup 2013, Sater 2012), Tunisia (Voorhoeven 2013), and Algeria (Benzenine 2013). They have also examined the PSC in Morocco (Cavatorta and Dalmasso 2009, Sadiqi and Ennaji 2006) and in Algeria (Bras 2007), and constitutional changes in Tunisia (Mersch 2014). Others have focused on the relationship between secular feminists and Islamists (Salime 2011, Gray 2013), and on women's movements in Morocco (Belarbi 2012, Salime 2011), Algeria (Allalou 2009), and Tunisia (Labidi 2017). While these studies are invaluable and I rely heavily on them, they are not situated in a comparative perspective that looks at commonalities and differences across cases in the context of regional dynamics, nor do they look at the overall patterns in legislative and constitutional reforms that would allow for greater generalizability, as this book seeks to do.

Cross-national studies on a global scale, on the other hand, have also provided important insights, but they tend to overgeneralize and do not allow for the kind of regional specificity that would help explain variance within the MENA region. Studies of this type have often focused on explaining female legislative representation globally but overlook the context of regional dynamics. For example, in Western Europe, the adoption of gender quotas is not always correlated with increased female representation as it is in Africa or the Middle East. Where quotas have been introduced in Western Europe, this has often happened after women have already attained 20–30 percent of parliamentary seats (Dahlerup 2006, Rosen 2012). According to the Inter-Parliamentary Union data, women in European countries with quotas hold, on average, 33 percent of the legislative seats, which is the same rate as women in countries without quotas. However, in Africa, countries with quotas have on average 30 percent women in legislative seats compared to 15.7 percent in countries without quotas. The gap is even larger in the MENA region: women hold 20 percent of the legislative seats in MENA countries with quotas and 5 percent in countries without.

Some cross-national studies have argued that religious attitudes influence gender equality, but at a level of generality that does not attempt to explain differences within regions (for example, Inglehart and Norris 2003, Kenworthy and Malami 1999, Alexander and Welzel 2011). In fact, it is not uncommon to find that Muslim countries, from Morocco to Somalia, Albania, Syria, Iran, and Indonesia, are treated as a monolithic entity in some of the literature. I am of the view that generally it is not possible to speak meaningfully about "the Muslim world" any more than it makes sense to speak of a "Christian world." Regardless of different political systems, cultures, languages, economies, and ideologies, 2 billion people in dozens of countries spanning the globe from the Americas to China become swallowed into an entity called the "Muslim world." This is not to say that there are no commonalities or shared global experiences (such as the spread of conservative Islam); nor should one deny the idea of the Muslim *ummah* (community). Rather, it appears that such categories prevent us from making meaningful social scientific comparisons and developing middle-range theories that help untangle complex realities.

When it comes to women's rights, one finds enormous variation among predominantly Muslim countries. For example, Senegal, which is overwhelmingly Muslim, has some of the highest rates of female legislative representation in the world with women holding 43 percent of the parliamentary seats, while Yemen has 0 percent, Oman 1.2 percent, and Kuwait 3.1 percent, among the lowest in the world. Muslim countries were among the first in Africa to adopt gender quotas to increase women's political representation. They were also among the first in Africa to adopt constitutional reforms regarding women's rights.

Much also depends on the issues at stake. In Egypt, for example, Muslims are more likely than Copts (who make up 10–20 percent of the population) to say that ensuring gender equality in the constitution is very important and to strongly agree that women should be allowed to work outside the home (Arab Barometer 2013). On other measures, like support for women in politics, Muslims are less supportive than Copts. In Lebanon, where Christians make up 40 percent of the population and Muslims constitute up to 54 percent, fifteen separate personal status laws regulate family law for Christian, Muslim, Druze, and Jewish confessional communities, all of which are administered by separate religious courts. In all sects, women are treated worse than men when it comes to divorce and child custody (Fakih and Braunschweiger 2015). This has led many gender scholars in the region to focus on patriarchy rather than religion, while at the same time recognizing the centrality of religion in shaping women's rights (Sadiqi and Ennaji 2011). Thus, the very fact that there is so much variance within the region, as well as change, suggests that we need to interrogate more carefully the many political factors that account for female subordination and the ways in which they interact with one another.

By focusing on regions and subregions, this book attempts to disabuse the reader of easily made generalizations about women's rights in the predominantly Muslim and Arab MENA region that suggest that there is something intrinsic about Islam that prevents progress in women's rights. This is not to deny that religion or, more specifically, religiosity is irrelevant to women's rights, but rather to argue for more contextualized explanations that account for political contestation.

In fact, my interest in variance between countries with large or majority Muslim populations started south of the Sahara in Tanzania, where I lived for fourteen years and where I carried out fieldwork for my dissertation and later for other projects. In Tanzania, where the Muslim and Christian populations are evenly divided, the backbone of the independence movement was led by Bibi Titi and a large number of other Muslim women, who went door-to-door to recruit people into the Tanganyika African National Union. Bibi Titi toured the country, giving fiery speeches demanding independence. She was as important a figure in the nationalist movement as Julius Nyerere, the country's first president (Geiger 1987). Muslim women supported independence because they wanted, among other things, more educational opportunities. The coastal Muslim women who helped galvanize the independence movement were largely from matrilineal societies, where they had relatively more freedom than others.

When the new women's movement emerged in the 1990s, it also had its start with a Muslim-led women's media organization. Moreover, Muslim women are more likely than Christians to support women's leadership in politics, according to the Afrobarometer Survey. Thus, it was clear to me that as important as religion is, there is much more that requires explanation beyond religion when it comes to women's rights, particularly as one moves to the Muslim-majority regions outside of the Middle East. And, indeed, this is what I found in my two years of research in the Maghreb.

Political Ritual and Symbolism of Those in Power

This book is written along two tracks: deconstructing the symbolic uses of women's rights along with a process tracing narrative. It follows Murray Edelman's (1964) counsel that political analysis must proceed on two levels simultaneously, examining how political actions allow groups to get concrete things from the government, but also looking at what they mean to the public, and how the public is mollified or energized by them. This book looks at the political symbols primarily of several groups: those in power, political parties, Islamist movements, and women's movements. It examines the outcomes of their interactions. Far from being simply rhetoric, rituals (i.e., behavior laden with symbolic meaning) and symbolic forms of communication have real-world implications for the everyday lives of women and men.

In other words, as Swedish sociologist Ulf Himmelstrand explained, political acts are both instrumental and expressive. Himmelstrand (1960) argued that non-verbal symbolic actions allow for greater "creativity and constructive transformation" since they allow people to project multiple meanings without the use of more direct and possibly more off-putting words.

Symbolic expression or rituals are not accompanied by long explanations, but their significance is universally understood. In most societies, people do not pay much attention to or carefully analyze events that affect them, but when communication is symbolic or enacted in a ritualistic fashion, they tend to comprehend the cues more readily, according to Edelman (1988). Politics is a spectacle that is reported in the media and witnessed by the public. It attracts attention because its inherent ambiguity allows it to be infused with meanings that reassure or threaten. Take, for example, Americans living in the age of Trump. We have been treated to more symbolic spectacle than many of us would wish to endure, and while for some it has met their collective need for recognition and retribution, for most it has been threatening, enraging, and disorienting. Perhaps at no other time in US history has the symbolic dimension of politics been more visible as one witnesses a relentless display of tweets, summits, trials, investigations, rallies, press conferences, and communication through hats, handshakes, flag hugging, backdrops to events, and other subtle and not-so-subtle forms of expression. The much-debated border wall was more symbolic than real in what it represented as a bulwark against people who were portrayed as a threat to the United States. The reality of the situation at the border was irrelevant.

This book is, in part, interested in the creation of meaning around women's rights as much as in the content of the rights themselves and why they are adopted in some places and not others. It looks at how women's rights came to be and how battles over the symbolic expression of those rights were part of that process. It examines the meanings of political events and how they have been constructed and changed through language, symbols, and ritual; how the meanings were evoked; and what values, ideologies, and worldviews were embedded in them. The meaning of the symbol cannot be found in the symbol itself, but rather in the observers and their environments. There are no objective meanings that can be given to symbols. Rather it is the interpretations of the symbols which shape behavior and vice versa.

For example, in January 2018, a new minister of education was appointed in Morocco after the unexpected firing of his predecessor and two other ministers over their failure to improve the economic situation in the northern Rif region, which had been facing unrest that had aroused Amazigh nationalist sentiments. When the new minister, Said Amzazi, attended the appointment ceremony, he bowed to the king and kissed his hand instead of his arm in a manner that caused a kerfuffle in Moroccan social media when the photo was released. (*Zunqat 20* 2018). Perhaps the firing of his predecessor had evoked extreme obsequiousness on his part. Nevertheless, the reaction was over the angle of his ritualistic bow, which had him folded over in a way that suggested servility rather than simply deference or loyalty to the king. His bow was compared to the posture of a diver set to race. Others commented that his "forehead almost touched the ground as he bowed." "He was probably looking for his wallet on the floor," remarked another in jest (*Article19.ma* 2018). While the discussion may have seemed lighthearted, it was intensely political, in a country where no one can openly criticize the king and the extent of his power. The significance of the reaction to the photo is not easily put into words, but was understood by all who reposted the image.

Political symbols are expressed through rituals such as voting, through oratory, legal language (including laws and constitutions), publicized consultations of interest groups with public officials, through acts of voting or boycotting elections, expressed rejection or critique of established policies by the opposition, acts of suppression and speech against or for particular groups, ritual trials that are carried out to set an example, attacks on a personified enemy, banal rhetoric that helps suppress public anxiety, and discussion of target groups as "us" or as an enemy (Edelman 1971). Harold Lasswell and Murray Edelman saw symbols as a way in which political elites could defend their interests, while at the same time providing a means for the mass public to release anxiety. Symbols can reassure people and thus discourage resistance (Klatch 1988).

Symbols can legitimize the distribution of power through rituals like elections, especially in authoritarian or hybrid countries, where elections may seem farcical, since the outcome may be preordained. Thus, symbols and their enactment can be a means of domination (Lukes 1975). Some, like Adorno et al. (1950), have regarded symbols as expressions of the irrational workings of the mind and as disguised representations of the collective unconscious. He argued that the political symbolism of Nazi Germany was a disguised latent desire of the unconscious. One might argue that the peculiar hold Trump has on a segment of the American population, in spite of his menacing and inexplicable actions and lies, has to do with the way in which he has captured their imagination, relating to them at a symbolic level rather than through rational argumentation and facts, and playing on their most base sentiments and fears. As such, political symbols can be a release for a social and psychic anxiety.

In the literature on gender and politics, symbolic politics has sometimes been tied to women's descriptive representation. Women's presence in politics has been seen as energizing other women to participate in politics, signaling that women too can be leaders and game changers (Alexander 2015, Celis et al. 2008, Franceschet and Piscopo 2008). Symbols can be measured prior to the act of representation, unlike substantive representation, which can be measured only after women have assumed office, by looking, for example, at how many pieces of woman-friendly legislation they have sponsored (Lombardo and Meier 2014). However, some have argued that the presence of women does not necessarily have this energizing impact and that it can also generate backlash, as has been the case in numerous Asian contexts (Liu 2018). The use of the concept of symbolic politics in contexts of representation is, nevertheless, generally seen as a positive influence on women's political participation, although presumably the failure of women leaders, as in the cases Liu looks at, could signal a warning to other women who venture into politics. This book shows that symbols can work in many different ways in the same polity, depending on how they are deployed. The symbolic uses of women, women's bodies, and women's rights can serve purposes that have nothing to do with women's political participation or rights. Moreover, they can be used by many actors, such as women's rights activists, autocrats, extremists, and Islamists.

Outside of political science, there is a rich literature on political symbolism that helps inform the many ways in which symbols are used. Some, like anthropologist Clifford Geertz, have argued that political symbols serve as an expression of solidarity and common feelings of identification. This could be the case with particular events, like a ceremony commemorating the death of a leader, raising awareness around a particular issue through a demonstration, marking a nationalistic identity, or providing a cognitive road map with which to make sense of the world (Geertz 1973).

Anthropologist Victor Turner (1982) believed that symbols both reinforce structure but can also serve anti-structural purposes and threaten social order by challenging the status quo. On one hand, they can unify society and provide a way to mobilize people around a particular set of moral and psychological appeals. On the other hand, they can also be used to divide groups, as the swastika was used by the Nazis, or as the Confederate flag is used in the contemporary United States. Symbols are an expression of political preference but also a means of mobilizing interests. They are used by both the elite to maintain the status quo (Edelman 1967) and by opponents to change society (Kowalewski 1980).

This book looks at a variety of ways in which gender-related symbols and rituals are used in politics. The central elements that I focus on are legislative and constitutional reforms around women's rights. Constitutional provisions, in particular, contain strong symbolic resonance, as evident in the fierce battles fought over the parity versus complementarity provisions proposed for the Tunisian constitution in 2014. The 2004 PSC or Moudawana in Morocco is another piece of legislation which most Moroccans have an opinion about, regardless of whether they understand its contents. I link these legislative reforms to other forms of political symbolism. For example, women's bodies are another arena where the battle lines are constantly being drawn and redrawn.

Symbolism of Women's Bodies

Few symbols engender as much debate or response in the MENA region as women's bodies and the virtue they are to embody. Battles over veiling, the protection of premarital virginity, and regulating women's presence in certain public spaces have been especially salient in this regard. These battles became especially fierce after the 1980s, with the spread of Salafi and conservative Muslim ideologies throughout the region. Transgressions and rejections of such manifestations of "honor" quickly became forms of protest. Women's bodies thus became symbols of continuity for some and of change for others, a canvas on which people projected their diverging visions for the future.

There are public discourses about women's rights, but there are also hidden ones, particularly those pertaining to sex, which most people prefer not to talk about or express publicly. As Algerian journalist and novelist Kamel Daoud wrote in a controversial essay:

> Today sex is a great paradox in many countries of the Arab world: One acts as though it doesn't exist, and yet it determines everything that's unspoken. Denied, it weighs on the mind by its very concealment. Although women are veiled, they are at the center of our connections, exchanges and concerns. Women are a recurrent theme in daily discourse, because the stakes they personify – for manliness, honor, family values – are great. In some countries, they are allowed access to the public sphere only if they renounce their bodies: To let them go uncovered would be to uncover the desire that the Islamist, the conservative and the idle youth feel and want to deny. Women are seen as a source of destabilization – short skirts trigger earthquakes, some say – and are respected only when defined by a property relationship, as the wife of X or the daughter of Y. These contradictions create unbearable tensions. (2016)[1]

[1] *Aujourd'hui le sexe est un énorme paradoxe dans de nombreux pays arabes : On fait comme s'il n'existait pas, mais il conditionne tous les non-dits. Nié, il pèse par*

As a visiting scholar at Al Akhawayn University in Morocco (2015–2016), I found myself often drawn into long discussions with female students about the angst they faced in having to conceal their sex lives, some even having multiple surgeries to reconstruct their hymens in order to "remain virgins" at marriage. The focus on virginity is primarily cultural, since women who are not religious also seek the same surgeries. Men have the freedom to do as they please. Girls and women, according to Leïla Slimani (2017), "have only one alternative: virgin or wife." The society and the law do not allow women to have sex outside of the context of marriage, regardless of age, marital status, or sexuality. Nevertheless, there are 8 million women who are single and independent according to a survey conducted by Ouest France and the average age of marriage for women is twenty-seven (Koundouno 2018b).

In Algeria and Tunisia, the stigma against premarital sex remains strong even though the law does not forbid it, as it does in Morocco (Penal Code Article 490). Similarly, adultery is against the law in all three countries, with heavier penalties for the woman than the man in Algeria, where a man, unlike the woman, would have a lesser sentence if he did not know the marital status of the woman (Penal Code Article 339). There are equal penalties for men and women charged with adultery in both Tunisia and Morocco. All same-sex sexual activity is illegal in both Algeria (Penal Code Article 338) and Morocco (Penal Code Article 489), however, in Tunisia the law bans sodomy but is silent on lesbian sexual relations (Penal Code Article 230).

Numerous scholars from Bordo (1993) to Crawford (1984) have depicted the body as conveying core social values as they relate to beauty, weight, eating disorders, and other such phenomena. In this case, the values of virtue and family honor take center stage in discussions of virginity. How women dress represents symbolic expressions of this honor, but they have real-world consequences that sometimes

son occultation. La femme a beau être voilée, elle est au centre de tous nos liens, tous nos échanges, toutes nos préoccupations.

La femme revient dans les discours quotidiens comme enjeu de virilité, d'honneur et de valeurs familiales. Dans certains pays, elle n'a accès à l'espace public que quand elle abdique son corps. La dévoiler serait dévoiler l'envie que l'islamiste, le conservateur et le jeune désoeuvré ressentent et veulent nier. Perçue comme source de déséquilibre – jupe courte, risque de séisme – elle n'est respectée que lorsque définie dans un rapport de propriété, comme épouse de X ou fille de Y.

Figure I.1 Cartoon: The debate that drives Algerian society.
Source: El Watan (Algeria) by Ali Dilem.
Le débat qui anime la société algérienne ("The debate that drives Algerian society"). *Ta jupe est trop courte* ("Your skirt is too short").

result in violence against women. Conservative young Internet users launched a web campaign in Algeria in 2015 called "Be a Man" (*Sois un homme*), also known as "Purity," inviting men to make sure that their wives and daughters wear "decent" clothes. "Do not let your women go out with a daring outfit," they implored their readers (*20 Minutes* 2015). The initiative was launched a few weeks after a student was denied access to an examination room because her dress was deemed "too short." "The inquisitors are back," announced the Algerian daily *El Watan* on March 25, 2015. Some promised that they would be "merciless" with those who would not hide their bodies enough. "We are going to take a picture and publish the pictures on the web so that it's a lesson for them," says one of them in a post in support of the campaign. "We are going to disfigure them by pouring acid on their faces," another wrote, according to the national newspaper (Verduzier 2015). Such threats are taken seriously in a country where during the Black Decade non-veiled women were beheaded and targeted by extremist Islamists. The Minister of Justice said that investigations into these threats were ongoing and promised that justice would face "those who want to take us back to the '90s" (*Algérie Monde Infos* 2018c). Nevertheless, some women responded by going to the beach in droves wearing bikinis, bringing a swift end to the campaign.

A similar campaign was launched in Morocco in 2018 also known as Koun Rajul ("Be a Man") with slogans like: "Be a man and do not let your wives, daughters, and sisters come out wearing tight, clingy, shocking clothes." The response from women on social media was fierce. A "Be a Woman" campaign was launched, defending the basic rights of women and insisting on a woman's right to dress as she pleases (*Algérie Monde Infos* 2018d). One woman wrote: "This campaign launched by obsessed sexual extremists . . . is too much. I am not veiled and yet I never thought, even for a second, to criticize my compatriots who made the choice to wear the headscarf." Another woman wrote an angry riposte: "Be a man and take care of your behind." Another said the campaign was launched to suppress Moroccan women because they were free. Another said she could not believe this was happening in 2018 (*Maroc Leaks* 2018). One wrote: "Be a woman and wear whatever you wish to." Some men turned the discussion around and asked what it means to be a man: "Be a man and curb your desire to control women and what they want to wear" and "Be a man and stop violence against women instead" (Ben Saga 2018). One woman wrote:

> Farewell beach of my childhood! Goodbye sweetness of life! Farewell carefree sunbathing. It is not the invasion of jellyfish, "Portuguese man o' war," or other marine creatures that threaten our Moroccan coasts, but an invasion of a different kind that is more insidious and more dangerous . . . men with naked torsos displaying women as submissive and inferior beings! (*Le Site Info* 2018)

Having discussed citizen-inspired campaigns to control women's dress, it should be pointed out that states too can regulate women's dress for symbolic reasons, as evident in the Moroccan government's efforts to ban *niqab* production and sales in 2017.

Women's right to enter public spaces is also of concern. Women and men constantly push back against these restrictions through daily acts of resistance. Two young women in Agadir, Morocco, were arrested in 2015 for wearing skirts that were deemed too short. There was a public outcry, including petitions and public statements by human rights leaders and activists. As a result, the women were acquitted as there is no law in Morocco requiring a certain dress code. Over 500 lawyers offered to defend the girls pro bono, in part because the arrests themselves flagrantly violated the law.

One woman in Algiers was verbally assaulted and beaten for jogging along the beach during Ramadan in 2018. When she went to the police to complain, they asked why she was jogging and did nothing. She then took to social media to complain. The next day, hundreds of women, men, and NGOs came out to run with her in protest (Rahmouni 2018). Thus, the body is not only a symbolic field for reproducing dominant values but also "a site for resistance to and transformation of those systems of meaning" (Crawford 1984, 95). Oldfield, Salo, and Schlyter (2009) look at how women and men use their bodies as tools of resistance and as sites of negotiating directly or through representation. As they explain, "We conceptualize 'body politics' as the negotiation of power via the body; processes that operate sometimes directly (for instance, violently), but also processes that work at a symbolic and representational scale" (3).

There is a large literature that looks at contestations in Africa, over clothing in colonial Lesotho (Comaroff and Comaroff 1992), the forcible fattening of girls among Azawagh Arabs in Niger (Popenoe 2004), female genital mutilation in many areas, and other such practices. In the MENA region, it is the debates over virginity, veiling, and women's presence in public spaces that prevail. These are intensely political debates, which have been instrumentalized. As a leader of a major women's rights organization in Morocco put it:

> The *hijab* [scarf] is not neutral, it is political, because we in Morocco have our traditional clothes. The scarf cannot simply be an Islamic identity, because we already have our identity as Muslims, so it is more than an identity. During the Islamist marches [against the revised PSC] they said, "All women who have a scarf belong to us." (M17.2.6.16)

But not all Moroccans see it this way. Avi Spiegel (2015) found that most, but not all, Islamist women veiled. Moreover, some veiled but not for religious reasons. One 2014 survey of 950 Muslim women throughout Morocco showed that age, marital status, and education had a far greater impact on a woman's choice of clothing than religiosity (Bachleda et al. 2014). Spiegel cites a study by Moroccan sociologists that found that 84 percent of young people were of the opinion that women should veil and two thirds supported this view for religious reasons. One third said they should veil for professional purposes, so they would be harassed less at work. Not all who said women should veil actually veiled themselves. According to Avi Spiegel (2015), women also veiled to be "cool," to follow fashion trends, family tradition, and some saw it as a form of empowerment. Others even used it as a "cover" for meeting romantic partners, believing they would be less suspect if they veiled. In one restaurant near my apartment in Rabat, sex workers wore the *hijab* while soliciting clients at nearby tables via Bluetooth. Thus, there are many different ways of regarding the purpose of the *hijab*, from piety to political expression to dissimulation. Nevertheless, at the end of the day, it is the meaning that people themselves give to their symbols that matters.

Thus, I build on the early recognition by Mary Douglas in her book *Natural Symbols* (1970) of the symbolic significance of the body. She argued that bodily symbols reflect the social and replicate the social situation and that the body symbolizes the social world. Bodies can reveal the core values of a society. Judith Butler (1990) captures this dual role of body symbolism as both a reflection of society and its agency, arguing that various acts or series of repeated performances of gender create gender. Building on these ideas from Butler and Douglas, several scholars have looked at the connection between women's bodies and their position in society and the ways in which the body-based functions of women in bearing and nursing children are used to justify a social artifice which becomes the seemingly unchangeable order of things (Devisch 1985, Reischer and Koo 2004).

Female Archetypes as Symbols

We are also interested in this latter symbolic aspect, which in general terms is akin to Carl Jung's (1980) notion of "collective unconscious" or archetypes. These are only revealed through stories, art, films, mythology, religions, statues, or famously in dreams. In today's commercialized societies, they also appear in jewelry, advertising, names of stores, and other such ventures.

References to archetypes help reinforce the roles that women are afforded in society. There are universal archetypes that appear in the Maghreb, as in most cultures around the world, in their infinite varieties: "the whore," "the virgin," "the good wife," "the difficult mother-in-law," "the nurturing mother," "the saint," "the sorceress," etc. But there are also archetypes that depict a rich history and mythology of female leadership and power in Maghrebian society, both in the public and private sphere. These women leaders are especially important as they are drawn on in contemporary political culture to remind people that women have a long history of prominent political leadership roles.

In my interviews I regularly heard about the red-headed "warrior queen" Amazigh Dihya (Al Kahina) (649–702) of the Aurès in eastern Algeria, who beat back the Muslim Umayyad invaders twice. Interviewees brought into our discussions mention of Sayyid al-Hurra, the famed sixteenth-century pirate queen of Tetouan. Tin Hinan, a Tuareg warrior queen of the fourth century, was frequently mentioned. There was also Zayneb al Nafzawiyya, who built Marrakesh. She married the conqueror Youssef Ben Tachfine and became the queen of one of Morocco's largest empires, the eleventh-century Almoravid Empire. Elishat (known to the Greeks as Elissa Dido) was the founding Queen of Carthage, a powerful city-state in Tunisia in the third century BC. To this day these women leaders are revered. There has been a renewed recognition of them because, as one leader of an Amazigh women's organization put it, "As in all other countries, even if the woman has done a lot of things, she is not put forward . . . it is always the man who is advanced . . . like Marie-Curie, it was her husband who received the glory, when it was she who had done everything" (M15.2.3.16).

Women's power is evoked in other ways as well. Some archetypes are female goddesses. A female Tunisian architectural student gave me a small parting gift of a *periapt* of Tanit, who she said held great significance to her as source of inspiration. Around 400 BC, the Amazigh people of Carthage, today Tunisia, were said to have worshipped a woman named Tanit. She was revered as the goddess of prosperity, fertility, love, and the moon. One finds her on necklaces, amulets, monuments, mosaics, as well as Amazigh ornaments (Naaim 2015).

Female saints are dominant female archetypes. Khalida Messaoudi describes how she grew up in Algeria revering the saint Lalla Yamina, who had her own mausoleum in Kabylia, in eastern Algeria. Yamina refused to marry and was a rebel and sage who had a rifle, which she used when an injustice had been committed and men had not corrected it (Messaoudi 1995).

In Algeria, the powerful women who fought in the struggle for independence are regularly commemorated for their contributions, women like Djamila Bouhired, Hassiba ben Bouali, and Zohra Drif who were among the 11,000 women fighters in the war against France. Earlier in Algeria, between 1850 and 1855, the Kabyle Lalla Fadhma N'Soumer had organized an armed resistance to the French along with the women of Ouled Sidi Cheikh.

Some archetypes are mythological. The most famous mythological figure in Morocco is Aisha Kandisha, the woman who lingers near deserted springs after dark. One foot or leg resembles that of a camel, donkey, or goat. She is adored and feared, and reveals herself in ritual possession. She causes death, illness, and madness but also can heal and bestow wealth, fertility, and fortune (Debbagh 2011). Her extreme beauty is used to seduce, captivate, and annihilate men. They are powerless as she seduces them with her soft and sweet voice, initially calling them by their first name, then starting a game of seduction, and finally killing them. This mythical creature has been revived by Fedwa Misk in a modern-day online zine which deals with current affairs, *Qandisha: Magazwine collaborative féminin*. Misk is a doctor by training and journalist by profession who started the zine in 2011 to discuss women's rights, human rights, and individual freedom. The contributors include journalists, writers, officials, business people, academics, and people of all different viewpoints.

In Morocco, there is also an archetypal woman, Châaibia Mokhlis, the rural woman who supports her husband in spite of everything. She endures his mocking assaults, but knows how to stand up and fight for herself. She is a symbol of strength, as she works in the fields day in and day out and then sells the crops. The woman is passionate: she fights for respect and dignity. The modern-day Châaibia Mokhlis is urban and independent, concerned about the right to choose her companion and provide for herself (Ziou Ziou 2015).

When taken symbolically, one enters another dimension of politics that is less quantifiable but replete with meaning. These symbols have consequences for the daily lives of women, particularly when policy is at stake. One cannot therefore read political pronouncements or legal texts simply as literal statements of fact. Rather, in order to understand their political and social significance, it is important to regard them also as communication at a symbolic level in order to better understand their purpose.

Thus, this book looks at political symbols and their ritual enactment. It looks at both the processes of women's rights reform in the Maghreb as well as the symbolic nature of the battles around legislative and constitutional reform. It also looks at the ways in which women's bodies are a battleground over political aspirations for power, control, religion, patriarchy, modernity, democracy, international acceptability, values, morality, and many other central concerns in the MENA region.

Research Design and Methods

This book asks, "Why do autocrats adopt women's rights?" The question is broken down into two components: The book asks why Tunisia, Morocco, and Algeria converged in the adoption of women's rights legislation after 2000 and why they diverged from the Middle East in moving faster to adopt legal and constitutional provisions regarding women's rights. In the Chapter 1, I look at the similarities and differences between the Maghreb countries and then contrast the Maghreb with the Middle East in terms of general women's rights outcomes. I focus on the different outcomes between the Maghreb and the Middle East when it comes to women's rights but also why the Maghreb countries converged in their women's rights agendas. I also discuss key alternative theories used to explain variance in women's rights in the region. Chapter 2 discusses various historical background conditions that contributed to the differences one sees between the Maghreb and the Middle East with respect to women's rights, from the adoption of a unified legal system and laws at the time of independence to the French legal legacy, cultural influences like the Amazigh factor, and the impact of political opening, however minimal, in the region. Chapter 3 goes further in depth in comparing the legislative and constitutional women's rights provisions between the two regions as well as variance more generally between countries that have been more successful than others with respect to women's rights. I also discuss why some areas of legal reform have seen more progress than others.

This study focuses on case studies of Morocco (Chapter 4), Algeria (Chapter 5), and Tunisia (Chapter 6). In each I show not only the processes of change, but how people have given meaning to these transformations though rituals and symbolic expression, and how those struggles for meaning influenced outcomes. The process of creating and expressing meaning is woven into the historical narrative. All comparisons are situated in broader comparisons in the region, focusing on legislative and constitutional reform. The Conclusions chapter revisits the hypotheses and takes a step back to further discuss the comparative dimension. Here, I make broader comparisons within the region as well as specific paired comparisons between countries. Lebanon is contrasted with Tunisia. Like the Tunisia, Lebanon has a francophone legacy and liberal views on women's rights. Egypt is contrasted with Algeria because in both countries the military is dominant and both have witnessed crackdowns on the political engagement of Islamists. Finally, I look at Jordan, which, like Morocco, has a modernizing monarchy that wants to see women's rights reforms, yet has not made as far-reaching changes as the latter. I use the findings of the study to explain why one sees the variation that has emerged in the region.

The case study chapters on Tunisia, Algeria, and Morocco look at the ways in which leaders have used women's rights to expand and solidify their authority at critical junctures. This analysis shows the role of women's movements in pressing for and shaping reforms, particularly in the post-2000 period. These reforms are situated within the context of earlier postindependence legislation relating to women's status, particular with respect to the PSCs in each country.

Process tracing of the history of women's rights legislation and constitutional reform in all three countries highlights the common patterns that distinguish the Maghreb from the Middle East: (1) the strategies of the political elite to use women's rights as a mechanism to counter extremist Islamist trends and present a modernizing image of their country abroad; (2) the political necessity for Islamist parties in the region to adopt women's rights reforms for their survival and how they changed their stated positions once in power; and (3) the role of women's movements in pressing for women's rights reforms to effect change at critical historical junctures for maximum effect. Finally, to understand why the Maghreb countries converged, one has to look at the collaboration between women's movements. The following hypotheses are elaborated on in Chapter 1.

The first hypothesis suggests that when modernizing leaders strategically use women's rights to counter extremist Islamist tendencies, they have been able to advance the cause of women's rights. In recent years, Islamist parties have adopted key aspects of reform, however reluctantly, and in so doing, have changed their rhetoric. Thus, the second hypothesis suggests that women's rights are more easily advanced when *not* supporting them becomes a political liability for political parties. It becomes a political necessity for the party in power to adopt women's rights reforms in order to remain in power, to exercise power, and to garner the votes of women. The third hypothesis focuses on the role of women's movements in advancing women's rights, particularly at critical junctures. I suggest that when there are abrupt changes in the authorities, these changes provide opportunities for gender reform. These hypotheses are examined historically through process tracing in the country case studies (Chapters 4, 5, 6). The case studies show the interactions between women's movements, Islamist movements and parties, and the political elite in making these changes. They also discuss the costs for women's rights activists of alignment with nondemocratic leaders around women's rights gains.

And finally, a fourth hypothesis suggests that the close cooperation between activists in the three countries resulted in an unmistakable pattern: a diffusion of goals, a convergence of legislative and constitutional reforms, and synchronicity in the timing of these reforms. This proposition is also analyzed through process tracing in Chapter 3.

The study draws on extensive interviews conducted in Morocco between 2015 and 2016, in Algeria in the fall of 2016, and Tunisia in the spring of 2017. Interviews in all three countries were conducted with leaders and members of a variety of Islamist, feminist, and Amazigh women's rights organizations; human rights organizations; members of parliament; leaders of the women's legislative caucuses; women's ministry representatives; party leaders; lawyers; religious leaders; academics; journalists; and representatives of donor and UN agencies. The interviews investigated questions ranging from different frames being used in advocating for and against women's rights to attitudes toward these rights, sources of legislative and constitutional reforms; the strength and autonomy of the women's movement over time; how different government leaders supported or resisted the adoption of women's rights; the role of donors and external actors; differences between the Maghreb countries; and causes of differences between the Maghreb and the Middle East when it comes to women's rights. The interviews conducted for this study in Algeria, Morocco, and Tunisia are anonymized for security purposes erring on the side of caution. They are indicated by country (A, M, T), interview number, month, day, and year of the interview.

In Morocco, my research assistant Sawsene Nejjar and I conducted eighty interviews with members and leaders of a variety of women's rights organizations, including key national organizations like the Fédération de la ligue démocratique des droits des femmes (FLDDF), Jossour forum des femmes marocaines, the Association démocratique des femmes du Maroc (ADFM), the Union de l'action féminine (UAF), as well as local organizations from the Middle Atlas. We also interviewed leaders of various coalitions and networks, including the Coalition printemps féministe pour la démocratie et l'égalité and the Islamist women's network Mountada Azzahrae pour la femme marocaine. We spoke with leaders and members of groups focusing on particular concerns such as those of Amazigh women (e.g., La voix de la femme amazighe and Observatoire amazigh des droits et libertés), women who had suffered from violence, migrants, rural women, and women in the southern provinces. We spoke with leaders of human rights organizations (e.g., the Association marocaine des droits humains) and religious institutions (e.g., Rabita al Muhammadia des Oulémas du Maroc). In addition, we interviewed representatives of governmental agencies, such as the Conseil national des droits de l'homme (CNDH), the Ministère de la solidarité, de la femme, de la famille et du développement social (renamed Ministère de la solidarité de la femme, de la famille et du développement social in 2017), and representatives of municipal councils, regional councils, and the national parliament, including the head of the Forum des femmes parlementaires. And finally, we interviewed women representatives of tribal councils, academics, journalists, religious leaders, and representatives of donor agencies. We conducted interviews primarily in Fès, Casablanca, and Rabat but also in other places around the country. For half a year, I lived in a rural area of Ifrane in the Middle Atlas, where I taught for one semester at Al Akhawayn University; I lived the other half of the year in Rabat. I conducted another fifty interviews in the southern provinces, in Dakhla and Laâyoune (Western Sahara), with the help of the lawyer Naima Korchi, who has lived in the region extensively while working with the United Nation High Commissioner for Refugees.

In Algeria, I carried out about forty interviews in Algiers, Oran in the west, and Tizi Ouzou in the east, with the help of Nourredine Bessadi. The interviews were conducted with leaders and members of organizations like the Association des femmes cadres algériennes (AFCARE), the Centre d'Information et de documentation sur les droits de l'enfant et de la femme (CIDDEF), Femmes algériennes revendiquant leurs droits (FARD), the Réseau Wassila, and Tharwa Fadhma N'Soumer. I interviewed representatives of various donors and UN agencies like UN Women, academics, journalists, bloggers, and many others.

Thirty-five interviews were conducted in Tunisia, primarily in Tunis, with the help of Nourredine Bessadi with parliamentarians, lawyers, artists, dancers, activists, journalists, human rights organizations like La ligue tunisienne de défense des droits de l'homme (LTDH), and women's organizations like the Fédération internationale des droits de l'homme (FIDH), the Centre de la femme arabe pour la formation et la recherche (CAWTAR), the Association des Femmes tunisiennes pour la recherche sur le développement (AFTURD), the Comité scientifique de l'institut arabe des droits de l'homme, the Association tunisienne des femmes démocrates (ATFD), the Association femme et progrès, El Kef, the Ligue des électrices tunisiennes, the Association Mawjoudin, and many others. The interviews in Algeria and Tunisia were conducted in French.

I also created an original database of legislation and constitutional reforms with the help of research assistants. It includes all legislative and constitutional changes made in the MENA region pertaining to women's rights as identified by women's organizations in the region since independence. This data informs Chapter 3. I also draw in Chapters 1 and 2 on data from Arab Barometer, Afrobarometer, the World Values Survey, V-Dem, the International Institute for Democracy and Electoral Assistance (International IDEA), the Inter-Parliamentary Union, and the World Economic Forum.

The project also draws on newspaper and magazine articles from the region in both Arabic and French as well as on secondary literature. The data on the countries paired with the Maghreb countries are derived from media accounts and secondary literature.

PART I

Comparing the Maghreb and the Middle East

1 *Women's Rights*

Comparing the Middle East and the Maghreb

After ten years of advocacy, thousands of women in Morocco's "Soulaliyate" land rights movement won the right to compensation for tribal lands in 2018. "Speaking up for my rights and going against my uncles and [other] male relatives was not only considered rude, but it was like declaring war [against] our tradition that has been favorable only to men," said Mahjouba Mhamda of the Ouled Mbarek tribe in the Kenitra region. "It was a long and difficult journey during which we were insulted and intimidated. But being here today, makes it all worth it" (UN Women 2018). About 42 percent of the land in Morocco is owned by tribes and with pressures for privatization, men were selling tribal lands to the government while women were receiving no compensation. Thousands of women were forced off their land until the Association démocratique des femmes du Maroc (ADFM) started what became a nationwide movement in 2007 to demand women's rights to land. Women succeeded in gaining compensation for their land taken by the government. This is, in part, a direct result of constitutional provisions for equality passed in 2011. These kinds of outcomes have been made possible by the new legal environment found in Morocco that is establishing new ground rules for women's rights in a country that has an Islamist party in power.

This chapter looks at this new disposition in Morocco and how and why it is part of a convergence of legal reform in the Maghreb countries. The chapter discusses the commonalities between the Maghreb and the Middle East and, most importantly, it asks why there has been a divergence between the two regions when it comes to advancing women's rights. I hypothesize several possible explanations for the divergence: (1) Maghrebi leaders adopted a political strategy to advance women's rights in order to present a modernizing image of their nation to the world and to neutralize Islamist movements, especially extremist ones; (2) the ruling parties, including Islamist parties, sought to stay in power by advancing women's rights, knowing it would cost them if they did not adopt such reforms; (3) women's movements exerted pressure, resulting in demands for greater accountability; (4) often these reforms occurred in the context of a critical juncture after a change of leadership, the end of a war, coup d'état, or other major social upheaval; and finally, (5) the women's movements in all three countries engaged each other, thus diffusing goals and strategies. The chapter briefly considers alternate explanations for women's rights reforms in the region.

Differences between Countries within the Maghreb

In explaining what sets the Maghreb countries apart from the Arab countries in the Middle East with respect to women's rights, one plausible argument might be that the Maghreb countries are distinct because they share a common French colonial legacy, as well as other historic, demographic, and geographical similarities. They share a common Amazigh (Berber) population mostly in Morocco and Algeria and common cultural influences that reach into Tunisia. The Arabic, French, and Tamazight (Berber language) languages are spoken to varying degrees in all three countries. The population of the Maghreb is a mixture of Amazigh, Arabized Amazigh, and many other peoples who invaded or migrated to the Maghreb, including the Arabs, Greeks, Phoenicians, Egyptians, Romans, Vandals, Europeans, and Africans from south of the Sahara. It was Islamicized by the thirteenth century with the exception of a few pockets of Jewish and Christian communities. In spite of these commonalities, there are enormous differences between the three countries, some of which account for their gender policies and how they evolved. I will return to the French and Amazigh influences in the Chapter 2.

Morocco

Unlike the other two countries, Morocco is the only monarchy, but it regards itself as a modernizing one. The king, under pressure from women's organizations, has been pushing for women's rights reforms along with other reforms, and has intervened at strategic moments to advance various reforms affecting women. Morocco was never part of the Ottoman Empire, which meant that it never operated under the millet system in which personal law was adjudicated by different courts based on their confessional community. This had implications later on for the creation of a unified legal system. Because of the conflict in the Western Sahara (southern provinces), which Morocco claimed militarily in 1975, Morocco left the African Union (AU) in 1984 when a majority of AU members voted to recognize the independence movement, Sahrawi Arab Democratic Republic or POLISARIO. It was not until 2017 that Morocco rejoined the AU, mostly because of its expanding trade, financial, and other ties with the rest of Africa and because these goals overrode other considerations. The POLISARIO by this time had weakened considerably, especially after the death of its leader Mohamed Abdul-Aziz in 2016. Having not been a part of the AU meant that Morocco did not experience the same pressures for gender reform as Algeria and Tunisia (e.g., the Maputo Declaration around women's rights). Morocco has one of the poorest educational systems in the Arab world, with some of the highest rates of illiteracy, particularly among women (Monjib 2011). Morocco is a semi-authoritarian regime that is neither fully democratic nor fully authoritarian. In 2016 it started slipping in its political rights and civil liberties rankings with Freedom House due to repression of the press and of protests.

Algeria

Of the three Maghreb countries, Algeria is the only one that was colonized by France and whose *départements* were fully integrated into France. The other two countries were protectorates of France. Algeria was under France's control for 132 years. The experience of Morocco and Tunisia with French colonialism was much shorter than Algeria's: forty-four years in the case of Morocco and seventy-five years in Tunisia. Unlike the other two countries, Algeria had a large French settler population of 1.6 million people, making up 15 percent of the total population at the time of independence. As a result of these differences in colonial relations, only Algeria fought a long and bloody war of liberation against France, obtaining its independence in 1962.

Algeria is the only country of the three which has twice in recent history experienced major war: the war of independence from 1954 to 1962 and the civil war from 1991 to 2002. The legacy of the latter war has important implications for women's rights and follows patterns of other postconflict African states after the 1990s (Tripp 2015). Countries in Africa that experienced extremely bloody wars or wars long in duration that ended after the 1990s have higher levels of representation of women in politics and in many cases more women's rights legislation.

Of the three Maghreb countries, Algeria has the most authoritarian regime. It also has had the weakest women's movement, in part because of its more limited political space. Whereas in Morocco, human rights lawyers and activists often see women's rights as an entry point into fighting for democracy, in Algeria civil society has often been more concerned with democratization and human rights than women's rights because it is seen as a prerequisite to women's rights (M2.1.26.16). It is the only oil producer of the three countries. Unlike Morocco and Tunisia, Algeria placed a premium on educating girls after independence and made education compulsory for all up to the age of sixteen. This had implications later on for women's entrance into professions and politics.

Tunisia

Of the three countries, Tunisia is considered the only democracy, albeit a fragile one. It earned this ranking in 2015 from Freedom House after having been considered an autocracy since independence in 1956. In 2011, Tunisia became an electoral democracy after the departure of President Ben Ali from office. In 2015, it gained democratic status due to constitutional reforms, improvements in governance, and the holding of free and fair parliamentary and presidential elections in 2014. Tunisia is also a semi-presidential republic and historically had a state that was more centralized than those of Morocco and Algeria (Charrad 2001).

Tunisia has had a more secular orientation than the other two Maghreb countries and is regarded as a leader in the MENA region when it comes to women's rights. In 1956, the country's first postindependence president, Habib Bourguiba, introduced a new family law or Personal Status Code (PSC), which established that family structures should be based on the legal equality of men and women. He abolished polygamy and introduced legal divorce, set a legal age for marriage, and gave women the right to work and to obtain an education. The 1959 constitution further institutionalized these rights. Women gained the right to contraception in 1961 and the right to abortion in 1973. The top-down nature of the women's rights reforms in Tunisia under presidents Habib Bourguiba (1956–1987) and Ben Ali (1987–2011) meant that the close connection between women's rights and authoritarian rule was exceptionally difficult to shake in later years even though women's rights activists also suffered under the Bourguiba and Ben Ali regimes.

Given these major historical, structural, and political differences between Morocco, Tunisia, and Algeria, it is interesting that these countries have now converged around constitutional and legal women's rights reforms as a result of elite competition and women's movement collaboration between these countries. Since 1956, Tunisia had led the way in the MENA region in adopting women's rights legislation. After 2000 we witnessed a convergence among the three countries in legal reform with constitutional reforms and legislation pertaining to the violence against women, quotas, sexual harassment, nationality laws, and other such reforms.

Commonalities between the Maghreb and the Middle East

In contrasting the Maghreb with the Middle East, it is important to point out that the two regions share much in common. When I refer to the Middle East in this book, for purposes of comparative analysis, I am referring to Arab countries, including the Levant, the Arabian Peninsula and Gulf, and Egypt, and I am not including the non-Arab countries, like Iran, Israel, or Turkey, that are part of the Middle East. Including these countries, however, would not change the basic argument. I do not use the term *mashriq*, which includes all countries east of Egypt up to Iran and Turkey, because it excludes Egypt and the Arabian Peninsula, which are part of my study. When I refer to the Maghreb in this book, I am referring to Tunisia, Algeria, and Morocco unless otherwise specified. Sometimes Libya and Mauritania are included as part of the greater Maghreb. Mauritania fits some of the patterns discussed in Chapter 3, while Libya does not, due to the disarray and political fragmentation the country finds itself in after the ousting of Muammar Gaddafi in 2011.

People in the Maghreb and Middle East are often referred to as belonging to a geopolitical region that is commonly identified as the Middle East and North Africa (MENA) region, even though people from the Maghreb do not always like to be lumped together in such a category. This objection in itself is telling, as will be evident when I contrast the regions.

Although people in Arab countries speak many dialects and languages, they share in common the written form of Arabic and its spoken literary variant, Modern Standard Arabic. Most Arab countries are predominantly Sunni Muslim, with the exception of Iraq and Bahrain, which are made up predominantly of Shia Muslims, and Oman, which is predominantly made up of Ibadi Muslims. Lebanon also has a large Shia population. With a few exceptions,[1] all Arab countries belong to the Organisation of Islamic Cooperation and all belong to the Arab League.

A large number of MENA countries share a Mediterranean heritage, which throughout history has had commercial, cultural, migratory, and political implications as well implications for the sharing of knowledge, philosophy, and religious influences. Historically, the Maghreb and the Middle East share common historical legacies of the Umayyads, who were at their height in AD 750; the Roman Empire in the coastal areas of the Mediterranean, at its height in AD 117; and the Ottoman Empire, which was at its height in the sixteenth and seventeenth centuries. The main colonial power in the region was Britain. Nevertheless, the Maghreb shares a French colonial past with Syria and Lebanon, which were French protectorates. There was also the earlier brief French occupation of Egypt under Napoleon (1798–1801). Spain controlled as a protectorate what is referred to today as Western Sahara from 1884 to 1975 and it still has protectorates in enclaves on the coast of Morocco (Ceuta and Melilla), and Libya was a protectorate of Italy from 1912 to 1934 and then a colony of Italy up to 1943.

A historic preference for marriage within the kin group, or kin endogamy along lines of patrilineage, is another commonality shared by people in this region (Charrad 2001, Patai 1965, Fernea and Malarkey 1975). This has the effect of strengthening ties among men in the lineage or tribe. The extended patrilineage historically was the basis for solidarity rather than the nuclear family, although this is now changing as nuclear families are slowly replacing extended families in importance. These lineage systems predated Islam in many places but were reinforced by Islamic law. Exogamy or marriage out of the kinship group has always been practiced in this region, but historically there has been a preference for marriage between the first parallel paternal cousin

[1] Syria is suspended at the time of writing.

and the father's brother's daughter. The benefit of this is that it keeps the property within the family. Endogamy today is not the dominant marriage system, but still around 30 percent of marriages in both the Maghreb and the Middle East are endogamous, although recent figures from Morocco show a drop to 21 percent (Koundouno 2018a).

According to French anthropologist Germaine Tillion (1966), the wearing of veils and the gendered use of space in architecture kept women from being available to men outside the kinship group, especially when groups felt their autonomy was threatened. Of course, veiling took on other meanings related to modesty after the coming of Islam, but this was perhaps the initial intent of veiling and may explain in part why it was historically so prevalent in this part of the world compared to others. All these commonalities relating to religion, language, and kinship make the divergences evident between the Maghreb and other Arab countries in the Middle East all the more significant.

The 1804 Napoleonic Code formed the basis for law in France and its colonies and was drawn on in establishing Ottoman law, specifically the criminal code. The Napoleonic Code reflects common historic Mediterranean sensibilities regarding honor, duty, and obedience in gender relations that spanned North Africa and Southern Europe. Napoleon articulated the view that "Women ought to obey us. Nature has made women our slaves!" In France, marriage mandated male superiority. The husband, who was the head of the family, was obligated to protect his wife while she was to obey him. The wife, who was basically a minor, could not travel, move, obtain a passport, or chose a doctor without her husband's permission (Mayer 1995, 436). If a man killed his wife for committing adultery, his sentence could be commuted. This provision was not repealed until 1975 in France. It is the legal source (via the Ottoman Empire) in countries like Jordan for the honor crimes legislation that allows for a reduced sentence for murders committed by men against female family members in the service of preserving the family honor (Warrick 2009).

Divergence of the Maghreb from the Middle East in Women's Rights

In spite of the aforementioned commonalities between the Maghreb and the Middle East, the Maghreb countries moved earlier and faster on women's rights legislative reform than most of the Middle Eastern countries. Chapter 3 details the sharp differences between the Maghreb and the Middle East when it comes to women's rights legislative and constitutional reform in virtually every area where we have seen reforms since the 2000s.

Some of the most dramatic changes for women in the Maghreb have been evident in the political arena, where we have seen steady increases in rates of female political representation. Due to changes in quota laws, women today hold on average 26 percent of legislative seats (lower house or unicameral bodies) in the Maghreb (Morocco, Tunisia, and Algeria) compared with an average of 11 percent in the rest of the Arab countries in the Middle East (Table 1.1). Tunisia and Algeria have the highest rates of female legislative representation in the MENA countries with 31 percent and 26 percent of their legislative seats held by women, respectively. The Maghreb countries exceed the global average of 22 percent and the US rate of 24 percent. Women hold as many as 47 percent of the seats in provincial councils in Tunisia as a result of the new quota law. Morocco was the first country to adopt quotas in the recent wave of quota law adoption in the MENA region, starting in 2002 (Egypt had a quota for a short period between 1979 and 1986).

Indeed, once one moves out of the Middle East, the picture regarding female legislative representation changes significantly. In examining some key variables for women's rights cross-nationally, Alice Kang and I found that quota adoption and region explained much of the global variance in female representation. At the time, the Middle East as a region had the lowest levels of female legislative representation and the Scandinavian countries the highest (Tripp and Kang 2008). The Middle East has now been supplanted by the Pacific region, which today has the lowest levels of female legislative representation.

The Maghreb countries were leaders in other areas related to legal reform as well. Tunisia, Algeria, and Morocco as well as Sudan have had women judges since the 1960s, long before other countries. Jordan appointed its first woman judge in 1996, Egypt in 2003, and Bahrain in 2006. Saudi Arabia announced that it would hire women judges as late as 2018 (Toumi 2018).

One attempt to quantify these broader differences between the Maghreb and the Middle East is through the Social Institutions and Gender Index (SIGI), which shows that on most measures the Maghreb

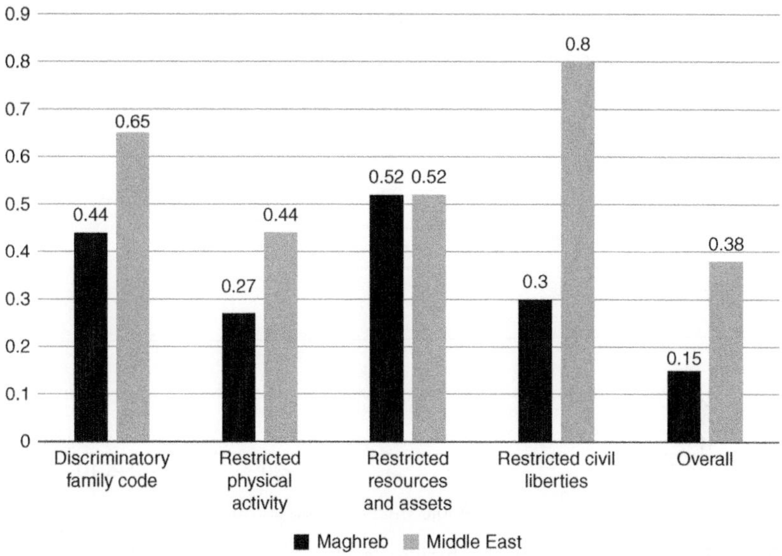

Figure 1.1 SIGI index of gender equality, legal framework, practices, and beliefs in Maghreb and Middle East (0 = low discrimination; 1 = high discrimination)
Source: Social Institutions Gender Index (SIGI), OECD Development Center, database, www.genderindex.org/
Discriminatory Family Code: norms and laws and practices: women's status in the household and the family; age of marriage, early marriage, parental authority, and inheritance.
Physical integrity: violence against women, laws on sexual harassment, attitudes toward violence, prevalence of violence in lifetime.
Restricted resources and assets: secure access to land and non-land assets, access to financial services.
Restricted civil liberties: access to public space; political voice; political representation.

countries do better than other countries in the MENA region when it comes to gender equality (see Figure 1.1). The two regions are the same when it comes to restricted resources and assets. The SIGI index combines both the women's rights legislation adopted and the implementation of policy within countries.

Varieties of Democracy (V-DEM) data, which similarly use a wide range of variables, also show the gap quite clearly. They pinpoint

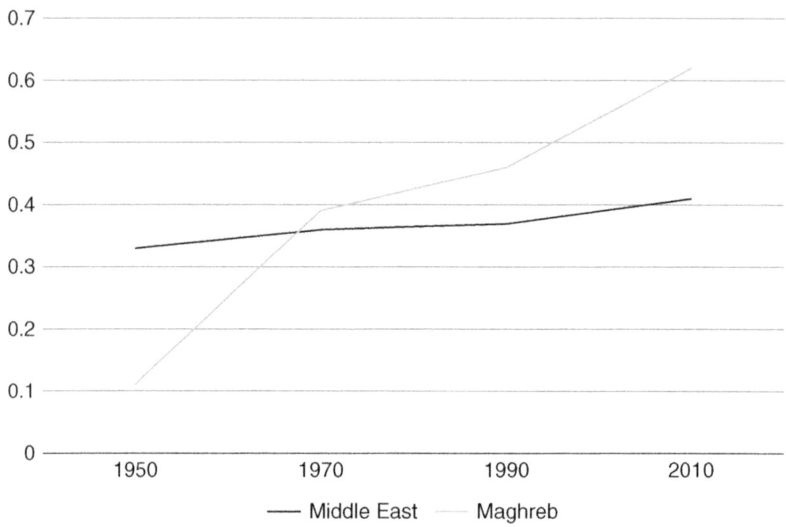

Figure 1.2 Gender equality (1 = highest level)
Source: Varieties of Democracy V-Dem Institute, Database, 2017, www.v-dem.net/en

roughly when the Maghreb countries overtook the Middle Eastern countries, starting in the 1970s but most clearly in the 1990s, when the convergence between the three Maghreb countries also took place (Figure 1.2). Up until then, only Tunisia was a leader in women's rights.

Chapter 3 looks in further detail at the same bifurcation between the Maghreb and Middle East when it comes to constitutional and legislative reform. But the data above suggest that the gap exists not just in legal reform but in gender outcomes as well in key areas.

Research Questions and Hypotheses

The two central research questions driving this project come from an interest in explaining subregional variation in the adoption of women's rights policy in the MENA region. With the term "women's rights," I am referring in this book to women's rights legislation and constitutional changes that are fought for and supported by women's rights organizations in the region. I show: (1) why there is a convergence between the Maghreb countries of Tunisia, Algeria, and Morocco when it comes to women's rights, and (2) why these countries, taken as a subregion, have pursued patterns that diverge from those found in most other Arab countries in the Middle East. This study helps explain the mechanisms for legislative change, aspects of which can be found throughout the Middle East, but not as consistently as in the Maghreb, which is why these countries were selected. Contrasting the Maghreb countries with the Middle East allows me to control for historical and cultural variance between them to help isolate which factors hold explanatory power.

This study provides two ways of thinking about variance in the region with respect to women's rights. The first is the aforementioned cross-national regional comparative dimension. The second is a temporal dimension, in which I am looking at the adoption of women's rights reforms over time as a reaction to the conservative Islamic trends that swept the region after the mid 1970s and 1980s and the ways those in power responded to various Islamist tendencies, especially extremist ones, using women's rights as a means of isolating them.

The three case studies of Morocco, Tunisia, and Algeria show how the convergence between the three countries occurred with respect to women's rights through competition and diffusion (see Table 3.4 in Chapter 3). In the Conclusions, these three countries are paired with Middle Eastern countries that have done less well in advancing women's rights to further tease out the differences between the Maghreb and the Middle East: Morocco with Jordan, which are two kingdoms with modernizing kings; Tunisia with Lebanon, two former French protectorates with populations who hold more liberal attitudes toward gender equality than most in the region; and Algeria with Egypt, two autocratic states where the military has excessive control.

Hypotheses

Women's Rights as Part of an Internal and External Strategy by Leaders

The rise of Al Qaeda and, later, Daesh put the spotlight on the Islamist parties and organizations in the region, particularly after two terrorist incidents carried out by local Islamists: a 2002 attack in Djerba, Tunisia, in which a truck rammed into a synagogue, killing twenty-one mostly European tourists, and another suicide bomb attack in Casablanca in Morocco in 2003. More attacks followed in 2007 in a Tunis suburb and in Algeria in a series of bombing incidents in 2006 and 2007 that appeared to be linked to external groups. In 2007, Al Qaeda in the Islamic Maghreb (AQIM) announced its establishment in Algeria. Later suicide operations involved an attack on a café in Marrakesh, Morocco, in 2011, and attacks in Tunisia, on the Bardo National Museum in Tunis, a hotel near Sousse in 2015, and an attack by a female suicide bomber in 2018 in Tunis. Except for the killing of two Scandinavian students by ISIS in a remote village near Imlil, there have been no attacks in Morocco since 2011 as a result of a state policy to dismantle jihadist militia cells, the numbers of which have dropped significantly since a high in 2014. Estimates of Moroccan fighters who went to Syria and Iraq range from 1,600 to 2,100 (Guenfoudi 2018). The number of fighters who went to fight in Syria and Iraq from Algeria was negligible, while the number of fighters from Tunisia (6,000) was the highest of the three countries (Bremmer 2017).

Those in power in the Maghreb used a variety of tactics including repression, co-optation, surveillance, and forms of accommodation to neutralize extremists. A dominant theme in these strategies was the use of women's rights as a moderating force. This had both beneficial and problematic consequences for women's rights and women's rights activists. The only leader in the Middle East to adopt this strategy was General Sisi in Egypt, but he did so while at the same time suppressing women's movements and civil society, making it nearly impossible for women's rights activists to effectively collaborate with the government in shaping women's rights reforms.

When the Islamist movements in the Maghreb started to grow in the 1970s, the governments tolerated and even encouraged them, often to offset the influence of the leftist and Amazigh movements. In all three countries, the state initially took control of many spheres that were traditionally the domain of the religious authorities, like religious educational institutions, the mosques and their personnel. The *'ulema* (علماء, religious scholars) were absorbed into the state administration as employees, particularly in the religious affairs ministries. They used to issue *fatwas* (فتوى, rulings on Islamic law) in support of government policies. Political authorities similarly used religious texts to justify their own policies. In all three countries, the Islamists mounted resistance to being sidelined and their ranks grew. Michael Willis (2012) argues that a vacuum was created between state and society as the '*ulema* were neutralized and co-opted, depriving them of their traditional role as arbiters between the state and society.

The Islamists began to fill this void. Most of the MENA region experienced the spread of Salafism, variants of the Muslim Brotherhood, and many other conservative Islamic movements after the mid 1970s and 1980s, sponsored by governments like those of Saudi Arabia, but also Qatar, the United Arab Emirates (UAE), and Kuwait. The governmental effort involved building colleges, schools, mosques, and religious centers in Muslim countries; the distribution of Qur'ans; the spread of various proselytizing organizations; and the widespread use of various media, starting initially with books and cassette tapes and later continuing with cable TV and social media. One of the most visible manifestations of this trend was the increase in veiled women throughout the MENA region and the spread of veiling to other Muslim countries. Opposition to women's rights advances mounted in the region, including the Maghreb, as the Islamist influence expanded, often with the assistance of oil money from countries in the Gulf. There are vast differences among the Islamists. Many were competing movements; some were based on Sufism and others were hostile to it; some used violence and others opposed the use of violence; and, finally, some wished to engage in contemporary legislative politics, while others did not.

As the conservative Islamist influences spread throughout the MENA region and became more powerful, governments adopted a dual policy. On the one hand, they fiercely repressed the Islamist movements. On the other hand, they sought to legitimize them, granting them various concessions. In Egypt, the Mubarak regime reversed a number of progressive laws that had been promulgated and ended up with a reactionary women's policy. The situation was the same in Iraq at the time of the war with Iran. The leaders sought conciliation with the conservative elements and in the process they made concessions by revoking various women's rights (T2.3.16.17). This occurred in the Maghreb to some extent and is evident in the passage of the 1984 PSC in Algeria, which was full of concessions to Islamists in that country.

Yet, after 2000, there was the beginning of a reversal as women's movements began to push back. The use of women's rights as a weapon against extremism was seen primarily in North Africa. This leads us to our first hypotheses:

H1a: Women's rights were more easily advanced where heads of state and other leaders used them as an internal strategy to neutralize extremist Islamist movements.
H1b: Women's rights were more easily advanced where heads of state and other leaders used them as an external strategy to present a modernizing image of their countries to the world.

Women's Rights as a Party Strategy of Survival

In the wave of expansion of Islamist influence throughout the MENA region, Islamist parties started making bids for power in North Africa. They were about to win the 1991 elections in Algeria but the government moved to keep them out of power by cancelling the second round of elections. A brutal civil war ensued that ended around 2002. A decade later in Egypt, Mohamed Morsi and his Muslim Brotherhood were elected in 2012. He remained in power for just over a year until he was forcibly removed from office in a military coup d'état led by General Abel Fattah el Sisi, who harshly suppressed the Muslim Brotherhood in the aftermath. In Morocco, the Party of Justice and Development (PJD) came to power in 2011, heading up a coalition government. Ennahda similarly was elected to office in 2011 in Tunisia. Both the Moroccan and Tunisian Islamist parties were challenged on their women's rights policies by women's movements. Realizing that if they were to have any staying power, they would have to make concessions in this area, both parties, perhaps defensively, have now adopted the language of women's rights through a process of what some have called "political learning" (El Hachimi 2015).

The Islamist party in Morocco, the PJD, made almost 180-degree turns from opposing the PSC reforms in 2004 to supporting the PSC; from opposing a World Bank gender reform policy, the Plan d'action national pour l'intégration de la femme au development (PANIFD, Action Plan for the Integration of Women in Development), to supporting a European Union-funded gender equality project; and from bitterly resisting pressures to comply with the United Nations Convention on the Elimination of Discrimination of Women (CEDAW) on women's rights reform to accepting CEDAW and going ahead with lifting many of Morocco's reservations. In Tunisia, in the face of massive protests and pushback, the Islamist party Ennahda conceded to a constitution that included a gender parity clause after much pressure and internal party dissent. Ennahda came second in the 2014 parliamentary elections and formed a coalition government with a larger secular party, Nidaa Tounes. It did not endorse a candidate to run for president in the 2014 elections, reflecting a retreat.

In addition to the women's movement, another element that factored into the changing positions of the parties was the fact that there was another concentration of power in politics. In Morocco, power was concentrated in the hands of the king, in Algeria in the hands of the military, and in Tunisia in the hands of the president and his hegemonic political party prior to 2011 (Willis 2002). The parties had to appease these power centers if they were to remain in power. In the case of Morocco, for example, this entailed going along with the PSC and the revised 2011 constitution.

This leads to a second hypothesis:

H2: Women's rights were more easily advanced when supporting them became a political necessity for a party in order to remain in power, to exercise power, and/or to garner the votes of women.

Women's Rights at Critical Junctures

All three countries experienced critical junctures in which women's rights hung in the balance, when women's rights were often pitted against conservatives and the Islamists, particularly the extremists. These moments were accompanied by major political change or changes in power. In Tunisia these moments came at independence in 1956, after the coup d'état in which Zine El Abidine Ben Ali ousted President Habib Bourguiba in 1987, and again after the Arab Spring in 2011, when President Ben Ali himself was ousted. In Algeria, the critical junctures came with independence in 1962, later with the death of Houari Boumédiène in 1978, the subsequent takeover of President Chadli Bendjedid, with the end of the Black Decade, which lasted from 1991 to 2002, and once again in the 2019 uprising when feminists combined demands for democracy with calls for women's rights. In Morocco, the critical junctures occurred with the ascent to power of Mohammed VI after the death of his father Hassan II in 1999 and then after the Vingt février movement at the time of the Arab Spring in 2011. In each of these transitions, women's rights were strengthened, with the exception of the period after independence in Algeria, which was marked by devastating setbacks for women's rights. In each case, it was up to women's organizations to press for change lest the Islamists and other conservatives claim the upper hand.

It is striking how many narratives of these critical junctures in the Maghreb have failed to account for the struggle of women's claims to citizenship. This is most notably evident in the literature about the Arab Spring, where discussions of women's rights have been siloed in books and articles about women, yet these struggles over women's rights were central to understanding the Arab Spring and its aftermath. Many of the legal changes I analyze in this book took place after the uprisings and were energized by them, particularly in Morocco (the Vingt février protests) and Tunisia. Women were at the forefront of protests in Morocco, Tunisia, Egypt, and Yemen during this period (Abounaï 2012, Bacha 2013, Desrues 2012, Ghorbani 2012, Mohsen-Finan 2013, Salime 2012, Tchaïcha and Arfaoui 2012). They were active in blogging and other social media, and they were also part of a cultural renaissance of graffiti artists, filmmakers, and musicians (Stephan and Charrad forthcoming, Khalil 2015).

While some have argued that women did not benefit from the sacrifices they made during the Arab Spring (Olimat 2013), this was not the case in Tunisia and Morocco, where women made important gains on the legal front as a result of legislative and constitutional reforms, as described above. Although Algeria did not experience an Arab Spring per se, the ripple effects were felt in legislative changes affecting women at this time. The diverse outcomes for women after the Moroccan and Tunisian uprisings contrast sharply, for example, with what happened in Egypt, which experienced a sharp deterioration of civil liberties and political rights after the military overthrow of President Mohamed Morsi by Gen. Sisi in 2013. The outcome in Morocco and Tunisia also diverges from the experience of Yemen, which fell into disarray after its Arab Spring. Nevertheless, most books on the Arab uprisings have ignored the central role of women in these movements and the impact of the uprisings on women (see for example Brownlee et al. 2015, Lynch 2013, 2014, Roberts et al. 2016).

In all three Maghreb countries, activists fought over legislative and constitutional reforms regarding women's rights. They were doing so in an environment where for many, women rights held symbolic meaning over and above the rights themselves. The struggles were over the broader question of the meaning of citizenship itself and what that meant for the rights and duties of women. The perennial question was, on what basis do women become citizens? Would it be based on complementarity, which values women's contributions as mothers and wives in the home, or would it be as equal citizens with parity with men in all areas of life? Would they be seen as full citizens or as minors in need of guardianship and as dependents of men because they were regarded as vulnerable and in need of protection?

In the early years after independence, the women's movements were curtailed in all three countries and as a result they had little influence on the adoption of women's rights in these countries. After the war of independence in Algeria, when women had fought on the frontlines and contributed in a wide variety of ways to the liberation effort, women leaders thought they would be rewarded with political positions and with equal rights. Instead, they were shown to the kitchen and told that their role was to serve as mothers and wives. Their status as virtual minors was enshrined in the 1984 PSC, which included a provision for male guardianship of women. The guardian or *wali* (الولي) was often the father, who oversaw the conclusion of a marriage contract and selected the bridegroom. It was not until after the civil war, which ended in 2002, that women's rights activists had some input into the PSC and as a result gained a slightly improved code in 2005 (although still with a modified guardianship provision), key legislation, and constitutional changes that gave them equality with men, with greater political representation.

Women's movements became more visible in the region after the 1990s. This was in part a consequence of the opening of some political space in each country, the existence of more educated women, the presence of more women in professions, the delay in the age of marriage, and smaller family sizes. The diffusion of international norms regarding women's rights after the Fourth United Nations Conference on Women in Beijing also contributed to greater pressures to increase women's political representation and women's rights. At the same time, the rise of fundamentalist movements in the Maghreb and across the MENA region more generally posed direct challenges to women's rights and in some countries, like Tunisia, they threatened to roll back hard-won gains. Women's organizations built inclusive alliances with each other, with left-leaning parties, human rights organizations, and other civil society organizations to demand legislative and constitutional reforms (Moghadam 2017).

In Morocco, the ascent of the new king, Mohammed VI, to the throne in 1999 saw increased focus on the status of women. He made his mark by facilitating the passage of the 2004 PSC (Moudawana), which was pivotal in establishing greater gender equality in the home by getting rid of guardianship. Under pressure from women's movements, he further helped expand rights for women by ushering in constitutional reforms in 2011, establishing women's right to parity with men in the political sphere. In Tunisia, women had legal equality with men in the home after independence with the 1956 PSC, but they had yet to claim political parity until after the Arab Spring, with the 2014 constitution. Reproductive freedom is key to women's capacity to exercise their citizenship in the home, in the workforce, and in politics. In Tunisia, this came early with the right to family planning in 1961 and the right to abortion without conditions in 1973, incidentally the same year that the US Supreme Court decriminalized abortion. Women's rights activists were energized during the 2011 Arab Spring protests in Tunisia and subsequently fought for constitutional and legislative reforms.

Women and women's rights have represented a central theme in the struggles for internal political legitimacy, modernity, international recognition, and dignity in the postindependence era. At each critical juncture, women's rights were thrust to the fore as a key battleground. Women, women's bodies, and women's rights became proxies for the state and for Islamists, standing in for other goals and objectives, which this book explores. At almost every critical juncture, women's movements helped shape this discourse and inserted their demands. Hence my next hypothesis:

H3: Countries in the MENA region experienced greater success in advancing women's rights where women's movements intervened at critical junctures after a change of leadership, a war, coup d'état, or other major social upheaval.

Women's Movement Collaboration across the Maghreb

One of the most striking features of women's rights legislative reform in the Maghreb after 2000 was the manner in which the three countries passed legislation in an almost synchronized fashion. Competition may have occurred at the level of policymakers. But the fact that women's rights legislation has been passed almost in tandem in all three Maghreb countries speaks mostly to the coordination among women's rights activists, which they confirmed in my interviews in all three countries. They have participated in networks throughout the Maghreb and the MENA region such as Collectif Maghreb-Égalité 95 (Collective for Equality in the Maghreb 95), Gender and Politics (WEP), the Arab International Women's Forum (AIWF), Karama, the Arab Network for Gender and Development, Mediterranean organizations like the Euro-Mediterranean Women's Foundation, the Arab Women Parliamentarians Network for Equality *Ra'edat* (Pioneers), and many other organizations and networks. The Union de l'action féminine (UAF) in Morocco formed the Court for Arab Women made up of researchers, journalists, lawyers, and policymakers to share experiences throughout the region.

Because the Maghreb has a triple identity as part of the African, Arab, and Mediterranean worlds, they often sit at the intersection of networks in these three regions. The UAF, for example, organized a preparatory conference of all the human rights NGOs of Africa for the World Conference on Human Rights in Geneva later that year. The UAF was also part of African women's rights networks like Femnet. One of the judges in the Court of Cassation, leading women's rights activist Malika Benradi, was president of the Association of African Women for Research and Development (AAWORD)/Association des femmes africaines pour la recherche et le développement (AFARD). The late Fatema Mernissi was a founding member of AAWORD and participated in its launch meeting in Dakar, Senegal, in December 1977. Benradi was the one who presented the report on parity in Africa to the International Conference on Parity held in Senegal in 2011 on behalf of AAWORD.

One activist who was involved in these various regional networks told me that "My Spanish and Italian friends tell me that we in the Mediterranean have more in common with you as Moroccans than we do with the English, Finns or Swedes" (M20.4.25.16). But Europe is important for other reasons. The European Union (EU) is a major funder of women's rights activities in the region, there are many exchanges between North African and European leaders around these issues, and the EU is the major trading partner of Morocco and Tunisia.

Because of the large number of immigrants from the region who live in Europe, the laws in the region matter to those who live abroad who may find, for example, that they can be polygamous in Morocco or Algeria but not in France, or they may find the inheritance laws differ from Morocco to Belgium.

The networks within the Maghreb itself have been particularly effective in sharing strategies. One Tunisian lawyer and women's rights activist explained:

> I currently participate in many meetings on law and when you attend these meetings you realize the rapprochement between the Maghreb countries and the legal difference between the Maghreb and the Middle East. First, the feminist movement appeared almost simultaneously in all three countries. For example, we conducted many meetings together on sexual harassment, and the three states at the same time changed laws to punish sexual harassment. When we established parity in our electoral law in 2011, in Algeria they modified the constitution and modified the electoral law to introduce the quota. Morocco introduced parity in the constitution and laws. So it is moving forward in a convergent way. (T1.3.16.17)

Although there are many autonomous organizations and networks within the region, one of the first and most influential organizations was Collectif Maghreb-Égalité 95, formed in 1991 by activists and researchers from Algeria, Morocco, and Tunisia at the invitation of the Moroccan Women's Democratic Association (ADFM). The collective was formed to coordinate activities leading up to the United Nations Fourth Conference on Women held in Beijing in 1995. They were united in the belief that the struggle for gender equality would allow women to achieve full citizenship. They plotted a strategy for bringing about gender equality in the region, drawing on their commonalities of history, language, and civilization to forge unity. They articulated this strategy in the document *Cent mesures et dispositions pour une codification égalitaire des relations familiales au Maghreb*. Their demands included gender equality before the law; abolition of the wife's duty to obey her husband and of the notion that there was only one head of household; allowing women to provide for the family like men; substitution of parental responsibility for parental authority; gender equality in inheritance and in passing one's nationality to one's children; elimination of all forms of racial and religious discrimination within the family; and legal recognition of children born out of wedlock. In compiling an overview of legislation passed in the Maghreb, it becomes clear how successful they have been in moving their agenda forward as each one of these agenda items has been tackled systematically. The most intense linkages are between Morocco and Tunisia because they have more active women's movements, but they have also collaborated extensively with Algeria (and Mauritania). As one Algerian activist who has been active in Collectif Maghreb-Égalité 95 from the outset put it:

Collectif Maghreb-Égalité 95 has been particularly effective in coordinating women activists in the three countries. The Maghreb countries, apart from Tunisia, which already had an advanced Family Code, worked on a code of the Maghrebian family which we call the 100 measures and which we went to present in Beijing. Through this Maghrebi Code, we have gone further than those of our respective countries and we have presented a document we called the White Paper, which included all the international conventions ratified by our countries and where we spoke of "Maghrebis under reservation," that is to say, the reservations made by our countries when ratifying these Conventions, in particular CEDAW. So we went to Beijing and organized a parliament that included more than 2,000 women and we presented the 100 measures with the obligation for each of us to return to our countries and work with this Code. The work of the Collectif Maghreb-Égalité 95 has served to support the work in each country. (A3.9.26.16)

Some of the linkages were bilateral between organizations. Women worked with organizations in other countries to learn their strategies firsthand. Starting around 2000, women's rights organizations participated in caravans in their own and neighboring countries, even in Spain and France, to carry out campaigns around specific issues and sometimes conduct surveys to learn about the conditions of women. A member of Morocco's Fédération de la ligue démocratique des droits des femmes (FLDDF) coordinated with Algerian associations around the violence against women law, and they worked together for a framework for the law (M3.2.26.16).

As a result of this collaboration, we see a pattern of convergence in legislation passed around quotas, sexual harassment, the prohibition on the marriage of victims to their rapist, nationality issues, violence against women, and other such legislation (see Table 3.4 in Chapter 3). This leads us to the final hypothesis, that:

H4: Women's rights legislation converged in the Maghreb because of the close cooperation between women's movements and the diffusion of goals and strategies.

Alternate Explanations

There are no major studies to my knowledge that tackle the exact same questions I am asking, but there are studies that speak to the broader question of what accounts for women's advancement in the MENA region. Below I explore two sets of explanations. One set relates to cultural factors like kinship and religion, and the other looks at structural factors relating to women's education, economic growth, the presence of oil rents, and international pressures.

Cultural Arguments

Kinship Systems

Mounira Charrad (2001) has argued that kin-based power systems have influenced women's rights outcomes in Tunisia, Algeria, and Morocco. This would have implications beyond the Maghreb as a factor in explaining divergences in gender policy. She found in the Maghreb that the more autonomous the state was from tribal kin groups, the more liberal the policies were toward women, particularly with respect to family law. In Morocco, the tribal structure was tied to the state and in Algeria the state depended on support from kin groups, whereas in Tunisia the state that emerged after independence was largely autonomous from kin groups. As a result, more conservative policies emerged in Algeria and Morocco than in Tunisia, which was able to adopt more progressive women's rights policies early on, particularly with respect to the PSC.

I build on Charrad's work extensively in this book, but her argument does not help explain why we now see the convergence between the three countries in the Maghreb, nor why the Maghreb region as a whole has moved along a different trajectory from the rest of the MENA countries with respect to women's rights. Tunisia, to be sure, is still the leader in women's rights reforms, but today the similarities between the Maghreb countries outweigh the differences in spite of historical and structural divergence. It might also be worth considering that the kinship structure may have eroded in all three countries with civil war in Algeria, with urbanization, and with the formation of more nuclear families at the core of the social structure. At least 61 percent of Morocco's total population lived in urban areas and cities in 2017, and 67 percent in Tunisia and 71 percent in Algeria as of 2016.

Religious Influences

Some have argued that Islam *and* autocracy make a potent combination that mitigates against the advancement of women's rights. When it comes to predominantly Muslim countries, some see authoritarianism combined with Islam as antithetical to women's rights or, at best, a challenge to them (Inglehart and Norris 2003). In fact, Steven Fish (2002) argues that predominantly Muslim countries are incompatible with democratization and that women's subordination helps explain this democratic deficit. He points to potential mechanisms that account for this link, from gender differences in literacy to the sex ratio imbalance that favors men due to the high number of male migrants working in oil-rich countries; the dominance of the father in the family, which is transposed to patriarchal governments; the segregation of sexes in schools, workplaces, and places of leisure; the removal of women's perspectives from politics and governance; male attitudes that favor authoritarianism; women's aversion to violence; and extremism in politics that tilts toward men.

Others dispute such linkages. Cesari (2017) argues that the arrows go the other way: that the deficit of women's rights in Muslim countries is tied to religiously based legislation. This is further elaborated on by Dawood I. Ahmed and Moamen Gouda (2015), who argue that the more constitutions in Muslim-majority countries are Islamicized, the less they adhere to women's rights, the less democratic they are, and the less politically stable. While agreeing that most Islamic countries are governed by authoritarian regimes and that women's status is worse in Islamic countries than in others, Daniela Donno and Bruce Russett (2004) find these patterns to be more likely in Arab countries, not Islamic countries. They also argue that these types of relationship are fluid and point out that Catholic countries at one time used to be even more likely to be authoritarian than Islamic ones, yet this changed after 1990. Contrary to Fish, Donno and Russett find that women's repression is *not* central to maintaining autocratic rule. When measures for women's status, such as education, political participation, health, and economic activity are disaggregated, democracy only has an impact on women's presence in government. They added to Fish's variables for women's rights the literacy gap, the sex ratio in society, and the percentage of women in government and parliament, the life expectancy ratio, the educational attainment ratio, and the ratio of economically active females to males. They find that Islamic countries are more likely to be autocratic, regardless of whether women's rights are restricted, and they argue based on their findings that Arab countries do not repress women because they are autocratic. They argue that Islamic or Arab culture is not an impediment to achieving women's rights either, but rather other factors relating to the Arab states would provide better explanatory power. They speculate on some of these factors (the role of religious groups, how secular the state is, the role of international and civil conflict, oil, etc.).

Another cross-national study conducted by Mala Htun and Laurel Weldon (2018) argues that the adoption of family law that upholds women's rights depends on whether religion is institutionalized in the state as doctrine. All Arab countries in the MENA region have a clause in their constitutions identifying Islam as the state religion. However, the institutionalization of a state religion does not tell us enough about the differences between the countries within the MENA region and why some have adopted more progressive policies than others when it comes to family law. The Nordic constitutions also invoke state authority over the Lutheran church in their respective countries and religion is also institutionalized in these countries, yet this has very different implications for family law than what one finds in the MENA region. In contrast, in much of Africa, including Muslim-majority countries, it is not institutionalized religion, but rather traditional authorities and customary law that shape family law in practice, even where they are limited by statutory law. These are not doctrinal entities.

In Muslim-majority countries, according to Cesari (2017), what matters is whether there is a hegemonic religion, where the state elevates a certain religious group with exclusive legal, economic, or political rights and denies these rights to other religions. It is not separation of religion from the state nor state cooperation with religious entities that matters, as one finds in the Nordic countries. Rather, it is the privileging of one religion over others and the exclusion of other religious groups at the expense of one religion that makes the difference. The hegemonic status of a religion, according to Cesari (2017, 19), involves the nationalization and management of official religious institutions, government regulation of religious activities, the teaching of one religion in schools, as well as restrictions on freedom of speech and women's rights based on that religion. Most Muslim-majority countries (with a few exceptions, like Lebanon, and Senegal) have two or three of these characteristics.

Cesari has argued that the secularization of Muslim-majority countries in the postindependence period led to the advancement of the political, economic, and social rights of women, while the expansion of Salafi movements led to the curtailment of women's rights in family law. This helps explain why – except for a few extreme cases, like Afghanistan under the Taliban and Iraq under ISIS control – women's rights generally expanded in education, employment, and political representation, but not in the area of family law. These advances were made in authoritarian contexts, which were different than what one saw in Europe, where women's rights expanded with democratization. The state itself became the most important agent in redefining Islamic law after the 1960s and in shaping Islamic norms. Women's bodies became a major site for politicizing Islam for both state and nonstate actors.

Cesari is correct in arguing that the presence of a hegemonic religion matters in most Muslim-majority countries for women's rights, but one still has to explain why there is so much variance across time and terrain among these countries. At the regional level of analysis, it is easier to see how historical practices have shaped different de facto practices determined by tribal and religious authorities, social movements, colonial policy, and state strength. But which practices matter the most when it comes to women's rights? And why have some Muslim-majority countries done better than others when it comes to women's rights? These are the questions this book sets out to answer.

Before testing our hypotheses, we must first discuss some of the common alternative arguments made to explain variance in the region when it comes to women's rights. Women's legislative representation is one measure that is commonly referenced in discussions on women's status and is discussed in the section that follows on alternative arguments.

Structural Influences on Women's Rights Reforms

Economic Growth

Higher GDP is associated with higher rates of female legislative representation globally (Tripp and Kang 2005) and some have argued that this is the case in the MENA region (Welborne 2010). In the MENA region, none of the five countries with the highest GDP per capita (over $20,000) have quotas, although Saudi Arabia, Bahrain, and the UAE have some appointed seats. Moreover, the countries with the highest rates of female legislative representation in the MENA region – over 25 percent – (Tunisia, Algeria, and Iraq) all fall into the bottom half of GDP per capita rates for the region (Table 1.1). The same lack of correlation is evident if one compares GDP per capita rates with the gender gap using World Economic Forum data. The causal pathways normally used to explain the relationship between GDP and women's rights are not evident in the MENA region. It is believed that a larger GDP expands the middle class, which then pushes for greater democracy, which in turn opens up political space for women's movements to demand representation. A higher GDP has not had these democratizing effects in the MENA region, which remains one of the most authoritarian in the world.

Female Labor Force Participation

The other suggested pathway regards an increase in GDP as an important factor in increasing women's labor force participation, which in turn is said to result in pressures on societies to grant women political power. However, female labor force participation is not a pathway for gender reform in the MENA region (Table 1.1), where changes in legislative representation, for example, are a result of the introduction of quotas, which are tied more to the role of the political elites who introduce top-down measures often as a result of pressure from or with support of women's movements. Only half of the countries with higher rates of representation (over 20 percent of legislative seats held by women) have higher levels of female labor force participation (over 25 percent), but of the countries with the lowest levels of representation (below 10 percent), half also have higher levels of female labor force participation (over 25 percent). Of our case studies, only Tunisia and

Morocco have among the highest rates of female labor force participation, with 27 and 26 percent of their women in the labor force respectively, while Algeria at 18 percent has lower female labor force participation. The case for female labor force participation rests on an unproven assumption that MENA legislatures will readily succumb to pressures to adopt women's rights legislation in response to mobilized women workers.

Female Education

Education is also commonly regarded as an explanatory factor in accounting for female legislative representation. Certainly, one needs women to be educated to serve in legislatures. There is no shortage of educated women in the region, but there is little if any difference between the Maghreb and the Middle East in this regard, which means that education cannot account for the differences between the two regions. Women with a university education are the most likely to serve in legislatures in the MENA region. The percentage of women in universities exceeds that of men in all MENA countries for which we have data, except for Morocco, where it is high at 48 percent. They also exceed male students in medicine and STEM fields in many MENA countries. Moreover, the gender gap in education in the MENA region has closed to 95 percent, according to the World Economic Forum data (see Chapter 3, Figure 3.11). The countries with the highest levels of women with BA degrees, with the exception of Tunisia, all have the lowest levels of female legislative representation, although the data are somewhat incomplete for the region as we are missing data for five out of eighteen countries (Table 1.1). Nevertheless, it is unlikely that any variance in education would account for differences in women's rights reforms.

Oil Rents

Some, like Michael Ross (2008), have argued that it is oil rents that suppress female labor force participation in parts of the world like the Middle East, thereby keeping female political representation low. Women in the labor force, according to this hypothesis, are once again seen as responsible for pressing for greater representation. However, this does not account for the pressure exerted by women's

Table 1.1 *Maghreb and Middle East female legislative representation, GDP per capita, labor force participation, tertiary education, and oil production*

	Rates of female legislative representation %	Quota	GDP per capita $	Female labor force participation %	Female tertiary graduates %	Oil production bbl/day 2016
Algeria	25.8	Yes	4,123	18	63	1,348,361
Bahrain	7.5		23,655	21	64	50,000
Egypt	14.9	Yes	2,413	23	54	494,325
Iraq	25.3	Yes	5,166	20		4,451,516
Jordan	15.4	Yes	4,130	18	56	22
Kuwait	2.5		29,040	28	73	2,923,825
Lebanon	4.7		8,524	24		
Libya	16.0	Yes	7,998	25		1,003,000
Mauritania	20.3	Yes	1,137	31		5,000
Morocco	20.5	Yes	3,007	26	48	160
Oman	0		15,668	13	64	1,006,841
Palestine	13.0	Yes	3,095	21	63	
Qatar	9.8		63,506	14	76	1,522,902
Saudi Arabia	19.9	Yes	20,761	16	57	10,460,710
Syria	13.2		2,058	14	60	

Tunisia	35.9	Yes	3,491	27	68	48,757
UAE	22.5		37,622	12	55	3,106,077
Yemen	0.3		990	8		

Sources by column: 1: Inter-Parliamentary Union (2008); 2 International Institute for Democratic and Electoral Assistance, Gender Quotas Database, www.idea.int/data-tools/data/gender-quotas; 3 World Bank Open Data, GDP per capita (current US$), https://data.worldbank.org/indicator/ny.gdp.pcap.cd; 4 World Bank Open Data, Ratio of female to male labor force participation rate (%) (modeled ILO estimate) https://data.worldbank.org/indicator/sl.tlf.cact.fm.zs; 5 UNESCO Institute for Statistics, Tertiary graduates by level of education, http://data.uis.unesco.org/index.aspx?queryid=162; 6 US Energy Information Administration, International Energy Outlook, "Production of Crude Oil including Lease Condensate 2016," www.eia.gov/outlooks/ieo/.

movements for quotas irrespective of women's labor force participation. In fact, we are seeing women becoming more active in politics in many oil-producing countries like the UAE and Algeria, mostly as a result of the introduction of quotas or appointed positions, support by political leaders for such reforms, and pressure from women's rights activists. This is happening even in the Middle East, where oil-producing countries are increasing rates of female representation. Of the countries in the MENA region producing over 1 million barrels a day, half have over 20 percent of their parliamentary seats filled by women (Table 1.1). Thus, when quotas are taken into account, the role of oil diminishes in importance and one has to look elsewhere for explanations of women's political representation. Algeria produces over 1 million barrels a day *and* has women in 26 percent of its parliamentary seats. The higher rates of representation in this oil-producing country have less to do with female labor force participation, which is relatively low, and much more to do with the role of the women's movements, the government's commitment to advancing women, as well as postconflict repercussions.

External Influences

While the main impetus for gender reform came from within the Maghreb countries, one of the factors that has contributed to the expansion of women's movements globally is the role of UN Women and other multilateral and bilateral donors. The 1995 UN Conference on Women in Beijing had a particularly salutary effect on women's political leadership globally and, as mentioned above, it helped spur collaboration between the three Maghreb countries. Almost all women's rights advocates interviewed pointed to the importance of UN treaties like the Convention on the Elimination of All Forms of Discrimination against Women (CEDAW), various UN agencies, and the establishment of the Millennium Development Goals, Sustainable Development Goals, and other initiatives which were invoked by domestic initiatives to increase women's political representation and address other concerns.

The proximity of the Maghreb to other Mediterranean countries and to Europe is also of consequence. Marseilles in France is only one hour from Algiers by plane. The ties which began in bitter colonial domination and are experienced through the continuing legacies of domination have also resulted in population flows and related exchanges of ideas. The extensive linguistic pluralism of the region has allowed North Africans to access and to contribute to the world of ideas through their facility with Arabic and French, but also Spanish and increasingly English. The French historically influenced leftist tendencies and feminism in the Maghreb, and both ideologies have influenced women's rights activism in the region (A7.11.10.16, A11.9.29.16, A25.10.9.16, A30.10.16.16). In Morocco, for example, two of the leading feminist organizations had such origins. The Association démocratique des femmes de Maroc (ADFM) was formed in 1985 by women in the Parti du progrès et du socialisme (PPS), while the Union de l'action feminine (UAF) was formed in 1987 out of the now defunct left-wing Organisation de l'action démocratique populaire (OADP).

Morocco, Tunisia, and Algeria have close relationships with the EU, which resulted in a series of new agreements around women's rights promotion after the Arab Spring in 2011. Morocco already had an advanced status with the EU in terms of political cooperation, which was established by the 2000 Association Agreement. In 2012, Tunisia signed a Privileged Partnership agreement with the EU for 2013–2017 in which the EU pledged support for the people's transition toward greater democracy, freedom, and social justice. It provided €169 million in bilateral aid with the emphasis on economic recovery and reforms in key sectors including gender equality. A similar agreement was signed between the EU and Algeria in 2017.

The ties between North Africa and Europe are especially strong in the Mediterranean region, as evident in the 1995 Barcelona conference on the Union for the Mediterranean,[2] where the Barcelona Declaration recognized "the key role of women" and the need to enhance women's social and economic roles, along with the importance of education and employment opportunities for women. In its communication "Reinvigorating the Barcelona Process" (2000), the Commission stressed that specific emphasis should be put on the enhancement of the role of women in economic development, along with the implementation of best practices on linking training policies with employment needs in the Mediterranean. It recommended greater attention to the

[2] The Union for the Mediterranean involves twenty-eight countries from the European side, fifteen from the Mediterranean side, and the Arab League.

sector of justice and home affairs, which includes seeking conformity of judicial systems, including family and inheritance law.

The Euro-Mediterranean Partnership also involved various forms of economic, political, and security ties between twenty-five EU countries and ten Mediterranean countries. These close ties have influenced collaborations in the area of women's rights in the Maghreb. The EU has supported Morocco's Government Plan for Equality (2012–2016) to the tune of €45 million, focusing on resolving serious gender inequalities as an essential prerequisite for achieving the objectives of the Barcelona Process. In addition, cooperation between Morocco and the Council of Europe has focused on key human rights issues, such as the prevention of and fight against violence against women and children and the fight against trafficking.

However, this international influence is not unique to the Maghreb, nor has the Maghreb benefited more than other countries in the Mediterranean region in financial support for women's rights activism, which suggests that external influence constitutes an important factor but not one that necessarily explains variance in the MENA region.

Some have argued that donor support plays a key role in gender quota adoption, which generally increases rates of female legislative representation (for example, Bush 2011). Bozena Welborne (2010) found a correlation between Overseas Development Assistance (ODA) and gender quotas in the Middle East by looking at the years 1990–2007. Mina Baliamoune-Lutz (2013) also found that ODA has increased women's political empowerment in a study of thirteen MENA countries covering the period 2002–2010. While the United Nations agencies have promoted quotas in the Maghreb and the Middle East more generally, if one takes a longer trajectory than the aforementioned studies, there appears, in fact, to be a downward turn in funding of general ODA between 1980 and 2011 in the Middle East (Figure 1.3) and in the Maghreb (Figure 1.4), particularly after 2000 in the Maghreb. This does not suggest an overall positive correlation between ODA and support for women's rights advocacy, given that funding has decreased as female representation has increased and reforms have been instituted.

However, aid directed at women's organizations has doubled since 2005 in the MENA region, so this targeted support may be what is helping fuel some of the changes. It certainly is the case that foreign donors – through United Nations and EU agencies and various international NGOs, like the National Democratic Institute, the

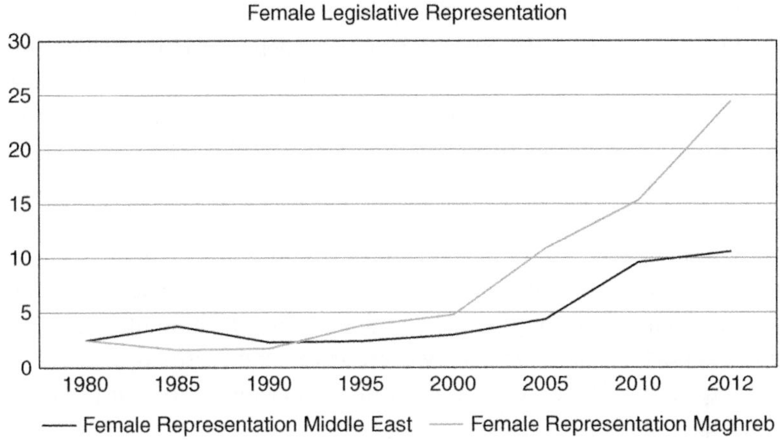

Figure 1.3 Rates of female representation, Middle East and Maghreb (1980–2012)
Source: Inter-Parliamentary Union (1995, 2012)

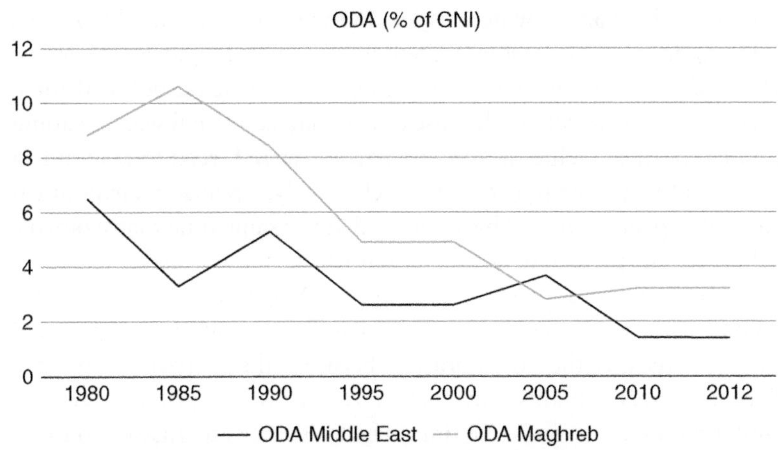

Figure 1.4 Overseas development assistance (% of GNI), Middle East and Maghreb (1980–2012)
Source: World Bank Open Data, Net official development assistance received (current US$) (percent of central government expense), https://data.worldbank.org/indicator/dt.oda.odat.cd

International Republican Institute (IRI), the International Foundation for Electoral System (IFES), the Konrad Adenauer Foundation, the Friedrich Ebert Foundation, and other such organizations – have played a role in supporting gender reforms in the Maghreb. However, since the aid is evident across the region, one would still have to explain what differentiates the Maghreb countries from the rest of the Middle East. For example, Bush and Jamal (2015) found in an experimental study that in the case of Jordan, foreign endorsement of women in politics had the effect of depressing Jordanian support for such reforms among women who opposed the regime, more so than among those who supported the regime. However, at the end of the day it is not popular opinion that creates policy, but rather the actions of political leaders.

Conclusion

The central argument of this book is that the outcomes we see in the convergence of constitutional and legislative reforms around women's rights in the Maghreb countries and the divergence of the Maghreb from the Middle East in this regard can be explained primarily by looking at the ways in which leaders in the region have used women's rights to drive a wedge isolating Salafis and other religious extremists, who had become a growing and sometimes menacing political force after the 1990s (which, in the case of Algeria, led to civil war). Leading political parties, including Islamist parties, were forced to respond to pressures for gender reform, often reluctantly, because their political survival depended on it. This happened at the same time that women's rights activists pressed to advance a reform agenda domestically and, in collaboration with activists, in neighboring Maghreb countries but also beyond. They were especially successful in doing so at times of national crisis. Moreover, the collaboration between the activists across the three countries explains why they started passing legislation around similar issues about the same time. The book seeks to answer an overarching question about why authoritarian regimes in the Maghreb adopt women's rights and it shows that they do so for political purposes of expediency to stay in power, to keep extremist elements at bay who might challenge their rule, and to respond to popular pressures. They are also seeking to create a positive international image of modernity that is tied to women's rights.

The decades since independence in the Maghreb have been largely defined by a tug of war between Islamists, religious extremists, and the political elite within each of these countries, vying for control of women's rights. Although the influence of Islamist extremist groupings in each of the three countries has been quite different, the responses of the governments follow similar patterns and the latter have learned from one another about how to respond to religious extremism. All three countries took measures to neutralize their Islamist extremist movements through a combination of tactics, ranging from repression to co-optation. Significant sectors of the population in all three countries, including women's rights activists and moderate Islamists, were fearful of the jihadist Salafis, and saw them as a threat to the creation of a secular, stable, and economically viable country. Thus, in all three countries, leaders adopted women's rights as a means of tempering the rising Islamist extremist movements. The leaders' promotion of women's rights represented a way to portray themselves as modernizers and to distinguish their politics from that of the conservative Islamists. It was also a way to signal to the world that these were modern countries that were complying with international treaties like CEDAW.

The Islamist parties themselves reversed their positions on key women's rights reforms in Tunisia and Morocco. In Tunisia this happened in the context of the 2014 constitutional debate and in Morocco after the PJD came to power and came under pressure from the king. Both parties faced considerable risk of losing support had they not adapted at least in their official rhetoric.

The presence of active women's movements in all three countries helped ensure that leaders stayed the course on their commitments to women's rights. They were particularly successful during moments of transition, or what I refer to as critical junctions that involved changes in power or followed periods of unrest. The close ties between feminists within the region through organizations like Collectif Maghreb-Égalité 95 helped forge common agendas between the three countries and facilitated friendly cooperation and perhaps even competition between the countries.

The extent to which women's rights legislation is being adopted in the Maghreb and the MENA region more generally serves as an important gauge for understanding where these societies are heading, as some of their leaders seek to engage the world, increase economic growth, modernize, and become more secular. The interactions between heads of state, ruling parties, Islamist and Salafi movements, and women's movements were played out through symbolic contestations as women's rights came to stand in variously as a proxy for notions of modernity, progress, nationalism, secularism, and other such ideas. Chapter 3 goes into further depth comparing the adoption of women's rights legislation and constitutional reforms in the Maghreb and Middle East.

Many of the discussions in the scholarly literature on women's rights focus on the role of religion or religiosity. However, this factor alone does not explain the enormous variance in the Middle East and North Africa when it comes to women's rights, which are contested in the political arena. A close look at some of the other alternate explanations for the adoption of women's rights in the MENA region explored in this chapter also shows that many explanations do not adequately account for the variance we find in the region, particularly some of the theories that focus on kinship, GDP growth, female education, labor force participation, and oil rents.

2 *Setting the Stage for Gender Reforms*

This chapter explores several key factors which created the conditions for the women's rights reforms that became evident after 2000 in the Maghreb. These include such factors as the French colonial legacy; the adoption of unified legal systems after independence; the growing secular Amazigh influence; the particular appeal of Sufism to women; the impact of political opening, however minimal, in the region; and finally attitudes toward gender equality and religiosity. In and of themselves, these factors do not explain the changes I am describing because many of them have been present since long before the changes, but they helped lay the groundwork for the reforms. Many of these factors are also evident in countries that have not undergone change, which is why they do not suffice as explanations. Nevertheless, they played a facilitating role in making the reforms more likely. What is important here is not just the role of these factors, but the *way* in which they mattered. For example, it was not the influence of France in general that affected women's rights reforms, but rather a specific class of migrants from a certain milieu who lived in France and brought back these influences, notably leftists and feminists.

It is also important to note that, just like elsewhere, the pathways to reform vary. Much of the reform in the Middle East has been piecemeal and not sustained in the way that we see in the Maghreb, even given all the constraints on reform in the three Maghreb countries that are detailed in this book. The United Arab Emirates has increased women's representation in its cabinet and parliament. Egypt has engaged in widespread constitutional reforms. Lebanon has begun to reform its legislation relating to violence against women. Saudi Arabia has launched an initiative to allow women to drive and participate in elections. Bahrain has adopted some important reforms. Many of these developments have taken place for reasons that diverge from what is being described in the Maghreb. Some of the developments in the Gulf, for example, have more to do with diminishing oil revenues, the need to diversify their economies, the difficulty of sustaining a large foreign workforce, and the need to replenish the workforce with women who are already highly educated. These suggest different pathways to gender reform from the ones found in the Maghreb countries.

The French Colonial Legacy

Perhaps the most obvious commonality between the three countries that might potentially affect legislation around women's rights, apart from their common culture, is their common colonial heritage. This legacy is shared with Lebanon, where the French ruled between 1920 and 1943; Syria, where the French had a mandate between 1923 and 1946; and Egypt, which endured a brief French occupation between 1798 to 1801. However, former French colonies in the Middle East and Africa do not stand out as having especially advanced legislation around women's rights. Lebanon and Syria have been especially slow in this regard, even taking into account the conflicts in Syria and the impact of regional instability on Lebanon. Lebanon has long had a diaspora, with over 14 million Lebanese living abroad today. This, coupled with the fact that Lebanon has a large educated class, may have influenced its stronger attitudinal support for women's rights, which is evident in surveys like the Arab Barometer. However, none of these factors have resulted in greater legislative reform. Thus, the French legacy and other external influences need to be interrogated more closely. If the French connection matters, then how does it matter?

Morocco and Tunisia had a different experience with French colonialism than Algeria, which accounts for the different impact of the French colonial legacy on the three countries. Algeria was an actual department of France, its colonization was much lengthier (132 years), and it had a huge settler population. Morocco and Tunisia were protectorates of France. As a result of these differences in colonial relations, only Algeria fought a long and bloody war of independence against France, obtaining it in 1962.

French Legal Legacy

With independence, all three countries faced several choices: they could (1) revert to the decentralized precolonial legal system characterized by Maliki jurisprudence; (2) follow the legally pluralistic French system that had separate family courts for the Imazighen, Arabs, and French, and a separation of family law from other areas of the law; or (3) create a unified and codified legal system, which inevitably would build on existing French law. They all chose the latter, allowing for centralized state control of the legal system in which all laws would be applied uniformly to all citizens rather than being under the influence of conservative clerics or *shariʿa* courts or subject to a model of separate family laws for different Muslim and non-Muslim confessional groups that one finds, for example, in Lebanon (Mayer 1995).

However, the French legal legacy, which dates back to the Napoleonic Code of 1804, was no gift to the Maghreb. It had basically created a bifurcated legal system in which family law was left to local Muslim and Amazigh courts, while the remainder of the legal system was under French law. The Napoleonic Code had unified the French legal system, giving France its first set of coherent laws regarding property, commerce, criminal law, colonial affairs, and family law. And while it strengthened individual rights for men, it reduced them for women, increasing male authority over women. Divorce by mutual consent was abolished. The Code enshrined the notion of maternal complementarity, which formed the basis for gendered citizenship in France until the 1960s (Wadowiec 2013). The laws were applied to all colonies but French family law was applied only to the French living in them and to the *évolués* (the educated "civilized" colonial subjects of France). After independence in Algeria, French law continued to be used as late as 1965, and even after 1965 the content of the law remained essentially French. Lawyers continued to be trained in French, and hence were heavily influenced by French legal jurisprudence (A7.11.10.16).

French family law itself was slow to reform relative to other European countries. It was not until the 1960s that laws in France regulating the status of women in the family incorporated the modern norm of equality, and up until that time male superiority was enshrined in the law. Men had juridical power over their wives within the family and the status of women as legal minors lasted until after World War II. French women were among the last in Europe to gain the right to vote in 1944 and to stand for election. Women did not gain parental authority equal to men until 1970, when men finally forfeited the rights that came with their status as head of the family (Mayer 1995). It was not until 1965 that women could work without obtaining permission from their husband and only in the mid 1980s were women granted autonomy in fiscal matters. By 1985 women could work freely, collect an income, and manage joint assets of the marriage. Even with the adoption of parity laws in 2000, women made up only 12 percent of the parliament in the subsequent election in 2002. As late as 2018 women only held 26 percent of the seats in the French parliament, which is lower than in Tunisia and the same as in Algeria, which had already exceeded this rate, with 32 percent, in 2014. France ranks 129th in the world in terms of gender wage inequality. It has, however, improved in other areas and today ranks 11th in overall gender equality globally compared with 57th in 2010, according to the World Economic Forum data. However, for most of the period in question, France was no role model for *la francophonie* when it came to women's rights.

Influence of North African Migrants to Europe

The Maghreb has several identities, unlike its neighbors to the north, east, and south. It is located on the southern shore of the Mediterranean, which has allowed for extensive interaction with Europe and the rest of the world both historically and today. The Maghreb shares a common language and religion with the Middle East. The Maghreb has been influenced by the cultures, trade, migration, and other interactions with people south of the Sahara. The wealthier and educated classes are quite mobile and travel frequently to Europe and elsewhere (A30.10.16.16; A25.10.9.16). All of these interactions have shaped the region and its peoples.

Some have argued that the region was more accepting of women's rights because of its proximity to Europe and the diffusion of ideas that might come with the flow of people to and from Europe, particularly between the Maghreb and France. However, many of the Maghreb populations living in Europe are more conservative than their counterparts in the Maghreb as a result of social withdrawal and isolationism due to the marginalization of migrants. There are many Maghrebi populations in Europe who migrated in different time periods for different reasons. Some from the educated classes left North Africa to study in France and many still do so. Others went to work in French mines and factories after World War II. Several "guest worker programs" in the 1960s also resulted in diversified migration to a variety of European countries, like Germany, Belgium, and the Netherlands.

Moroccan migration to Europe slowed down after the 1973 oil crisis, when European countries started closing their borders due to growing unemployment and economic stagnation. Family reunification or marrying a partner in Europe became one of the only ways to migrate and thus this wave of migration was completed mostly by the end of the 1980s (Bilgili and Weyel 2009).

Even with the slowdown in legal outmigration, the Maghreb today has one of the highest percentages of emigrants from the MENA region, with most of them living in Europe, particularly France. By 2015, at least 8 percent of Morocco's population lived abroad, 89 percent of them in Europe; 6 percent of Tunisians and 4 percent of Algerians lived abroad, and of these similarly 91 percent and 90 percent lived in Europe, respectively. Only Syria and Lebanon had proportionately more emigrants in the MENA region.[1]

While many North African immigrants in France (46 percent) regard themselves as completely secular, even when religion occupies an important place in their lives, other North African workers live in enclaves in France and are quite conservative in their outlook. This is borne out in surveys of Muslims living in France, the majority of whom have come from the Maghreb (Tabet 2017). While the Moroccan and Algerian governments monitor and regulate the imams and the content of preaching within mosques, the number of Salafi places of worship increased by 170 percent in France between 2010 and 2016 (*Algérie Monde* 2018a). Except for Corsica, every region in France has Salafi prayer halls, some of which are located in apartments, houses, old shops, gyms, and even garages and basements.

Nevertheless, as Table 2.1 below shows, in France citizens who speak Arabic at home appear to be more supportive of women's rights than people living in the Maghreb, but less supportive than those who speak French at home. Given the large number of people of Maghrebi origin living in France (4 million), it is safe to assume that the majority of Arabic speakers in France are of North African descent (20 percent of immigrants in France are from Algeria, another 15 percent from Morocco or Tunisia, making up nearly 35 percent of the total immigrant population, according to the National Institute of Statistics). Thus, it is plausible to assume that migration plays a role in influencing developments in the Maghreb. But how

[1] International Organization for Migration, www.iom.int.

Table 2.1 *Support for women's rights in the Maghreb and France (%)*

	Algeria (2010–2014)	Morocco (2010–2014)	Tunisia (2010–2014)	France: Arabic speakers (2005–2009)	France: French speakers (2005–2009)
Agree: An essential characteristic of democracy: Women have the same rights as men	30.6	46.4	36.4	44.4	49.9
Disagree: When jobs are scarce, men should have more right to a job than women	19.3	31.1	17.2	56.6	73.8
Disagree/Strongly disagree: On the whole, men make better business executives than women	32.2	29.6	34.5	71.1	85.3
Disagree/Strongly disagree: On the whole, men make better political leaders than women do	25.1	25.1	22.6	71.1	77.5

Source: World Values Survey Database, Wave 5, 2005–2009, www.worldvaluessurvey.org/wvs.jsp; Algeria N = 1,200, Morocco N = 1,200, Tunisia N = 1,205, France N = 1,001

* Language spoken at home. Arabs who speak French at home are not captured in this survey.

Note: Survey questions asked in Wave 6 for Algeria, Morocco, and Tunisia and in Wave 5 for France.

much influence is the question, especially since there is little correlation between attitudes and policies in the Maghreb given the top-down nature of policymaking in this part of the world. In other words, many of the policies that are adopted are more progressive than positions taken by the general population.

Given that the Maghreb does not stand out in any particular way in the MENA region when it comes to support for gender equality (see Table 2.8), it appears that these population flows themselves have not generally resulted in significant differences in outlook between the Maghreb and the Middle East, at least not among ordinary citizens. Nevertheless, many of the political elite and women's rights activists I interviewed in the Maghreb referenced feminist and leftist ideas they had acquired while studying or working in France, so the influences may be primarily at the elite level both in government and the women's movements and among people who have studied in France and other Western countries. This is further confirmed in Table 2.2, which shows that those Moroccans who speak French as their first language are more supportive of women's rights.

Unified Legal Systems

Some aspects of the adoption of women's rights legal reforms may have been tied to a reaction to French colonialism, which had fragmented the legal system in these countries, dividing the adjudication of family law from the rest of the legal system. The nationalists wanted to give women recognition, at least at the symbolic level, and they did this, in part, through the legal system (A31.10.20.16).

The adoption of unified legal systems and unified laws helps account for the greater ease with which women's rights policies have been adopted in the Maghreb countries relative to other parts other Middle East without such a system. They were a *necessary but insufficient condition* for later women's rights reforms. The centralized state control of the legal system applies all laws uniformly to all citizens and can be contrasted to the more common model in which family law is subject to clerics in *shari'a* courts, while civil courts oversee civil and criminal matters. In some countries, there are separate family laws and courts for different confessional groups (Mayer 1995) and the separation of family law under the jurisdiction of *shari'a* courts.

The French had played a game of divide and rule in Morocco and Algeria, pitting Imazighen against Arabs and pitting Islamic law against customary law and Amazigh codes. They kept the framework of Islamic law in all three countries. The French did not try to unify the legal system because they thought it would inflame anti-colonial feelings. So Algerian law basically remained a patchwork of customary, Islamic and French law, as did Moroccan law under French rule. The French tried to formalize Amazigh law in a decree of 1930, which resulted in a huge blowback, as it was seen as an attack on Islam and an attempt to divide the country into two blocks, Amazigh and Arab, even though in reality the Imazighen did not follow Islamic law at the time. Of the three Maghreb countries, Algeria was most influenced by French law due to the long duration of colonial rule in the country.

With independence, all three countries adopted unified legal court systems and unified laws. They not only reformed the judicial and legal systems, but unified them, creating one set of courts and legal codes for all. In Tunisia, the French courts were eliminated in 1957 and a system similar to that in Morocco was established, eliminating the religious courts. In Algeria, the judicial system was unified under the ordinance of 1965 and the system was streamlined, borrowing the Supreme Court model of Morocco. The Tunisians also abolished the religious courts. New civil, penal, and commercial codes were enacted, following German, Swiss, and French templates (Liebesny 1972).

In Morocco, the Unification Law of 1965 integrated the Islamic *qadi* courts and the courts of the Jewish community into the national system as part of a nationalist impulse that allowed only Moroccans to be eligible for the post of judge and integrated Islamic law into the statutory legislation. However, even though King Hassan II insisted that the unification of laws had been done in accordance with Islamic legal principles, the process in fact allowed for the secularization of legal institutions, of which women's rights was one aspect (Sharia Source 2016).

New personal status codes were also enacted to cover marriage, divorce, and inheritance matters. Unlike other aspects of law, the underpinning of many of these early personal status codes was Islamic law. Morocco's first 1958 Personal Status Code (Moudawana) incorporated some Maliki Islamic patriarchal judicial provisions, as did the 1984 Algerian Personal Status Code (PSC), while Tunisia's PSC of 1956 departed from this tradition most radically. The Islamic influence was reduced in later versions of the PSC in Morocco, but there are still clear traces of Maliki jurisprudence within the family laws. Maliki law is one of the four Sunni Islamic schools of jurisprudence (*fiqh*) prevalent in West Africa and North Africa and the southern part of Egypt. Some authors have claimed that the influence of Maliki jurisprudence has made the legal system in these three countries more supportive of women's rights (Terem 2014). It is unclear how Maliki law favored women compared with the other schools of *fiqh*, but it is possible that it acquired this reputation because it was integrated into various legal systems that were attempting to reform women's rights.

The fact that all three Maghreb countries ended up with unified courts and a unified legal system made it possible for them to adopt common laws affecting all women. A unified legal system in and of itself is not sufficient to ensure the enactment of women's rights reform, but it is a necessary condition. There are countries with unified legal systems that have not made progress with women's rights reforms, but without such a system, women's rights reforms are nearly impossible to pass uniformly since every religious group has its own courts and laws.

The Amazigh Dimension

One of the explanations for the divergence between the Maghreb and the Middle East is the claim that, unlike parts of the Middle East, the Maghreb is a homogenous entity which employs Arabic and French, which adheres to Sunni Islam, and in which the people are a mixture of Amazigh-Arab descent. However, there is enormous diversity in the region, with people speaking different dialects of Arabic within a country, different Tamazight dialects, other languages like Tamashaq, which is the Tuareg dialect related to Tamazight, and Hassaniya. Not all identify as Arab, and only some identify as Amazigh (M13.2.26.16).

In recent years, the Amazigh identity has been strengthened. In Morocco, for example, new cultural organizations have emerged since the 2000s, including Amazigh teachers', film, theater, writers', and women's associations, to promote Amazigh culture (M15.2.3.16). The movement also has a political dimension, which infused protests around Morocco against the alleged police complicity in the killing of a fishmonger in Al Hoceima in 2016. The Amazigh flag was visible in many of these protests, which were concentrated in the Rif, home to one of the three main Amazigh groups in Morocco and which has historically been neglected by the state. To this day, Imazighen from the Rif area recall demonstrations that Riffians held in the late 1950s, which were brutally suppressed by the authorities.

According to the 2016 Arab Barometer, 13.7 percent of those surveyed in Algeria said that Tamazight was their first or second language, while in Morocco the figure was 28.8 percent. The Imazighen have a very small presence in Tunisia. The number of Imazighen in Morocco is largest, ranging from 13 to 20 million out of 35 million people, and the number in Algeria ranges from 9 to 13 million out of a population of 41 million. Many, if not most, Imazighen are of mixed heritage and many no longer speak Tamazight. In fact, beyond those who speak Tamazight, it is virtually impossible to distinguish between Arabs and Imazighen except by how people self-identify. But even that is challenging. As a senior academic said to me, "I always thought of myself as Arab. I had not really thought about the fact that my family was Amazigh until recently, since the changes in the constitution. We don't speak Tamazight at home although my grandmother did" (M37.2.25.16). The professor did not identify as Amazigh, but clearly this was part of the identity of her family. Many families did not speak Tamazight to their children because they were concerned they would have a hard time getting an education and finding a job. Some felt their Amazigh identity was devalued by society and so they hid it (M15.2.3.16). Thus, there are many reasons the identity has receded even as some are trying to revive it.

This Amazigh identity may help explain, in part, why the Maghreb countries have always regarded the notion of Pan-Arabism, as espoused by Egyptian President Gamal Abdel Nasser, with some skepticism, unsure if they could reconcile their Amazigh identity with Arabism.

It is true that the overwhelming majority of the Amazigh population is Muslim, but the extent to which the Imazighen adhere to Islam and want to see a state based on Islamic principles and law varies throughout the region. Some people I interviewed saw the perceived secular orientation of the Imazighen as a bulwark against religious extremism. As one Algerian women's rights activist explained:

> We often rely on our local cultural and religious values – traditional Algerian Islam – to counter extremist discourse. There is the famous phrase by Khalida Messaoudi [a prominent Algerian politician, and feminist activist]: "Islam of my mother." There are specific characteristics of the practice of Islam in the Maghreb region. We have, for example, no difficulty in saying that the *chador* [full face and body veil] is not part of our culture and that we have

our own traditional Algerian and Maghrebian clothes. These values are imbued within the population. We also have our own female historical figures like Dihya, Tin Hinan, the *moudjahidates* [who fought during the war of independence]. (A7.11.10.16)

A central element of this identity is the role played by women in resisting Muslim encroachments historically. Amazigh women's rights activists I interviewed frequently highlighted key roles played by women in their historically matrilineal societies. They pointed to mythic and historical leaders like Dihya (also known as Kahina in Arabic), an Amazigh warrior queen who lived in the seventh century in the territory that today is known as Algeria. She is said to have twice beaten back Umayyad (Arab and Muslim) invaders in Eastern Algeria and Western Tunisia, pushing them back to the borders of modern Libya. Some claim she was Christian, others say that she was Jewish and some say animist. To this day there is a statue that commemorates her in Béjaia, Algeria, and she continues to be portrayed on Amazigh websites and in graffiti and songs. Her name can be found on pizza restaurants, clothing stores, children's books, movies, museums, and in literature in Algeria. She has come to symbolize, as Cynthia Becker (2015) puts it, "a liberal-oriented transnational Berber movement that emphasizes gender equality as well as religious and ethnic tolerance. She symbolizes Berbers as a people who refuse to be subjugated, free and willing to fight to retain their freedom against outside invasion." Dihya is believed to have been buried in Khenchela, a city in modern Algeria.

One leader of a Moroccan Amazigh women's organization explained the significance of these symbols of Amazigh female empowerment:

We have always respected women's rights. We had queens, we had Dihya and other Amazigh queens. We never said women had to be covered, that they were destined to stay home, or that they must not work . . . this is a culture that came from the Middle East and it is not our culture. We, Amazigh countries, we do not have the problems of the Middle Eastern cultures with Islam . . . we are always open and we are secular by definition. My grandmother was Jewish, and we have always lived with Muslims and other religions peacefully. There are Amazigh people who are atheists. It is a personal choice and they must not be bound to follow other religions. (M9.2.24.16)

She and other Amazigh I interviewed identified more with being part of Africa and regarded Arab culture as alien. For example, one women's organization, Tamazgha Amazigh Women's Forum, is active in all the countries where Amazigh is spoken in its various dialects, including Algeria, Morocco, Tunisia, Mali, Niger, and Burkina Faso (M15.2.3.16).

Other Amazigh women talked about certain contemporary practices like veiling as imported. As one woman explained:

> Moroccan women wore headscarves, but the scarf was to gather their hair, because with the exception of Fès and other cities where one found notables, women in all other regions of Morocco worked outside. They did the farming, the gardening, they took care of the livestock and the trees. The woman's body was not considered something that must be hidden. (M13.2.26.16)

As suggested above, women in rural areas worked in the fields and tended livestock in addition to their household responsibilities. This meant that the division of labor was less limited than it was for women in an urban setting, where men worked outside the home and women inside. This may have also afforded rural women greater freedoms.

Others I interviewed highlighted the continuing encroachments on their culture such as religious prohibitions on tattooing. Many Amazigh women, especially the older ones, have tattoos on their faces, feet, and elsewhere. These are marks of beauty and tribal affiliation. Sometimes they are inscribed for healing purposes. Dancing and singing are also integral to celebrations in their cultures, but at times have been shunned by religious authorities. Today they integrate Islamic practices but continue with their own customs (M15.2.16).

One of the earliest women leaders who is still recalled is Tin Hinane, a Tuareg warrior queen who lived in the fourth century. In Tamazight she is known as Tamenukalt, which means "leader," "mother of the tribe," or "queen of the camp." Her reputation spread as far as Mali, Niger, Nigeria, Libya, and Algeria. She is said to have been of the Amazigh Braber tribe, which came from a Tafilalt oasis in the Atlas Mountains in Morocco. To this day, she is regarded as a symbol of the social, political, and spiritual stability of Tuareg tribes.

Part of this valorization of Amazigh women leaders feeds into a popular argument one hears today that focuses on the distinctiveness of the Imazighen, whose ancestors lived in a matrifocal and matrilineal society with many prominent leaders. They argue that this, coupled with their more secular orientation, makes the Imazighen more inclined to support women's rights today (M13.2.26.16). They point to the traditional Amazigh practice in the event of a divorce of dividing marital assets based on what is brought into the marriage by the husband and wife, a right which is enshrined in the 2004 Moroccan Family Code, but which Amazigh women had benefited from as long as people could remember (M15.2.3.16). A young Algerian feminist activist explained:

> Now, I would say that the dimension of identity is very important for us since we are part of a history that goes back to the ancient Amazigh kingdoms with queens like Tin Hinane, Dihya, and all the women who have marked the history of this continent. I think that all aspects of my identity – Amazighnity, Kabylity, Algerianity – make me the African that I am today. (A22.10.20.16)

The claim that the Imazighen are more open to women's rights than those with an Arab identity, however, is not borne out by Afrobarometer and Arab Barometer surveys conducted in Algeria and Morocco. For example, it is not possible to discern different attitudes toward women in politics when comparing tribal affiliations within the region (see Tables 2.2, 2.3, 2.4, 2.5). If one looks at this in terms of linguistic groups, the results show that on average 25.4 percent of Amazigh-identifying people (Chaoui, Kabyle, Mouzabit, Tergui) and 34.7 percent of people who identify as Arab agree that women should have the same chance of being elected to political office as men (Figure 2.1), while 41.5 percent of those who identify neither as Arab nor Amazigh, responded that they "Don't think of self in those terms." It is possible that because of the centuries of intermarriage the attitudinal differences between the various groups are irrelevant.

What does emerge from Table 2.3 in the case of Morocco, and to some extent Algeria (Table 2.4), is support for the earlier claim that it is primarily the elites and educated people who have ties to France and their associates who have driven the women's rights reforms. French-speaking people in Morocco and Algeria are better educated than most and they are wealthier urban dwellers. In Algeria they are primarily of the Kabyle Amazigh grouping. They appear to be more supportive of women's rights than others. In both Morocco and Algeria they self-identify as less religious than those whose first language is Arabic or Tamazight.

Some Moroccan women's rights activists, particularly Amazigh activists, have suggested that the Imazighen adopt a more secular orientation

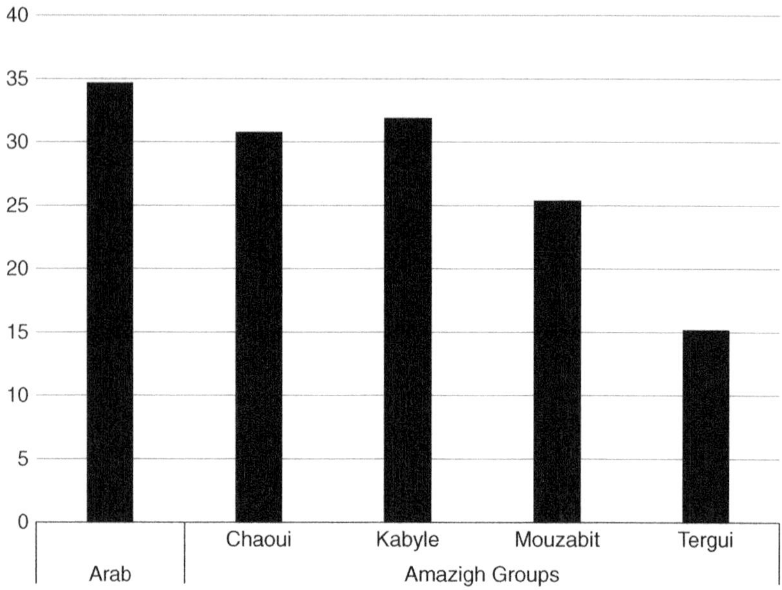

Figure 2.1 Support for women leaders in Algeria by ethnic group, 2014–2015 (%)
Agreement with statement: "Women should have the same chance of being elected to political office as men."
Source: Afrobarometer Database, Round 6, 2014–2015, www.afrobarometer.org/online-data-analysis/analyse-online, N = 1,199

because of their awareness of the multiple religious and ethnic heritages one finds in the region. They argue that this cultural pluralism has allowed for greater openness to women's rights as well. Algerian historians like Si Ammar ou Bouli have argued that women played the most important political roles in Amazigh history (Merolla 2001). However, the surveys do not indicate that the Imazighen are any less attached to Islam than Arabs in the region (Table 2.5). This is no doubt a product of centuries of intermarriage and syncretism. Nevertheless, the belief in cultural pluralism is strong. For example, one Amazigh woman who grew up in Agadir told me her father was a devout Muslim. She continued:

The generation of my grandparents always lived with Jews and my father was born in a big village that was half Jewish, half Muslim. They always lived quietly together. My father always had his friends who were Amazigh Moroccan Jews. So for us it was not a problem. Everyone respected each

Table 2.2 *Support for women's rights by first language, Morocco, 2016 (%)*

	Morocco			
Question	Total	Arabic	French	Tamazight
Agree strongly: Married women can work outside home	23.4	24.1	38.2	20.5
Disagree strongly: Men are better political leaders	15.0	14.6	23.6	16.1
Agree strongly: A woman can become President or Prime Minister of a Muslim country	27.4	26.9	76.4	28.7
Strongly disagree: University education more important for males	47.9	49.5	100.0	41.1
Agree strongly: Women should wear modest clothes without needing to wear *hijab*	15.9	17.3	–	11.2
Agree strongly: Women and men should have equal inheritance rights	85.3	85.8	100.0	82.9
Strongly disagree: Husbands should have final say in family	11.4	12.4	76.4	7.0

Source: Arab Barometer Database, Wave IV, 2016–2017, www.arabbarometer.org/; Algeria N = 1,199, Morocco N = 1,199, Tunisia N = 1,201

Table 2.3 *Support for women's rights by first language, Algeria, 2016 (%)*

	Algeria			
Question	Total	Arabic	French	Tamazight
Agree strongly: Married women can work outside home	25.9	26.6	30.4	17.9
Disagree strongly: Men are better political leaders	5.0	5.3	8.8	1.6
Agree strongly: A woman can become President or Prime Minister of a Muslim country	13.9	13.9	27.8	11.2
Strongly disagree: University education more important for males	34.7	34.0	26.8	43.2
Agree strongly: Women should wear modest clothes without needing to wear *hijab*	19.0	18.3	24.5	24.8
Agree strongly: Women and men should have equal inheritance rights	61.5	63.5	56.7	41.8
Strongly disagree: Husbands should have final say in family	4.9	5.3	7.4	1.1

Source: Arab Barometer Database, Wave IV, 2016–2017, www.arabbarometer.org/, Algeria N = 1,199, Morocco N = 1,199, Tunisia N = 1,201

Table 2.4 ***Support for women as leaders, Algeria and Morocco, 2014–2015 (%)***

	Algeria				
Question	Total	Arabic	French	Tamazight	Hassaniya
Agree strongly: Women should have the same chance of being elected to political office as men	16.5	16.8	15.3	13.6	NA
			Morocco		
Agree strongly: Women should have the same chance of being elected to political office as men	33.3	35.5	NA	19.4	55.7

Source: Afrobarometer Database, Round 6, 2014–2015, www.afrobarometer.org/online-data-analysis/analyse-online; Algeria N = 1,200, Morocco N = 1,200

other. They did their Bar Mitzvah, we went. They did their Rosh Hashanah, we said to them "Happy New Year." We had our religious holidays, they came to say good day. The people accepted you as you were, and you accepted them as who they were, and at the same time they were our best friends. My grandfather's accountant was a Moroccan Jew and his cashier was a Moroccan Jew, and they worked side by side peacefully. (M15.2.3.16)

In response to a 2014–2015 Arab Barometer question asking about the extent to which the respondent agreed with the statement that "Religious practices are private and should be separated from social and political life," those who said that Tamazight was their first language were just as likely to agree with this statement as those who identified as Arabic speakers, who tended to agree even more strongly with this statement that was trying to probe secular orientations. Because the identities are so blurred in this

Table 2.5 *Religiosity by first language, Morocco and Algeria, 2016 (%)*

Question	Morocco			
In general, would you describe yourself as . . .	Total	Arabic	French	Tamazight
Religious	45.1	42.0	0	57.6
Somewhat religious	46.8	48.9	61.8	38.9
Not religious	7.9	9.0	38.2	3.2
Don't know	0.2	0.2	–	0.3
Question	**Algeria**			
In general, would you describe yourself as . . .	Total	Arabic	French	Tamazight
Religious	32.6	32.6	28.2	34.6
Somewhat religious	55.1	55.6	45.0	52.2
Not religious	11.6	11.1	26.8	13.2
Don't know	0.7	0.8	–	–

Source: Arab Barometer Database, Wave IV, 2016–2017, www.arabbarometer.org/, Algeria N = 1,199, Morocco N = 1,199

region and language is not necessarily a proxy for identity, it may be that one cannot extrapolate too much from these survey results.

It is also possible that secular attitudes are sentiments shared by the Amazigh women's rights activists and more educated Amazigh, who appear to be attached to this evolving imaginary. For example, when I asked a leading women's rights activist in Algeria about the "Amazigh dimension," as they call it, she replied:

> At this moment, the people are recovering an identity that politics has stolen from them. The French Jacobin model – all Arabs and all Muslims – it cannot work. And although we talk about relations between men and women in the Maghreb, the Imazighen have their specificity of being always in search of change and evolution. Elsewhere [a reference to Islamism], there is the fatalism of religion. The Imazighen know how to distinguish earthly affairs from spiritual affairs. It is linked to the way in which religion is understood, which is different from those who are inhibited by religion. (A3.9.26.16)

Another scholar explained that:

Among the Imazighen, one finds everything. There are Marabout Sufi families among the Imazighen who are more attached to Islam. This does not prevent them from being very modern and not at all fundamentalist. We also have Amazigh minority groups who are very Arab in orientation and very Islamist. But generally, the peculiarity of the Imazighen in Algeria is that they are very rooted in Algerian nationalism. And even when they are devoutly religious, they are much more tolerant than the Arabs. It is a very stable society thanks to the collective culture ... The control mechanisms are so strong that even when they are Islamists, they will respect order. (A30.10.16.16)

Amazigh activists I interviewed also spoke at length about loyalty to nation, particularly in the struggle against colonialism. The Kabyles in Algeria were especially proud of their role in the resistance to the French. As one activist explained, the name of her organization, Fadhma N'Soumer, is not tied to her tribal Kabyle identity, but rather refers to a woman "who represents the figure of the struggle against oppression, the figure of a spontaneous feminist who broke all taboos by fighting against colonialism and emancipating an entire nation with it." Fadhma N'Soumer was a leader of the resistance to the French colonial takeover of Algeria from 1854 to July 1857. She was captured by French forces and died six years later. She was said to have supernatural powers of healing and predicting the future.

Women have found a place in Sufi practices quite unlike other parts of the MENA region, where women do not feature prominently in Islamic institutions. Amazigh women are said to have played central roles in pre-Islamic rituals associated with healing, fertility, lamenting the dead, and passage through liminal transitions. Sufism is fairly strong in the Maghreb and women are afforded roles as leaders in several *zawiyas* (religious monasteries) and mosques (ElBoudrari 1993, Rausch 2006, Sadiqi 2017). Sufism is one area where women have sought self-realization, independence, alternatives to dominant patterns of local patriarchal culture, and perhaps an escape from convention. Hagiographic accounts of historic female saints in Morocco show how they escaped male domination, marital relations, and even traditional gender roles at times through their religious pursuits. Women went to shrines and venerated female saints, asking them to intervene on their behalf with God to provide them with assistance. They engaged in various rituals involving *dhikr* (الذكر,

a form of worship involving rhythmic repetition of the name of God or God's attributes), sacrifice, and trance. They would go to the shrines seeking help with fertility, marriage, or other troubles. Although more orthodox Muslims do not approve of saint veneration and would not visit such shrines, many Islamist women leaders privately value the role of women saints as symbolic figures and what they represent in their capacity to break with and challenge patriarchal norms.

Moroccan historic texts are full of hagiographic descriptions of devout Sufi women going back to the thirteenth century. Women like Mina Fassi Fihri, who lived in the eighteenth century, are praised for their asceticism, devotion to silence, and removal from bodily attachments. Hamza Al Kattani's work *Salwat al-Anfas* depicts women figures like the seventeenth-century Sayyida Aisha Bint Chaqroun al-Fakhar, who were devoted not only to their work as mothers and wives, but also to worship and reaching high spiritual status. Some, like Sayyida Aisha Bint Ali Bounafi in the eighteenth century, were seekers of knowledge (El Haitami 2014).

I regard this link between the Amazigh identity and women's status as an imaginary or an idea that has fueled women's rights activism in the Maghreb and helped shape it. A renewed awareness of the role of women and identification with powerful women has energized both the Amazigh and women's movements. As such, it is a contributing factor in influencing the advancement of women's rights in the region, but it is not possible to explain the changes that have occurred on the legal front in the Maghreb by drawing on these imaginaries. One cannot draw a straight line from these ideas about Amazigh women to legislative outcomes.

Nevertheless, the growing Amazigh activism may impact women's rights in the region in the long run. The Amazigh dimension is emerging as an important counterweight to Islamism, particularly the extremist variant, even though the political elite treat these Amazigh movements with reserve and sometimes repression because they have the potential for great unrest and disruption. In this sense, the Amazigh movements are different from the women's movements. However, like the women's movements, they represent another pillar of secularism in society. The

Maghreb seems to be moving now into a post-Islamist era, particularly with the rise of the Amazigh identity movements. Protests in Kabylia, Algeria, in 2001 and continuing in Morocco in 2011 with the Vingt février protests and the Hoceima protests in Morocco in 2017 as well as in Tataouine, Tunisia, have highlighted some of the tensions between the Imazighen and the states in the region. These protests have sometimes been linked to women's rights since these are two groups that lost out with the ascent of the Islamists. The Vingt février uprisings in Morocco highlighted the common cause of both Amazigh and women's rights activists. In 2011, the Moroccan king included Tamazight as one of Morocco's official languages in the same constitution that expanded women's rights. This was an important recognition of both Amazigh and gender identities. At the same time, however, an Amazigh party was banned in 2008 in Morocco and the aforementioned protests and Amazigh leaders have faced severe repression and imprisonment.

Political Opening

Historically, democratization has been linked to the improvement of women's rights, especially in Europe. With the exception of countries in conflict, in the MENA region we have seen some women's rights reforms being adopted, however limited, even as civil liberties and political rights worsened, often in a top-down and piecemeal fashion. Saudi Arabia today is a case in point. As the current regime has eased restrictions on women's travel, driving, and voting rights, it is also repressing women's rights activists. Egyptian President Sisi has done much the same in restricting women's rights activism, having pursued extensive constitutional reforms involving women's rights. This brings us to the core question in this book: Why do authoritarian leaders adopt women's rights reforms?

Part of the answer in the Maghreb has to do with a change in strategy that took place after the 2000s. After independence and especially after the 1980s, the leaders of the Maghreb countries sought to appease the Islamists, who were rapidly growing in influence. As political liberalization took hold in the 1990s in the MENA region, Laurie Brand (1998) argues that it gave rise to conservative Islamist forces, which threatened women's rights and women's rights movements. Hatem's (1994b) study of political liberalization in Sudan, Tunisia, and Egypt drew even more dire conclusions than Brand, arguing that the state and Islamists had converged around a view of women's rights that drew on traditional notions of domesticity and gender and that their position on women's roles did not substantially differ.

In the case of Tunisia, Brand suggests that Ben Ali sought to curry favor with the Islamists while discouraging independent women's mobilization. Algeria is perhaps the most vivid example of this: when the country opened up to multipartyism, leading to the electoral successes of Islamic Salvation Front (FIS), the government could not in the end accept this, resulting in the shutting down of the FIS. This led to a civil war.

By the 2000s, leaders in the Maghreb had seen the limits of this strategy of trying to appease the Islamists, particularly extremists. In all three

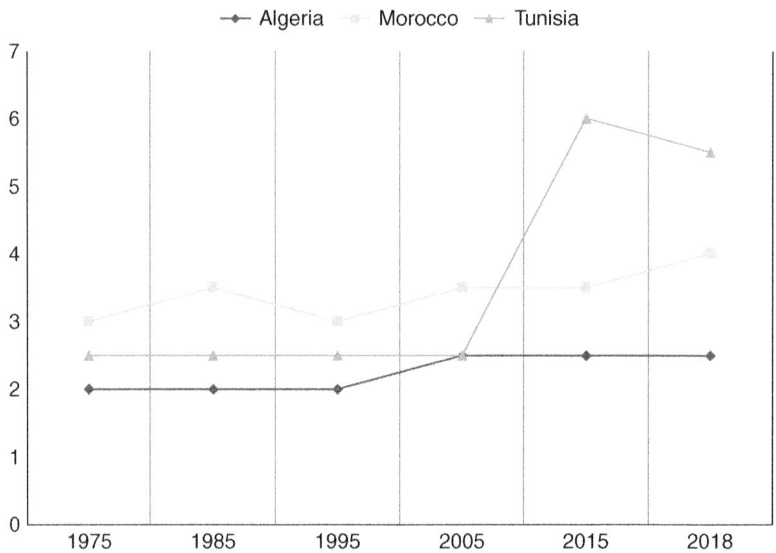

Figure 2.2 Political rights and civil liberties, Algeria, Morocco, and Tunisia, 1975–2018

Note: Inverse of Freedom House index for purposes of presentation (5.5–7 = Free, 3–5 = Partly Free, 1–2.5 = Not Free)

Source: Freedom House, Freedom in the World database, https://freedomhouse.org/

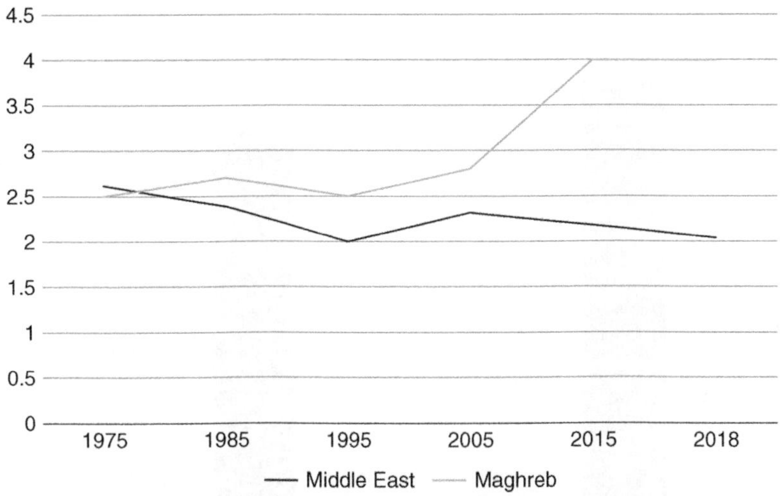

Figure 2.3 Political rights and civil liberties, Maghreb and Arab Middle East, 1975–2018
Note: Inverse of Freedom House index for purposes of presentation (5.5–7 = Free, 3–5 = Partly Free, 1–2.5 = Not Free)
Source: Freedom House, Freedom in the World database, https://freedomhouse.org/

countries, leaders started using women's rights as a way of neutralizing the Islamist extremists, along with other tactics of co-optation, surveillance, and outright repression. Women's rights were not used in the same way in other parts of the Middle East, not even in Egypt. While there is no question that Salafis and other conservatives had gained ground in the Maghreb after the 1990s, it is also the case that conservative trends were evident throughout the region and one would still have to explain how, in that context, the Maghreb countries were able to produce a stronger women's rights regime.

Part of the explanation has to do with the fact that the Maghreb countries opened up slightly more than their Middle Eastern counterparts even as they remained authoritarian or hybrid regimes (neither fully democratic nor fully authoritarian). This allowed enough political space for women's organizations to mobilize and engage the state. In looking at the longer trajectory of political liberalization, the Maghreb countries overall were more repressive than the Middle East until the late 1970s,

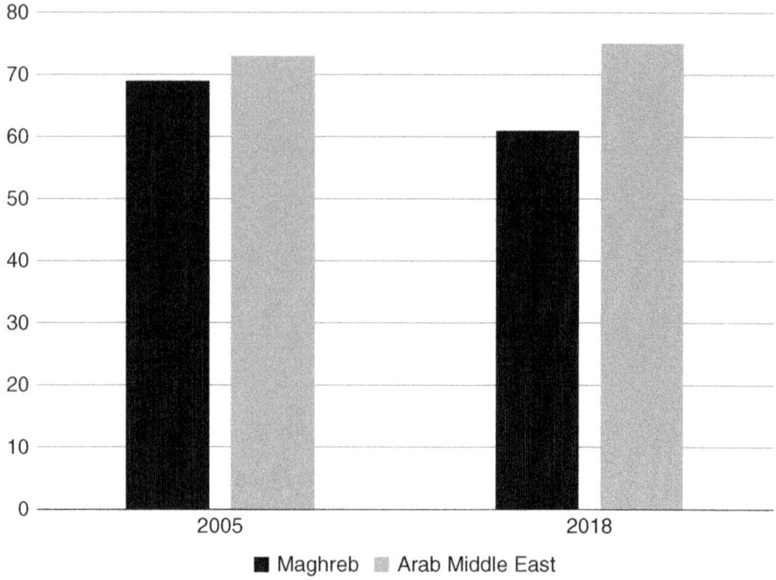

Figure 2.4 Press freedom in Maghreb and Arab Middle East, 2005 and 2018
Note: Inverse of Freedom House index for purposes of presentation
Free (F): 61–100; Partly Free (PF): 31–60; Not Free (NF): 0–31
Source: Freedom House, Freedom in the World database, https://freedomhouse.org/

but since then they have steadily opened up politically to a greater extent than the Middle East, which has remained doggedly authoritarian for the most part (Figure 2.3). As one leader of a women's rights organization in Morocco explained:

Morocco has widened this path that allowed for a diversity of opinion, freedom of expression, freedom to carry out advocacy, the right to strike, and freedom to use Facebook and Twitter. Morocco has been open for a long time. There is an opposition that expresses itself freely, and then there is the government that acts. There is the voice of civil society that is heard. (M4.2.12.16)

She pointed to the existence of seventeen trade unions and dozens of parties in Morocco. Among the twelve parties with seats in parliament, she said multiple interests are represented, from Islamists to conservatives, environmentalists, royalists, and socialists. She also gave the example of the Vingt février protests that were followed by a constitution-making process in which the king called for proposals and advocacy for change. This appeased many forces, at least temporarily, including the Amazigh movement, the Sahrawi movement, the women's rights movement, environmentalists, political parties, trade unions, and others who had not felt listened to in the past. But there are limits to this openness, as is evident in the repression of the Rif Movement (Hirak Rif) since 2016. There are limits to reforming the king's status and limits of response to certain areas like corruption. Human rights groups point to increasing limits to their freedom to operate and that of investigative journalists since 2011 (M12.2.25.16). Nevertheless, Morocco's relative openness compared with other MENA countries has had a positive impact on the women's movement.

In the Middle East, only Jordan, Kuwait, and Lebanon could be considered hybrid regimes today. Of the Maghreb countries, Algeria remains authoritarian and Tunisia is the only country that could be considered democratic in the entire region. Morocco has remained a hybrid regime with basically the same level of civil liberties and political rights since the 1970s, with a few moments of liberalization in the late 1970s, in the 1980s, and after the 2000s. Tunisia was an authoritarian regime until the 1980s, when it became a hybrid. It became more repressive, reverting to autocratic status in 1993. Its record worsened in the 2000s until after the Arab Spring in 2012, when it reverted to being a hybrid, and then in 2015 it claimed democratic status. Algeria has been authoritarian since independence and had a brief opening in the early 1990s before it plunged into civil war. It remained autocratic up through the end of the Bouteflika presidency. Massive demonstrations starting in February 2019 succeeded in ousting the president and have continued to press for democratization and regime change. The outcome at this writing is uncertain. But generally, the fact that there was a modicum of political opening in all three countries created opportunities, as limited as they were, for reforms to be made.

The other explanation for the difference between the regions has to do with the women's movement, which pushed for reforms at critical moments of transition and turmoil. Women were no strangers to working in unfavorable conditions, and demanding reforms under authoritarian or semi-authoritarian rule at times even proved advantageous. Women's rights activists have been part of movements demanding greater democratization, but they have also, at least in the Maghreb, historically benefited from authoritarian means of adopting women's rights policies, with autocratic leaders often overriding popular sentiments to implement a policy that benefited women (Cavatorta and Dalmasso 2009). One of the perennial challenges for women's rights activists in this region has been to try to extract reform from leaders while distancing themselves from authoritarian rule. Referring to Tunisia, Morocco, and Algeria, Daniel Brumberg argues that: "In all three countries, many secular elites have seen autocracy as a necessary evil sheltering them from the prospect of uneven democratic contests with Islamists" (2013, 90).

Since the 1970s there has been slightly more political space in the Maghreb that has allowed for greater mobilization by women's organizations to press for reform. Nevertheless, with the exception of Tunisia after 2015, all three countries have had either authoritarian or semi-authoritarian regimes. While leaders in the region had initially sought to appease Islamists and extremists, they shifted course after 2000 (in the 1990s in Algeria) and sought to rein in these forces through outright repression, co-optation, and other means. One of the strategies involved using women's rights to neutralize the extremist groups. The rise of Islamist parties in Morocco and Tunisia after the early 2010s saw yet another dynamic of Islamist parties trying to accommodate demands around women's rights while maintaining their own platform (see Chapters 4, 5, and 6).

Attitudes toward Gender Equality

Some cross-national studies have argued that cultural attitudes influence gender equality and gender-related policy (Inglehart and Norris 2003, Kenworthy and Malami 1999). Inglehart and Norris, for example, argue that "Islamic religious heritage is one of the most powerful barriers to the rising tide of gender equality" (2003, 49). Some studies have found more support for patriarchy in Arab Muslim societies than in non-Arab Muslim societies (Rizzo, Abdel-Latif, and Meyer 2007, Angrist 2012, Caris and Hayo 2012).

However, the way in which women's rights reforms have been implemented, often in a top-down fashion, makes popular attitudes less relevant. The Lebanese, for example, are the most supportive of women as political leaders in the MENA region, yet Lebanese women hold 3 percent of the legislative seats in their parliament. The Lebanese have some of the most favorable views on women's rights overall in the region, yet their policies in this area remain weaker than those found in the Maghreb and even in other Middle Eastern countries.

Attitudes in the Maghreb are more supportive of gender equality on some measures and less so on others when compared with the Middle East. This is borne out by data from both the Arab Barometer and the World Values Survey (Tables 2.7, 2.8). When levels of education are taken into account, there is stronger support for women's rights among the more educated, but even here the differences between the Maghreb and the Middle East, while visible on some measures, are not sustained across the board (Table 2.7).

A 2013 Pew Survey of selected Muslim countries found that the Maghreb countries were the most tolerant when it came to veiling. When asked if women should decide whether or not to veil, 89 percent in Tunisia and 85 percent in Morocco said it was a woman's choice (Pew 2013), compared with an average of 50 percent for countries surveyed in the Middle East. Respondents were more likely to agree in Tunisia (81 percent) and Morocco (73 percent) that women had the right to ask for a divorce, compared to an average of 29 percent in Middle Eastern countries. However, they were slightly more inclined than Middle Easterners to agree that a woman must always obey her husband. Of all the countries PEW surveyed, the Maghreb countries were the least supportive of allowing sons and daughters to have equal inheritance rights (15 percent in both Tunisia and Morocco), while 30 percent in the other MENA countries surveyed supported equal inheritance, although Arab Barometer shows that attitudes to gender and inheritance are roughly the same in the two regions (see Table 2.6).

The Arab Barometer data similarly show a mix of attitudes with slightly more people in the Maghreb believing that men are *not* better leaders than women, and that women should have the right to choose if they want to wear the *hijab*. Equal numbers in the Maghreb and Middle East thought that a university education was not more important for men and that women and men should have

Table 2.6 *Attitudes toward gender equality, Maghreb and Middle East, 2013 and 2016*

Question	Algeria	Morocco	Tunisia	Maghreb	Middle East
Agree/Agree strongly: Married women can work outside home [1]	70.6	78.1	87.8	78.9	85.3
Disagree/Disagree strongly: Men are better political leaders [2]	18.8	40.7	42.8	34.1	29.5
Agree/Agree strongly: A woman can become president or prime minister of a Muslim country [3]	35.7	49.2	62.6	56.2	66.8
Disagree/Strongly disagree: University education more important for males [4]	73.5	87.2	88.2	83	84
Agree/Agree strongly: Women should wear modest clothes without needing to wear *hijab* [5]	51.7	54.5	89.2	65.2	53.6
Agree/Agree strongly: Women and men should have equal inheritance rights [6]	95.3	96.4	97.6	97.1	96.3

Table 2.6 (*cont.*)

Question	Algeria	Morocco	Tunisia	Maghreb	Middle East
Disagree/Strongly disagree: Inheritance laws should be in accordance with Islamic law [7] 2013	4.2	7.3	14.8	8.76	12.5
Disagree/Strongly disagree: Husbands should have final say in family [8]	22.4	41	41.5	35	42.7
Very important/ Somewhat important: Gender equality in constitution [9] 2013	69	86	78	78	85

Source: Arab Barometer Database, Wave III, 2012–2014; Wave IV, 2016–2017, www.arabbarometer.org/; Algeria 2013 N = 1,177, Algeria 2016 N = 1,199; Morocco 2013 N = 1,080, Morocco 2016 N = 1,199; Tunisia 2013 N = 1,168 Tunisia 2016 N = 1,201; Middle East 2013 N = 4618, Middle East 2016 N = 5,397

1. A married woman can work outside the home (Agree, Agree strongly)
2. In general, men are better at political leadership than women (Disagree, Strongly disagree)
3. A woman can become president or prime minister of a Muslim country (Agree, Agree strongly)
4. University education for males is more important than university education for females (Somewhat disagree, Strongly disagree)
5. Women should wear modest clothes without needing to wear the *hijab* (Agree, Agree strongly)
6. Women's share of inheritance should be equal to that of men (Agree, Agree strongly)
7. Inheritance laws should be in accordance with Islamic law (Disagree, Strongly disagree)
8. Husbands should have final say in all decisions concerning the family (Disagree, Strongly disagree)
9. New constitution draft: what is the importance in insuring equal rights between men and women? (Very important, Somewhat important)

Table 2.7 ***Attitudes toward gender equality and college-level education (bachelor's degree), Morocco and Algeria, 2013 (%)***

	Algeria	Morocco	Middle East
Question	BA education	BA education	BA education
Important/Somewhat important: Gender equality in constitution [1]	80	90	88
Agree: Married woman can work outside home [2]	98	84	89
Disagree: Men better political leaders [3]	44	61	33
Disagree/Strongly disagree: University education more important for males [4]	97	89	79
Agree/Agree strongly: Women should wear modest clothes without needing to wear *hijab* [5]	69	69	57

Source: Arab Barometer Database, Wave III, 2012–2014; Wave IV, 2016–2017, www.arabbarometer.org/; Algeria N = 1,177, Morocco N = 1,080, Middle East N = 4618
1. New constitution draft: what is the importance of insuring equal rights between men and women? (Agree, Agree strongly)
2. A married woman can work outside the home (Agree, Agree strongly)
3. In general, men are better at political leadership than women (Disagree, Strongly disagree)
4. University education for males is more important than university education for females (Somewhat disagree, Strongly disagree)
5. Women should wear modest clothes without needing to wear the *hijab* (Agree, Agree strongly)

the same inheritance rights. On all the other questions, Middle Eastern opinions were more favorable to women's rights than those in the Maghreb (i.e., women working, women being president or prime minister, husbands having a final say in the household, and constitutional provisions on gender equality) (Table 2.7). These attitudes in the two regions, surprisingly, do not match the

Table 2.8 *Attitudes toward gender equality, Maghreb and Middle East, 2012–2014 (%)*

Question	Maghreb	Middle East
Disagree/Disagree strongly: Men are better political leaders	24.2	20.3
Disagree/Strongly disagree: University education more important for males	67.7	65.8
Disagree: When jobs are scarce, men should have more right to a job than women	22.6	18.5
Disagree/Strongly disagree: On the whole, men make better business executives than women do	13.1	32.8
Women have the same rights as men. Agree/ Strongly agree that this is essential characteristic of democracy	37.8	26.7
Disagree: If a woman earns more money than her husband, it's almost certain to cause problems	28.5	31.8
Agree: Having a job is the best way for a woman to be an independent person	48.4	49.5
Never justifiable: For a man to beat his wife	55.2	57.4

Source: World Values Survey Database, Wave 6, 2010–2014, www.worldvaluessurvey.org/wvs.jsp; Algeria 2014, Egypt 2013, Iraq 2013, Jordan 2014, Kuwait 2013–2014, Libya 2014, Morocco 2011, Palestine 2013, Qatar 2010, Tunisia 2013, Lebanon 2014, Yemen 2014
N = 15,222

comparative reality of gender equality in the Maghreb and the Middle East in that women in the Maghreb generally have more rights than those in the Middle East.

Religiosity

Religiosity is the only relevant area where one sees a slight difference in attitudes between the Maghreb and the rest of the MENA region. Lower levels of religiosity are frequently associated with higher levels of support for women's rights (Htun and Weldon 2018, Inglehart and Norris 2003). Most Moroccans consider themselves to be devout religious people. However, when asked about their beliefs and practices, people in the

Table 2.9 *Religiosity: Practices and beliefs, Maghreb and MENA (%)*

Question	Algeria	Morocco	Tunisia	Maghreb average	Middle East
Read or listen to Qur'an or Bible: Always	22	11	33	22	38
Pray daily: Always	64	61	62	62	74
Are you a religious person?	24	36	33	31	39

Source: Arab Barometer Database, Wave III, 2012–2014, www.arabbarometer.org/; Algeria N = 1,177, Morocco N = 1,080, Middle East N = 4618

Maghreb countries overall exhibit less religiosity than other parts of the MENA region (Table 2.9). Because attitudes toward gender equality are not that different between the two regions, it is unlikely that existing differences around religiosity influence these attitudes. Ultimately, in order to explain the variance between the two regions when it comes to women's rights, it is more important to look at the political strategies of political leaders and women's movements than attitudes of ordinary people toward religiosity, or gender equality for that matter. Certainly religion plays a role, but mainly it is invoked as part of a political contestation.

Conclusion

This chapter has discussed some of the background factors that provide the context for the changes being discussed in Chapter 1. It shows how the newly independent countries in the Maghreb rejected the French legal system that had been imposed on them and adopted unified laws and a unified legal system that made it possible to adopt laws that would affect all women (and men) and placed family law into the statutory courts rather than the Islamic courts. The large North African presence in France and other European countries also resulted historically in a cross-fertilization of ideas, particularly among leftists and feminists, who were influenced by like-minded French thinkers and activists.

Claims are often made about the Imazighen being more secular and more open to women's rights because of their long history of warrior queens and other women leaders in a society that once was matrilineal and matrifocal. Imazighen women also have found a place in Sufi practices that is denied their counterparts in other Islamic religious institutions in the MENA region. Amazigh women's rights activists draw on this imaginary as inspiration for their cause of promoting an Amazigh identity and fighting for women's rights. The Amazigh and women's movements form two strands of secular post-Islamist mobilization and their causes have often been intertwined. While this imaginary is a popular one, it would be difficult to link it directly to the legal changes that have occurred in the Maghreb.

The MENA region has remained stubbornly undemocratic, but the Maghreb overall has seen the opening of a little more political space since the 2000s, especially Tunisia, while the Arab Middle East became even more authoritarian. The political opening in the Maghreb, however limited, allowed for greater women's mobilization. At the same time, women's movements in the region have benefited from top-down women's rights policy measures adopted by leaders to neutralize Islamists and present a more democratic face to the world. This has sometimes put them in the awkward position of being associated with repressive regimes while fighting for political liberalization.

Finally, the Maghreb appears to be less tied to religiosity than the Arab Middle East, according to an Arab Barometer survey. Generally, levels of religiosity are related to openness to women's rights. Attitudes towards gender equality in the Maghreb, however, are mixed. In some areas they are more progressive than the Middle East and in other areas less so. In both the case of religiosity and gender equality, attitudes remain unrelated to actual policy outcomes around women's rights.

While the unified legal systems in the Maghreb, the Amazigh cultural influences, the slightly greater political space, and attitudes towards religiosity are all quite diverse background factors, they may have helped shape the changes described in Chapter 3.

3 *Legislative and Constitutional Women's Rights Reforms in Arab Countries*

Amina Filali, a sixteen-year-old girl from a village near Larache, Morocco, had reached her limit with her husband's constant beatings. According to one account, she walked to the local *souk* (market), bought a bottle of rat poison, swallowed it, and died. After her death, it came to light that she had been raped in the street and when she reported the rape and went to court, she was told by the prosecutor to arrange for a marriage contract with her rapist. And so her family married her off to the rapist even though she was a minor. In Morocco, as in many MENA countries, losing one's virginity outside of marriage, even through rape, is regarded as sullying the family honor, which can be regained if the rapist marries the woman. "I had to marry her to him, because I couldn't allow my daughter to have no future and stay unmarried," said Amina's mother. "We would be the laughingstock of our neighbors" (Allison 2012). The husband started beating Amina and soon thereafter she took her own life.

Amina's act of desperation stunned the country and protests in the streets and furor in the media against the law led to its repeal in 2014. Women's organizations like the Association démocratique des femmes du Maroc (ADFM) held protests in front of the parliament. They issued press releases, sent letters, alerted the media, and lobbied hard to change the penal code. In the end, the government was forced to amend the code. Women's organizations continued to push for a complete overhaul of the penal code so that it would be in line with the constitution (M17.2.16). The passage of legislation in Morocco was followed by similar legal reforms in Tunisia and then in Jordan and Lebanon.

The passage of such women's rights reforms is one of the most important ways in which the Maghreb differs from the Middle East, in terms of the quantity, content, and timing of women's rights legislation. Overall, the Maghreb countries have adopted more women's rights legislation and have done so earlier than Middle Eastern countries. The pattern of coordination between Algeria, Tunisia, and Morocco is quite clearly a result of collaboration by activists and efforts by government leaders to stay abreast of their neighboring countries. This collaboration and diffusion has been mediated by United Nations Women and other regional and international organizations. When one of the three Maghreb countries has passed women's rights legislation, often the other two have followed suit within a few years. This is evident in the legislation passed on violence against women, trafficking, quotas, sexual harassment, the rape loophole, nationality, and other such reforms.

In this chapter I treat constitutional and legislative reforms, my main dependent variables, in two ways. I look at them as symbols of the direction a country is moving with respect to women's rights. Sometimes the reforms are only aspirational. Often they are the culmination of political battles over the future of the country. But these reforms also have real-world impacts, which is why they matter. They are not only representative of a vision; they also influence people's daily lives to one degree or another, although often leaving much to be desired in the way of enforcement.

This chapter shows how constitutional and legislative women's rights reforms have converged in the Maghreb region, but also how the Maghreb has diverged from the Middle East in this regard. I discuss the adoption of unified legal systems, which set the stage for future women's rights reforms. I then examine constitutional reforms followed by a discussion of key areas of legislative reform since 2000, particularly areas with variation within the region and where we have seen legislative reforms improving women's status. I leave out or discuss only briefly legislation where we see uniformity in the MENA region, either for or against women's rights. This allows us to identify the key differences between the Maghreb countries and the Middle East, but also where variance cuts across the entire region.

Unified Legal System

One way in which the Maghreb and Middle East part ways when it comes to women's rights is related to the creation of unified legal systems in all three Maghreb countries. While several scholars have used unified legal systems as a way to explain variance in the adoption of women's rights reforms, the fact that countries with unified legal systems have just as poor a record on women's rights as countries without them suggests that there are additional factors at play and that such systems alone cannot explain the adoption of women's rights reforms. Nevertheless, as with other constitutional reforms and legislation, a clear pattern emerges, with the Maghreb countries following a similar path of adopting unified legal systems (see Table 3.1).

Most countries in the MENA region have dual legal systems in which "modern law" coexists with *shari'a* law. In countries like Jordan and Qatar, separate laws and courts are maintained. Family law is generally adjudicated based on *shari'a* law, although these laws have evolved over time based on diverse principles. The laws are influenced not only by religion but also by the cultures of the Mediterranean region. Perhaps the main distinction between these two legal traditions is that *shari'a* law is unlegislated whereas modern law is legislated (Warrick 2009).

Some have argued that women have gained broader civil rights in countries with unitary legal systems (Engelcke 2014, Maktabi 2012). It is argued that this allowed the king to have more influence in Morocco, while in Jordan the *shari'a* court administration has had more influence over family law (Engelcke 2014). However, if one looks beyond the Maghreb, one finds that Iraq and Kuwait also have unified laws and a unified court system, and Libya, Yemen, Oman, and Egypt have unified courts (but not unified laws) (Table 3.1). Yet none of these countries have made the same types of gains found in the Maghreb with respect to women's rights. Members of the Shia religious establishment and Islamic parties in Iraq have even been trying to revoke the country's Personal Status Code (PSC), which was established in 1959 to provide a unified legal framework for family law, and to replace it with sectarian religious law. Iraq is one of the few MENA countries whose legal system is not based in *shari'a* law. The changes the Islamists are seeking would violate the constitution and would affect inheritance, marriage, and divorce provisions. One of the proposed amendments would allow child marriage of girls as young as nine. It would allow sectarian religious authorities to adjudicate cases and would remove protections of women from polygamy and various forms of abuse (Ali 2017). Women's organizations have thus far successfully pushed back against such modifications, but efforts to roll back women's rights continue.

Given the fact that nine countries in the region have a unified court system and most have not made significant women's rights reforms, it is more likely that a unified court system and unified laws are a necessary but not sufficient condition for establishing a stronger footing for women's rights. In other words, in and of themselves, unified court systems are not guarantees of such reforms. And while such systems do not fully explain why some countries have advanced in terms of women's rights, the fact that the Maghreb countries have adopted a unified legal system and used it to advance women's rights lends itself to the argument that it was a necessary precondition for further legal reforms. Although the existence of these systems in the Maghreb does not demarcate the region from the Middle East in this regard, it does lay the basis for women's rights reforms.

The adoption of unified legal systems occurred at the same time in all three Maghreb countries after independence. This might be seen as an assertion of autonomy from the French system of legal pluralism. At independence, Maghrebi legal systems were a mixture of French, *shari'a*, and Amazigh courts. In Algeria, the French replaced the Ottoman courts with secular courts and introduced French law. Most Algerians were under *shari'a* or Amazigh courts, which could be reviewed by the French courts. After independence in 1962, the Algerian government sought to eliminate the French influence, announcing a new unified legal system in 1965 and new civil and criminal codes in 1975 under President Houari Boumédiène. The Algerian government later introduced a highly controversial Family Code in 1984, which women's rights groups felt was a betrayal of the revolution.

Similarly, in Morocco, the entire legal system was unified in 1965 and the *shari'a* and Amazigh courts were abolished. All citizens were subject to the same law. A new Moroccan Family Code was issued that applied to all citizens to reform the French strategy of using multiple legal systems (Engelcke 2014). Unlike countries that have multiple court systems, in Morocco, the unitary courts have been less autonomous than they are in countries like Jordan. Moreover, they are subject to universal legal reforms affecting all citizens. The courts have thus been able to curb the conservative influence of clerics over family law.

The patterns found in the Maghreb countries contrast sharply with what is found in countries with multiple courts. Lebanon, for example, has fifteen different personal status laws and multiple courts, one for each confessional group. Even though the constitution does not mention *shari'a* law as the basis of its legal system or of family law because of the various confessional groups, and because it does not specifically mention inheritance laws (as do most other constitutions in the region), its multiple-court system makes it exceptionally difficult to bring about universal legal reform for all women in the area of family law. All of the personal status laws are discriminatory toward women. All efforts to introduce a unified civil status have failed, including the most recent one in 2010. In effect, what one has, as Suad Joseph explains, is the "elevation of religious identity to civil status," which makes religious law the state's official law (cited in Maktabi 2012, 100). Family law not only differs from one confessional group to another but within each group, women are afforded different rights than men. They are assigned at birth to a religious group status, from which they cannot remove themselves. This is the case in both Muslim-majority states and multifaith states like Lebanon (see Table 3.1, columns 5 and 7).

Table 3.1 *Unified courts and laws in MENA region, 2018 (Maghreb countries highlighted)*

Country	Unified courts	Unified laws	Source of family law	Basis of family law/Personal Status Law	Islamic inheritance mentioned in constitution	Laws for separate religious groups
Algeria	Yes	Yes	Personal Status Code (1984, amend. 2008)	Constitution	No	No
Morocco	Yes	Yes	Personal Status Code (1957, 2004)	Constitution	No	No
Tunisia	Yes	Yes	Personal Status Code (1957)	Constitution	No	No
Iraq	Yes	Yes[1]	Personal Status Law (1959)	Constitution	No	Yes
Kuwait	Yes	Yes	Personal Status Law (1984)	*Shari'a* law	Yes	No
Libya	Yes	No	Family Law (1984)	*Shari'a* law	No	No
Oman	Yes	No	Personal Status Law (1997)	*Shari'a* law	Yes	Yes

[1] According to Article 41 of the 2005 Constitution, each religious group has jurisdiction over its own personal status affairs. However, this provision has not been implemented due to pressures from women's rights organizations against Article 41.

Table 3.1 (*cont.*)

Country	Unified courts	Unified laws	Source of family law	Basis of family law/Personal Status Law	Islamic inheritance mentioned in constitution	Laws for separate religious groups
Egypt	Yes	No	Personal Status Law (1920, 1929, 1985)	*Shari'a* law	No	Yes
Yemen	Yes	NA	Personal Status Law (1992)	*Shari'a* law	Yes	No
Bahrain	No	No	Personal Status Code (2009)	*Shari'a* law uncodified	Yes	Yes
Jordan	No	No	Personal Status Law (2001, 2010)	*Shari'a* law	Yes	Yes
Lebanon	No	No	15 different personal status laws (1936)	NA	No	Yes
Palestinian Authority	No	No	1976 Jordanian Personal Status Law in the West Bank; 1954 Egyptian Family Law in Gaza	*Shari'a* law	**No**	Yes
Qatar	No	No	Family Law (2006)	*Shari'a* law uncodified	Yes	No
Syria	No	No	Personal Status Law (1953)	*Shari'a* law	Yes	Yes
UAE	No	No	Personal Status Law (2005)	*Shari'a* law	No	No
Saudi Arabia	No	No	No codified family law	*Shari'a* law	No	No

Sources: Brown (2001); Engelcke (2014)

Constitutional Reforms

It is interesting to note the changes in the Maghrebi constitutions with respect to women's rights provisions and how they expanded over time with each constitutional revision. Although Tunisia had advanced

Table 3.2 *Convergence of gender-related provisions in Maghrebi constitutions (shaded areas 1 = adopted, 0 = not adopted)*

Country	Year	Labor or work	Political representation	Gender equality	Nondiscrimination clause	Mention of gender pronouns
Algeria	**1963**	0	0	1	0	0
Algeria	**1996**	0	1	1	1	0
Algeria	**2008**	0	1	1	1	1
Algeria	**2016**	1	1	1	1	1
Tunisia	**1958**	0	1	0	0	0
Tunisia	**2014**	1	1	1	1	1
Morocco	**1962**	0	0	1	0	0
Morocco	**2011**	1	1	1	1	1

Sources: Compiled from Women, Global Gender Equality Constitutional Database, http://constitutions.unwomen.org; Constitute database, www.constituteproject.org; Constitution Net, www.constitutionnet.org/; Constitutions du Monde database, http://mjp.univ-perp.fr/constit/constitintro.htm

earliest in terms of legislation, Algeria was the first to incorporate explicit women's rights provisions into its constitution in 1996 in the middle of the Black Decade. Most changes were adopted in Morocco and Tunisia after the Arab Spring and reforms regarding women and work were adopted in Algeria after 2016, also in response to civil society pressures and unrest related to the Arab Spring (Table 3.2). Thus, one sees a convergence in women's rights constitutional reforms in the Maghreb over time.

If one compares the constitutions of the Maghreb countries with those of other MENA countries with respect to women's rights today, the former have charted a significantly different path from most of the MENA region, Morocco and Tunisia especially, representing a new set of political accommodations between Islamists and secularists. These accommodations are critical to the prospects of stability and democracy in the region.

Tunisia's 2014 constitution is one of the most radical in the world when it comes to women's rights. In Tunisia, women's rights activists fought back hard against Islamist efforts to introduce a complementarity clause in the new constitution that would value women's and men's equal but different contributions to society. Feminists won a major victory when they were able to introduce Article 46, which says: "The State engages in protecting achievements in the field of women's rights and in reinforcing them." The constitution includes gender-sensitive language following Morocco and Algeria. It provides a positive rights frame for women's rights, which is virtually unprecedented anywhere in the world. The state guarantees gender equality of rights and duties and opportunities in all domains (Preamble, Article 21, Article 46), and equality of both genders before the law without any discrimination (Article 21). It mentions both women and men specifically in relation to the right to work, the right to decent working conditions and to a fair wage (Article 40). The state seeks to guarantee women's representation in elected bodies (Article 34) and to attain parity between women and men in elected assemblies (Article 46). The state commits to take all necessary measures in order to eradicate violence against women and to protect women's accrued rights, and to work to strengthen and develop those rights (Article 46). Although gender is not mentioned specifically, all are guaranteed an education up to the age of sixteen (Article 39) and promised access to water (Article 44) and basic health services (Article 38).

In Morocco, the constitutional changes were precipitated by the 2011 Vingt février (February 20) protests, which represented a coming together of feminist, Amazigh, Islamist, and pro-economic rights advocates, along with other secular and leftist concerns (Salime 2011). The protests took place in the context of the Arab Spring, although they were not as large as the protests in Tunisia or Egypt. The king responded quickly and sought to address some of the protesters' concerns through constitutional reforms. The new 2011 constitution, which many felt did not go far enough in democratizing the political system, expanded the powers of the prime minister, made Amazigh the official state language along with Arabic, and guaranteed women "civic and social equality with men." The new constitution, which was voted on in a referendum, also allowed for an increase in the number of seats reserved for women in parliament to 15 percent.

Of the three constitutions, the gender reforms were the most limited in the Algerian case. Up until 2008 there were no provisions in the Algerian constitution specifically mentioning women's political rights. This changed with the 2008 constitution. For example, Chapter IV, Article 31bis states: "The State shall work for the promotion of the political rights of women by increasing their chances of access to representation in elected assemblies."

Contrasting Constitutions in the Maghreb and Middle East

The women's rights provisions in Maghrebi constitutions exceed what one sees in other MENA constitutions, with the exception of Egypt and perhaps Iraq. What has to be factored in is not only what the constitutions say regarding women's rights explicitly, but also what other provisions there are regarding how family law is adjudicated, how motherhood is depicted, and ultimately the extent to which the constitutional provisions are translated into law. For example, although the 2014 Egyptian constitution gave women unprecedented rights (Table 3.3), these have not been followed up with legislative or other policy changes. The most challenging deficiency is in family law, where there is no unified Family Code in Egypt. Personal Status Law governs Muslim women's rights within marriage and the family, where the principles of Islamic *shari'a* law are the main source of legislation (Article 2). Other faiths apply their own community's religious standards to family matters (Article 3).

In contrast to the Maghrebi constitutions, there is no mention of women's rights in the constitutions of Kuwait, Lebanon, Saudi Arabia, the United Arab Emirates (UAE), or Yemen (Table 3.3). Yemen's constitution refers to women as "sisters of men" and guarantees their rights and duties assigned by the *shari'a*. Jordan's constitution refers to women only by saying that the law will protect "motherhood." The constitutions of Bahrain, Jordan, Libya, Mauritania, Palestine, Qatar, and Syria make only one or two references to women's rights while those of Egypt and Iraq make slightly more. But in all cases, they have considerably weaker provisions than what one finds, for example, in Tunisia's constitution (see Table 3.3).

A generic statement about gender equality and a clause opposing gender discrimination is found in most African constitutions today. All three Maghrebi constitutions contain these two clauses. However, this is not the case in all Arab MENA constitutions, of which only six contain both these basic provisions (Table 3.3). Bahrain qualifies gender equality to say that women can have equality with men in political, social, cultural, and economic spheres as long as it does not

Table 3.3 *Constitutional provisions regarding women's rights (Maghreb countries highlighted)*

Country	Year constitution passed or amended	Labor or work	Parity or quota in political representation	Equality of all citizens	Gender equality	Antidiscrimination clause with reference to gender	Gender-based violence
Algeria	2016	X	X	X	X	X	
Bahrain	2002	X		X	X	X	
Egypt	2014	X	X	X	X	X	X
Iraq	2005	X		X	X	X	X
Jordan	2011	X		X			
Kuwait	1962			X			
Lebanon	2004			X			
Libya	2012			X		X	
Mauritania	2012			X	X	X	
Morocco	2011	X	X	X	X	X	
Oman	1996			X		X	
Palestine	2003			X	X		
Qatar	2003			X	X	X	
Saudi Arabia	2013						
Syria	2012			X	X	X	
Tunisia	2014	X	X	X	X	X	X
UAE	1971/1996			X			
Yemen	2001			X			

Sources: Women, Global Gender Equality Constitutional Database, http://constitutions.unwomen.org; Constitute database, www.constituteproject.org; Constitution Net, www.constitutionnet.org/; Constitutions du Monde database, http://mjp.univ-perp.fr/constit/constitintro.htm

breach "the provisions of Islamic canon law (*Shari'a*)" (Article 5.b). Libya, Oman, Jordan, Lebanon, Kuwait, the UAE, and Yemen have general equality clauses that do not mention gender specifically. Only Saudi Arabia does not have any form of such an equality provision, neither for all citizens nor in reference to gender. Feminists in the region are quick to point out that even though most MENA constitutions hold out the promise of equality for all citizens, many legal provisions in all countries stand in sharp contrast to this promise by relegating women to secondary and minor status when it comes to family law in particular. There is a bifurcation in the legal framework, which allows for education for all, the right to government employment, the right to work, and the right to vote, but at the same time creates serious inequalities within the private sphere and within the home. It is this paradoxical imbalance that is beginning to change, especially in the Maghreb countries as laws are reconciled with constitutional provisions for gender equality.

Although a few constitutions in the Arab MENA region mention women's right to political participation, only the Maghrebi constitutions (and the Syrian) mention that the state will proactively work for the promotion of women's political rights by increasing their access to representation. In the cases of Morocco and Tunisia, the constitutions mention that the state works toward gender parity in politics, which is a much higher bar than one finds in most constitutions. The only other constitutions globally that mention gender parity are those of Ecuador (2008), Bolivia (2009), and the Democratic Republic of Congo (2011). Of these countries, only Bolivia has attained parity, with women holding 53 percent of the country's legislative seats. As for economic rights, Algeria, Morocco, and Tunisia all have gendered provisions pertaining to the right to equal access to work. The only Middle Eastern countries with these provisions are Bahrain, Egypt, Iraq, and Jordan.

There are a few areas where constitutions address women's rights in other Arab countries but not in the Maghreb. For example, Egypt allows citizenship to be transferred from both the mother and father to the child, as do Iraq and the Palestinian territories. However, this is provided for in legislation in all three Maghreb countries – Algeria (2005), Morocco (2007), and Tunisia (1998) – in addition to Bahrain.

The Maghreb countries stand out also for what they do not say in their constitutions. Most MENA constitutions focus on women's roles as mothers and on the protection either of mothers or motherhood, with the exception of the Maghrebi, Lebanese, and Saudi constitutions. The Egyptian constitution of 2004 has many provisions regarding women, however, many of them are cast within the framework of motherhood and women's roles in the home. For example, it declares that: "The state ... ensures women empowerment to reconcile the duties of a woman toward her family and her work requirements. The state ensures care and protection and care for motherhood and childhood, and for breadwinning, and elderly women, and women most in need" (Chapter 2, Article 11). Placing women's rights alongside children's rights infantilizes women and reduces them to the same category of dependence that children and the elderly often fall under.

Ten of the MENA constitutions mention the need to protect mothers or motherhood, often along with childhood, but unlike children, the implicit assumption is that mothers raise the young and form the values of the nation. As the Bahraini constitution says, the mother "tends the young and protects them from exploitation and safeguards them against moral, bodily, and spiritual neglect." Women are placed on a par with children, the elderly, and the disabled as vulnerable populations in need of protection rather than as citizens in their own right. The equation of women with children is evocative of their status as minors who are not accorded full citizenship but, rather, are in need of protection and special consideration. For example, the UAE constitution says:

> The community shall care for children and *mothers*, and protect minors and others who are unable to look after themselves for any reason, such as illness or incapacity or old age or forced unemployment, assist and rehabilitate them for their own interest and for the interest of the community. Welfare and social security laws regulate these matters. (Part II, Article 16)

This relegation of women to the category of vulnerable people in need of protection is not found in the three Maghrebi constitutions. Although the Moroccan constitution mentions mothers, it specifies that not all mothers across the board require protection, only "certain categories of women and of mothers." This is an important recognition that not all women are the same: single mothers, widows, and very poor mothers face particular challenges in Moroccan society and bear a double burden given gender inequality.

Another major distinction between the constitutions relates to religion. Generally, religiosity (in any religion) is associated with fewer women's rights globally (Inglehart and Norris 2003). Although constitutions in all countries in the region, except for Lebanon, specify that Islam is the state religion, it is only the Maghreb countries and Lebanon that do not mention Islamic jurisprudence as a source of law (Table 3.1). This has implications for women's rights, particularly family law. Tunisia historically had one of the most "modern" constitutions among the Muslim-majority countries, written in 1861 under pressure by the competing British and French consuls (Ahmed and Gouda 2015) at a time when the earliest debates were being had over how to combine constitutionalism with Islam. Ever since then, a perennial struggle has ensued over the extent to which political authority should be accountable to Islamic law or to the constitution. The meaning of references to Islam differs from country to country and they have greater salience in some. In a country like Tunisia, the insertion of references to Islam in the constitution historically may be seen more an attempt by reformers to appease the religious conservatives who feared that modern constitutions were a way of perpetuating Western, European, and colonial dominance (Ahmed and Gouda 2015, 18).

The problem for women's rights is not religiosity per se, as some have argued, because Islam influences all law to one degree or another in these countries. Tunisia is the only country in the region where the *shari'a* plays little role in the legal system, and in Morocco and Algeria there are references to Islamic law but also to other more universal aspirations that have been incorporated into the constitutions. Similarly, provisions on inheritance in the constitution, for example, provide little information about women's rights outcomes since five countries mention it in their constitution and six do not (including the Maghreb countries), yet all MENA countries rely on Islamic jurisprudence to dictate inheritance laws for women. Central to Islamic jurisprudence around inheritance is the notion that women can inherit only half of what men can inherit.

The real question, then, is how religion is used to influence women's rights. Thus, the mention of *shari'a* law in the constitution as the basis of personal law is perhaps the most important measure to understand women's rights outcomes (see Table 3.1).

Legislation

One of the most striking features of women's rights legislative reform in the Maghreb after 2000 was the manner in which the

Table 3.4 *Convergence of women's rights legislation in the Maghreb (2003–2018)*

Legislation on women's rights	Morocco	Algeria	Tunisia
Family Code	2004	2005	1993
Sexual harassment	2003*		
	2004	2004	2004
	2016	2016	2017
Quotas	2011	2012	2011
Prohibition of marriage to rapist	2014		2017
Prohibition of domestic violence	2017	2014	2017
Nationality of children to follow both husband and wife	2007	2005	1998
Violence against women	2018	2015	2017

Sources: WomanStats Project, www.womanstats.org/
* Sexual harassment at work.

three countries passed legislation in an almost synchronized manner. Competition may have occurred at the level of policymakers, but the fact that women's rights legislation has been passed almost in tandem in all three Maghreb countries speaks mostly to the coordination among women's rights activists in Morocco, Algeria, and Tunisia, particularly through organizations like Collectif Maghreb-Égalité.

The pattern of convergence is evident in legislation passed around quotas, sexual harassment, the prohibition of the marriage of victims to their rapist, nationality issues, and violence against women among other areas (see Table 3.4). In the discussion that follows, I focus on legislation in every major area where there are notable differences among the MENA countries.

Political Empowerment

One of the areas where we see the biggest divergence between the Maghreb and the Middle East is in the political sphere. Here the introduction of quotas, in particular, has pushed the Maghreb countries to the fore in the political empowerment of women in the region.

Table 3.5 *Quota adoption in MENA (%)*

	Women in legislature (%) average
Quotas	20
No quotas	5

Source: International Institute for Democracy and Electoral Assistance, Gender Quotas Database, www.idea.int/data-tools/data/gender-quotas/country-resources/142/35

Table 3.6 *Types of quotas adopted in Arab MENA countries (%)*

Type of quota	Women in legislature (%) average
Legislative quotas	23.0
Reserved seats	17.0
Voluntary quota	17.0
Appointed seats	8.5

Source: International Institute for Democracy and Electoral Assistance, Gender Quotas Database, www.idea.int/data-tools/data/gender-quotas/country-resources/142/35

In the Maghreb, women have increased representation primarily through the introduction of various forms of gender-based quota laws, which generally improve women's chances of being elected. Morocco, which adopted quotas in 2002 through an agreement between parties, served as a reference point for other Arab countries (Abou Zeid 2006). Today in the MENA region, countries with quotas have four times the level of representation of countries without, especially where legislated quotas are adopted, creating incentives for parties to increase the number of female candidates or place them more favorably on the party list (Tables 3.5 and 3.6). Tunisia today has the highest rate of female legislative representation at the national level (31 percent). Voluntary quotas and reserved seats have similar results for female representation in the MENA region. Voluntary quotas are those adopted by parties with or without the presence of legislation. Reserved seats are seats for which only women can run, regardless of party. And finally, appointed quotas are found where the ruler appoints individuals to the legislature. Given the low numbers appointed on average, it is hard to regard this last type of quota as anything more than tokenism. The adoption of quotas is also evident at the local level.

After the adoption of quotas with the aim of achieving parity, and with alternation between men and women on candidate lists, a stunning 47 percent of local Tunisian council positions were held by women following the May 2018 elections. This is higher than the rates found in France (40 percent), Britain (33 percent), and Germany (27 percent) (*Business News* 2018). A member of the Islamist Ennahda party was elected as the first woman mayor of Tunis. At the local level, women in Morocco won 38 percent of the commune council seats in 2015, nearly three times as many as in 2009. However, only twenty-one women assumed the presidency of 1,538 municipalities and only one woman was elected district president (*Aujourd'hui Le Maroc* 2018).

In the case of Algeria, the changes in representation were dramatic and can be linked not only to the adoption of quotas but also to postconflict effects found in other parts of Africa (Tripp 2015). After the civil war ended in 2002, women's proportion of legislative seats in Algeria increased from 2.4 percent in 1987 prior to the civil war to 31.6 percent after the 2012 elections. In 2014, Algeria had a cabinet in which women held 30 percent of the posts, which was the highest percentage among the Arab countries. The figure for women's legislative representation subsequently dropped to 26 percent in the 2016 election.

If one looks at the overall picture of the impact of quotas in national-level legislatures (Table 3.7), and the influence of subnational-level quotas (Table 3.8), and executive-level ministerial appointments (Table 3.9), the Maghreb countries stand out from the rest (Figure 3.1). If one includes Mauritania in the mix of Maghreb countries, the pattern is even more distinct when it comes to political empowerment. Moreover, if one examines World Economic Forum data on the rate of change in closing the gender gap in the MENA region, the gap has closed almost entirely in the fields of health and education, less so in economic opportunity and least in the area of political empowerment (a measure based on a composite of subnational, national, legislative, and executive leadership) (Figures 3.2, 3.3, 3.4, 3.5, 3.6). It is here in political empowerment that we once again see that the Maghreb has made some of the biggest gains over time.

Table 3.7 *Quotas, electoral system, and female representation in MENA legislatures (lower house), 2018*

Country	Lower or single house % women 2018	Year quota adopted	Quota or appointed seats	Electoral system	Chambers in legislature
Algeria	25.8	2012	Legislated	Mixed	Bicameral
Bahrain	7.5		No quota	Plurality/Majority	Bicameral
Egypt	9.0	1979–1986	Reserved seats	Plurality, PR after 1983	Unicameral
	12.7	2010/2014	Reserved seats	Plurality/Majority	
Iraq	25.3	2005	Legislated	PR	Unicameral
Jordan	15.4	2012	Reserved	Mixed	Bicameral
Kuwait	3.1		No quota	Plurality/Majority	Unicameral
Lebanon	3.1		No quota	Plurality/Majority	Unicameral
Libya	16.0	2012	Legislated	Mixed	Unicameral
Mauritania	25.0	2012	Legislated	Parallel	Unicameral
Morocco	20.5	2011	Reserved seats	PR	Bicameral
Oman	1.2		Appointed	Plurality/Majority	Bicameral
Palestine	13.0	2005	Legislated	PR	Unicameral
Qatar	9.8		No quota	Not applicable	Unicameral
Saudi Arabia	19.9	2013	Appointed	Not applicable	Unicameral
Syrian Arab Republic	13.2		No quota	Plurality/Majority	Unicameral
Tunisia	22.8	2004	Voluntary	PR	Unicameral
	31.3	2011	Legislated	PR	
United Arab Emirates	22.5		Appointed	Election by electoral college	Unicameral
Yemen	0.3		Appointed	Plurality/Majority	Bicameral

Sources: International Institute for Democracy and Electoral Assistance, Gender Quotas Database, www.idea.int/data-tools/data/gender-quotas/country-resources/142/35; Inter-Parliamentary Union (2018); Inter-Parliamentary Union, Parline database, Structure of parliament, https://data.ipu.org/compare?field=country%3A%3Afield_structure_of_parliament#map

Table 3.8 *Adoption of quotas at municipal or regional level in MENA countries (Maghreb countries highlighted)*

	Quota in municipal or regional council	Year quota adopted
Algeria	30–35% quota in regional councils, depending on the number of seats in each electoral district, and 30% quota in municipal councils.	2012
Bahrain	No quota	
Egypt	25%	2014
Iraq	33% quota in provincial, district and sub-district elections.	2008
Jordan	30% of all municipal council seats.	2012
Kuwait	No quota	
Lebanon	No quota	
Libya	Council of Ministers Decision (No. 161) on the Adoption of Principles and Procedures for Municipal Election mentions quota provisions but no specific percentage or means of calculation is provided.	2013
Mauritania	20% of seats on municipal councils	2012
Morocco	33% quota in regional councils Lower district and communal councils, additional electoral constituencies are reserved for women to be elected through a proportional representation system	2011
Oman	No quota	
Palestine	Approximately 20% quota in local council	2005
Qatar	No quota	
Saudi Arabia	No quota	
Tunisia	Parity for men and women	2014
United Arab Emirates	No quota	
Yemen	No quota	

Source: Inter-Parliamentary Union (2018)

According to World Economic Forum data, the gender gap closed four times faster in the Maghreb between 2006 and 2017 than in the Middle East when it came to political empowerment.

Table 3.9 *Appointment of women ministers (%) in MENA countries (Maghreb countries highlighted)*

Country	2008	2017
Mauritania	23	44
UAE	17	36
Tunisia	4	30
Algeria	4	15
Morocco	11	15
Egypt	9	13
Jordan	7	8
Kuwait	7	7
Oman	9	7
Qatar	0	7
Syria	6	6
Yemen	6	6
Bahrain	11	5
Lebanon	7	4
Saudi Arabia	0	0

Source: World Bank, Gender Data Portal, Proportion of women in ministerial positions (%), https://databank.worldbank.org/Data/indicator/SG.GEN.MNST.ZS?id=2ddc971b&report_name=Gender_Indicators_Report&populartype=series

Family Law

Family law has always had a particular place in the legal history of the Maghreb, as mentioned at the start of the chapter. The colonial influence ensured that while other areas of law were transformed, family law remained subject to Islamic jurisprudence (*fiqh*). Even though unified legal systems and personal status codes were introduced after independence, the imprint of Islamic law and the historic centrality of the family in the Mediterranean region weighed heavily on the new legal frameworks, although to a lesser extent in Tunisia. Historically, the family was based on blood relationships, which is why adoption was not permitted. To this day, adoption is prohibited in Algeria and Morocco based on understandings of Islamic law, although

Table 3.10 *Women (%) in legislature (lower house or unicameral) in MENA countries (Maghreb countries highlighted)*

Country	1990	2000	2010	2018
Tunisia	4	12	28	31.3
Algeria	2	3	8	25.8
Iraq	11	6	26	25.3
Mauritania	–	4	22	25.0
UAE	0	0	23	22.5
Morocco	0	1	11	20.5
Saudi Arabia	–	–	0	19.9
Libya	–	–	8	16.0
Jordan	0	0	6	15.4
Syria	9	10	12	13.2
Palestine	–	–	–	13.0
Egypt	4	2	2	12.7
Qatar	–	–	0	9.8
Bahrain	–	–	3	7.5
Lebanon	0	2	3	4.7
Kuwait	–	0	8	3.1
Oman	–	–	0	1.2
Yemen	4	1	0	0.3

Source: Inter-Parliamentary Union (2018)

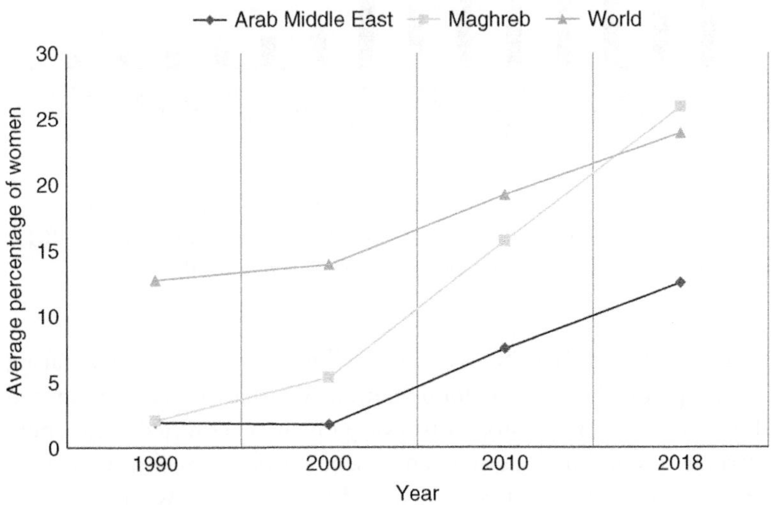

Figure 3.1 Average percentage of women in legislature by region (lower house or unicameral), 1990–2018
Source: Inter-Parliamentary Union (1995, 2019)

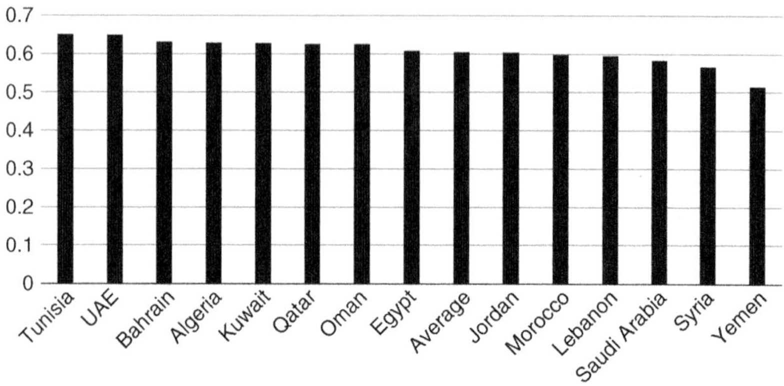

Figure 3.2 Overall gender gap in MENA countries, 2017 (1.0 = no gender gap)
Source: World Economic Forum, Global Gender Gap Report, 2017, www.weforum.org/reports/the-global-gender-gap-report-2017

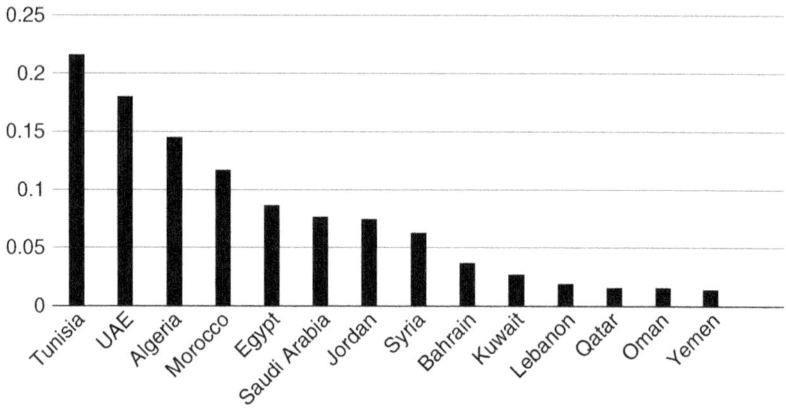

Figure 3.3 Gender gap in political empowerment, 2017 (1.0 = no gender gap)
Source: World Economic Forum, Global Gender Gap Report, 2017, www.weforum.org/reports/the-global-gender-gap-report-2017

guardianship (*kafala*, الكفالة) is allowed, which involves raising or caring for an orphan who is not a blood relation. Tunisia, however, permitted adoption after 1957. Historically, polygamy was permitted, weakening marriage ties and making women dependent on the will of their husband, who could relatively easily divorce them. Women found

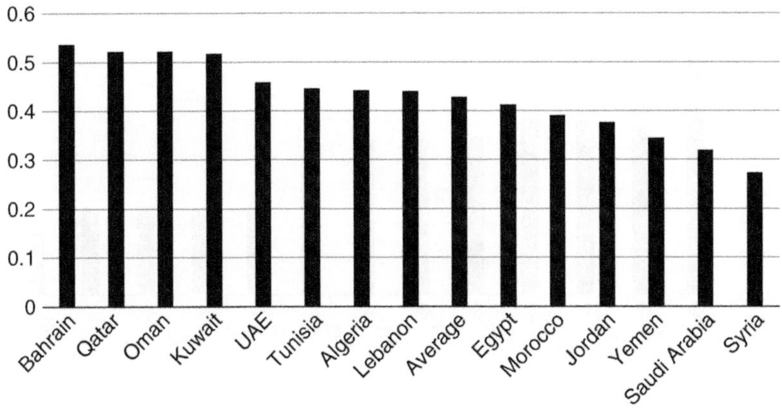

Figure 3.4 Gender gap in economic participation, 2017 (1.0 = no gender gap)
Source: World Economic Forum, Global Gender Gap Report, 2017, www.weforum.org/reports/the-global-gender-gap-report-2017

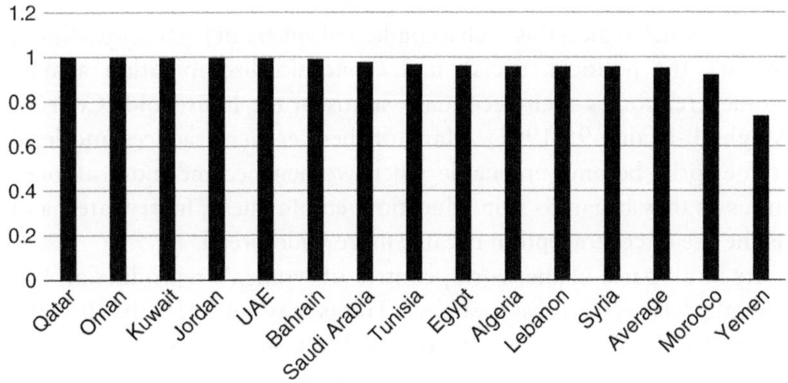

Figure 3.5 Gender gap in educational attainment, 2017 (1.0 = no gender gap)
Source: World Economic Forum, Global Gender Gap Report, 2017, www.weforum.org/reports/the-global-gender-gap-report-2017

themselves vulnerable to men in the family in various ways: The father decided on the daughter's marriage; she was to obey her husband; she could only have custody of young children; and was subject to unequal inheritance. Women activists regard the legal inferiority of women, which continues to this day, as the basis of discrimination in the public

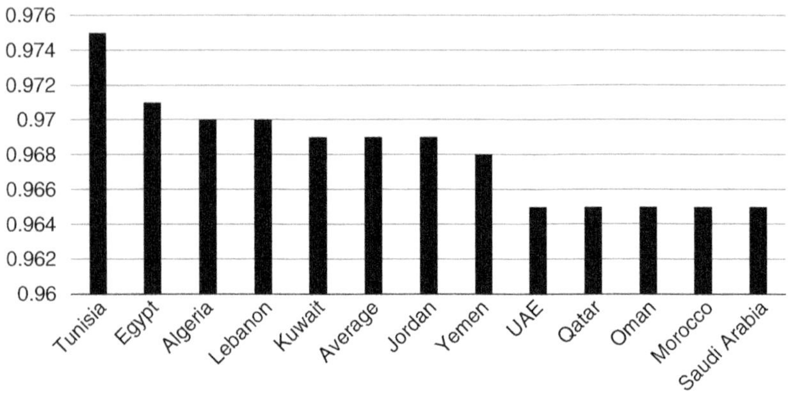

Figure 3.6 Gender gap in health and political empowerment, 2017 (1.0 = no gender gap)
Source: World Economic Forum, Global Gender Gap Report, 2017, www.weforum.org/reports/the-global-gender-gap-report-2017

sphere, which makes this such a conflictual sphere of legal contestation. In turn the political, social, and economic discrimination against women reinforces their secondary status in the household (Collectif Maghreb-Égalité 95 1991). Many of these earlier practices and legal frameworks became untenable when women became more autonomous as they began to gain education, employment, marry later, and as the use of contraception became more widespread.

As in all parts of the world, control of women's reproduction historically has been critical to society. This is why family law has become such a focal point for the state and for Islamists, who want to control this domain, but also for feminists, who seek to defend women's rights to control their own bodies and lives. It is also what makes laws relating to marriage, divorce, child custody, and inheritance so central to women's rights in the MENA region and elsewhere. It animates debates and practices around virginity and veiling in the MENA region and the many ways in which women's sexuality is controlled. Legislation around LGBTQ rights is related to reproduction because such arrangements historically did not result in children. Even whether the wife can marry someone of a different religion and pass on her nationality to her husband are related to controlling the nationality and religion of the offspring.

It has been widely acknowledged that the PSC promulgated in Tunisia in 1956 was the most progressive Family Code in the region, with its abolition of polygamy, a woman's duty to obey her husband, customary (العرف, *urf)* marriages, marital repudiation,[2] and the marital guardian. The PSC allowed for the practice of free and full consent in marriage, civil marriage, and judicial divorce. In Morocco and Algeria the PSCs could be seen as accommodations between the state and the Islamic authorities, particularly within the framework of the Maliki school (المذهب, *madhhab)* of Islamic jurisprudence, as they incorporated aspects of Islamic law.

In Morocco, the 1957 Moudawana was generally a codification of Maliki *fiqh*, although it recommended the adoption of modern legislation in line with new social realities. In 1993 it was partially reformed, doing away with matrimonial guardianship for women without fathers, giving the mother legal custody in the event that the father dies or becomes incapacitated, and abolishing the need for a woman to seek her husband's permission to work. A new PSC (Moudawana) in Morocco was passed in 2004, marking a watershed in women's rights in the country (see Chapter 4). It gave women the right to divorce, raised the legal age of marriage from fifteen to eighteen for girls, allowed women free choice of their spouse, and abolished polygamy. The provision that put the family under the direction of both spouses was seen by some to make this the most progressive PSC in the region. Even the Tunisian PSC did not have such a provision (M20.4.25.16).

In Algeria, the 1984 family law was regarded as a harsh setback for women, who had hoped for greater recognition of their efforts in fighting for independence. Instead, they were handed a PSC which enshrined polygamy, guardianship, female obedience, marital repudiation, and established the husband as the head of household. The subsequent 2005 PSC borrowed heavily from its Moroccan counterpart of 2004. Nevertheless, many feminists felt that the 2005 amendments did little to improve the code, and thus it remained highly contested. Some feminists sought to abolish it and others to reform key provisions. The code forbids women from marrying without the presence of their guardians, whom they can choose. They cannot be forced to marry against their will. The code no longer states that the wife must obey her

[2] An informal *talaq* divorce, which allows a man to divorce his wife by saying "I divorce you" three times.

husband. Instead, spouses have reciprocal rights and duties. Both parents are responsible for the protection and education of children, but the father is their guardian. In cases of divorce, the judge grants custody and guardianship of the children in the following order of preference: to the mother, the father, the maternal grandmother, the paternal grandmother, the maternal aunt, the paternal aunt, and then the closest relative in the best interest of the child. The parent without custody has visitation rights. If a woman remarries, she loses custody of her children, which is not the case for the father. Only men have the right to divorce without cause, although the 2005 code expanded the circumstances under which women could ask for divorce. Because of the substantial inequalities in the PSC, President Bouteflika announced in 2011 that he would abolish the code. This has yet to happen.

Although all three countries increased gender equality with their PSC reforms, the Maliki imprint was still evident, even in Tunisia, where the Code upheld traditional interpretations regarding inheritance. In 2018, the Council of Ministers voted to equalize inheritance rights between men and women but at this writing the parliament has yet to pass it. Article 58 of the Tunisian PSC gives judges the discretion to grant custody of children in the event of a divorce to either the mother or the father based on the best interests of the child, but it prohibits a mother from having her children live with her if she remarries. No such restriction is applied to fathers.

It has been the task of subsequent legislation to address these remaining inequalities, often by arguing that these reforms are within the spirit of Islamic jurisprudence and through a rereading of *shari'a* law. Feminist activists have often reacted with suspicion to such claims and fear that they serve as justification for a patriarchal and conservative view of the family.

Marriage and Divorce Laws

Marriage and divorce laws continue to pose impediments to reform in family law even in the Maghreb (Table 3.11). In 2017, Tunisia overturned a 1973 law banning the marriage of Muslim women to non-Muslim men. This makes Tunisia the first MENA country to introduce such a law. In the past, a non-Muslim man who wished to marry a Tunisian Muslim woman had to convert to Islam and submit

Table 3.11 *Marriage laws in the MENA region, 2018*

Country	Legal age of marriage: women	Legal age of marriage: men	Is polygyny illegal?	Restrictions on polygyny
Algeria	19	19	No but restricted	The man must first obtain permission from the first wife to marry others and a civil marriage is required to precede a religious one.
Bahrain	16	16	No	The man is required to inform his wife of his new marriage only if their premarriage agreement forbids him from taking another wife.
Egypt	18	18	No	The man has to state whether he is already married while registering his marriage. The first wife is informed of the new marriage and can divorce him within a year of being informed.
Iraq	18	18	No	The man needs approval from a judge, who considers the legal justification and his financial capacity.
Jordan	18	18	No	The man is required to inform his wife of his new marriage only if their premarriage agreement forbids him from taking another wife. Violation of such a clause in the premarriage contract entitles the wife to divorce him.
Kuwait	15	17	No	
Lebanon	None	None	No	
Libya	18	18	No	
Mauritania	18	18	No	

Table 3.11 (*cont.*)

Country	Legal age of marriage: women	Legal age of marriage: men	Is polygyny illegal?	Restrictions on polygyny
Morocco	18	18	No but restricted	The man must provide evidence to a judge that he has the means to sustain two wives and that he has permission from the first wife.
Oman	18	18	No	
Palestine	16	16	No	
Qatar	16	18	No	
Saudi Arabia	10	10	No	
Syria	17	18	No	The man needs approval from a judge, who considers the legal justification and his financial capacity.
Tunisia	18	18	Yes (1956)	
UAE	18	18	No	
Yemen	None	15	No	

Source: WomanStats Project, Database, www.womanstats.org/

a certificate of his conversion as evidence. Tunisia has small Christian and Jewish populations.

The only countries in the MENA region that limit polygyny (marriage of men to multiple women) are Tunisia, where polygyny was banned in 1956, and Morocco and Algeria, where it was restricted. After the passage of the 2004 Moudawana in Morocco, a man can take on another wife if he can provide evidence to a judge that he has the means to sustain two wives and that he has permission from the first wife. The judge meets in camera with both parties before making a decision. In 2005, the law on polygamy was amended in Algeria, requiring men to first obtain permission from their first wife to marry another and requiring a civil marriage to precede a religious one. The judge also has to determine whether the man has met the "legal condition of equal justice" to all wives. If the first wife does not approve, she can initiate divorce proceedings.

Polygynous marriages are relatively rare in the Maghreb; however, Algeria has experienced a surge of informal and temporary marriages like *nikah al-misyar*, or traveler's marriages, that are imports from the Gulf states. They are popular among the Wahhabis and are a form of marriage in which a man and a woman agree to marry in the presence of two witnesses. *Zawadj al-moutaa* is a variant of this type of marriage, which is not recognized by Maliki jurisprudence, but is found in other parts of the Middle East although it was practiced in Algeria during the Black Decade. It is a form of marriage for a few hours or days that served to bypass laws against prostitution. It was introduced to Algeria via the Islamist FIS militants who had participated in the Afghan conflict or had been to Iran. Women who refused to participate in this form of marriage were sometimes brutally raped and killed in this dark period of Algeria's recent history. *Nikah al-harb* is yet another variant of this type of informal marriage, found particularly in Syria and Iraq, where some women volunteered for sexual relations with Daesh fighters (to be distinguished from the rape and forced marriages that occurred). There is no sanction against such informal forms of marriage, but they are still relatively rare in the Maghreb.

In the MENA region, only Egypt does not allow exceptions to the legal age of marriage. In other countries, people can petition a judge for an exception. Those marrying under the legal age without permission can find their marriage voided in Algeria, Tunisia, Jordan, Palestine, and Qatar. Lebanon has no set age for marriage as each confessional group has its own laws, some of which allow girls to marry at the age of fifteen. Early marriage often means the end of a girl's education, thus diminishing her potential in employed work. It leaves her at risk of marital rape, domestic violence, fistula, and other health problems. Marriage to an older man, which is frequently the case, often results in the wife being treated as a child, diminishing her agency in the marriage.

In Morocco, at least 16 percent of teenage girls who marry do so under the legal age of eighteen compared to 3 percent in Algeria and Tunisia, which have the same minimum age of marriage for women. One reason for this higher rate of underage marriage may be that sex outside of marriage is illegal and so girls in rural areas, where such mores are more strictly observed, may marry their boyfriends with the understanding that the marriage may not last since there is less of a taboo for divorce. In Morocco the number of underage girls who marry has increased by nearly 50 percent since 2004, to 27,205 in 2016, according to the Justice Ministry. Alarmed by these high numbers, the prosecutor general called on the courts in 2018 not to hesitate "in rejecting marriage demands that undermine the minor's interests" (Abdennebi 2018). Nevertheless, the average age of marriage in Morocco has gone up considerably, partly as more women are pursuing secondary and higher education and are seeking employment. Morocco's average marriage age is now twenty-seven for women and twenty-eight for men. This suggests that families are not playing such a large role in personal decisions, although anecdotally most single women will tell you that the pressure to marry increases with each year and can be quite intense. According to Family Optimise, a British NGO, the number of single women has increased to 60 percent or 8 million in Morocco, which is only surpassed by Tunisia (81 percent) and Lebanon and Iraq (85 percent) (Koundounou 2018a).

Women can initiate divorce in almost all MENA countries, but often in an unequal way through the *khul'* (الخلع), system by which the woman can divorce her husband by returning her dowry (*mahr*, المهر) or another mutually agreed upon sum to the husband. In Egypt, *khul'* was adopted in 2000, but even then it was difficult to get such cases approved in Egyptian courts. Most women who pursued these cases were poor (Sonneveld 2012). Some have used it to obtain a no-fault divorce. Between 2000 and 2010, at least six Arab states adopted *khul'* provisions in their family codes, including Egypt, Syria, Jordan, Iraq, Saudi Arabia, and Yemen. Another three adopted a provision but did not name it *khul'*. *Khul'* has long been in the PSCs of Morocco, Algeria, and Libya, all of which follow the Maliki school of *shari'a*. Tunisia, in contrast, has equalized access to divorce for both men and women early on in its PSC (Warrick 2009).

Mobility of Women

Some of the most severe restrictions globally on women's mobility can be found in the Middle East. While women are free to travel outside the country in Algeria, Morocco, and Tunisia (as well as Libya, Mauritania, and Lebanon), they must obtain the permission of their husband or another male guardian in all other Arab MENA countries (World Bank 2019). This has implications for women who wish to pursue higher education, conferences, or business-related activities abroad.

Inheritance

Perhaps the most challenging area for women's rights in family law is the issue of equality in inheritance. No Arab countries allow sons and daughters the same right to inherit assets from parents. Nor do spouses have equal rights to inheritance, according to the World Bank database on Women, Business, and the Law (2018). There has been considerable debate on inheritance, particularly in Tunisia and Morocco. According to the Qur'an, male relatives receive double the inheritance of women and the son inherits twice as much as the daughter, while the brother inherits twice as much as his sister. As families have become more nuclear in formation and women marry later and are employed, many of the rationales for inheritance operating the way it has in the past have become less compelling, even if one leaves aside the issue of equity.

The issue of inheritance was debated in the Tunisian parliament in 2018 alongside several other provisions. Proposed legislation stipulated that women and men would be able to choose ahead of time the system of inheritance they preferred, be it Islamic or gender-equal. The new legislation proposed that the family was to be headed by both the father and the mother, that the dowry be abolished in the marriage contract, and that the family name can be chosen to follow either the father or the mother. In the same year, the Tunisian cabinet agreed to legislation that would equalize inheritance rights for both men and women, however, it is unclear whether the parliament will pass it.

In Morocco and Tunisia there has also been a debate around the *ta'asib* (التعصيب), which is the residual inheritance that goes to distant relatives of the deceased, who benefit after the immediate family members have received their share. Some have argued that the inheritance should go solely to the nuclear family and not to those who have weak ties to the family and will not support the family. This has taken on urgency as widows are increasingly being left as the sole supporters of their families. A woman may have contributed significantly to the household income and then find herself forced to relinquish her earnings to distant relatives upon the death of her husband. Thus, the *ta'asib* only compounds their financial difficulties after the death of a husband. This is recognized even by some prominent Islamists and Salafis as unjust.

Table 3.12 *Legality of Abortion in the MENA region, 2017 (Maghreb countries highlighted)*

Country	Abortion legality score (2017)
Tunisia	6
Bahrain	6[1]
Algeria	4
Morocco	4
Jordan	3
Kuwait	3
Qatar	3
Saudi Arabia	3
Lebanon	2
Libya	2
Oman	2
Syria	2
UAE	2
Yemen	2
Egypt	1
Iraq	1
Mauritania	1
Palestine	N/A

Source: Singh, Remez, Sedgh, Kwokand, and Onda (2017)

[1] Abortion is legal but subject to authorization by a panel of physicians.

Key

1 Prohibited altogether (no explicit legal exceptions)

2 To save the life of the woman

3 To save the life/preserve the physical health of the woman

4 To save the life/preserve the physical and mental health of the woman

5 To save the life/preserve the physical and mental health of the woman/on socioeconomic grounds

6 No restriction as to reason (with gestational and other requirements)

Table 3.13 *Contraceptive use among women of childbearing age, 2017 (%) (Maghreb countries highlighted)*

Country	All methods	Modern methods
Morocco	68	61
Tunisia	66	57
Bahrain	65	45
Algeria	63	57
Jordan	62	46
Lebanon	62	46
Egypt	61	59
Palestine	59	47
Syria	58	44
Iraq	56	43
Kuwait	56	49
UAE	50	42
Libya	49	32
Qatar	47	41
Yemen	40	34
Oman	36	24
Saudi Arabia	30	26
Mauritania	17	16

Source: UNFPA (2017)

Reproductive Rights

As with family law, reproductive rights legislation is another area that has been fairly contentious in the MENA region, particularly abortion. Contraceptive use is fairly widespread, especially in urban areas. The highest rates of contraception use in the MENA region can be found in the Maghreb countries (Table 3.13). UNFPA data from 2017 show that 63 percent of married women of child-bearing age use contraception in Tunisia and 67 percent in Morocco, while for the remainder of the Arab countries in the MENA region the average is 50 percent. The major constraint for the Arab states is not legal but rather financial, and for some it is their religious beliefs (UNFPA 2017).

However, the legal framework for abortion is of importance. Within the MENA region, Tunisia, Bahrain, Algeria, and Morocco have the most lenient abortion laws, and only Tunisia allows abortions without restriction (Table 3.12). Tunisia is an outlier in the region, having granted the right to legal abortion without conditions up to the twelfth week of pregnancy in 1973. The first abortion law in Tunisia was passed as early as 1965, legalizing abortion for women with more than five children. Eight years later, this right was extended to all women, regardless of the number of children. In Bahrain, abortion is legal, but a panel of physicians must approve each case. Morocco recently revised its abortion law. In the past, it was allowed only if the mother's health was threatened. The new law allows abortion in cases of rape, incest, and fetal impairment. Even though many argue that Islamic law forbids abortion on the grounds that it violates the sanctity of life, some Moroccans appeal to another Islamic law that allows abortion if the pregnancy threatens the life of the mother, a law premised on the idea that one is choosing the lesser of two evils.

Violence Against Women

The Maghreb countries stand out in the region for the amount of legislation regarding violence against women (VAW), and are alone in possessing comprehensive legislation regarding VAW (Table 3.14). The Maghreb countries converged when it came to these general laws regarding violence against women. Algeria passed a law regarding violence against women in 2015; Tunisia followed suit in 2017, and Morocco in 2018. Tunisia's legislation, for example, covers a wide range of forms of violence in addition to physical violence. It recognizes economic, sexual, political, and psychological violence. It allows victims to access a variety of legal and psychological services. It repeals the penal code provision that allows a rapist to marry his victim to escape prosecution. The legislation is the product of years of advocacy by women's rights organizations, civil society organizations, national institutions, and international organizations like UN Women and other UN agencies like the Development Programme (UNDP), the Office of the High Commissioner for Human Rights (OHCHR), the Population Fund (UNFPA), and the Office on Drugs and Crime (UNODC), together with the Council of Europe and the European Union (UN Women 2017).

Only Algeria and Tunisia have passed legislation around marital rape at this time and a similar provision is being debated in Morocco. However,

Table 3.14 ***Policies regarding violence against women in the MENA region (Maghreb countries highlighted)***

Country	Domestic violence	Law against sexual harassment	Comprehensive VAW law	Law against marital rape	Rape law loophole abolished
Algeria	2016	2004, 2015, 2016	2015	2015	No
Bahrain	2015	No	No	No	No
Egypt	No	2014	No	No	1999
Iraq	No	2016[1]	No	No	No
Jordan	2008, 2016	Yes[2]	No	No	2017
Kuwait		No	No	No	No
Lebanon	2014	No	No	No	2017
Libya	No	No	No	No	No
Mauritania	No	No	No	No	No
Morocco	2018	2003, 2004, 2016, 2018	2018	No	2014
Oman	No	No	No	No	No
Palestine	No	1998	No	No	2018 only in West Bank[3]
Qatar	No	No	No	No	No
Saudi Arabia	2013	2018	No	No	No
Syria	No	Yes	No	No	No
Tunisia	2017	2004, 2017	2017	2017	2017
UAE	No	2017	No	No	No
Yemen	No	No	No	No	No

Sources: WomanStats Project, Database, www.womanstats.org/; UN Women (2017); *Al Jazeera* (2018); BBC News (2017a, 2017b)

[1] The law prohibits sexual harassment at the workplace. But there is no comprehensive law.

[2] The Jordan 2017 Human Rights Report states: "The law strictly prohibits sexual harassment and does not distinguish between sexual assault and sexual harassment. Both carry a minimum prison sentence of four years at hard labor" (US Department of State 2018).

[3] It was abolished in the part of Palestine under Jordanian law. However, articles 290 and 291 of the old Egyptian Penal Code are still applied in the Hamas-controlled Gaza Strip.

Table 3.14 excludes legislation where there is little to no variance. For example, anti-trafficking legislation was introduced in most MENA countries after 2009, Tunisia being the most recent country to adopt it, in 2016. Only Yemen has no legislation pertaining to trafficking.

One of the areas where we have seen reform is in the repeal of laws that allow rapists to marry their victims. Here the diffusion has spread from the Maghreb to other MENA countries. Morocco passed a law in 2014 that repealed Article 475, which protected a rapist from prosecution if he married his victim. This came after protests erupted when sixteen-year-old Amina Filali committed suicide in 2012 after being forced to marry her alleged rapist. Tunisia similarly abolished this law in 2017 and Jordan and Lebanon followed suit that same year. In the Maghreb, this law was a relic of French law, and even France had abolished it only as recently as 1994. It was imported into the 1911 Ottoman Code from the Napoleonic Code of 1810, which allowed a man who kidnapped a girl to escape prosecution if he married her. This explains the existence of this provision in other legal codes in the region, including both former British and French colonies (Begum 2017, Osman 2017).

Citizenship Rights

One of the areas where there has been increasing legislation in the region relates to women's citizenship rights (Table 3.15). Only Algeria and Tunisia allow women to pass their citizenship to both their husbands and children. Morocco, which allows citizenship to be extended to the woman's children, has been debating extending citizenship from wives to husbands. Qatar, Kuwait, and Lebanon do not allow mothers to confer their nationality to their children. Bahrain, Iraq, Jordan, Libya, Oman, Saudi Arabia, and the UAE only allow mothers to confer nationality to their children if the father is unknown or stateless. The Iraqi Nationality Law (2006) limits the ability of women to confer their nationality to children born outside the country. In such cases, the child of an Iraqi mother may apply for Iraqi nationality within one year of reaching majority age where the father is unknown, stateless, or of unknown nationality (UNHCR 2014). There have been efforts to reform the citizenship law in Lebanon and a new law was drafted in 2018. If passed, Lebanese women will not pass their citizenship to their children if they marry a Palestinian or Syrian. But here, again, the Maghreb countries stand out in providing

Table 3.15 ***Women's citizenship rights in the MENA region***

Country	Can woman confer citizenship to her children?	Can a woman confer citizenship to a non-national spouse?
Algeria	2005	2007
Bahrain	2007	No
Egypt	2004	No
Iraq	2006 partial	No
Jordan	No	No
Kuwait	No	No
Lebanon	No	No
Libya	No	No
Mauritania	2010 partial	No
Morocco	2007	No (under consideration in parliament)
Oman	No	No
Palestine	No	No
Qatar	No	No
Saudi Arabia	No	No
Syria	No	No
Tunisia	1998	2002[1]
UAE	No	No
Yemen	2010	No

Source: WomanStats Project, Database, www.womanstats.org/
[1] A Tunisian woman can only give her nationality to her husband after he has lived in Tunisia five years.

more extensive rights for women and Tunisia, in particular, was a leader in this regard (Table 3.15).

Economic Rights

The record regarding economic rights for women in the Maghreb is mixed and does not fit the overall patterns described in this chapter. All MENA countries allow women (married and unmarried) to sign contracts, register businesses, open bank accounts, and have equal ownership rights to property. Only Mauritania does not allow married women equal ownership rights. When it comes to pursuing a trade or

Table 3.16 *Property and employment rights (scores based on comparison of 198 countries, highest score = 100)*

	Using property	Accessing institutions	Building credit	Getting a job	Providing incentives to work	Total
Morocco	40	100	50	67	60	317
Egypt	40	100	25	59	60	284
UAE	40	100	50	20	60	270
Palestine	40	64	50	49	60	263
Lebanon	40	100	0	54	60	254
Algeria	40	82	0	51	80	253
Tunisia	40	91	25	52	40	248
Bahrain	40	100	25	41	40	246
Libya	40	100	0	64	40	244
Qatar	40	100	0	40	60	240
Kuwait	40	100	25	13	60	238
Mauritania	20	100	0	57	60	237
Saudi Arabia	40	91	50	16	40	237
Oman	40	91	0	50	40	221
Jordan	40	45	0	41	80	206
Syria	40	64	0	33	40	177
Iraq	40	36	0	38	60	174
Yemen	40	45	0	43	40	168
Average	39	84	17	44	54	238

Source: World Bank (2018)

profession the same way as a married man, Algeria, Morocco, and Tunisia, in addition to Egypt, Iraq Lebanon, Libya, Oman, and Saudi Arabia, allow married women equal rights in this area, although the practice may depart significantly from the letter of the law. With the exception of Morocco, the law does not prohibit discrimination by creditors on the basis of gender or marital status in accessing credit in other MENA countries (Woman Stats Project, www.womanstats.org/).

The table above (Table 3.16) shows that the Maghreb countries do better than most MENA countries in the areas of property rights, accessing institutions, building credit, getting a job, and providing incentives to work, and Morocco does best in this regard. However, other countries like Egypt, the UAE, Palestine, and Lebanon do somewhat better than Algeria and Tunisia. The UAE incidentally is the only MENA country with a quota for women on corporate boards (20 percent) (World Bank 2018).

Labor rights are very uneven in the MENA region and the Maghreb does not stand out in any particular way in this area, with the exception of Morocco, where the law does not allow discrimination based on gender in employment, hiring, promotions, or dismissal, including dismissal of pregnant women. Algeria, Morocco, and Libya are the only countries in the region where the law mandates equal remuneration for work of equal value. When it comes to the legal mandate of nondiscrimination in employment, all but Lebanon, Algeria, and Oman require that employers provide break time for nursing mothers. The mandatory age of retirement is lower for women than men in Algeria, Iraq, Libya, and Saudi Arabia.

Only a few Arab countries meet the international standard of a minimum of fourteen weeks' maternity leave. The only countries which meet the standard are Maghreb countries: Algeria and Morocco as well as Libya and Mauritania. Tunisia is an outlier here with only four weeks of paid maternity leave. Syria provides coverage of seventeen weeks, but only for the first child. It is much shorter for other children (Table 3.17). The maternity leave provisions in most MENA countries create disincentives for women to work.

International Treaties

The existence of international treaties regarding women's rights has provided added impetus for governments to put forward legislation in this area. Foremost among these is the United Nations Convention on the Elimination of All Forms of Discrimination Against Women (CEDAW), adopted in 1981. It addresses all major aspects of gender equality from discrimination to gender stereotyping, women's rights in the public sphere, political representation, nationality rights, economic and social rights, rights to equality in family law, and reporting procedures and implications for other treaties. The first countries to ratify the treaty were Egypt (1981), Yemen (1984), and Tunisia (1985), and Qatar was the last to do so, in 2009. All Arab countries in the MENA region are signatories to the CEDAW treaty, but all have reservations, with the exception of Tunisia. The majority of these reservations concern provisions that might conflict with *shari'a* law, especially those pertaining to family law and inheritance.

Table 3.17 *Maternity leave benefits in the MENA region, 2017*

	Duration of paid maternity leave per legislation in weeks	% of earnings covered	Source of coverage
Algeria	14	100	Social insurance
Bahrain	9	100	Employer liability
Egypt	12	100	75% Social insurance; 25% employer liability
Iraq	9	100	Employer liability
Jordan	10	100	Social insurance
Kuwait	10	100	Employer liability
Lebanon	7	100[1]	Employer liability
Libya	14	50[2]	Employer liability but social insurance for self-employed women
Mauritania	14	100	Social insurance
Morocco	14	100	Social insurance
Oman	7	100	Employer liability
Palestine	10	100	Employer liability
Qatar	7	100	Employer liability
Saudi Arabia	10	50–100[3]	Employer liability
Syria	17[4]	100	Employer liability
Tunisia	4	66.70	Social insurance
UAE	6	50–100[5]	Employer liability
Yemen	9	100	Employer liability

Source: Economic and social Commission for Western Asia (2016)

[1] The International Social Security Association reports that these benefits are not implemented in practice.

[2] 100 percent for self-employed women for thirteen weeks.

[3] Women in Saudi Arabia receive 50 percent of their salary during maternity leave if they have completed between one and three years of service before the commencement of maternity leave. They receive 100 percent of their salary if they have over three years of service.

[4] In the Syrian Arab Republic, women are entitled to 120 days of paid maternity leave for the birth of their first child. The duration of paid maternity leave is shorter for other children.

[5] In the UAE, women who go on maternity leave before completing one year of continuous employment receive only 50 percent of their salary in cash benefits, otherwise they receive 100 percent.

In 2011, Tunisia became the first country in the region to withdraw its reservations to the CEDAW, which took effect in 2014. This was the result of a major campaign organized by the Fédération internationale des droits de l'homme and its member organizations the Association tunisienne des femmes démocrates, the Ligue tunisienne de défense des droits de l'homme, and Doustourna. Tunisia's transitional government adopted Decree-Law No. 103, lifting the reservations to articles 9, 15, 16, and 29 of the CEDAW. These reservations had made it possible for Tunisia to opt out of key provisions in family law affecting women. The reservations pertained to equal rights for women in passing on their nationality to their children; responsibilities in marriage and divorce; guardianship and adoption of children; choosing a family name, profession, and occupation; and property rights. The lifting of the reservations opened the door to important reforms in Tunisia's Family Code.

In 2011, Morocco finally lifted the reservations on the contentious articles 9(2) and 16 after the constitution and nationality laws were passed. However, it maintained reservations on three other provisions. Morocco has been steadily working toward lifting its reservations as it passes legislation that would allow it to do so. It has indicated its intent to ratify the Optional Protocol, which would allow individuals or groups to bring complaints to the Committee on the Elimination of Discrimination against Morocco. Tunisia and Libya are the only other countries in the MENA region that have signed this protocol. Official speeches by the king and other Moroccan leaders reference international treaties like the CEDAW, suggesting that they are concerned about their international image when it comes to women's rights.

Conclusions

By surveying constitutional and legislative reforms from across the Arab MENA countries in key areas where we have seen changes – from political empowerment, to family law, violence against women, reproductive rights, citizenship laws, and economic rights – we see evidence of a convergence in women's rights reform within the Maghreb countries and a divergence between the Maghreb and most of the Middle East in this regard. No one measure would suffice to make such a claim, but when taken as whole, the pattern is distinct and one that requires explanation, which is the task of much of the rest of the book.

Constitutional reform is important to look at as a measure of societal change, not only because it has implications for the parameters of broader legislative change, but also because it can be taken to be a normative statement about how a society sees itself and what it aspires to. As such, constitutions are a reflection of these norms and the battles over wording and substance are a reflection of what one could regard as changing norms. Legislative reforms similarly are a way to gauge a society's commitment to women's rights reforms. These reforms open the door to the possibility of accessing legal instruments to effect changes in behavior. They signal expectations of what is acceptable behavior and what is sanctioned. They also give activists a standard to which they can hold their leaders accountable.

However, the ability of people to realize their rights through legal means often remains elusive and the capacity of the most vulnerable in society to access the legal system can remain equally challenging. This is, in reality, the gold standard for evaluating the passage of legislation. Here, the challenges are far greater given the lack of resources on the part of women, poorly trained judges, gaps in legal literacy, and conservative perspectives among the population. One of the activist lawyers I interviewed in Morocco pointed to these dilemmas:

> The area of access to justice for women is an area that has risen to the top in the Middle East and North Africa, because we have all these countries that are slowly passing legislation, but now we've reached the point where we say, well, do women actually benefit from these laws? What are the issues related to accessibility? How do we define and conceptualize access to justice in our country? What is access to justice? Is it empowering women and giving them information about the laws? Or is it just the normative protection? So we've made the changes, we have the piece of law, but then what about the administration of justice, what about the procedural fairness? What about informational justice? These are issues that we haven't really worked on yet. (M40.5.13.16)

The next three chapters explore case studies that show how Morocco, Algeria, and Tunisia were able to bring about legal reform in women's rights and the challenges they encountered. They also show that even though these reforms were important markers of achievement in the area of women's rights, they were also symbolic of many other values in society, which is why they were often so contested. They stood in for a wide variety of ideas ranging from modernity and progress to nationalism, democracy, and secularism.

PART II

Case Studies

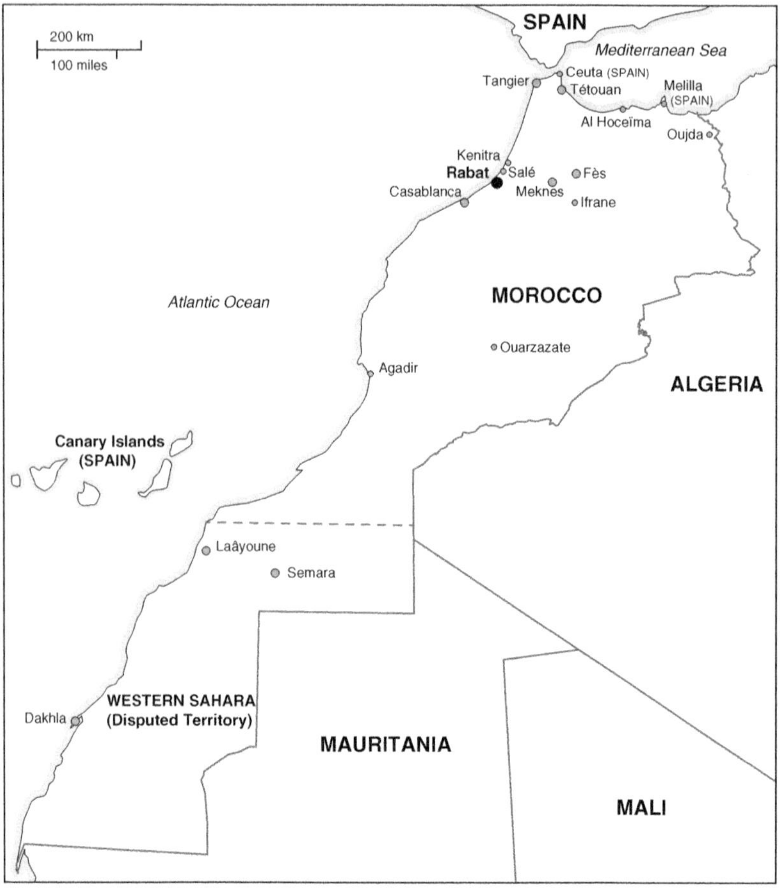

Map 4.1 Map of Morocco
Credit: Eva Swantz

4 *Morocco*

The US President Franklin Roosevelt hosted the Allied powers' Casablanca Conference in 1943. Two Moroccan royals addressed the conference: the sultan (who later became Mohammed V) and his daughter Lalla Aïcha. Both called for Morocco's independence. Journalists at the time noted that she was unveiled. She boldly stated: "Our Sultan, may Allah glorify him, expects that all Moroccan women will persevere on the road to education. They are the barometer of our Renaissance." Enormously popular in Morocco, she came to symbolize sentiments of nationalism and feminism. Her brother, King Hassan II, later appointed her ambassador to London (1965–1969), making her the first female ambassador in the Arab world.

Seventy-five years later, the palace continues to use public appearances of the king, his wife, and sisters to make statements about women and women's rights, sometimes in speeches, but often through the rituals of public engagement. The king's sister, Princess Lalla Meryem, like her aunt Lalla Aïcha, describes herself as a "women's and children's rights activist." For example, on International Women's Day in 2018 she gave a speech in Marrakesh on behalf of the king, calling for reforms of the Family Code, arguing that there was a large gap between the 2004 law and the reality, that women in rural and remote areas were unaware of the code and family courts were ignoring the law or required translation. She said the king intended to ask the government to undertake measures to remedy this situation (*Medias24* 2018). His agenda regarding women's rights has evolved over time, as evident in the debates over the Personal Status Code (PSC) and other women's rights legislation. It has been influenced by feminists and tempered by the Islamist Party for Justice and Development (العدالة والتنمية, Parti de la justice et du développement, PJD).

While Hassan II saw his mission as balancing the modernist elements of society and the traditionalists and conservatives, this has been less important to Mohammed VI, who has sought legitimacy from his religious role,

Table 4.1 *Heads of state, Morocco*

King	Years
Mohammed V	1927–1953 (deposed)
Mohammed Ben Aarafa	1953–1955 (abdicated)
Mohammed V	1955–1957 (proclaimed King of Morocco in 1957)
Mohammed V	1957–1961
Hassan II	1961–1999
Mohammed VI	1999–present

but he has used it to pursue what he sees as a thoroughly modern agenda regarding women's rights, thus challenging the conservative elements. Mohammed VI, like the kings before him, is the *amir al-mu'minin* or Commander of the Faithful (all believers) and is of "sharifian" lineage as a descendant of the Alawite dynasty's Sharif ibn Ali, who is said to be descended from ʿAli ibn Abi Talib, the Prophet Mohammed's son-in-law and cousin. Sharif ibn ʿAli became Prince of Tafilalt (in southeastern Morocco, near Sijilmassa) in 1631. Thus Mohammed VI is said to be in possession of a divine blessing (*baraka*, بركة) through his lineage. In Morocco, the dominant symbolism centers around religion and the monarchy monopolizes the production of religious symbolism, while maintaining religious pluralism (Naciri 1998). The king capitalizes on this religious authority to advance his objectives, but he is also leader of the country's secular government.

In this chapter, I show how and why the Islamists' official position regarding women's rights has changed fairly dramatically since the PJD came to power. They appear to have continued to make legislative changes around women's rights and have worked with other parties in crafting this legislation. They have adopted an equality approach to women's rights in spite of their own inclination to support complementarity.[1] Perhaps most importantly, their changing position was a result of pressure from the king, who was, in turn, influenced by the activism of women's movements and international agencies. The changes in PJD policy were a product of divisions within the PJD after 2011 over how to respond to internal pressures for reform. They were

[1] Women and men are equal in their own areas of competence, women in the private sphere of the home and men in their public roles.

Table 4.2 *Heads of government, Morocco*

Mbarek Bekkay	1955–1958	Independent
Ahmed Balafrej	1958	Istiqlal Party
Abdallah Ibrahim	1958–1960	Istiqlal Party
Mohammed V	1960–1961 (died in office)	Independent
Hassan II	1961–1963	Independent
Ahmed Bahnini	1961–1963	Front for the Defense of Constitutional Institutions
Hassan II	1965–1967	Independent
Mohamed Benhima	1967–1969	Front for the Defense of Constitutional Institutions
Ahmed Laraki	1969–1971	Istiqlal Party
Mohammed Karim Lamrani	1971–1972	Independent
Ahmed Osman	1972–1979	National Rally of Independents
Maati Bouabid	1979–1983	Constitutional Union
Mohammed Karim Lamrani	1983–1986	Independent
Azzeddine Laraki	1986–1992	Independent
Mohammed Karim Lamrani	1992–1994	Independent
Abdellatif Filali	1994–1998	Independent
Abderrahmane Youssoufi	1998–2002	Socialist Union of Popular Forces
Driss Jettou	2002–2007	Independent
Abbas El Fassi	2007–2011	Istiqlal Party
Abdelilah Benkirane	2011–2017	Justice and Development Party
Saadeddine Othmani	2017–present	Justice and Development Party

also a result of the party's reading of the tea leaves and their interpretation of the fate of Islamists in the region, in Tunisia, Algeria, and Egypt, where much of their future hinged on their positions regarding women's rights as a result of pressure from women's movements and international norms. They were also a product of a long process of political learning, as El Hachimi (2015) calls it, and moderating their Islamist positions in response to the broader authoritarian political environment in order to survive politically. The PJD was also reacting in a pragmatic fashion as the governing party to the need to conform to international treaties, in spite of their stated aversion to perceived external influences, particularly Western ones. In this chapter I also show some of the limitations of the PJD's legislative record, which has been reluctant to address marital rape and inheritance issues. The shift we have seen in the PJD's approach, however, is a far cry from 2000, when the party and other Islamists organized mass demonstrations against the PSC, also known as the Moudawana.

This chapter looks at these developments, focusing first on the women's movement, then the king, and finally the Salafis, Islamists, and the PJD. It shows how the symbolic uses of women's rights made women and women's rights a focal point of the contestations between the palace and the parties and a key instrument in the struggle against religious extremism. It explores the role of the women's movement in the middle of this unfolding contest. This chapter looks at the transformation of these events to show how they were a product of and reflected the symbolic discourse between the palace, the Salafis, and the PJD as they interacted with the women's movement. The chapter thus takes us through the main elements of the hypotheses outlined in Chapter 1 as they apply to Morocco.

Turning Points in Women's Rights

One of the main themes in this book relates to the role of the women's movement, which asserted itself at critical junctures or turning points in Morocco's recent history for maximum impact. In Morocco, these included the succession of Mohammed VI in 1999, which was followed by the passage of a new PSC, and later the Vingt février (February 20) protests in 2011, or Morocco's Arab Spring, which resulted in constitutional reforms regarding women's rights. The next section provides a background for these changes.

The Rule of Hassan II (1961–1999)

The Akhawat Al-Safaa (Sisters of Purity) Association was among the earliest advocates of women's rights reform. The association was part of the secular Istiqlal (Independence) party and was made up of the daughters of notables from Fès. In 1946, they were already lobbying around education for women, the abolition of polygamy, and a greater public presence for women (Sadiqi and Ennaji 2016). Later the

Progressive Women's Union, which was formed in 1962 and was affiliated with the Moroccan Labor Union, led marches in Casablanca that year to call for gender equality (Kadiri 2017). In the 1970s and 1980s, women activists worked within the leftist parties, the Democratic Popular Action Front, the Party of Progress and Socialism (PPS,) and the Avant-Garde Social Democratic Party, but found that their agendas were being sidelined. Many of these women had studied in France and had been influenced by the 1968 student protests and the leftist movement in France as well as the French feminists. Their frustrations with the Moroccan parties led to the emergence of new independent women's organizations in the late 1980s. Thus, it was not until the 1980s that women's mobilization was revived in earnest, particularly around reform of the 1957 PSC. As the debates shifted away from creating a nation in the early years after independence toward protecting the rights of individual citizens, this opened the door for demands for the secularization and universalization of women's rights (Zeghal 2005).

Unlike Tunisia and Algeria, both Morocco's urban elite that had studied in Egypt and Europe prior to independence and its conservative circles drew on Islam to establish legitimacy in formulating a nationalist response to colonialism. These elements were ultimately embodied in the 1957 PSC, which was based on Islamic law and Maliki jurisprudence. All other legal provisions were secular and became part of a unified legal system. The 1957 code put women under male guardianship for the duration of their life and women could not enter into marriage of their own accord. Under the PSC, the legal age of marriage for girls was fifteen; a man could divorce a woman by repudiation; and the man was the head of the family and responsible for maintaining his wife and children, while the wife had duties toward her husband. Other legislation such as the Public Freedom Law (1958) and the Penal Code (1959) were similarly biased against women.

One of the first organizations to be formed in this period was the Union de l'action féminine (UAF), established in 1987. It was made up of women from the now defunct leftist Organisation de l'action démocratique populaire (OADP), which did not seem to be serious about women's concerns, according to the UAF activists. One of the founders of the UAF, Fatima Maghnaoui, created the *March 8th* newspaper in 1993, which focused on raising public awareness of women's rights. It covered the experiences of ordinary women such as teachers, housewives, and women working in the *hammamat* (الحمامات, public baths). They targeted political parties, unions, and public opinion more generally. They stated that they were not against men, but rather that they were fighting structural violence against women, which included illiteracy and poverty. The central objective of UAF at the time was to oppose all forms of discrimination against women through legislative reform, relying on international conventions as points of reference.

The conditions under which women started mobilizing were unfavorable. Nevertheless, in 1985 feminist groups started to create structures to help women, starting in Casablanca. The UAF started another two centers in March 1996 to help women victims of violence, one in Rabat and the other in Casablanca. These centers were funded by a Spanish organization, Movimiento por la Paz, el Desarme y la Libertad. They also created an associative space (a set of offices) for several women's rights, human rights, development, and other associations that formed part of a larger coalition. This facilitated the opening up of debates on social issues, democracy, freedom of associations, financing of associations, and other such issues. Today the space brings together more than one hundred associations (M16.2.3.16).

By the early 1990s, two other organizations were formed, the Democratic League for Women's Rights and the Moroccan Association for the Defense of Women's Rights. Mobilization around the PSC dominated the early women's rights movement in Morocco. The PSC was their first target. In 1992, the UAF had collected 1 million signatures for a petition to reform the code, and formed alliances with parties, unions, and other organizations. Among their demands was gender equality in inheritance, a demand that was radical for its time given the prevalent thinking among Islamic jurists. As one UAF leader explained, "We had a lot of resistance and controversy and we were often told, 'You are importing ideas from the West that have nothing to do with us. You are imitating European or American women. Here we are Arabs and Muslims and we have our culture.'" To the feminists, the movement was clearly homegrown and had emerged in response to the Moroccan realities, while at the same time incorporating universal principles of human rights (M20.3.4.16).

In response to the UAF's mobilization around the PSC, Islamist leaders like Abdelilah Benkirane and Mustapha Ramid started attacking the feminists. They came to UAF conferences and assemblies and accused the women of being prostitutes, Zionists, Masons, and atheists. When the UAF organized a campaign around the PSC that attracted 1 million signatures in 1991 and 1992, Benkirane published a *fatwa* ruling, in this case a death sentence, against all UAF leaders. Islamists pursued and harassed the women when they collected signatures in the neighborhoods and villages (M20.3.4.16).

Women's organizations sought out King Hassan II in 1992 to press their demands for reform of the PSC and to talk about the harassment they were facing. Hassan II responded with a speech in which he addressed women directly for the first time, saying that their demands were legitimate and the Family Code was not fair to women. He said he would change it. No one else had the right to speak in the name of Islam since he was the Commander of the Faithful. This finally put an end to the Islamist harassment (M20.3.4.16).

Hassan II formed a council of twenty male and one female religious scholars, but the changes they made to the PSC were minimal: doing away with the father's prerogative to marry his daughter without her consent and ending male guardianship if the father died and the woman was an adult (twenty-one years). Husbands would need permission from a judge to repudiate their wives. These reforms fell far short of what women were demanding (Sandberg and Aqertit 2014). The first headway in PSC reform for the feminist movement occurred in 1993. An orphaned woman was given the legal right to get married without a guardian even though the PSC was regarded as sacred and based on the Islamic *shari'a* law and therefore unchangeable. A small door had opened that paved the way for further reforms of the PSC.

Although Morocco had signed the main UN women's rights treaty, the Convention for the Elimination of All Forms of Discrimination against Women (CEDAW), it finally ratified it in 1993 with some reservations. That same year, a "Committee for the Participation of Women in Political Life" was formed in Casablanca to lobby for a quota for women. After the UN's Fourth World Conference on Women in Beijing in 1995, the momentum picked up around the issue of increasing the representation of women in parliament and in 1997 a coordinating committee of women's organizations started pressing for a proportional representation system and a 20–30 percent quota. Up until that time there had been only two women parliamentary representatives (Latifa Bennani Smir and Badia Skalli of Istiqlal), who were elected in 1993 to a body of 333 members. In response to this initial pressure, political parties adopted an internal voluntary quota of 10–20 percent women in their own leadership (Darhour and Dahlerup 2013).

In 1998, women's rights activist Rabéa Naciri wrote that by focusing so much on women's identity and denying women equality in the family, the growing Islamist influence in the 1990s had inadvertently opened the door to a political debate on the role of Islam in society, thus paving the way for the secularization of women's rights. It resulted in a broader shift within the country that led to the implementation of a secular PSC in 2004. The women's movement responded in two ways. One response of the secular element was to promote a universalist philosophy of the rights of the individual, both of men and women. This included the major women's organizations, but also Amazigh activists. The other response was to look to the Qur'an and sacred texts to highlight the egalitarian nature of Islam in order to carve out a more public role for women, while arguing that it was patriarchal culture that had distorted this egalitarian essence of the Qur'an. This had required wearing a *hijab* (head scarf) and demonstrating one's religious devotion as a way to access the public sphere. It was possible to make this argument in the Maghreb (unlike in the Gulf countries, for example) because the Islamist discourse in the Maghreb was generally not premised on women's exclusion, seclusion, or inferiority, only their difference from men in their own sphere of competence (Bessis and Belhassen 1992).

The Personal Status Code

Pressure from secular women's organizations continued to mount after the death of Hassan II and the ascent of Mohammed VI to the throne in 1999. Over the last two decades Mohammed VI has sought to adopt reforms that would improve Morocco's image abroad, strengthen Morocco's economic competitiveness and role as a trade partner, particularly in Africa, and have Morocco play the role of promoting a moderate Islamic vision of religious tolerance in the Muslim world and beyond. He did this through a variety of strategies, including isolating and neutralizing religious extremists in his own country, incorporating political opponents into national politics, playing off political parties and factions against one another, and promoting women's status to drive a wedge between Islamists and secularists.

Certain moments of Mohammed VI's rule have been punctuated with uses of women and women's rights, particularly after bombings by religious extremists in Casablanca in 2003 and again after the 2011 Vingt février protests. Key women's rights reforms occurred after both events with the passage of key legislative reforms after 2003 and constitutional reforms after 2011 to improve women's status. The king was especially keen to see equality measures incorporated into the constitution.

Morocco opened up politically after the succession of the new king. The years 1999 to 2002 were particularly important in this regard. Mohammed VI announced from the outset that he wanted to promote human rights, rule of law, and women's rights. He released 46,000 prisoners, many of whom had been imprisoned for political reasons. Hassan II had already started aspects of this process with the policy of *alternance*, allowing for an opposition party to assume power in 1998 and a prime minister to be selected from the leading opposition party, the Union socialiste des forces populaires (USFP). It was the first time since 1960 that a prime minister had the ability to implement some reforms, even if the king had ultimate authority. But even at this time, when it appeared that there was more freedom, the government banned newspapers and journalists lost their jobs and went to prison or exile.

The PJD was granted legal status at this time. This represented a sea change in the king's orientation, although he did not allow any fundamental changes in the institution of the monarchy (Dennerlein 2012). He sought to make changes in women's status, in part as a response to international pressures and from a desire to assert modernity but mostly as a way of isolating the Salafis and other radical Islamist and conservative forces. In 1999, he launched the World Bank-funded Plan d'action national pour l'intégration de la femme au development (Action Plan for the Integration of Women in Development, PANIFD), which called for greater reforms in women's education, reproductive health, and economic and political empowerment. He also wanted to see a revision of the PSC (Sater 2012). The PANIFD was written by leading Moroccan women's organizations like the Association marocaine pour les droits des femmes, the UAF, and the Association démocratique des femmes du Maroc (ADFM), but it was never adopted despite years of protests and petitions in support of it. Islamist influences had increased in the 1990s and the plan was seen by Islamists as promoting a vision of progress and modernization as defined by international agencies (Dieste 2009). The king was careful not to close down debate on important subjects like the Family Code, but he was also keen to see the reforms implemented (Cavatorta and Dalmasso 2009).

Pressures to improve women's status continued to mount. Women's organizations like the ADFM, UAF, and the Ligue démocratique pour les droits de la femme (LDDF) lobbied the government to expand women's rights. In 2000, a coalition including the PPS, trade unions, human rights organizations, development associations, and sixty women's rights groups demonstrated in support of gender reform in Rabat, while the Organization in Defense of the Moroccan Family (which included two main Islamist associations and the PJD) led massive demonstrations in Casablanca against the proposed reforms to the PSC. The Islamists' demonstrations opposing the reforms were significantly larger, suggesting that they had grown in strength since the time of Hassan II. A network of feminist organizations called Printemps de l'égalité (Spring of Equality) pressed the king to support the reforms, while recognizing that most Moroccans and most parties would resist such change (Cavatorta and Damasso 2009).

A key part of the king's strategy involved expanding women's rights. A bombing in Casablanca in 2003 by Salafi jihadists gave him an opening to move ahead with the PSC reforms, which were passed by parliament in 2004 (Dennerlein 2012). He handpicked commissioners to work on the reforms and saw to it that conservative Islamist scholars were less influential than the academics and the women's and human rights specialists. In the past, the PSC had never been discussed in parliament; the king had the parliament pass it, reminding people that he was the Commander of the Faithful. Mohammed VI said in an historic speech of October 10, 2003, that "I do not forbid what the *shari'a* authorizes and I do not allow what the *shari'a* forbids." Both houses unanimously passed the PSC.

Meanwhile, the palace successfully co-opted the PJD, whose leader, Abdelilah Benkirane, became head of government from 2011 to 2017. The king neutralized the Salafis, repressed those who were considered most threatening, and brought a handful of Salafis into the political process. At the same time, the king marginalized and weakened the largest Islamist movement, al-'Adl wal-Ihsane (جماعة العدل و الإحسان, Justice and Charity Association, AWI). The PJD Islamists eventually came to support the PSC reforms because the final text contained references to Islamic values and traditions (Cavatorta and Damasso 2009). The king sought to capitalize on the code to gain greater international legitimacy.

The 2004 PSC gave women additional grounds to divorce, made both spouses responsible for the family, raised the legal age of marriage from fifteen to eighteen for girls (with exceptions), allowed women free choice of their spouse, and allowed them to sign their own marriage contract without a guardian. The PSC gave children born outside of marriage the right to the acknowledgement of paternity and to granddaughters the right to inherit property. It strengthened women's control of the assets within a marriage, equalized rights to child custody, and restricted polygamy.

It should be pointed out that in spite of these significant advances in women's rights, women and men still remained without equal access to divorce, with women having to resort to the *khulʿ* process, which required offering the husband financial or other compensation (see Chapter 3). The PSC gave judges discretion to waive the minimum age to allow minors to be married. This disproportionately affected young girls married to older men. Inheritance rights still differed between men and women, and men could marry other wives in spite of the new restrictions. Nevertheless, the law was hailed at the time as a major landmark in women's rights and to this day is referenced as a turning point in women's struggle for rights.

The passage of the PSC further emboldened the king and allowed women's rights activists to make gains that had been challenging in earlier periods. Women gained equal access to the courts when the Code of Criminal Procedure was reformed in 2002 to allow women to take civil action against their husbands without prior authorization of the court (Article 336). Amendments were made to the Labor Code in 2003 to prohibit discrimination against women in employment, salaries, and promotion. Paid maternity leave was also increased to fourteen weeks for women working in both the private and public sectors. Sexual harassment was made a workplace crime. The Penal Code was modified in 2003 to impose heavier penalties on a spouse who injured their partner. The Penal Code was revised to allow health care workers to waive professional confidentiality rules if they suspected violence between spouses or gender-based violence, and they were allowed to report such incidents to judicial or administrative authorities (Article 446). The king also launched a national campaign to combat violence against women in 2004. A law allowing children to take not only the nationality of the father but also that of the mother was announced by the king in 2005 and passed by parliament in 2007.

In 2002, political parties agreed to reserve thirty seats for women in the lower house through a special women's list. After this, a group of twenty women's, human rights, and party organizations formed a Monitoring Committee to push for a proportional list system and the adoption of a quota setting aside 30 percent of seats for women and alternating the positions of men and women on the lists (Tahri 2003).[2] Because there had been some dispute about the constitutionality of the provision, the seats were intended for women, but men could also use them. Women parliamentarians, through the Women's MP Forum, also worked together to get a proposal rejected that would have put business leaders and other professionals on a national list but would have diluted the women's list. As a result of the new law, 697 women and twenty-three men contested for these national-level seats, resulting in the election of thirty-five women, thirty through national lists and five through local lists (Storm 2007). Women were not placed high on the local lists and were often put in losing districts. Moreover, they represented only 4.6 percent of local lists, as political parties did not believe they needed to include women on these lists (Tahri 2003). As a result of the creation of the national list, however, women more than doubled their representation from two women (0.66 percent) after the 1993 elections to 10.8 percent in the 2002 elections, remaining at 10.5 percent in the 2007 elections. Similarly, they worked together to get a 12 percent local quota for municipal elections. This allowed the number of female local representatives to increase from 0.03 percent in 2003 to 12 percent in 2009 (Sater 2012).

[2] The monitoring committee was composed of women's organizations, including the ADFM, the Association marocaine pour les droits des femmes, Joussour, Espace point de départ, the Union action féminine, the Ligue des femmes fonctionnaires du secteur public et semi-public, the Ligue démocratique des droits des femmes, and Amal. It also included five women's committees of political parties (Istiqlal, the Union constitutionnelle, the Union socialiste des forces populaires, the Front des forces démocratiques, the PPS) and three civil society associations (Alternatives, Afak, EDF).

Vingt Février Protests

Women were at the forefront of the Vingt février Arab Spring protests in 2011, which called for democratic change, a reduction in the king's power, and the creation of a constitutional democracy, freedom of speech, the liberation of political prisoners, Amazigh rights, jobs for youth, and lower food prices. The movement also demanded increased female representation in the parliament and improved women's rights more generally (Salime 2012). Women's organizations did not participate but individual women activists did. The movement included a wide conglomeration of activists representing different interests, from the Amazigh to the socialist, women's rights, human rights, land rights, and many other movements. Islamists also participated. The PJD had neither officially supported the Vingt février movement, because they did not want to be seen as against the palace, nor criticized it. This way they stayed in the good graces of both the movement and the king. Some party members joined the movement, including the current prime minister, Saad Eddine Al Othmani, and Mustafa Ramid (Ait Dada and van Schaik 2012).

Unnerved by the Arab Spring events in neighboring countries, after Morocco's Vingt février movement protests, the king appointed a royal commission to inform a constitution revision process. The commission listened to all political parties. Women's organizations formed a large coalition, Printemps féministe pour la démocratie et l'égalité (Feminist Spring for Democracy and Equality), which produced memoranda and petitioned the commission. As one leading activist explained in an interview, "In the end, the results were very positive thanks to this work and thanks to the dynamics of the social movement, and also to the royal will to receive our input in order to guarantee human rights" (A3.2.1.16).

The king approved key reforms and a referendum was held on the constitutional changes in which 72.65 percent of the population turned out to vote despite calls for a boycott, and 98.5 percent of those who voted approved the reforms. The constitutional changes included expanding the powers of the prime minister and allowed for greater parliamentary oversight. It made Tamazight an official state language along with Arabic. The 2011 constitution guaranteed women "civic and social equality with men" beyond the political equality that had already been guaranteed. The constitution also required the state to promote gender equality and to end sex discrimination. It was to foster women's participation in political, economic, social, and cultural life, work toward parity between men and women, and comply with all international conventions ratified by the government. At the same time, the new constitution kept the monarchy intact, allowing the king to hold onto his key powers (i.e., the ability to dissolve parliament and government, and control of the military, foreign policy, and Islamic affairs). Since the passage of the 2011 constitution, activists have been working on bringing the Penal Code, the PSC, and other legislation in line with its equality provisions (M21.4.29.16).

After the 2011 elections, the PJD, as head of a coalition, became the dominant party in parliament and head of government. The PJD, which had opposed the PSC, changed its orientation toward women's rights, albeit reluctantly, in response to pressure from the king, but also from the women's movement, donors, and from a sense that in order to stay in power it would need to adopt more women's rights. Chastened by the losses of Ennahda in Tunisia, the PJD opted to make important concessions. This is evident in the quantity of legislation passed after 2011 and in changes in rhetoric.

The electoral law was reformed in 2011 to allow sixty seats to be reserved for women elected through a proportional representation system based on national closed party lists (Article 23 (2) of the Organic Law No. 27-11 on the House of Representatives). As a result, sixty-six women were elected in the 2011 legislative elections (16.7 percent of MPs), compared with thirty-four (10.5 percent) in 2007 (Organize Law No. 27-11 on the House of Representatives). By 2018 they had reached 20.5 percent. At the local level, at least one third of all seats were allocated to women in the regional councils, which are directly elected (Law N° 59-11, articles 76 and 77). Similar provisions were made to the lower district and communal councils (Article 143) (IDEA 2018).

As a result of heavy pressure from women's organizations, Article 475 of the Penal Code, which protected a rapist from prosecution if he married his victim, was repealed in 2012, making Morocco one of the first countries in the MENA region to repeal this law. Other legislation has incorporated an awareness of gender equality, such as the 2014 law approving Convention N° 97 on migrant workers and Organic Law N° 130.13 relating to the Finance Act, and the Communal Charter of 2008 which devolved political power to the municipalities and gave people in the southern provinces (Western Sahara) more control over their affairs.

Legislation was passed in 2016 to give more protections to domestic workers. Morocco also voted to endorse the international Decent Work Convention for Domestic Workers in 2011 and plans to become the first country in the MENA region to ratify it. Only twenty-five countries have ratified it globally. The law sets eighteen as the minimum age for domestic workers, who are mostly women in Morocco. It limits the number of hours to forty-eight a week and guarantees one day of rest and a minimum wage of $158 a month. The law also provides for financial penalties for employers who violate these provisions. Many of these provisions still fall below what is permissible by the Moroccan Labor Code, however.

Morocco also passed an anti-trafficking law in 2016 that has implications for women. After strong pressure from women's organizations, a major law 103-13 on the Elimination of Violence Against Women was passed in 2018. It criminalizes "any act based on gender discrimination that entails physical, psychological, sexual, or economic harm to a woman." It addresses domestic violence, and for the first time penalizes forced marriage, preventing a violent spouse from returning home and avoiding payment of maintenance after a divorce, and sexual harassment in public spaces as well as cyber harassment.

Efforts had been made by activists to get the law passed, starting with Yasmina Baddou, Minister of Family Affairs under the Istiqlal-led government in 2004. They worked on changing the law and also on finding ways to protect women through the existing legislation. Efforts continued during the era of Nouzha Skalli, who was PPS Minister of Solidarity, Women, Family, and Social Development from 2007 until 2012 and served in the coalition government of Abbas El Fassi (M21.4.29.16). However, it was not until an Islamist party took over that the Elimination of Violence Against Women Law was finally passed.

The law requires public authorities to take preventive measures, including establishing programs to raise awareness of violence against women and to assist women and children in courts, government agencies, and police affairs. However, critics find that it does not go far enough in providing protections for victims of domestic violence: it does not address marital rape, or establish funding for the agencies that are to provide support services to women (health services, mental health care, legal advice, and hotlines). They claim that the law is not detailed enough in specifying the duties of police, prosecutors, and investigative judges in domestic violence cases, and that it does not fund women's shelters (Human Rights Watch 2018). There has already been quite a bit of coordination between these agencies in dealing with violence against women at the local level. Nevertheless, this was one of the few such comprehensive laws in the region.

Various institutional measures were also adopted, including the creation of an independent entity, the Autorité de la parité et de lutte contre toutes formes de Discrimination (Authority for Parity and the Fight Against All Forms of Discrimination), provided for in articles 19 and 164 of the constitution, to oversee the implementation of constitutional provisions regarding discrimination of women. Two long-term policies were adopted by the Ministry of Family, Solidarity, Equality, and Social Development, in collaboration with various ministries to promote women's rights and parity by setting measurable goals and objectives for an Initiative Concertée pour le Renforcement des Acquis des Marocaines (Concerted Initiative for Strengthening Moroccan Achievements) otherwise known as the Government Plan for Equality: ICRAM I (2012–2016) and then ICRAM II (2017–2021). It is interesting to note that the explicit goal of these projects was to serve as a "framework for different initiatives aiming at promoting equality between women and men and integrating women's rights in public policies and development programs." The National Action Plan on Democracy and Human Rights (2018–2012) also incorporated women's rights as part of its mandate.

The name of the Ministry of Solidarity, Women, Family, and Social Development was changed in 2017 with little fanfare, replacing "women" with "equality" so that it now is the Ministry of Family, Solidarity, Equality, and Social Development. The Inter-Ministerial Consultation Network for gender equality continues to function and coordinate gender related activities between the various ministries. The Gender Observatory in the Public Service was created in 2016 to promote modernization and democratization and to institutionalize gender equality in the civil service.

It should be pointed out that in spite of these advances in legislative and policy reform, there are still significant limitations on the actual realization of these rights. These formal changes are only a first step.

Without adequate measures to see that they are realized, many of these reforms can only benefit women with means. As Leila Hanafi and Danielle Hites (2017) have argued, there is still inadequate judicial oversight and accountability, there is a lack of police enforcement, and inadequate legal aid and information. Judges, particularly in rural regions, sometimes permit waivers for early marriage and restrict female-initiated divorces. Even if the ruling favors the woman, there is no assurance that it will be enforced. Social and cultural considerations as well as illiteracy and lack of resources among women create additional barriers for gender equality and inherent rights. Poverty puts pressure on families to marry their daughters early, thereby forfeiting an education and employment, and some girls end up married to older men, making it more difficult to have a marriage on an equal footing. Moreover, many of the laws do not go far enough, as activists have pointed out. Marital rape is still permitted. Polygamy has not been abolished and by some accounts is increasing, although overall it is rare in Morocco. Men and women still have unequal access to divorce, and minors are still being married (M40.5.13.16).

In spite of these limitations, Morocco has accomplished a considerable amount relative to its neighboring countries and the commitment to women's rights, however problematic in some areas, is still moving in a forward trajectory in spite of the fact that this is a deeply conservative society with an Islamist party in power.

The Symbolic Politics of the Monarchy

The king has heavily influenced the changes that have occurred with respect to women's rights in Morocco. There have been a number of elements to the king's promotion of women's rights. One has involved the promotion of key women's rights-related constitutional and legislative reforms along with policies that would address women's education, the economic marginalization of women, and other such concerns. The second element involved promoting women as part of the king's religious strategy to advance "moderate Islam," as he puts it. And finally, a key element of this strategy has been the promotion of women in general as leaders and greater involvement of them in public life.

Although the promotion of women's rights was a central component of Mohammed VI's efforts to advance Morocco when he took over, the use of women in symbolic ways is not new to the monarchy. Even his grandfather, Mohammed V, publicly unveiled his eldest daughter in 1957 and called for the emancipation of women. Following this symbolic gesture, thousands of women followed suit and the image of the unveiled woman came to be associated with working outside the home. Women's rights became incorporated into the party platforms of both conservative and less conservative parties, even if somewhat peripherally. The main goal was to signal that women were part of a remedy to the backwardness of the nation and that progress necessitated women's education and training (Sadiqi and Ennaji 2006).

One particular feature of the monarchy in Morocco is that the king is the final arbiter of societal tensions. If there is a conflict, all parties look to the king to resolve it. Social forces influence him, including women's and Islamist organizations, but he has the final word. Once the king proclaims a policy change, like those regarding women's rights, the Islamists generally accede even if they do not agree with it (M31.3.22.16).

Hassan II spoke of women as pillars of the family and society and as protectors of the national identity. In his later years, he emphasized their role as ramparts against terrorism (Naciri 1998). Mohammed VI's early speeches depict Moroccan women both as heroines and victims. On the one hand, women were valorized for their "firm will," "seriousness," "realism," "integrity," and "righteousness," all of which he claimed made women's emancipation necessary for development and democracy, according to Yasmine Berriane (2013), who studied speeches made by the king between 1999 and 2004. At the same time, women appeared both as "vulnerable" and "victims," alongside street children, the disabled, and the elderly, and as individuals who suffered from violence, discrimination, injustice, and poverty. Women were typically described as a homogenous category, although on occasion they appeared as "the rural woman" or "heads of deprived families." Mohammed VI commented from time to time on the need to harmonize national legislation with international conventions in order to improve "the image of Morocco abroad" but also that Morocco should "position itself as an active partner on the international chessboard," according to Berriane (2013).

At the time of the PSC reforms, the king vacillated between a feminist frame of reference based on the notion of equal rights and a maternal frame of complementarity in which women play their designated roles in the family, a frame which is generally embraced by Islamists. He said that with respect to the Family Code, according to a complementarity perspective, it is in the family that the woman assumes "her duties" in occupying "the place that suits her and of which she is worthy," while accomplishing her mission. The king also underscored in his speeches that Islam is not the cause of women's problems. These arguments are similar to those of Islamic feminists who blame culture for women's low status and who seek inspiration for a more egalitarian order from a rereading of the Qur'an (Berriane 2013).

By 2013, the king's speeches had shifted away from the victim trope and from women's role in the family to putting women and men on an equal footing. Much of the language appeared to be adapted from international women's rights and development discourse. For example, at an international conference on human rights, the king made a typical speech extolling the country's goals and accomplishments around women's rights: "My country has made this question [of women's rights] one of the pillars of its public policies, promoting, to this end, gender budgeting, which is recognized by the United Nations as a pioneering approach." Women are portrayed as active and as catalysts and agents of change. They are no longer members of a vulnerable group but, instead, they are actively contributing to the welfare of vulnerable groups through their women's rights struggle. However, they are still "selfless." Women are linked to independence, modernity, nation building, development, and democracy. For example, in a message to participants at the sixty-first Global Women Entrepreneurs Congress in Marrakesh in 2013, the king declared:

> We are well aware of the important role played by Moroccan women in the national movement as part of the struggle for Morocco's independence as well as their significant contribution to building a *modern nation* ... I would like to commend the Moroccan *women's struggle for their rights* and wish to pay tribute to their *selfless* involvement in national associations, especially community organizations concerned with children, handicapped people and vulnerable women ... Women have been playing an *active role* in every single region in the Kingdom – whether in urban, peri-urban or rural areas. *They have thus become real catalysts for comprehensive and sustainable development* and this is truly a source of pride and hope. (September 25–27, 2013; emphasis added)

The King's Religious Strategy Regarding Women's Rights

After the 2003 Casablanca bombings, the king undertook a massive project of restructuring religious authority in Morocco to project the "spiritual security" of its citizens, which was another way of saying he sought to prevent the ideas of Al Qaeda from taking hold. The king took a number of symbolic steps involving women to further chip away at Islamic extremism. He has enormous latitude in religious affairs as chair of the Higher Council of the *ʿulema*s (religious scholars), the sole body empowered to issue religious rulings that are approved by the monarch. The king reserves the exclusive right to issue *dahir*s or religious decrees, according to the constitution. The king also appoints the minister of religious endowments and Islamic affairs, who reports directly to him and not to the prime minister.

Since the 1970s, a conflict emerged between the palace and Islamists over who was in control of religious authority both at a spiritual and symbolic level (Daadaoui 2016). A major part of the current king's modernizing strategy has been to find ways to moderate the Salafi and Islamist influences. He has sought to do this by reinforcing his religious authority through constitutional mechanisms; through repression of Salafi-inspired violence, while offering incentives to nonviolent Salafis; and through a series of reforms, including those pertaining to women's rights. Wainscott (2018) argues that Morocco has adopted a unique approach to counter-terrorism by bureaucratizing religion. The regime has used religious institutions to reward loyalty and discourage dissent.

The king has taken various symbolic measures to signal his desire to sideline religious extremists. One such measure was banning the production and sale of the full-body and face covering, the *niqab* (النقاب), in 2017. The *niqab* is generally associated with extremist religious fundamentalists and is seen as an import from the Gulf region. The government argued that this was a security measure, and that bandits and terrorists had used the *niqab* as a disguise in order to perpetrate their crimes. The Moroccan government stopped short of banning the wearing of the *niqab* in public places, a measure adopted by France, the Netherlands, Austria, Belgium, and Germany. The various responses to the banning are indicative of the fault lines in Moroccan politics. It was welcomed by feminist activists like former Minister of Family and Social Development Nouzha Skalli, who regarded it as "an important step in the fight against religious extremism." Amazigh researcher and activist Ahmed Assid similarly welcomed the move. The Islamist PJD remained silent because, as a PJD leader told Mohammed Masbah, "it did not want to provoke the government formation by creating an ideological contradiction with our secular partners" (2018b, 140). However, some Salafi Muslim groups like Annahda wa Al Fadila (Renaissance and Virtue) strongly criticized the ban and Salafi Abu Naim called those who made this decision "infidels, apostates and renegades who are leading a war against God" (*Al Jazeera* 2017). The decree did not affect most ordinary women in Morocco, who prefer the *djellaba/jalbab* (الجلباب) or hooded robe with a scarf, if they veil.

A key part of Morocco's identity is Sufi and the king has also been strengthening this dimension by promoting Sufi music and other cultural festivals like the Essaouira-Mogador cultural festival, the Mawazine world music festival in Rabat, and the Fès Festival of World Sacred Music that prominently feature Sufi musicians. He has given prominence to the Boutchichiya *zaouia* (زاوية) or religious schools and sanctuaries.[3] He appointed a Sufi follower of the Boutchichiya Tariq (Brotherhood), Ahmed Taoufiq, Minister of Islamic Affairs, encouraged the Brotherhood to appear at public events, and has made donations to popular mausoleums and Sufi shrines across the country. Sufism is often regarded as antithetical to Salafism (or Wahhabism) and according to Ben Issa Zemrani Chahbouni, the rector of the Darqawouia *zaouia*, "Sufism is considered as a tool to get out of the framework of a strict and literal form of orthodoxy and a powerful weapon to fight extremist ideologies thanks to its moderation and rich history" (Guerraoui 2016). As Asma Lamrabet, the Islamic feminist, put it

> We have in Morocco what I called popular Islam like Sufism, which is very tolerant, very open ... it is not like the Wahhabis, who do not believe in culture. What they have is ideology. So, they try to disturb everything that is cultural. Moroccans have this culture of tolerance and diversity, and we should preserve it. (M8.2.22.16)

[3] A *zaouia* (spiritual hostel) can serve a variety of purposes. It can be a place of prayer and ceremonies, but also a place where people seek accommodation, training, social services, and neighborhood jobs (Toutou 2012, 110).

While many of the king's religious gestures were directed at the Salafis, they were also aimed at suppressing another popular Sufi movement led by Sheikh Abdessalam Yassin, the AWI. It is also interesting to note that Sufism is one of the main ways that women have engaged in spirituality in Morocco historically (Dwyer 1978). The new prominence of Sufism has thus given women greater visibility in the religious sphere (El Haitami 2014) (see Chapter 1).

Since 2003, the Ministry of Religion has had eighty local councils that oversee the content of the sermons in the country's 50,000 mosques. It appoints the religious personnel in mosques as well as the Quranic schools. Some mosques and Quranic schools have been closed as a result of this oversight. More militant religious elements have been arrested and vigorously repressed, while those who complied with the king's policies were left alone. For some people this resulted in a lack of trust in the mosques because they felt the imams were compromised by the government and not independent in their thinking. Thus, some sought out independent mosques which tended to be more radicalized. Overall, however, the policy has had a moderating effect.

A key dimension of the king's use of women has been filling religious institutions with women leaders. Most notably, the king established a program to train women *mourchidates* (المرشدات, female religious leaders) in 2005. The Minister of Islamic Affairs stated in a 2008 televised interview that their presence was a strong symbol which would encourage other women to engage in public Islamic action and debate while fostering moderate Islam (Eddouada and Pepicelli 2010). According to El Haitami (2012), the *mourchidates* were heralded as "the new face of Moroccan Islam, moderate, tolerant and modern." Trained in the *shari'a* and social psychology, over 500 such spiritual guides are assigned to mosques throughout the country today (El Haitami 2012). They work in public schools, prisons, hospitals, workplaces, and in communities and give public speeches (Dirèche 2010). However, as Islamist feminist Asma Lamrabet observed:

> The only positive thing I can say is that the symbolism of the *mourchidates* is important for an illiterate woman who enters the mosque and finds a literate *mourchida* ... But on the empowerment side at the religious level, on the side of independence, autonomy, and knowledge, what they offer is

patriarchal. They just convey a very misogynist orthodoxy. That, for me, is a pity. (M8.2.22.16)

In spite of claims that the *mourchidates* are something new and unprecedented (Batha 2015), it should be pointed out that although this particular initiative is new, the idea of women religious scholars is not. Women of both Amazigh and Arab backgrounds were involved in Islamic education as far as back as the year 859, when Fatima bint Muhammad Al Fihri built the first university or center of Islamic learning in Morocco, Qarawiyyin. According to UNESCO, this was the first degree-granting university in the world and housed the first library in the world.[4] Nevertheless, the king's initiative in launching the *mourchidates* program was a bold and ambitious move in the current context.

In 2003, in an unprecedented gesture, the king invited a woman, Dr. Rajaa Naji el-Mekkaoui, a professor at Mohammed V University in Rabat and one of the architects of the *mourchida* initiative, to deliver the Ramadan Islamic lesson, *durus al-hassaniyya*, at the royal palace (El Haitami 2012). The annual event is highly stylized: the king sits on the floor on a carpet; the lecturer sits on what looks like a golden throne dressed in a white *jellaba*[5] facing the king and his son; and the audience is seated on both sides. The event receives wide media coverage and is attended by Islamic scholars from Morocco and around the world. Since the first lecture by Dr. El-Mekkaoui, the event has included women. Even the Minister of Endowments and Religious Affairs, Ahmed Taoufiq, gave his 2016 lecture on "women's contribution in building Islam's spiritual culture," in which he talked about equality between men and women in Islam, drawing on Quranic verses to make his case (Ministère de la Culture 2016).

The king also placed the first woman, Fatima al-Kabbaj, on the sixteen-member Council of Religious Scholars. She is a graduate of

[4] Women taught Islamic sciences in the Tashelhit dialect of Tamazight at female-run *zaouia* in southeastern Morocco as far back as the eleventh century. They engaged in Islamic reform movements in the fifteen century and there are multiple examples of women active in education in the mosque in Fès in the 1800s documented in *Salwat al-Anfas*, the Sufi biographical dictionary written by Mohammad Ibn Ja'far Kattani (1899). In Fès, there were schools for girls that went by the name of *dar al faqiha* (house of the female jurist) and were run by women according to AbdelHadi Al-Tazi (Ahmed 2016).

[5] A loose garment with sleeves and a hood.

the Islamic Theological University of Qarawiyyin. Kabbaj provided instruction to the king and his siblings on the *shari'a*.

As mentioned in the Introduction, in 2018, the king issued a royal decree allowing women to hold the position of *'adoul* or public notary, an official who draws up marriage documents and manages inheritance cases. Ultraconservative Salafis immediately condemned the policy (*The New Arab* 2017). But women were eager to step into these new positions. In the first year, 40 percent of those taking the test to become an *'adoul* were women.

In 2011, Mohammed VI established the Rabita Mohammadia des Ulemas (Mohammadia League of Religious Scholars), a center that aims to publicize the tenets of Islam following the principles of moderation, making it the first of its kind in the region. It has positioned itself as a leader and convener of ecumenical dialogue in the Moroccan context but also beyond to the broader Muslim world, organizing conferences that include people of different religions and different Muslim orientations with the idea of spreading religious moderation. It was seen as challenging Wahhabism, a radical import from the Gulf. Its secretary general, Ahmed Abbadi, has talked about how the center draws on Morocco's Maliki tradition of *fiqh* (jurisprudence), which it regards as a more moderate tradition that focuses on Islam as a practicing religion attuned to an ever-changing society (Moroccan American Center for Policy 2013). Some have argued that although Maliki jurisprudence is patriarchal in tone, it has at times accounted for the fact that women's experiences are more restricted than men's. Some religious scholars in this tradition, for example, have been critical of inheritance arrangements that perpetuate the inferior status of women and their descendants, particularly widows, divorcees, and unmarried women, who have been seen as especially vulnerable (Terem 2014).

In 2010, the Center of Studies and Research on Women's Issues in Islam was formed in the Rabita, headed by an Islamic feminist, Asma Lamrabet, until 2018. The Center is unique in that it does not have an equivalent in the region, not even at the Egyptian Al Azhar, the leading Islamic studies center in the region. The research centers in Tunisia regarding women and gender are all secular.

Lamrabet helped set religious policy regarding women's rights as someone who had adopted an Islamic feminist position, or what she refers to as the "third way" (Gray 2013). This orientation has primarily gained popularity internationally through organizations like the

Musawa Network and Karama and through the works of Ziba Mir-Hosseini, Amina Wadud, and others. However, it has not taken hold as a movement in Morocco, although Lamrabet finds there is receptivity to her ideas. As Lamrabet explained to me:

> We have an Orthodox Islamic discourse and above all the Wahhabi Islamic discourse, which is literalist . . . and which marginalizes the reformist reading. But this third way is a way that reconciles everyone. It reconciles the Muslim with herself, with her identity, with the universal and with others . . . We have been with this classic vision for centuries. Especially on the issue of women. We cannot continue like this. (M8.2.22.16)

Abbadi gave Lamrabet independence in charting her course at the institute. He told her that what was needed was to reform the institutions from within, and this was also her vision. As she explained, "I know that today in religious institutions, we are not yet ready for equality of inheritance, but I say it outside, and I try to work from the inside." She made clear in an interview that her goal was to reinterpret Islam in a way that highlighted its emancipatory aspects for women (M8.2.22.16). For her, it is not religion that poses problems, but rather its interpretation. She also opposes the instrumentalization of religion by orthodox Islamists. She is not as sanguine about Maliki *fiqh* as others when it comes to its implications for women, although she argues that this *madhab* (school of jurisprudence) is useful in fighting radicalism. She finds it to be quite patriarchal and misogynistic and would prefer the school of Abu Hanifah, who "told women that you are free to marry without guardianship." She added, "He believed in egalitarian divorce." She is a researcher but distinguished herself from the *ʿalimat* (women religious scholars), who she felt were quite patriarchal and were not feminists. Her departure from the Center in 2018 came amidst a fierce debate in Morocco over the need to reform inheritance law for women to bring it into line with the constitution, particularly the requirement that women inherit half of what men inherit (Kasraoui 2018).

This issue of female secular leadership has also been central to the project of the king, who helped facilitate the introduction of legislation that further institutionalized the quota in 2011. He has sent strong signals through palace events to promote women's leadership, not only in religious institutions but also in political appointments over which he has control. In an October 2016 palace ritual, sixty-five newly appointed ambassadors lined up at the royal palace in Casablanca to be sworn in by the Mohammed VI. Among them were thirteen women, the most women in such a post in any MENA country. They included the king's cousin Lalla Joumala Alaoui, the first woman to serve as Moroccan ambassador to the United States. The king regularly deploys his wife, sisters (Lalla Zineb, Lalla Hasnaa, Lalla Meryem, who is Chairwoman of the National Union of Moroccan Women), and other women from the palace to officiate at formal functions on his behalf, particularly at women's organizations and initiatives.

Journalist and blogger Zineb Ibnouzahir described the wife of the Moroccan king attending the inauguration of an exhibit dedicated to Alberto Giacometti at the Mohammed VI Museum of Modern and Contemporary Art in Rabat in 2016 in this way:

> At a time when the Arab-Muslim culture seems to be reduced for obtuse minds and media about the wearing of the veil and terrorism, the appearance of Princess Lalla Salma, dressed in a satiny chic ensemble, her long red hair blowing in the wind, reminds Moroccans and the world that this is Morocco! . . . Princess Lalla Salma was able to embody, with great elegance, the image of a Morocco open to the world, passionate about art, culture and resolutely enlightened. (Ibnouzahir 2016)

And indeed, Ibnouzahir's description of Lalla Salma picked up on precisely the message the royal establishment has chosen to convey about Morocco and how it wishes to be seen by the world: as a modernizing forward-looking country whose elite women look like privileged women in any international metropole. In fact, the image of the princess is carefully choreographed by the palace. Mohammed VI is the first king to give public visibility to his wife, breaking with a tradition of secrecy surrounding the identity of kings' wives. Even his father, Hassan II, declared that "in Morocco, there is no queen." The visibility of the king's wife was interpreted by many observers as a sign of modernity, while others suggested that it reflected his desire to see changes in the status of women in Morocco (Berriane 2013). Even women's rights activists saw the king in much the same vein. As one leading women's rights activist put it, "The king promotes gender equality, parity, diversity, and modernity, which are the values of Moroccan society. He has great respect for women. His wife is very active and in many aspects she is an example for Moroccan women" (M42.12.16). Thus, the use of symbolism and ritual allows for ambiguity in interpretation, and sometimes allows one to convey messages more powerfully than if they were clearly stated.

The Salafis

While the promotion of women leaders and women's rights forms one part of the king's policy, the other is directed at the Islamists, particularly the extremists. Islamists do not form a united movement in Morocco, nor do they share a similar vision. Rather, they are part of a dynamic and ever-changing landscape of competing organizations with diverse orientations and goals. Salafis form the most politically extreme element in this landscape and at times elements among them have resorted to violence. Women's rights are a key focus of their activities.

Since the 1990s, but especially the 2000s, the Salafis (Wahhabis) underwent a process of radicalization following global trends and then de-radicalization through the king's initiatives targeting them, according to Mohammed Masbah (2016). Salafis are Sunni Muslims who wish to see society revert to the imagined values of the time of the first three generations after the Prophet. In general, Salafis in Morocco have a shared identity around a broad set of ideas and have often coalesced around a particular *sheikh*. Ironically, although they claim they are about *tawhid* (توحيد, unity), a common pattern among such groups is fragmentation: power struggles break out within the group and factions break off and form their own groups.

The Salafis came to Morocco in the 1970s and 1980s and their influence intensified in the 2000s as a result of the spread of satellite TV, videos, CDs, and the Internet. Women were particularly susceptible to these preachers because they were often at home watching TV as they carried out their household chores. Some Moroccans had gone to work in Saudi Arabia and returned inspired by Salafism. But unlike the many Egyptians who studied and worked in Saudi Arabia, only hundreds of Moroccans did so. They returned to teach in mosques and Quranic schools. Initially they were primarily focused on separating religion from politics, but after the mid 1990s a new breed of Salafi jihadists appeared, bent on altering the political order. Their ranks expanded after the 9/11 attacks in 2001 and they were especially energized after the US invasion of Iraq in 2003.

As mentioned earlier, in 2003 these jihadists carried out suicide bombings in Casablanca at a time when the regime had been attempting to reform the PSC. This became a turning point for the Salafis. Up to two thousand were jailed for their activities. In the late 1990s and early 2000s, some became a menace in their communities, where they harassed and whipped people they found smoking and drinking or not conforming to their dress code. They sometimes set up makeshift jails. This happened in the rural towns and suburbs of Casablanca and Fès, as they moved into areas where the police presence was sparse. Sometimes people called these self-appointed Salafi militias in the absence of state security. After Al Qaeda groups had morphed into what is today known as ISIS or Daesh after 2006, the Salafis gravitated toward this fighting force in Iraq. Thousands either went to Iraq to fight or tried to. By this time, many of the fighters from Morocco were being lured not so much for religious reasons but by promises of money and wives. Morocco and Tunisia became two of the biggest external suppliers of fighters for Daesh. About one fifth of those who went to join Daesh were women and most went as wives or for the purpose of marrying (M35.4.4.16).

The PJD lobbied for the Salafis' right to exist and criticized their repression and the closing of their Quranic schools. After the Vingt février movement, the king released 190 political prisoners, including Salafi leaders, some of whom were on death row. He allowed Salafi scholar Mohammed Maghraoui to return to Morocco from exile in Saudi Arabia, where he had fled after issuing a *fatwa* allowing the marriage of underage girls, which contradicted the PSC of 2004. The policy shifted from isolating Al Qaeda influences to targeting Daesh and preventing its expansion. This involved stepping up security within the country, preventing potential recruits from leaving, and arresting fighters who returned. It also involved suppressing AQUIM (Al Qaeda in the Islamic Maghreb), a military force in the Sahara that claims allegiance to Daesh.

As a result of the king's carrot-and-stick policies, the Salafi jihadists have softened some of their positions. After spending time in prison, many made a pragmatic calculation. They wanted to make it clear they were not interested in subverting the regime and that they rationalized their support for Al Qaeda as having to do with its anti-imperialist stance. Many were also chastened by the prison experience and decided they wanted to live normal lives with their families. A few, however, became even more radicalized in prison (A35.5.5.16).

Today there are many Salafi groups. They believe that the religious texts have a single meaning and that only Salafi scholars can correctly interpret this truth. They also believe that strictly and literally following God's words will allow them to enter paradise. Some, like Sheikh Mohammed Maghraoui, are traditionalists and primarily scholars who focus on teaching and studying religious texts in the mosques and Quranic schools. Sheikh Mohammed Fizazi represents another strain of Salafism and had been considered one of the most radical *sheikh*s in Morocco. He was sentenced to thirty years in prison for having inspired the Casablanca bombings, but was released in 2011 by royal pardon. Since then, surprisingly, he has agreed with almost all government positions, including the ban on the sale of the *niqab* in 2017. A third group involves the *haraki* (movement) of civil society activists. This group is made up of former prisoners who focus on providing social services, including well-known *sheikh*s like Mohammed Rafiki Abou Hafs and Hassan Kettani. A fourth group is made up of jihadi prisoners and their supporters and families, including the Joint Committee for the Defense of Islamist Detainees. Because they have refused to renounce violence and recognize the monarchy, they have yet to be released (Masbah 2013, 2017).

After 2011, when the regime released a large number of Salafi ex-jihadists from prison and opened up political space for them, it hoped to contain their political ambitions. Mohammed Masbah argues that at that time most Salafis had been persuaded of the need to participate in the public sphere and to accept plurality, the rule of law, and political freedom in general. They watched the Tunisian and Egyptian dictators being overthrown by peaceful protests rather than violence, and this also had an impact on them (Masbah 2013).

After 2011, Sheikh Mohammed Maghraoui and his followers supported the PJD but then in 2016 he gave his backing to PJD's opponent, the secular Authenticity and Modernity Party (PAM), which is backed by the palace (Masbah 2018a). Abou Hafs first joined the Party of Renaissance and Virtue (PRV), a small offshoot of the PJD, and then the secular Istiqlal party. In May 2015, another ex-jihadi, Sheikh Abdelkerim Chadli, joined a party aligned with the palace, the Democratic and Social Movement (MSD). Others joined smaller parties (Masbah 2017).

However, no sooner did the Salafi ex-jihadis try to engage political parties than they ran into difficulties. They hoped to use their newfound political "freedom" to expand their influence and avoid government harassment. However, much to their dismay they found it difficult both to form their own parties and to bring the rank and file of their movements with them into the parties they joined. This led to further divisions within the Salafi movements and deepened the divide between the leadership and their followers. This may lead, as some have suggested, to the further radicalization of young Salafis and those supporting jihadi causes (Masbah 2017).

The Islamists

Two other key elements of the religious landscape of Morocco are the two Islamist movements, the AWI and PJD, both of which have engaged in nonviolent opposition strategies. The AWI has for the most part stood against state corruption, stayed away from political engagement, and challenged the legitimacy of the monarchy, which has brought it into the crosshairs of the government. The PJD, in contrast, has pursued a political strategy and has led a coalition in parliament since 2011.

Al-ʿAdl wal-Ihsane

The AWI movement was founded in 1987 by Sheikh Abdesselam Yassine, who had once been a member of the Boutchichiyya Sufis. This movement gained support among the middle classes, particularly university students, teachers, doctors, lawyers, and engineers. The AWI became a political party in 1989 but did not engage in the political process in Morocco and boycotted elections because it considered them fraudulent. Yassine's writings reflected a combination of Sufism, Marxism, secularism, and nationalism, including the ideas of Hassan al-Banna, the Egyptian founder of the Muslim Brotherhood, and the militant Islamist Sayyid Qutb (Daadaoui 2016). He was especially hostile to monarchy as a form of government and advocated for the establishment of a republic. The AWI is concerned with providing social services like food and clothes to the poor as well as providing spiritual education. Yassine had a particular animus against Hassan II, whom he considered a ruthless autocrat who ruled with an iron fist during the "years of lead," which involved the imprisonment, torture, and disappearance of tens of thousands of members of the opposition (Clark and Young 2008). Yassine was put under house arrest from 1989 until 2000, after the death of Hassan II, following which he appeared to take a less militant stance against the government, even though he had issued a letter earlier in the year asking King Mohammed VI to repatriate the massive fortune his father had amassed to pay off the national debt, thus violating a taboo against speaking about the wealth of the king.

Nadia Yassine, the daughter of Abdesselam Yassine, was head of the women's section of the association. She led the massive demonstrations against the reform of the Family Code in 2000 in Casablanca. She opposed the top-down nature of the PSC reforms and the fact that the process had not included all women's voices or taken the *shari'a* as its inspiration (Salime 2011). Nadia Yassine felt that the reforms had been introduced by Westerners trying to meddle in Moroccan affairs. The women's section of the AWI later pursued a campaign to "clean up the beaches," demanding that women not wear swimsuits and remain fully clothed (Gray 2013).

Nadia Yassine sought to promote women's leadership within the organization. She often served as a spokesperson of the AWI, especially to international audiences. Some have suggested that she offered a more palatable version of conservative Islam, particularly to Westerners who were impressed by an "intelligent, strong woman representing an Islamist movement and making a case for a conservative Muslim lifestyle" (Dilday 2007). Many had thought that she would succeed her father as leader of the association, but when he died in 2012 she was sidelined by the organization as it became clear that men in this movement would not accept the leadership of a woman. Instead Mohamed Abbadi was elected secretary general.

Nadia Yassine had a vision of women's emancipation that was not focused on changing legislation but rather on changing mentalities (Gray 2013). She saw the Qur'an as the basis for changes that would liberate women and felt that male interpretations of the Qur'an had stood in the way of these realizations.

After Abdesselam Yassine's death the association was divided over whether it should enter politics and possibly even reconcile with the palace, neither of which occurred (Daadaoui 2016). The AWI's influence diminished after 2000. The organization resurfaced again publicly with the Vingt février protests, hoping to tap into the anti-monarchy anti-corruption element, but by this time it had become less militant and was struggling for its existence. The AWI's youth wing joined the demonstrations but ended up pulling out partly because they struggled to work with the secular leftists who were leading the movement. The AWI also did not want to be seen as part of a waning movement after the demonstrations started to dwindle (Daadaoui 2016). In any case, by this time the PJD was starting to attract more adherents with its strategy of participating in elections.

The PJD

The PJD is an Islamist party that is often compared to Recep Tayyip Erdogan's Justice and Development (AKP) party. It also has an affinity to the Muslim Brotherhood in Egypt. It is the only Islamist party in the Arab world that has survived a full term in office and been reelected with a larger majority (Masbah 2018b). In a country where the king holds enormous power, the party has been able to navigate a pragmatic course that has afforded it some independence, while making sufficient concessions to the king to win the trust of the palace. At the outset in the early 2000s, the PJD had less room to maneuver, but it has stayed the course and after the Vingt février protests, it managed to gain slightly more leverage.

In 2017, a government was formed after much wrangling and many delays because some PJD leaders felt their party would be weakened by sharing power with four smaller parties. In the end, under the leadership of a new prime minister, the PJD coalition was made up of royalist parties Rassemblement national des indépendants (RNI, National Rally of Independents), the Union constitutionelle (UC, Constitutional Union), and the conservative Mouvement populaire (MP, Popular Movement), as well as two socialist parties, the PPS and USFP. Prior to this, the PJD was in a coalition with Istiqlal in 2012–2013, but the coalition fell apart over disagreements relating to economic policy.

One of the most interesting changes has been the transformation of the party's position from opposing women's rights reforms to placing them at the center of its platform, even if only rhetorically. The PJD had its origins in the Islamic Youth Association and Jamaʿat Al-Islamiyya (Islamic Group), whose members regrouped in 1996 to form Harakat al-Tawhid wal-Islah (Movement for Unification and Reform, MUR).

Unlike the AWI, it participated in the 1997 elections under the auspices of the Mouvement populaire démocratique et constitutionnel (MPDC), winning nine seats in parliament in 1997. In 1998, it officially changed its name to the PJD. Today it claims more than 10,000 members, with a base made up of students, teachers, and nurses in urban areas and teachers in the countryside.

The MUR opposed the PSC reforms being proposed in the late 1990s and was critical of all reforms that it feared would Westernize Moroccan women and diminish their religious affinities. But the MPDC, which put up three female candidates, emphasized in its 1997 election campaign that it was against all forms of exploitation of "femininity" and supported women's economic participation in professions and maternity leave of six months (Willis 1999).

The PJD was particularly bothered by the aforementioned PANIFD. They opposed it because the World Bank had funded it and provided logistical support. They felt that religious scholars had not been consulted, and that the process had been dominated by feminist organizations and the socialist-led government of the time without adequate input from other groups. PJD leaders also noted that it referenced international human rights and women's rights documents, such as the CEDAW, and they were concerned that this would lead to "the unrestrained Westernization of Moroccan society" (*La Gazette du Maroc*, 1 September 1999, cited in Clark and Young 2008). The Plan was subsequently dropped.

During the early years of the PJD's parliamentary presence (1997–1999), the party supported the left-led *alternanc*e government, which was necessary in order to establish that it was a constructive and conciliatory movement that supported King Hassan's II efforts to create a consensual government. Hassan himself supported the PJD because he saw it as a safety valve for the growing Islamist sentiment emerging in the country and hoped to use it to force the *Koutla* (كتلة, coalition) parties[6] into the government (Willis 2012). This was a precondition for Hassan's toleration of the PJD. However, the king's support was short-lived. The *alternance* government sought to reform the Family Code and supporting the government would have required the PJD to support this bill that it had bitterly opposed. The PJD opposed the abolition of polygamy, the right of women to arrange marriages without

[6] The *Koutla* is made up of Istiqlal, the USFP, and the PPS.

a guardian, and resisted the influence of what it perceived as the secularist and francophone elites and Western powers (Wegner and Pellicer 2009). The current Minister of the Family, Solidarity, Equality, and Social Development, Bassima Hakkaoui, and Khadija Moufid advocated to preserve polygamy and spoke of "the danger of a new law that simply wants to please the West" (Lamlili 2018).

The party increased its number of parliamentary seats after the 2002 elections from fourteen to forty-two, but refused to join the cabinet because its rank and file resisted being part of a cabinet that did not uphold Islamist causes and values. PJD members also wanted to maintain their image of not being corrupt and worried that joining the government would lose them electoral support. After the bombings in Casablanca in 2003, the government, with the support of many leftists and civil society activists, passed an anti-terrorism law that gave it the authority to override civil liberties. Because of the 2003 Casablanca bombings, the regime interfered in PJD affairs and sought to neutralize some of the more outspoken critics within the party. Even though the PJD saw itself as a force for moderation, the state accused it of giving moral support to violence and threatened to ban the party. The palace set out to "tame" the PJD, as one interviewee put it, but at the same time the PJD sought to prove itself as a trustworthy political actor. Part of the king's strategy has involved playing parties off against one another, primarily to ensure that no one player monopolizes the political scene. This has long been a standard operating procedure of the palace (M31.3.22.16).

The Makhzen (the network of actors close to the palace associated with the minister of the interior) forced Mustapha Ramid to resign as head of the parliamentary group and warned against making him secretary general of the party. It only allowed the PJD to run in 18 percent of the seats contested in 2002, ensuring that it would not win a majority. Through heavy-handed gerrymandering of constituencies and a new electoral law, the PJD gained five seats less than Istiqlal, even though it won most votes. Had the PJD gained more, it would have been able to lead a small government coalition and its strength would have made it difficult for the Makhzen to control the political order.

In response to the Makhzen's actions, the PJD became more conciliatory, publicly denouncing terrorism and religious extremism and highlighting its support for the king and democracy. After the bombings in Casablanca in 2003, the PJD separated its religious movement (the MUR) from the party and called for a separation of politics from religion, resulting in the secularization of the party (Masbah 2018b). The MUR's leadership was increasingly pressuring the party not to work with the left and was beginning to question the authority of the king. It opposed the PSC, especially the provisions restricting polygamy, the right of women to arrange marriages without a guardian, and what they perceived to be secular and foreign influences on the bill. The PJD did not want to be seen as the "party of refusal" (Wegner and Pellicer 2009). Like Ennahda in Tunisia, it started focusing more on economic liberalization and economic growth in order to gain greater support and adopted more pragmatic positions.

Recent appointments to key positions in the party are indicative of this shift. Rather than attribute this simply to an internal conflict within the party, it may be more useful to think about how the broader political environment contributed to this shift. To stay in the political game the PJD has had to abide by the wishes of the palace and to work in a coalition with other political parties, many of which diverge quite significantly from its own core principles. It has also learned by watching the fate of Islamist parties that veered too far from the sentiments of the population, the military, or those in power in Algeria, Tunisia, and Egypt. It soon realized that if it was going to stay in power, it would have to be more responsive to the other political parties in its coalition and to broader social forces like the women's movement. In Morocco, by law no party can win an absolute majority in parliament, thus making it necessary to form a coalition government. Moreover, key ministries are appointed by the palace (justice, foreign affairs, Islamic affairs, and interior).

The PJD differs from the AWI in that it is a secular party with an Islamic orientation and unlike the AWI, it has participated in electoral politics rather than boycotting it. Also unlike the AWI, it supports the monarchy but at the same time walks the fine line of trying to distance itself from the Makhzen by criticizing corruption, human rights abuses, and other autocratic measures. The king, in turn, has gone out of his way not to alienate the PJD as long as it abides by the palace's rules (Masbah 2015, 2018b). As analyst Intissar Fakir put it, the PJD treats "the monarchy as both an obstacle and a source of validation" (2017, n.p.). A key part of this accommodation has been the PJD's willingness to go along with the reforms the king has been pushing, including gender reforms. At the same time, the PJD has been able to carve out a larger role for the parliament and for party politics since 2011, at which time it won enough parliamentary seats to lead the government.

Like AWI, the PJD also participated in the massive demonstrations against the PSC in 2000. However, by 2004 it had made a 180-degree turn and began to support the PSC. No doubt the prospect of going against a plan sponsored by the Commander of the Faithful was a sufficient incentive in bringing about the turnaround. PJD leader Mustapha El-Khalfi explained in an interview that in contrast to the PANIFD, the party felt the PSC was a product of a democratic process, working through a Consultative Commission followed by a parliamentary vote. They also said they appreciated the inclusion of religious language and the absence of any reference to the CEDAW or other international treaties (Clark and Young 2008), although their objections to the CEDAW were to change with time. Leaders of one of PJD's women's organizations, Mountada Azzahrae, also told me that since a large part of the PSC is based on *fiqh*, they found it acceptable (M6.2.22.16).

Reflecting on the about-face on the PSC, Lahcen Daoudi, a member of the PJD General Secretariat and Vice-President of the House of Representatives, explained how the PJD was a mediator between the Makhzen and ordinary citizens:

> Our mission, the most difficult, is to develop a culture of moderation. The PJD sees itself as a dam against excessive interpretations of Islam. It played an important role in the debate on the reform of the status of women. Without the PJD, the situation could have turned into a quasi-civil war. There is a leftist current evident in Moroccan concepts developed in the West. I respect the West, but to transpose Western ideas and practices to Moroccan society as they are, causes them to be rejected. Moroccan society reacted in response to the proposed reform of the status of women. The PJD has played a mediating role between the authorities and the population by participating, modeling, and especially by endorsing this reform. We voted on behalf of all the people who demanded Islam.[7] (Gaouane and Elie n.d.)

[7] Notre mission, la plus difficile, est de développer une culture de la modération. Le PJD se considère comme un barrage contre les interprétations excessives de l'islam. Il a joué un rôle important lors du débat sur la réforme du statut de la femme. Sans le PJD, il aurait été possible que la situation vire à la quasi guerre civile. Il existe un courant gauchisant qui importe au Maroc des concepts élaborés en Occident. Je respecte l'Occident, mais transposer telles quelles des idées et des pratiques politiques occidentales dans la société marocaine provoque leur rejet.

The PJD changed its position on other women's rights issues in addition to the PSC, but the process was far from linear and was gradual and uneven. In 2002, Bassima Hakkaoui, who was in the PJD leadership and head of the Organization to Renew Female Consciousness, explained that the PJD was against the gender quota because it felt that women should gain political office as a result of their competence and not any special provisions like the quota (Chaarani 2004). By 2011, the party had adopted a completely different position on quotas as it had been its biggest beneficiary in the elections. Several secular women's organizations worked with Islamist organizations to bring about these quota reforms in spite of their differences (A3.2.1.16).

When the PJD came into power in 2011, the symbolic politics of women's clothes was one of the first ways in which the new Prime Minister, Abdelilah Benkirane, sought to reassure the country as well as foreign investors and tourists about the nature of his administration. He said that he would not force women to dress modestly. "We are proud that our point of reference is Islamist," he said, but added that, "I will never be interested in the private life of people. Allah created mankind free. I will never ask if a woman is wearing a short skirt or a long skirt" (Abdennebi 2011).

Early on in the PJD administration the party leaders ran into difficulties around statements they made. Minister of Family, Solidarity, Equality and Social Development Bassima Hakkaoui came under severe criticism during the debates around Article 475 of the Penal Code, which protected a rapist from prosecution if he married his victim. This article was repealed after protests surrounding the suicide of sixteen-year-old Amina Filali in 2012 after being forced to marry her alleged rapist. The website Yabiladi cited Hakkaoui as saying, "Parfois le mariage de la violée à son violeur ne lui porte pas un réel préjudice" ("Sometimes, the marriage of the rape victim to her rapist does not do her real harm") (Belabd 2012). Later she claimed that she had been misquoted: "A lot was said about me and a lot was attributed to me that I did not say or believe in, in the first place. They said that I back the idea of the rapist marrying his raped victim. This is not true; it does not even cross my mind [*sic*]" (*Asharq Al-Awsat* 2012). The Justice

La société marocaine a réagi, en réaction, contre le projet de réforme du statut de la femme. Le PJD a assuré un rôle de médiation entre le pouvoir et la population en participant, modelant et surtout en cautionnant cette réforme. Nous avons voté au nom de tous les gens qui se revendiquaient de l'islam.

Minister Mustapha Ramid was similarly vilified when he said, "the young Amina had a relationship outside marriage in which she lost her virginity." He never used the term "rape" in the context of what happened to Filali.

The government spokesperson and Minister of Communication Mustapha El Khalfi (PJD) tried to mollify the critics of Hakkaoui and Ramid, saying: "This girl was raped twice, the last [time] when she was married . . . We cannot ignore this tragedy" (Bruneau 2012).

Other PJD statements regarding women also drew criticism. In 2014, Prime Minister Benkirane told parliament that:

> There is a problem with the role of women in the modern family. When the women left their homes [to work], they [the homes] became dark. You who are there, you were educated in houses where there were chandeliers. These chandeliers were your mothers . . . We are proud because God honored us to defend this dimension.

Denouncing the "European model," he said that women in Europe "don't even find time to get married, to be mothers or to educate their children. Why don't we embrace this sacred status that God gave to women?"

Benkirane's comments immediately triggered fiery protests on the part of women's rights activists, many of whom protested in front of the parliament. Party leaders from royalist and leftist parties told him to focus instead on the application of Article 19 of the new Constitution, which provided for gender equality. The traditional and social media along with ten human rights and women's associations announced plans to take the prime minister to court for failing to apologize for his speech, which they considered "prejudicial against women" (Alami 2014, *France24* 2014). One leading women's rights activist explained to me that Benkirane did not necessarily speak for the entire party when it came to women's rights. There are divisions within the party and "there are officials who are aware that Morocco needs to be changed," she said. "He did everything to show his superiority. He humiliated women activists and women's associations. It's my personal opinion, there are women in the PJD and men too, who are for women's human rights" (A3.2.1.16).

Perhaps no one in the administration has come under as much criticism for her comments on women's rights as the Minister of Family, Solidarity, Equality, and Social Development Bassima

Hakkaoui. Yet by 2014 Hakkaoui was boasting about Morocco's gender policy. She was quoted as saying that "Morocco is a pioneer country in the Arab world in promoting the rights of women" (Ministère de la Culture 2014). By 2015, the PJD had changed its tune and was no longer using the language of complementarity, but had switched to parity, at least in their official pronouncements. Hakkaoui, for example, was holding up the 2004 PSC and the new generation of legislation around women's rights that her party had endorsed as evidence of the PJD's commitment to women's rights. This "legal arsenal" that followed the new constitution, she explained, included the nationality law that allows women to pass on their nationality to her children in the case of a mixed marriage, the Law on Presenting Petitions and Motions in Legislative Matters, the Parity and Anti-Discrimination Proceedings, the Advisory Council on the Family and Children, the Act to Combat Violence Against Women, and the gender budgeting provisions in the Finance Act. She also spoke of plans to complete the women's rights project ICRAM II (Gattioui 2018).

The prime minister, Saad Eddine El Othmani, likewise adopted a tone that was quite different from his predecessor, who had been suspicious of foreign influences. At a meeting to discuss ICRAM II the prime minister said that is was the best framework for all initiatives aimed at strengthening the rights of women and advancing the principle of equality, particularly in strengthening women's economic integration and strengthening their status in decision-making and development. His comments highlighted all the key changes that have become evident in the PJD's policy toward women's rights. He went on to recall the constitutional provisions for the establishment of the principle of parity between men and women, the king's focus on the importance of the role of women in society and contribution to the development of the country, as well as the kingdom's international commitments, in particular the CEDAW. El Othmani stressed that the question of women is at the heart of the government's concerns, notably the intersection of interests having to do with the strengthening of democratic choices, the rule of law, and advanced regionalization (*Le Matin (Maroc)* 2018).

After 2013, the Moroccan government created an intergovernmental commission on policy dialogue with civil society to come up with these new laws, so that civil society organizations could make petitions if unsatisfied with a certain law, and to advance public consultations with civil society. Women's organizations and activists reported participating in these dialogues, which gave them greater input into the policy-making process (M40.5.13.16).

Secretary of State for Crafts and Social Economy Jamila El Moussali was named the new head of the women's section of the PJD in 2018, replacing Bassima Hakkoui, who had held the post since 2011. A historian by training, she was one of the PJD stalwarts who had fought against the PSC in the early 2000s. Yet today she is a leader of the Renewal of Women's Consciousness, the ideological arm of the PJD on women's issues (Lamlili 2018). Her election represents a shift in orientation for the organization. El Othmani removed Hakkaoui and all the pro-Benkirane women, including the former prime minister's relatives, from leadership positions in order to reinvigorate the organization.

Feminist associations have consistently criticized the PJD government for dragging its feet on legislation regarding women's rights and trying to water down the 2017 bill that was passed regarding violence against women. Critics argue that the PJD has been especially slow to address the issues of single mothers, the right to equal inheritance, and sex education in schools (Darhour 2016).

At the same time, however, the government has not undone any of the international treaties, the constitution, or other laws that are in place regarding women's rights and has moved ahead with passing new women's rights legislation. The Government Plan for Equality (ICRAM I and II) continued with the program set in motion by the previous Istiqlal-led government. Its goal was to institutionalize the principles of fairness and equality and to establish the foundations of parity and promote *karama* (كرامة, dignity). Building on the 2011 constitution, the UN Millennium Development Goals, and the UN Sustainable Development Goals, the Plan sought to eliminate all forms of discrimination against women and to amend national legislation to protect women against all forms of violence. It attempts to advance gender mainstreaming in ministries, parliament, and in the public as well as increase female political participation.

The PJD has been making progress on numerous gender-related issues in what is a deeply conservative country, even if the outcomes are not as far-reaching as the secular feminists would like. For example, on abortion, the government passed a series of amendments to the country's Penal Code, which in the past only allowed abortion if the mother's health was threatened (Article 453). The new amendment allows abortion in cases of rape, incest, and fetal impairment and was aimed at bringing the law in line with the constitution. Moroccan Health Minister al-Hussein Louardi had voiced support for legalizing abortion, saying that he believed a woman should have control over her own body: "I think it is absolutely necessary to legalize abortion, because it is not only a medical problem but also a social problem" (M3.24.16).

The king had initiated the debate on Morocco's abortion law in 2015 after the Moroccan Association for the Fight against Clandestine Abortion and its founder Dr. Chafik Chraibi reported that 800 illegal abortions were being performed daily nationwide. The king formed a committee to investigate the issue. As a result of his TV exposé on unsafe abortions, the founder of the Association was fired from his job as a gynecologist, which he had held for thirty years.

Another hot button issue has been inheritance, which in the past no one could even broach in public discourse. When the UAF first discussed the matter in the early 1990s it was accused of heresy, and Benkirane and other Islamists issued a *fatwa* against its leaders and the newspaper *March 8th*. A leader of the UAF said: "We were able to break the silence and lift the taboo against the subject and today we are ready to fight for the issue of inheritance." She went on to explain that the times had changed and it is not possible to be governed by the same laws as in the past – such as cutting off hands for stealing, the death penalty for murder, lending money without interest, and other such practices mentioned in the Qur'an (M18.3.4.16). And indeed, today the issue of inheritance is being widely discussed in Morocco (M3.24.16).

Several PJD parliamentarians have expressed support for changing laws around women's inheritance. During a 2016 lecture in Salé, PJD parliamentarian and preacher Abouzaid El Mokrie El Idrissi called for the reform of the laws regarding the issue of inheritance. The MP said that certain principles of the Islamic heritage are now incompatible with the values of society, including those related to "custody and pensions which men had to pay towards women" (*Huffpost Maroc* 2016). Because women have the same financial and household responsibilities as men today, he felt it was unfair that they did not inherit as much. He advocated a reform that was based on an interpretation of religious texts in the light of lived realities: "Change must come through religious texts and take account of their specificity, and not be imposed by the West or international NGOs."

These changes were reflected even in the positions of a Salafi Moroccan religious scholar, Mohamed Abdelwahab Rafiki. Rafiki, also known as Abou Hafs, was among the 8,000 people arrested after the Casablanca bombings in which forty-five people were killed. He appeared on a prime-time TV show in 2017, arguing that the social roles of men and women had been transformed since the early days of Islam, and suggesting that it was time to debate inheritance rules. He indicated publicly that he was in favor of reform in inheritance laws, an area which has often been regarded as the most challenging to reform for Islamists: "In the society we are living in nowadays, *taʿasib* is unfair to women and girls." He added that it is unfair to distribute a family's hard-earned wealth among distant relatives. Hafs said that many things in Islamic law have changed over time, such as widespread gender segregation. His statements drew the ire of other Salafis like Mohamed Fizazi and Hassan Kettani, who said that he had crossed "not just a red line but an impassable wall."

Increasing numbers of *ʿulema* have expressed support for changing the laws on inheritance. A book, *Men Defend Equality in Inheritance*, was published in which one hundred leading public figures, writers, journalists, and artists, including Abou Hafs, talk about the importance of female inheritance. However, after Abou Haf's statement, Nouzha Skalli, the former minister of women and the family, observed that the lines of the debate were shifting. In the past, she noted, "as soon as you said the word 'inheritance' you were accused of blasphemy. Today, the debate can be held openly. The time has come to break the taboo, which hides major injustices against women. The Qur'an says that God is against injustice" (Mekouar 2017). The king himself, has already called for a religious *ʿulema* to give him a *fatwa* about women and equal inheritance.

Although there has been a clear movement in the positions taken by PJD when it comes to women's rights, some of the rhetoric changes depending on the audience. When in 2019 the daily *Al Akhbar* published a photo of a PJD parliamentarian, Amina Maelainine, posing without a veil and wearing a T-shirt and jeans in front of the Parisian cabaret Moulin Rouge, PJD supporters reacted with outrage on social media and in the traditional media. Commentators mocked and ridiculed her and advised her that it was in her best interest as a woman to conform. Some attacked her for hypocrisy. Feminists and progressives condemned the online shaming and criticized society for being given license to censure women's bodies and comment on their personal lives and choices. The former PJD Prime Minister Abdelilah Benkirane responded that this was not a matter of concern for a political party and that the PJD was even trying to find women leaders who did not veil. Both he and his successor as prime minister, Saadeddine El Othman, emphasized that this was a privacy issue (Barbouch 2019). However, the tone of El Othman's speech directed at party stalwarts at the January 12, 2019 party congress was slightly different. He stated that:

> The PJD will remain attached to its Islamic reference system. It is a choice of its constitution that is irreversible, which is even mentioned in its statute. The party's attachment to its Islamic referential is real and not an illusion. We must set an example, especially those who are in the front line of public opinion. (Kabbadj 2019, Koundouno 2019)[8]

Islamist Women's Organizations

The aforementioned change in the Islamists' official position is also evident in the women's associations tied to the PJD. The two main organizations with links to the PJD are Mountada Azzahrae (the Zahra Forum) and Tajdid al-Waʿi al-Nisaʾi (Renewal of Woman's Awareness). The Zahra Forum, which is a coalition of 113 organizations, focuses on the development of rural women (organizing listening centers for victims of violence, conducting family counseling and family mediation, supporting women's economic ventures, and promoting the schooling of girls in rural areas). Renewal of Women's Awareness is more concerned with women's legal rights. Both are still concerned with women's central roles as mothers and wives and with ensuring that the laws reflect Islamic values. But, like the PJD, their emphasis has changed noticeably. In the past, they lobbied against laws which conformed to international treaties, arguing that they were Western imports. They marched against the PSC in 2000 and against

[8] Le PJD restera attaché à son référentiel islamique. C'est un choix de sa constitution qui est irréversible, qui est même mentionné dans son statut. L'attachement du parti à son référentiel islamique est un exercice et non une illusion. Nous devons donner l'exemple, en particulier ceux qui sont en première ligne de l'opinion publique.

the rights of women. As one women's rights leader put it, "there was a fierce offensive on the part of the Islamist PJD organizations against modernist and legal associations" (M3.24.16).

Indeed, the current and two previous leaders of the women's organizations most closely affiliated with Islamist PJD party, the Zahra Forum, told me of their acceptance of the Moudawana and the constitution. As one leader put it, "Our main objectives are to defend the rights of women and fight discrimination against women." They appeared to be very much engaged with the UN's Economic and Social Council[9] and in support of the CEDAW. They also focus on religious principles, which they consider the basis for the promotion of women's rights and emphasize the fact that the principles of Islam are not in contradiction with the CEDAW. This is a dramatically different stance from that adopted earlier on by Islamist women's rights activists and shows that even if there are huge ideological differences between them and feminists in their strategies and understandings of equality, they have substantially shifted their thinking on key concerns.

Much like the feminist organizations, the Zahra Forum has been involved in legislative and policy reform, submitting memoranda around constitutional reform, the Government Plan for Equality (ICRAM), the establishment of the Authority for Parity and the Fight Against All Forms of Discrimination, the establishment of the Advisory Council of the Family and Children Morocco, and other such interventions. They lobby around legislation such as the civil service law, employment legislation, criminal law, and other such issues. They took part in the Ministry of Justice's assessment of the PSC and helped identify some of the loopholes in the code. They organized a caravan called Zahra Caravan to encourage female political representation. They encourage women to run for office and join political parties and to participate in the public sphere more generally (M7.2.22.16).

One of the strengths of the Islamist women's organizations is that they have resources and are well organized. They work with women on the ground in the rural areas, slums, and *medina*s (old quarters at the center of large metropolitan areas, often surrounded by a wall). As one feminist lawyer put it, "Their speech is simpler. They talk in a way that

[9] The main UN forum for discussing international economic and social issues and formulating policy recommendations. A large number of NGOs have consultative status with the council and participate in its deliberations.

goes directly to the heart." They are effective, she explained, "since we have a population that is illiterate, uneducated. They are able to win their votes in this way" (M21.4.29.16).

Many feminists, however, are deeply suspicious of the Islamist organizations, but even they concede that changes have taken place as a result of the PJD's need to comply with international treaties. As one leader of the LDDF put it:

> They have adopted the concept of equality of women, especially in the political field, but they still have reservations about the civil rights of women. For us, we cannot be for equality in some areas and not in others. A vision for equality must be comprehensive. One cannot pick and choose.

But she remained optimistic:

> I think that it will go forward, because there are also constraints at the international level, and Morocco has international commitments ... When the government has commitments, I do not believe that Mountada Azzahrae will contradict them. So for us these changes are good and positive and they will impact the evolution of women's rights in Morocco. (M3.24.16)

I spoke with the current and preceding two leaders of the Zahra Forum and asked about their points of commonality and difference with feminist organizations, with whom they collaborate in a number of symposia, national bodies, and international bodies. There was wide agreement around issues of political engagement, working women, and economic empowerment in terms of proposals and strategies. As one put it, "all these are common points. We work in the same way, with the same ideology." As far as differences go, they felt that it was more a question of emphasis. For example, they focused more on the family, and they felt that the Forum's position reflected more of a popular consensus in society. They were concerned with underage marriage, but they felt that the feminist organizations made too much of this issue. They saw this as a problem of poverty and education and felt that tackling these causes of the problem was the best approach. They did not feel that polygamy was a big problem in Morocco and said it was addressed in the Moudawana. Another difference concerned the issue of violence against women, which affects 62 percent of women in Morocco (2010 figures), according to the Moroccan Association of Human Rights. Their approach to the problem was family mediation, family counseling, and reconciliation in order to prevent divorce and the break-up of the family.

When asked about their Islamist orientation, they felt their views were a reflection of the broader Moroccan society's orientation. They also noted the convergence between the Islamist and feminist positions in Morocco as they have engaged around policy initiatives such as the PANIFD and other issues. Aziza El Bakali, the president of the Forum, explained:

> Here, I quote one of my friends who is a leftist and one of the pioneers of the feminist movements. She used to tell me that in the beginning of the feminist movement, they believed that the cause of women's problems was religion. After a while in the second phase they started using Qur'anic texts to respond to Islamists. So they started using Islam in this way [to defend women's rights], and we also took from religion in the same way. Now in the third phase, the feminist movement is convinced that Islam is not the root cause of women's problems, and that the problem is the manner in which religion is practiced but not religion per se. (M6.2.22.16)

The Islamist women's organizations, El Bakali said, have "reconciled with the universal ideology of human rights relating to international treaties, since international treaties are not the devil; they have positive and negative aspects. At the same time, the women's secular movements have reconciled with religion" (M6.2.22.16).

Nevertheless, there are still important differences between Islamist women's rights advocates and feminists. While for the secular feminists, the individual woman and her rights is at the center of their analysis and the struggle for legal reform, for the Islamists, the starting point is the family and its preservation or solidarity as they put it. One of their foci is equality through strategies like the eradication of violence in the family and the promotion of family consulting centers, where women experiencing violence can be counselled on how to keep their family together and seek mediation. Equality for them cannot exist without solidarity in the family (M32.3.4.16).

When I asked secular women's organization leaders about whether they had changed their position on the role of religion in influencing women's rights, several noted that religion could not solve women's problems with inheritance or poverty, violence against women, or child marriage. One leader of a major women's organization said that she had no issue with Islamic values or a family approach to dealing with violence in the family, but not at the expense of the woman. In other words, women need the right to leave an abusive marriage as well, not just help in reconciliation (M17.2.16).

At the same time, feminist organizations have by and large accepted that the problem in Morocco is patriarchy, not Islam. Many organizations directly engaged in legal reform prefer not to engage with questions of religion because they do not see its relevance to the law or women's welfare, although some concede that in opening a dialogue around inheritance they will need to engage religious thinkers and opinion leaders. Many feminists, especially those in academia, have found it necessary to shift their focus to discovering and emphasizing positive elements within the Qur'an that support gender equality. Thus, there is a growing convergence between these two tendencies in the women's movement, despite their continuing and major differences (Salime 2011). The synergy is stronger in Morocco than in Tunisia or Algeria, partly because Tunisia has a longer history of secular feminist mobilization and Algeria went through ten years of brutal civil war between Islamist extremists and those who opposed their agenda. Some have suggested that the synergy in Morocco is due to the fact that Morocco was a protectorate and was not colonized like Algeria, where the religious and cultural identity of the country was destroyed by colonialism (M8.2.22.16).

Conclusions

The key actors in this drama – the king, the Salafis, the Islamist PJD, and the women's movement, both secular and Islamist – have symbolically used women, women's bodies, and women's rights as a way of "drawing a line in the sand" or of expressing the contours of their differences with one another. This line has shifted significantly since Mohammed VI claimed the throne. It has not moved fast enough or far enough for the secular feminists, but for some of the Salafis and the PJD it has moved quite dramatically to the point that issues that once elicited death threats and harassment are now being discussed openly by the PJD and Islamists. This chapter has shown how and why this shift took place.

First, the passage of legislation around women's rights, the use of women in religious institutions, and the promotion of women leaders more generally, became a key part of the king's arsenal of neutralizing the most extreme Salafi tendencies in the country and moderating the Islamists. It strengthened secular constituencies and allowed Morocco to present a modernizing image of itself to the world. Second, the PJD, in responding to the king and popular pressures, was forced to present a new image to donors and international audiences who might have been reluctant to engage it given its Islamist orientation. The PJD changed its position with respect to international treaties like the CEDAW and legislation like the PSC because it was politically expedient to do so. A refusal to support these gender reforms would have risked the same fate that befell Islamists in Tunisia and Algeria. Moreover, it helped garner support in the voting booth.

Third, the women's movement in Morocco played a key role in bringing about these reforms. It was more active than in the other two Maghreb countries and was able to engage the government effectively. Leaders of the movement were consulted on key pieces of legislation, especially after Mohammed VI took over. This allowed them a voice in helping shape the legislation, even if they had to compromise with competing interests. There were moments when they were more successful than others. Their successes generally followed critical junctures such as the Casablanca bombing in 2000, after which the PSC was passed along with other legislation, and the Vingt février movement, after which the new constitution was passed, followed by other legislation to reconcile the constitution with existing laws.

Fourth, the women's movement and elites in Morocco were influenced by neighboring countries. Activists shared strategies and agendas with those in neighboring countries and vice versa. This explains the synchronicity in the timing of many of the reforms and also the willingness to engage in some of the reforms.

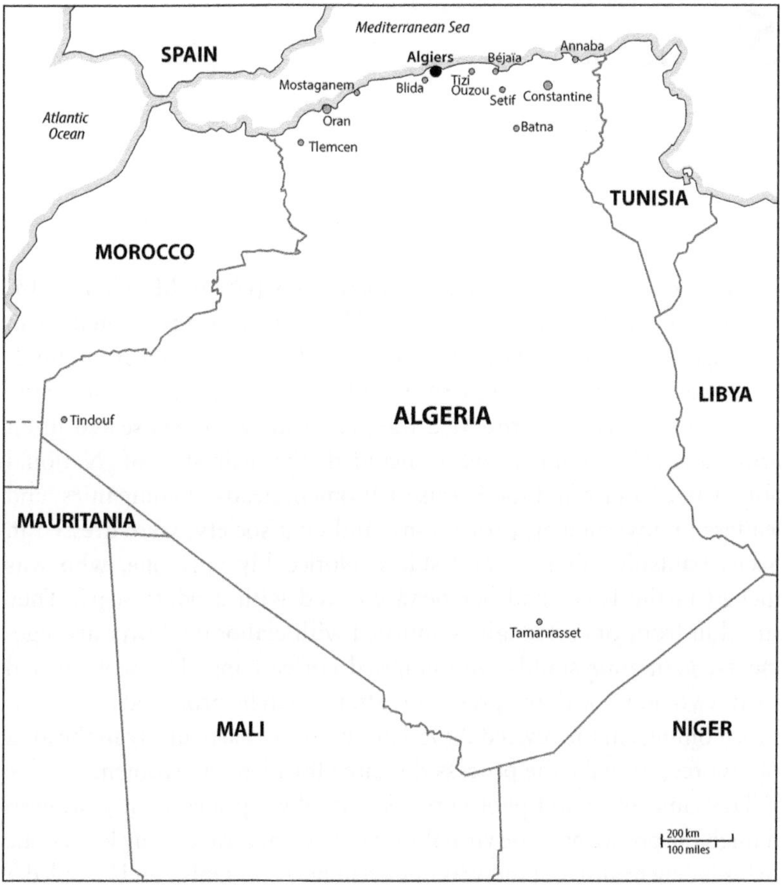

Map 5.1 Map of Algeria
Credit: Eva Swantz

5 Algeria

The occasion was International Women's Day (IWD), March 8, 2015, and the scene was the residence of Algerian President Bouteflika in Zéralda. Posing for a photo, twenty-one Algerian women stood holding bouquets of red and white roses with green sprigs – the colors of the Algerian flag. They surrounded the president, who was seated in an armchair. The women, who included the Minister of National Solidarity, Family and the Status of Women, heads of companies, and leaders in government, professions, and civil society, were dressed in heels, pantsuits, dresses, and skirts. Noticeably only one, who was tucked in the back, had her head covered with a white scarf. They stood in front of coffee tables adorned with elaborate flower arrangements, *petit four* stands, and emptied coffee cups. The women had spent two hours with the president, after which he promised to address shortcomings in the revised 2005 Family Code, particularly in the area of divorce, to make the process the same for men and women.

The same event and photo-op was dutifully repeated each year, even though the president made virtually no public appearances any longer due to his failing health. But this was one event he did not miss, and he called it an "essential meeting" (Bouteflika 2018). The annual ritual was a way for the president to reaffirm and underscore his commitment to women's rights as a centerpiece of his agenda. The symbolism of the requisite photo was not lost on anyone, even if subliminal: The women holding the roses stood for the nation. Their garb, although typical of women leaders, was also strikingly not Islamist. The message was simple and clear: women fought in the war for independence. The government has the political will to advance women's rights, but it must do more. Women need to play more public roles as they are key to the economic development and security of the country.

What was not said was as important as what was said at these events, which were televised with different versions of the same basic photo splayed across the newspapers the following day. Women were not just

Table 5.1 *Heads of state in Algeria since independence, 1962–present*

Head of State	Position	Years in power	Party affiliation
Abderrahmane Farès	Chairman of Provisional Executive	1962	National Liberation Front
Ferhat Abbas	President of the National Constituent Assembly	1962–1963	National Liberation Front
Ahmed Ben Bella	President of the Republic	1963–1965 (deposed)	National Liberation Front
Col. Houari Boumédiène	Chairman of Revolutionary Council	1965–1976	Military
Houari Boumédiène	President of the Republic	1976–1978 (died in office)	National Liberation Front
Rabah Bitat	Interim President of the Republic	1978–1979	National Liberation Front
Chadli Bendjedid	President of the Republic	1979–1992	National Liberation Front
Abdelmalek Benhabylès	Chairman of the Constitutional Council	1992	National Liberation Front
Mohamed Boudiaf	Chairman of the High Council of State	1992 (assassinated)	National Liberation Front
Ali Kafi	Chairman of the High Council of State	1992–1994	National Liberation Front
Liamine Zéroual	January 1, 1994 Head of State November 27, 1995 President of the Republic	1994–1999	Military (until November 27, 1995) National Rally for Democracy (from February 21, 1997)
Abdelaziz Bouteflika	President of the Republic	1999–2019	National Liberation Front
Abdelkader Bensalah	Acting Head of State	2019–present	National Rally for Democracy

fighters in the war of independence. They also stood up to violent extremists during the Black Decade,[1] as women were among the first targeted by the Islamist fighters for teaching, running businesses, driving, some for not veiling, and engaging in the public sphere.

Fast forward to International Women's Day in 2019, which could not have been more different from the earlier IWD celebrations. "No Democracy Without Gender Equality" read the placards of women and men demonstrators who descended on cities throughout Algeria in the hundreds of thousands to demand gender equality and democracy. This became a watershed moment in the struggle for women's rights in Algeria, as women reclaimed public space in unprecedented numbers in the 2019 Algerian uprising. The uprising started on February 22 as a protest against President Bouteflika's announcement that he was running for a fifth term. When he stepped down, the protesters continued to target the regime in power. They demanded democracy, freedom, dignity, and government transparency.

This chapter shows how Algerian women reached this moment of massive defiance in 2019, having been a focal point of the tensions between the Islamists and those who opposed extremism both symbolically and existentially during the Black Decade. It shows how in the post-civil war period women, their bodies, and ultimately women's rights, became a centerpiece of the regime's fight against *intégrisme* or fundamentalism. Legal reform, which included an emphasis on political rights, was part of a strategy against extremism which also had a negotiated and military dimension (Messahel 2018). In more recent years the struggle has shifted to the cultural arena as women, including young women, push back against Islamist proscriptions on women's dress. As a consequence, Algeria has seen the demise of militarized and political Islamist influences. It is impossible to understand what transpired in the dark years of the Black Decade or in its aftermath without accounting for the central role of women, yet most of the literature of this time period surprisingly treats this aspect as peripheral to these events.

Islamists' Expanding Influence (1962–1992)

The origins of political Islam in Algeria date back to 1931, when Abdelhamid Ben Badis formed the Association of Algerian Muslim

[1] The civil war between 1992 and 2002 between factions of Islamist groups, the military, and the government.

Ulema (AAMU), which became the country's leading Islamic reformist organization. Throughout his career, he sought to protect Algeria from domination by French values and culture, although initially he had not sought independence from France and thought the AAMU could serve as an intermediary between the French authorities and the Algerian people. By 1954, the AAMU had built 181 schools around the country, promoted the study of Arabic, and advocated for making Arabic a required language of study in primary and secondary schools. It did so with what some considered missionary-like zeal, bound and determined to destroy local practices and cultures. The AAMU clashed with the Sufi brotherhoods, and its ascent represented the sidelining of the older rural religious leaders affiliated with Sufism, *marabouts* (المرابطون, teachers), and other leaders of popular Islam, whose doctrines it considered questionable. Even as it promoted a more modern individualistic vision of Islam that appealed to literate urbanites, the AAMU also came into conflict with the Algerian *évolués*, the elite who had been assimilated into French culture and did not regard French language and culture as incompatible with Islam. Later the AAMU announced its allegiance to the National Liberation Front (FLN) in 1956 and fought with the FLN in the independence struggle. This helped the FLN gain religious legitimacy, which was important for its overall claims to authority (Roberts 1988, Willis 1996).

Algeria had the largest colonial French presence, which included almost 1 million settlers, originally from France and elsewhere in Europe. They settled in the most fertile parts of the country from Oran in the West to Constantine in the East, displacing 3–4 million of the indigenous population. This, coupled with the brutality of colonial rule, led to one of the fiercest wars of liberation on the continent, resulting in the deaths of over 400,000 on both sides. It was only in 2018 that the French government admitted to the use of systematic torture during this war. Already during this horrific war, rape and violence against women were strategies used by the French to dishonor the family and the tribe, resulting in increased veiling and seclusion of women (Salhi 2010).

After independence, the country was divided between three groups: (1) the Muslim, Arab, and conservative elements, (2) the secular, leftist, and modernist tendencies, and (3) the Amazigh cultural movement, which opposed the Islamization and Arabization project of the state. The state repressed the Amazigh demonstrations in April 1980 and accused the Imazighen of being separatists and puppets of the French.

The regime tried to drive a wedge between the Islamists and the Amazigh (Salhi 2011).

After independence, the first president, Ben Bella, banned the AAMU, but gave its members jobs in the education and religious affairs ministries, ostensibly to silence them (Willis 1996). As Michael Willis (2014) argues, the *'ulema* lost their role as arbiters between the state and the people and were weakened until the 1970s, leaving a vacuum into which the more radical Islamists moved. However, as early as 1962, the regime began to cede the cultural sphere to the Islamists. It made an implicit deal with the Islamists: the regime would maintain political power and the Islamists could do as they pleased with society (A8.10.30.16).

Ben Bella (1963–1965) sought to revive the education system with the departure of the French. Arabic was to become the national language and all Algerians were to study it at all levels. However, they lacked a sufficient number of teachers to teach the language. At the same time, they required the French to run the administration. The French were to control 600 primary schools and eight high schools, where the instruction would be in French. However, because of limited capacity, only the first two grades of primary education were in Arabic. Between 1966 and 1976, a plan was put into effect that gradually Arabized the primary schools one year at a time. At the secondary level, the humanities were taught in Arabic and all other classes in French. In 1970, the government administration started to be Arabized. Other institutions like the press and the military were to be Arabized as well (Abdulrazak 1982). Egyptian teachers, as well some Syrian, Iraqi, and Palestinian teachers, were seconded to help teach in the Algerian school system in the mid 1960s and to help promote Arabic as part of creating an Algerian national identity. Many of the teachers were Muslim Brotherhood sympathizers and were known to be poorly educated themselves (perhaps Egyptian President Nasser's intent was to offload them as the Brotherhood was banned in Egypt). But as Heather Sharkey observes, according to critics, these imported Egyptian teachers "seeded Islamism among Algerian schoolchildren in ways that bore bitter fruit during the Algerian civil war of the 1990s, when discontented and underemployed 'Arabized' youth filled the ranks of the agitators while standing on Islamist platforms" (Sharkey 2014, 317). To this day, deep tensions exist between those who were Arabized and Islamicized and the rest (Benrabah 2013).

Another part of ceding control of society and the cultural sphere to the Islamists involved making concessions when it came to women's rights. Women first broke key gender barriers during the Algerian war of independence when they joined the fight against France. By the end of the revolution, there were almost 11,000 *moudjahidates* (المجاهدات, women freedom fighters) of whom 1,755 were in the Armée de libération nationale (National Liberation Army). In addition, there were another 2,388 civilian workers of the resistance who provided food and shelter for the insurgents (Daoud 1996, Salhi 2010). Women fought shoulder to shoulder with men and fully expected to be rewarded with political positions after the war. Yet, after independence in 1962, women found themselves abruptly pushed out of public life (Ahmed 1982b). There were a few exceptions. For example, the wife of a former foreign minister, Fatima Khemisti, drafted legislation to raise the minimum age of marriage to sixteen for girls and eighteen for boys. This law, known as the Khemisti Law, was passed in 1963. But by and large women's participation was curtailed.

The FLN sought the support of women for their socialist government by creating the Union nationale des femmes algériennes (UNFA, National Union of Algerian Women). On International Women's Day, March 8, 1965, nearly 6,000 women participated in the first march organized by the Union. But the organization never really generated any further interest among most Algerian women.

Houari Boumédiène had been Ben Bella's defense minister. He deposed Ben Bella in 1965 in a bloodless coup and served first as chairman of the ruling Revolutionary Council between 1965 and 1976, and then as Algeria's president between 1976 and 1978. Neither Ben Bella nor Boumédiène had the political will of Tunisia's Bourguiba to advance women's rights. In 1976, a National Charter recognized the legal equality between men and women and women's right to education, but few women were employed relative to men. Although the government promised the creation of several hundred thousand jobs for women, these did not materialize. The 1976 constitution promised political rights for women. Women could be active in politics as long as it was in the service of the FLN, which was the only party. The 1976 constitution's Article 81 stated that "All the political, economic, social and cultural rights of Algerian women are guaranteed by the Constitution" (Algerian Constitution 1976).

In 1965, Boumédiène suspended the People's National Assembly (APN) and thus women did not join the body until it was reinstated in 1976, when nine were elected to positions. One woman was appointed to the cabinet in 1984. Only a few women held legislative seats in 1992 when the parliament was dissolved. When it was reconstituted in 1997, only twelve seats (3 percent) out of 380 were held by women. No women were affiliated in any capacity with the six-member Haut comité d'état (HCE) that ruled Algeria from 1992 to 1994, although seven women sat on the sixty-member legislative body, the Conseil consultatif national, established by the HCE after the electoral process was halted in 1991. Women's involvement at the local level was no better in this period. Women were active at the local level as far back as 1967, when ninety-nine women candidates were elected to communal assemblies (out of 10,852 positions). By the late 1980s, the number of women in provincial and local assemblies rose to almost 300, still a negligible number (Cheref 2006).

Boumédiène had the goal of Arabization, but not Islamization. However, the education program previously started under Ben Bella had resulted in both Arabization *and* Islamization to the point that the two identities were regarded as two sides of the same coin (Oulahbib 2016). The Islamists' reach expanded during the Boumédiène period and they were able to influence restrictions on women's freedoms, particularly in the areas of family planning and abortion (Ahmed 1982, 165). Boumédiène's successor President Chadli Bendjedid (1979–1992) faced even greater pressures from the Islamists and started caving into them through various policies. At the same time, there was an expansion of the Amazigh movement as well as the independent women's movement, which were both on a collision course with the Islamists (Willis 1996).

The women's movement at this time included organizations like the Algerian Association for the Emancipation of Women, SOS Women in Distress, and the Committee for the Legal Equality of Men and Women. Women's organizations pushed back and in 1980 they overturned a travel ban on women without a male relative. They also struggled against efforts to allow husbands to vote in place of their wives and defended co-educational schools between 1989 and 1991 (Lalami 2014). The biggest setback for women, however, was the threat of the imposition of a conservative Family Code.

In an especially pivotal moment in 1981, the younger independent feminists were joined by thirty women veterans who had fought in the liberation war to protest the proposed Family Code, which they felt was a betrayal of the revolution for women. Five hundred women protested in front of the national assembly. The *moudjahidates* wrote an open letter to President Benjedid in which they demanded that women should have the same age of legal majority as men, they should have unconditional rights to work, and should enjoy equality in marriage and divorce. They called for the abolition of polygamy and demanded that common inheritance be provided. They also advocated for the protection of abandoned children and for giving single women legal status.

Benjedid backed down at the time, appearing to concede to the women's rights activists, but then in 1984, much to their horror, the Family Code was enacted, clarifying irrefutably that the state was beholden to the Islamists (Salhi 2010). The Code institutionalized polygamy and made women minors under the law. Women could only marry under the supervision of a guardian. They could not divorce their husbands (although men could divorce their wives) and they could only obtain a divorce through the informal mechanism of *khul*ʿ, through which they would be obliged to give up their legal rights and claims to alimony (see Chapter 3). Breastfeeding and caring for children until adulthood were a woman's legal obligation. They had to obey and respect their husband and could only work with the latter's permission. Women were reduced to daughters, sisters, mothers, and wives, and as far as activists were concerned, they were not considered citizens in their own right.

The Family Code represented an effort by the government to sacrifice women's rights in order to appease the Islamists. Thus, the FLN played off secularists and Islamists against one another in order to mediate the different political tendencies within Algerian society. To enhance their legitimacy, they supported Islamist politicians such as Nait Belkacem and Boualem Baki, and allowed them political space to hold seminars and develop their ideas. The FLN thus helped the rise of the Islamic fundamentalists, who then later turned against the regime (A30.10.16.16).

However, the Islamists were not the only force behind these regressive policies regarding women. Since independence, the authorities had decided that the Algerian state should first be established and the country developed. Women's rights would be addressed later, as happened in so many newly independent countries in Africa at the time, particularly where the ruling party had waged a war of liberation. In Algeria, there was a conservative secular current that felt that women's rights were not a priority. As one activist put it, "Today I think that some currents in the government can hide behind the Islamists to say: 'It's not us, it's public opinion!' But even if elements in the government were not responsible for such views, there were few efforts at the time to change public opinion" (A30.10.16.16).

Women demonstrated in response to the 1984 Family Code, and three protesters were placed in solitary confinement without due process at this time. Algerian activists worked together with the international organization Women Living under Muslim Laws (WLUML) to campaign in their defense.

Since independence, the FLN had systematically eliminated any democratic opposition as it solidified its position in the one-party state. It rewrote history while suppressing cultural and political expressions it opposed. It choked civil society and permitted only the registration of sports and religious organizations. As Messaoudi explained in 1995, "Apart from the Berber cultural movement, it has been the women, and they alone – who have been publicly questioning the FLN since 1980–1981." She criticized Algerian and French historians, particularly the leftists and academics, for writing women out of Algeria's history, and proclaimed that any woman "whose public pronouncements do not correspond to their scheme of things is immediately doomed to symbolic lynching and stoning" (1995, 57).

Rise of the Front for Islamic Salvation

Algeria adopted a new constitution in 1989 under President Chadli Bendjedid, allowing for the formation of multiple parties beyond the FLN. This political opening allowed for the formation of all kinds of associations too. Modest political liberalization made it a little easier for civil society and women's organizations to mobilize. Three legal changes had opened up the political space: The Political Associations Act (1989), which led to the emergence of twenty-eight political parties; the 1990 Associations Act, which allowed for the legal formation of organizations with the permission of the local prefectures (ولايات, *wilayat*) in rural areas and of the Ministry of Information in the case of national organizations; and the 1990 Information Act, which allowed for freedom of the press. These legal reforms facilitated the creation of three women's associations: the Association for the Emancipation of Women, the Association for Equality before the Law between Women and Men, and the Association for the Defense and Promotion of Women's Rights. These organizations were particularly concerned with the rise of the Islamists as well as the Family Code and violence against women.

However, the opening of political space also allowed the Islamist groups to increase in influence. In 1989, the Front for Islamic Salvation (FIS) was formed and had soon gained a following of tens of thousands of supporters, drawing particularly from the urban poor. It emerged as the leading Islamist party, having grown rapidly in a relatively short period of time as a result of the networks of mosques it controlled and the social services it provided to the poorest, taking advantage of the economic crisis in the 1980s. Although the government controlled the mosques, the Islamists found ways to circumvent restrictions and thousands of places of worship emerged where imams preached sermons against women's rights, music, drinking, and "Western values." The government had legalized the FIS thinking that it would make it easier to control the party and prevent the further radicalization of society. But the FIS quickly took control of 55 percent of the communal councils and 80 percent of the regional councils (Willis 2012, 170). Soon it was poised for similar victories in the national assembly. The authorities started arresting and imprisoning most of the party's leaders. The FIS nevertheless claimed the majority of votes in the first round of the 1991 election. The party was certain to win in the second round, but the authorities annulled the results of the first round and cancelled the second altogether. The FIS was banned in 1992, President Benjedid was forced out of office, and a state of emergency was declared.

The FIS's two central concerns had to do with (1) Islamicizing and Arabizing the educational system and (2) focusing on the role of women in society with the aim of keeping them in the home to fulfill what they perceived to be their central roles as mothers and wives. The party also sought to dictate their clothing and social relations. They felt women and men should not work together and should not mix in schools and universities. They opposed birth control. The party's platform, Project de programme du Front islamique du salut, even argued that women should be given a pension for their social and educational functions in the home. They saw women in the workforce as taking jobs away from young men (Willis 1996, 1999). The Islamists targeted women's rights, in particular, and demanded changes to the Family

Code, arguing that educated women were French stooges. Many of the Islamists wanted (and still want) a return to the perceived golden age of Islam at the time of the Prophet Mohammed. For the Islamists, power is unjust, not because of a lack of democracy, as secularists would argue, but because it does not apply Islam properly, hence their focus on the term "justice" (A30.10.16.16).

At the heart of the FIS preoccupation with women was an obsession with sexuality, according to Messaoudi:

> The fundamentalists, like any totalitarian movement, want to exercise absolute control over society, and they fully realized that the place to start was by seizing control of women's sexuality, something Mediterranean-style patriarchy facilitates. In addition, like all purifiers, they hate and persecute difference, which inevitably accompanies democracy. Now, what women represent is desire, seduction, mystery, trouble, and also alterity, which is immediately visible on their bodies. That is why the Islamists are so anxious to hide the female body, to veil it, to make biological difference disappear from the body's external signs. The women who refuse to submit to this become perfect targets, because they embody the Other that the fundamentalists need to mobilize and rally people to their cause. This was even easier in Algeria during the time when the fundamentalists were gaining influence, because women were the most vulnerable members of society and had been made even more vulnerable by the pre-existing systems, colonization and then the F.L.N. (1995, 109)

Algeria was fertile ground for such a movement also because, as Messaoudi elaborated, "sexuality is taboo in our societies, but you don't have to listen to [Islamist] speeches to know that this frustration exists, and that it is deep ... This sexual distress had dramatic consequences. All that produced a very disturbed society, and the FIS took advantage of it" (1995, 109).

The Islamist movement regarded the women's movement and the Amazigh movement as beholden to the West. This had what was tantamount to treasonous implications given Algeria's bitter war of independence against France. The Islamists portrayed themselves as the true nationalists and Islam as a religion that had helped Algerians fight for their independence. Women were attacked with acid and knives in public spaces for dressing "indecently." When women went to the police, they were told they had brought it on themselves. The passage of the regressive 1984 Family Code did not seem to satisfy the Islamists, even though it contained major concessions to them. Nevertheless, they felt it was not Islamic enough, calling for *shari'a* law and the creation of an Islamic state.

Women's rights activists, at the same time, were galvanized and protested the Family Code, which had effectively declared them to be minors (Salhi 2011). Women were thus pushed into the crosshairs of the Islamists and the government. With the political opening in 1989, women's organizations began to mobilize and coordinate activities among themselves, even though the organizations were still informal and had not established their legal status. Nevertheless, women were among the first to protest the ascent of the FIS and called for the cancellation of elections because they felt that many women's votes were stolen by proxy FIS votes (men saying they were voting on behalf of their wives), bringing Algeria to the brink of becoming another Islamic republic like Iran and Afghanistan (A16.10.11.16). They had watched what had happened in these countries and had seen their own society being slowly "Talibanized," as some explained in interviews. At the time of the FIS's rise, about 3,000 Algerians who had fought in Afghanistan returned to Algeria, adding fuel to the growing civil conflict.

Women's rights activists felt that the FIS had planned to use democratic means to undermine democracy. As feminist author Cherifa Bouatta cautioned, "Winning elections alone is not democracy" (Bennoune 2013). Islamist violence directed particularly at women further convinced women that the FIS had never had any real democratic aspirations. The prospect of a second-round FIS victory brought over a million citizens to protest in the streets of Algiers, and women were at the forefront of these demonstrations. Women feared the Islamists were threatening to do away with the constitution, women's rights, and other freedoms. Many women and men felt physically threatened by the impending victory of the FIS.

Meanwhile, as the FIS grew in influence, they targeted women. They used mosques to preach their views and were able to convince large numbers of unemployed youth that women should return to their homes to produce fighters for the cause of Islam and leave their jobs to the men. They sought a moral cleansing of society and women were the prime focus of this project. The opposition of many women to the 1984 Family Code was seen as evidence of the moral corruption of secular women since they opposed polygamy. Women's rights activists who demonstrated against the Islamists were seen as the epitome of the repudiation of national values, as Abbassi Madani, the FIS leader, put it (Salhi 2011).

"Women mobilized, they protested. They were in the vanguard in confronting the Islamists. Indeed, they played a big role and gained the respect of everyone, including those in power," explained one activist (A8.10.30.16). Women led the civil society movements against the Islamists in the early 1990s, undoubtedly because they were among the groups first targeted. As one activist said, "We had nothing to lose, we had absolutely no other choice" (A8.10.30.16). Algerian women had seen what happened to women in Iran and Afghanistan, and they were determined that Algeria would not follow suit. As one activist said, "At the time, women were already emerging on the streets to shout 'neither Iran nor Afghanistan, Algeria is Algerian!'" (A2.10.31.16).

The most active women's organization at the time was the now defunct Rassemblement Algérien de femmes democrates (RAFD). Other groups also resisted the Islamists, among them the leftists like those in the Parti avant-garde socialiste (PAGS), journalists, trade unionists, and people who called themselves "les démocrates." Some leftists had originally opposed the closing down of the elections, but after the attacks by the Islamist militias, they changed their mind even as other foreign democracies condemned the actions of the Algerian government. Although there are human rights activists who today believe that the government committed abuses in its suppression of the Islamists, there are few Algerian feminists who would argue against the government's decision to suppress the Islamists, even if they recognize that democracy was obstructed in the process. As one feminist explained, "When I realized what the Muslim fundamentalists were capable of doing, I realized we did not have any other choice." (A2.10.31.16)

The first attacks by the FIS were cultural. They took down satellite dishes, which people used to watch cable TV from around the world and installed loudspeakers through which they preached hate and threatened those who did not follow their edicts. Men who wore beards started wearing Afghani garb and women also started wearing the *hijab*, *niqab*, and *chador*, all of which had previously been alien to Algerian society. In some areas, they segregated boys and girls in schools and forced girls out of physical education. One women's rights activist described what happened in her neighborhood:

The following day after the election, I had to go to the Assemblée populaire communale [APC], the local authority, to get some documents. The first thing they did was to separate men and women. It was a real shock to me when they said we had to queue separately. I said I will queue as usual with men. It was the first day of this, so they said OK. But after that things changed quickly and they were not so lenient. (A2.10.31.16)

They harassed people on beaches and in swimming pools and prohibited wedding ceremonies and celebrations involving music. They issued death threats against singers and actors and closed down cinemas and theaters. Fear was pervasive in the towns where the Islamist extremists were in control (Salhi 2011).

These forms of cultural control were soon followed by attacks on police and state officials, especially after the state of emergency was declared in 1992 and the government banned the FIS after annulling the December 1991 parliamentary elections, fearing that the Islamists would win. Top FIS leaders were arrested. Soon several armed organizations emerged, including the Groupe islamique armé (GIA, Armed Islamic Group), the Armée islamique du salut (AIS, Army of Islamic Salvation), and the Mouvement islamique armé (MIA, Armed Islamic Movement) between 1992 and 1995 (Salhi 2011).

After the attacks on state security personnel, students, journalists, intellectuals, feminists, leftists, and others became targets. Lists of women who were to be killed were posted at the entrances of mosques. Women were the key civilian targets and they were killed in the most brutal ways: They were decapitated in front of their children, tortured, and then killed, gang-raped, and shot in broad daylight. Female teachers were killed in front of their students. Thousands of schools were burned down. Leaders of feminist organizations were targeted. The prime targets included women who worked: women who worked in government, women who owned businesses and beauty salons in particular, teachers and university lecturers, as well as artists and singers. They also targeted women who were unveiled. Women were forbidden from going to the *hammam* (public bathhouse), where they could congregate and talk among themselves.

Then the killings became massacres, bus bombings, attacks on whole villages, kidnappings, and rapes of young girls. Girls were abducted to become sex slaves. Today there are thousands of parents who still do not know where or why their children were taken. Women were killed in the most horrific ways to send a message to others (e.g., tying victims to two vehicles which drove in opposite directions, taking fetuses out of women's bellies and throwing them against the wall). Women's bodies, in particular, were targeted as a means of terrorizing their communities and controlling women.

Women formed organizations like Djazairouna in Blida, which was established by women whose families had been targets of Islamist terrorism. The overall objective was to provide moral, psychological, and legal assistance to victims of the Black Decade. When Djazairouna was formed in 1996, few people were attending funerals because if they attended the burial of someone who had been killed by the Islamists, they would later find themselves on a list to be targeted. As one Djazairouna leader explained:

> There is the example of a twelve-year-old girl who was removed from her classroom and dragged by her hair through the school yard and outside. She was decapitated and her head was placed in front of the mosque the next day. Once the body was in the hospital, the nurses had refused to sew her head to her body and hand it over to the family on the pretext that she was an atheist. The ambulance which had recovered the girl's body was intercepted and burned, and the terrorists threw the body into a ravine. We had to wait another day to intervene so that we could finally give the body back to the family. She was eventually buried in the presence of an imam, her mother, sister, and uncle. This was not an isolated case, but I give this example to say that it was a little girl who did not belong to politics, who was neither with nor against the Islamist movement. It also shows that people refused to help or simply do their job for fear of reprisals. (A19.10.17.16)

The association's members, who included both men and women, attended the funerals of the victims of violent extremism. In the past only men had attended funerals, but women now started going as an act of protest to insist that the victims were not guilty and that the only culprits were the extremists. They also provided comfort to the families of the deceased.

It was not just women who were targeted; men were also attacked. Sometimes they were targeted through the abuse of women. The Islamists forced husbands to witness the rape of their wives, and fathers to witness the rape of their daughters. Often women who had been abducted by armed Islamist groups were physically reduced to an animal state. Their heads were shaved and they were forced to live naked among the rebels. They were used as beasts of burden to draw water, wash, and cook.

All these were unspeakably dehumanizing acts, but the violence was as much symbolic as corporeal. Cutting off the nose of those who smoked was an assault on pride, given the symbolism of the nose; as was cutting off a man's penis and putting it in his mouth or mutilating women's genitals. The violation of a woman, especially virgins, was seen as a humiliating assault not just on the woman but on all her relatives, especially the men (fathers, brothers, and husbands). She became what some regarded as "stinking flesh." She had been socially killed even though she was alive. This derives from a popular saying in Algeria that "when the carrion stinks, only those concerned, the parents, take care of it" (*al-lḥam ilā khnaz ma yarfdūh ghayr umm maḥḥ*). This saying is generally a reference to a woman who has yet to be married and whom only the parents can save from rotting by marrying her. A woman or girl who had been raped or sexually humiliated was socially destroyed and could not be redeemed because the honor of her family had been destroyed. She would forever remain a symbol of the power of her aggressor. Rape is tantamount to the murder of the group and the only way to repair it is through retribution in this symbolic language of violence (Moussaoui 2004).

The Black Decade almost destroyed all women's associations. In 1994, there were fourteen nationally registered organizations. Of these, only two or three remained at the end of the decade. Activists were either killed, they ceased their activities, or they fled the country. It was not until the 2000s that the movement reappeared (A3.9.26.16).

Many of the links with the international community were severed in this period. There were no efforts by international organizations to support the victims of Islamist extremism (A3.9.26.16). The women's organizations felt isolated. As one feminist explained:

> They laughed at me when I was invited to a feminist meeting in Europe and testified against terrorism as being responsible for the killings and deaths of my brother and sister. I was insulted when they said that I was sent by the generals and by the Algerian authorities. At the time, Amnesty International said their charter did not provide for victims of non-state entities. As the Islamists were victims of the Algerian state, they were defended instead of the

victims of the Islamists. I have never heard that victims of terrorism were contacted by international NGOs as the Islamists were. (A19.10.17.16)

In 1997, a series of large-scale massacres near the capital city of Algiers focused world attention on the civilian toll in the conflict. Yet the government never properly investigated these crimes against humanity or brought anyone to trial. The attacks were attributed to Islamist armed groups but they were carried out within a few miles of military bases, making many wonder who the perpetrators really were. The same goes for the assassination of leading cultural figures, intellectuals, and some sixty journalists: most of these crimes remain unsolved and unpunished. Algeria's privately owned press has reported on the discovery of numerous mass graves. But the bodies they hold have never been properly exhumed and forensically analyzed (Goldstein 2006).

The Black Decade took an incalculable toll on Algerian society. Fighting between the government and Islamist groups resulted in the deaths of approximately 200,000 people and the disappearance of 7,000 others. Fighting diminished after 1997 but many citizens remain traumatized for life. Some people came out of this period atheists, believing that if God existed, he would not have permitted such things. Others became more radicalized and more women, including even young girls, started veiling. For some it was a question of projecting a certain image. As one woman explained, "Islam has become a matter of appearances more than anything else, we want to be as Muslim as possible in relation to others. Before terrorism, Islam was present but it did not represent the radicalism it does today. Religion was not a constraint. Rather, it was a culture" (A19.10.17.16). Many felt abandoned or let down by the international community, including the international human rights NGOs. They felt and feel to this day that international opinion was unduly shaped by the foreign media, which portrayed the cancellation of the elections in 1991 as undemocratic at the time.

The Bouteflika Era: First Term (1999–2004) and Second Term (2004–2009)

Former foreign minister Abdelaziz Bouteflika won the elections in 1999, 2004, 2009, and 2014 and attempted to stabilize the country.

Part of this effort involved neutralizing the Islamists. Algeria pursued a policy of reconciliation and reintegration with Islamist fighters after the civil conflict. At the same time, there was investment in housing, jobs, health, infrastructure, and youth policies in order to pacify the citizens, who had been traumatized by the war.

In 2005, Algeria signed a Charter for Peace and National Reconciliation with Islamists and granted amnesty to former fighters who agreed to stop fighting. The Charter was passed on February 27 while the parliament was in recess. A public referendum was held in which 97 percent of the electorate voted in favor of a reconciliation charter. Those deemed to have violated the Charter could be imprisoned for up to five years for any statement or activity concerning "the national tragedy" which "harms" state institutions, "the good reputation of its agents," or "the image of Algeria internationally."

This was not the first time that Algeria had swept its uglier truths under the rug. After independence in 1962, Algeria and France agreed to an amnesty regarding the 1954–1962 war of liberation. Along with the amnesty, Algeria's leaders promoted a singular narrative glorifying the heroism, sacrifice, and unity of the fighters for independence. However, they also suppressed stories about the many massacres and assassinations perpetrated against fellow Algerians in the course of the war. It is only recently that historians have started to reveal these realities (Goldstein 2006, Stora 1991).

Bouteflika advanced this charter on the heels of a series of Family Code reforms in June 2005. Some have argued that the president had used women's rights as a bargaining chip in negotiating this charter and buying the silence of civil society. They felt he had broken his promises to women's rights organizations in order to appease the Islamists and gain their backing for the amnesty (Rachidi 2007).

Prior to the referendum, President Bouteflika and the state media campaigned in favor of the Charter, stating that those who opposed it were the enemies of peace and reconciliation (Goldstein 2006). The Charter promised to forgive and forget all crimes committed on all sides during the Black Decade, including the government security forces, who are known to have committed atrocities. The Algerian government argued that its approach to combating terrorism combined diplomatic, legal, and military solutions rather than pursuing simply a defense-based strategy. They claimed they were targeting the root of the problem, rather than the symptoms.

For the victims of this era, the reconciliation was a finger in their eye. As one victim said:

> We cannot talk about reconciliation of the people when there is a category of murderers and criminals who have committed criminal acts against a whole society who suffered the crimes. How can we then reconcile these two categories without recognizing the right of the second party to the memory, the right to the truth, and the right to reject the criminal? Yet the criminal is elevated to the rank of public figure ... We had to forget everything because of the Charter. It restored three principles which are the principle of amnesia, the principle of impunity, and the refusal of truth. The international mechanisms proposed within the framework of transitional justice include another three principles: truth, justice, and memory. (A19.19.17.16)

There is little about this period in Algerian history books. Some of the perpetrators of violence are described on TV as national figures and their taking up of arms is often justified. As one activist for the rights of victims explained to me:

> It is imperative that the new generations know what has happened. People must see the criminals judged on behalf of the people. It is also necessary to grant a real status to the victims of terrorism, to allow families to commemorate their loved ones, to set up a day of memory or have days of demonstrations. (A8.10.30.16)

For many there has been a price to pay for this collective and deliberate amnesia. As one activist put it:

> You must know that there has never been a debate about any historical event. The story is falsified and those in power only tell the story that suits their purposes. The Black Decade is no exception to this rule. From the moment we decided to give amnesty to the terrorists, we stopped talking about the Black Decade. The [authorities] did not see the utility of asking the opinion of the people. It is an authoritarian power that does what it wants and never solicits the views of the people. (A8.10.30.16)

The charter was opposed by human rights groups like Amnesty International, Human Rights Watch, the International Center for Transitional Justice, and the International Federation for Human Rights. They issued a joint statement saying that the law would "consecrate impunity for crimes under international law and other human rights abuses, and even muzzle open debate by criminalizing public discussion about the nation's decade-long conflict." The charter was also opposed by groups of victims like SOS Disparu(e)s, Somoud (families of people kidnapped by armed groups), and the National Association of Families of the Disappeared (ANFD).

According to Human Rights Watch, the law granted a sweeping amnesty both to the security forces for abuses as well as to Islamist militants for atrocities committed against Algerian citizens. As noted above, large-scale massacres carried out near military bases in 1997 were attributed to Islamist armed groups, but it is not clear who was really responsible. Numerous mass graves were uncovered, yet no action was taken to identify the bodies or those culpable. Many journalists and intellectuals were assassinated, yet most of these crimes were not investigated and went unpunished.

Women victims and the families of those who disappeared during the civil conflict continue to protest and demand answers. They are often beaten by the authorities and arrested because they refuse to seek authorization for their protests on the principle that what they are doing is legitimate, and as such should not require authorization. For example, activists from the Tharwa Fadhma N'Soumer and Djazairouna associations were arrested while protesting near the Grande Poste in Algiers on March 8, International Women's Day, in 2017 to denounce inequality in Algerian society and to honor the women who died during the Black Decade of Algeria's 1990s civil war.

No real dissent has been permitted in the broadcast media and the jailing of several journalists has served as a warning to others. A nineteen-year state of emergency was finally lifted in 2011 as a concession to the opposition at the time of protests against the government during Algeria's mini Arab Spring. The opposition argued that the terrorist threat was minimal and that the emergency was being used against those demanding greater democratization.

The government claimed that the continuing amnesty had been successful. "According to official figures ... between 2006 and 2015, 15,000 armed Islamists have been 'integrated in society,' while 17,000 were 'eliminated' between 2006 and 2012" (Meddi 2015). There has been a steady decline in fatalities due to Islamist attacks, dropping from 153 in 2009 to nine in 2016, but there are still concerns about Daesh (ISIS) fighters returning from Syria and Iraq. However, only 170

Algerians joined Daesh, compared with 3,000 Tunisians and 1,500 Moroccans. As a result, only eighty-seven have returned to Algeria compared with 800 Tunisians and 198 Moroccans (Bendaoudi 2018, Ghanem-Yazbeck 2018, Meko 2018).

The 2005 Family Code

After election to his second term in 2004, President Bouteflika committed himself to women's rights reforms despite fierce opposition from the Islamist parties. In particular, he sought to reform the Family Code of 1984, which treated women as minors. He sought to ban men from divorcing their wives without cause and to allow for alimony. He wanted to ban the provision that required women to ask for permission to marry from a male guardian and sought to require that those pursuing polygamous relationships seek approval from a magistrate.

For years, Algeria's brand of socialism had cut the country off from the influences of the international women's movement and human rights discourses. This had gradually changed as women's organizations linked up in 1995 with the Collectif Maghreb-Égalité Network, which helped them in their efforts around the Family Code. They also began to connect to the Western media and participated in various UN and international human rights conferences and events (Salhi 2010, 122). Algerian women's organizations also collaborated with the WLUML, which today is found in seventy countries with coordination offices in Senegal, the United Kingdom, and Pakistan. According to Algerian sociologist and WLUML founding member Marieme Hélie-Lucas, the organization connected Algerian activists with international counterparts and provided them with a platform to voice their concerns about crimes against women perpetrated by the FIS and other armed groups. The WLUML helped them gain access to various international women's conferences and the United Nations' World Conference on Women in Beijing in 1995 (Allalou 2009).

The focus of women's mobilization had long been on violence against women and on reforming the Family Code. The Collectif 20 Ans Barakat (20 Years Is Enough!) had been active in 2003 trying to overturn the family law. In the summer of 2003, twenty women musicians from Algeria, France, and Argentina recorded the song "Ouek dek yal qadi" (What Came Over You, Judge?) demanding: "This law must be undone and never done again!"[2] The press began to cover the Family Code around this time. In 2005, under pressure from women's organizations, Algeria amended the 1984 Family Code, but it was still far from acceptable to most feminists.

With the 2005 reform, women gained more rights in marriage, divorce, and citizenship, bringing the Family Code further in line with the international treaty of women's rights, the Convention on the Elimination of All Forms of Discrimination against Women (CEDAW). Consent became an important part of the marriage contract. The notion of women's obedience to men was abolished and replaced by reciprocal rights and duties in the marriage. The male guardian's role became symbolic as he could no longer force a female relative to marry against her will or oppose her choice in marriage. The legal age for marriage was changed from twenty-one for men and eighteen for women to nineteen for both sexes. The new code no longer prevented women from marrying non-Algerians and Algerian women married to foreigners could transmit their citizenship to their children. Men and women had reciprocal rights and duties and were to share their roles as head of household. This replaced an earlier clause which required the wife to obey her husband, who was regarded as head of household.

Many of the reforms in the 2005 Family Code appear to be a compromise between the Islamists and the women's right advocates. Algeria abolished repudiation as a form of divorce, but polygamy was still legal, although subject to conditions. The husband would have to secure the permission of the first wife/prior wives in order to marry another wife. He would also need the permission of a magistrate (Marzouki 2010). As was the case with the 1984 Family Code, the new Family Code was adopted by order of the Council of Ministers and then voted on without debate by both houses of parliament on February 22, 2005.

Many women's rights activists were unhappy with aspects of the 2005 Family Code. But there were limits to what Bouteflika was willing to advocate given the pressure from the Islamists: he told activists, "You have obtained vested rights today. Do not demand more" (Montenegro 2014). While some women's rights activists praised the

[2] www.youtube.com/watch?v=CKcwiBwtBqk.

law, others found it lacking. Some, like the Socialist Forces front (FFS) and the Workers Party (PT), felt that the entire code needed to be repealed and replaced, while others believed it should be amended. The Islamists, however, would have liked to see a Family Code based on the *shari'a*.

The objections by women's rights activists centered on several key provisions. One of the main concerns has to do with divorce by *khul'* (Article 54), which allows a wife to divorce her husband only if she pays for the divorce (at a price usually not exceeding the sum of her dowry). As the law stands, even if she has a third witness, the woman can be repudiated, while she herself cannot ask for divorce other than through *khul'*. Many women's associations found this provision to be degrading, because the woman was obliged to pay for her freedom. Custody of children is given to the wife and the husband is asked to provide rent or housing. However, the Penal Code and the Family Code have yet to be reconciled, and so the husband cannot be prosecuted if he does not provide housing (A7.11.10.16). Thus, some argue that the code has left hundreds of women homeless after divorce, resulting in many women living on the street, often with their children. There are many women with dependent children but no fixed home because they cannot return to the family home with their children as was the case in the past. And even women who can afford to rent encounter difficulties in renting apartments as divorcees. This is also the case for single mothers. There are few homes for women in distress. A woman still needs a guardian when she marries, even if his role is intended to be a symbolic one and his rights limited. Although technically the new Family Code allows women to choose their guardian, it is not clear that in practice they are able to do so given familial pressures (A3.9.26.16).

While some feminists seek to abolish the Family Code and others want to amend it, there is a third proposition for the Family Code, which women's rights activists reject. It is the "optionality" proposition by Hocine Zehouane, president of the Ligue algérienne pour la defense des droits de l'homme (LADDH), which consists of giving families the choice to be governed either by the Civil Code or by *shari'a*. As one feminist explained:

> For us, it would be very serious given the Algerian context. This option assumes that the Algerian woman has a real choice, but this is not the case. In fact, women are always under social and cultural pressures and all the

decisions they make in their lives do not result from their own choice but rather are imposed. We consider that this is a dangerous route. (A7.11.10.16)

Bouteflika's Third (2009–2014) and Fourth Terms (2014–2019)

With Bouteflika's third and fourth terms, we saw an increase in legal, constitutional, and policy measures to expand women's rights, matching the patterns in other Maghreb countries. This was coupled with women's rights rhetoric. The best sources on government self-representation include a series of predictably dull government press releases about its position on the status of women. The Algerian government saw the promotion of women's rights as a way of trying to convince the world that it was interested in democracy (APS 2018c), and to win acclaim internationally for putting Algeria on the map when it came to women's rights, particularly political rights.

It is interesting to note that of the key issues listed on the website of the Embassy of Algeria to the United States, the four main themes are: counter-terrorism, women's promotion, human rights, and the constitution. The fact that it gives such prominence to women's rights in this venue is indicative of the high symbolic importance the regime gives to women's rights, but also of what it is trying to signal to countries like the United States and the West more generally, even as US priorities are shifting globally away from human rights, women's rights, multilateralism, and international engagement.

Many of the postings on the site underscore Algeria's commitment to international treaties. For example, one article quotes Minister of National Solidarity, the Family and Women's Affairs Ghania Eddalia's speech to the sixty-second Commission on the Status of Women (CSW) (APS 2018a). She is cited as emphasizing Algeria's commitment to UN resolutions promoting women's rights like the Sustainable Development Goals (SDGs) by 2030. At another event, the Director of Local Governance, Fatiha Hamrit, lauded Algeria's achievements when it became the Arab country to attain the highest levels of female representation in local assemblies. As a result, in 2012 Algeria ranked twenty-sixth globally in female political representation (APS 2017).

Another key theme is the explicit link that is made between women, stability, and security. One press release refers to women as the leading initiators of reform today and "one of the guarantors of our country's stability and progress." Women reinforce the efforts of schools to promote civic feeling and "civil harmony and the national reconciliation triumph over discord (*fitna*) and destruction, and have worked to reconcile the Algerians with themselves and with their homeland." Women are seen as particularly adept at helping build a country that is "authentic and modern, tolerant and united, founded on the Rule of Law," according to President Bouteflika and his regime. As mothers, women are seen as socializers of the next generation through their role in the family, and as such they help preserve the identity of the country based on "Islam, Arabic, and Tamazight" components. Oddly, women in particular are also seen as key to building a decent and proud Algeria "free of excessive dependence on hydrocarbons" (APS 2018b). Although Bouteflika referred to the Qur'an in his speeches, he would have rather seen women's rights detached from fundamentalist influences, which he referred to as a "foreign religion." He said he did not want women to be treated as minors.

This emphasis reflected the growing interest of the regime in presenting itself as a champion of women's rights, especially in the area of political rights. Soon after Bouteflika's initial election in April 1999, he appointed the first female provincial governor and the first two female presiding judges. The number of women judges (district attorneys) increased in August 2001 from fifteen to 137, out of a total of 404 judges, or 34 percent. Prime ministers Ali Benflis and Ahmed Ouyahia[3] both included five women ministers and secretaries of state in their respective governments from 2000 to 2003 and 2003 to 2006 (Dris-Aït-Hamadouche and Zoubir 2007), bringing the number of female cabinet members to 25 percent. Bouteflika's 2014 cabinet included seven women out of thirty-four (30 percent), which was the highest percentage in the MENA region at the time. They became ministers in the fields of education, family, and immigration, even minister of finance (Karbea 2009, 19).

The Algerian military promoted a woman to the rank of general for the first time in 2009. Subsequently three other women were named generals. Algeria has the most women police officers in the Muslim world, 8 percent of its police force. A woman was named the head of

[3] Ouyahia has been prime minister four times, 1995–1998, 2003–2006, 2008–2012, and since 2017.

the Algerian police academy in 2009 (Media Line News Agency 2009).

Women are better represented in civil servant positions and in positions in government administration than in the private sector. This is in part because since 1974 men have been required to enroll in the military at the age of nineteen for two years of mandatory service. They have often deferred their military service for studies or spent time waiting for their deferment to clear and they are not allowed to work in the public sector during this time. This has made it easier for women to find employment in the public sector but harder to find employment in the higher-paying private sector, where men predominate.

Up until 2008 there were no provisions in the Algerian constitution specifically mentioning women's political rights. This changed with the 2008 constitution when the following clause was added: "The State shall work for the promotion of political rights of women by increasing their chances of access to representation in elected assemblies" (Algérie 1996) Additional amendments to the constitution in 2016 included several other key provisions, including the following: "Citizens shall be equal before the law without any discrimination on the basis of birth, race, gender, opinion, or any other personal or social condition or circumstances" (Article 32). This required the state to take positive action to ensure equality of rights and duties of all citizens, men and women. In February 2016, parliament introduced an article indicating that the "state works to attain parity between women and men in the job market," and "encourages the promotion of women to positions of responsibility in public institutions and in businesses."

Women's organizations became more active after 2011 with the formation of the Association indépendante pour le triomphe des droits des femmes and the Organisation de l'égalité devant la loi entre les femmes et les hommes (women's organizations affiliated with the Front des forces socialistes and the PAGS), the Rassemblement contre la hogra et pour les droits des algériennes (RACHDA), Reseau Wassila, and others. Women gained greater access to the media. They took on numerous concerns including quota legislation, reform of the Family Code, legislation around violence against women, and the nationality law, among other things.

At the same time, new restrictions were imposed on civil society which affected women's associations. A 2012 law required associations to register, while authorities arbitrarily rejected or refused to process their registration applications. This put many well-established organizations, including women's organizations, into legal jeopardy and made it difficult for them to receive foreign funding or hold public meetings (Human Rights Watch 2014). Some organizations operated without official accreditation, because the wait was so long, but that risked arbitrary closure. Organizations like Algerian Women Claiming their Rights (FARD) and the Association for the Development of the Person and the Exercise of Citizenship (AFEPEC) were closed by the governor (الوالي، *al-wali*) in Oran, claiming they were operating outside of the 12/06 law of 2014 (Boualem 2018a). They reopened a few days later but remained in a precarious situation without formal approval of their application to operate from the authorities (*Dernières Infos d'Algérie* 2018).

Quota Laws

Quota laws are examples of women's rights legislation introduced in the post-2011 period. The government supported these changes, in part as a response to pressure from some women's groups and from women parliamentarians close to the ruling party but also in response to international pressures and to improve its image abroad (Lalami 2012).

As a result of pressure from women's organizations supported by donors, a quota law was passed in 2012 for women in the national, regional, and local assemblies. Algeria, which has a proportional representation electoral system, adopted a somewhat unique quota arrangement that includes both legislated candidate quotas and reserved seats. Women must make up 20 percent of the candidates on party lists for the APN when the number of seats a party wins is equal to four; a 30 percent rate when the number of seats is five or more; a 35 percent rate when the number of seats is fourteen or more; a 40 percent rate for thirty-two or more seats. A 50 percent rate is applicable to seats reserved for nationals living abroad. The law does not specify where the women are to be positioned on the list. A similar system is in effect for the Wilaya People's Assemblies (WPA) elections. In elections for the Communal People's Assemblies (CPA), women's representation is set at a minimum of 30 percent in areas with a population greater than 20,000. One women's rights activist explained:

We launched an advocacy campaign in partnership with political parties and with civil society to tell the president that we want a quota of women in parliament and not less than 30 percent. We first had the constitutional revision in 2008 and then we had the law in 2012, so it's a process. There is the work done by the associations, but a political will is needed to make it work. (A3.9.26.16)

Even Islamists worked on this issue with secular feminists as they had at times on issues of violence against women (A3.9.26.16). It was rare in Algeria to find Islamist and feminist organizations working together like this, but the Islamists also stood to gain from this policy.

As a result of the introduction of the quota, the number of women members of the APN increased from 2.4 percent in 1987 prior to the civil war to 31.6 percent in the 2012 legislative elections, the highest proportion for women in the Middle East and the Maghreb at the time (Table 5.2). Of the 25,800 candidates in these parliamentary elections, 7,700 or 30 percent were women (Table 5.3). There were also many young female candidates: over 62 percent of the women running for office were under forty years of age, while only 44 percent of the men were under forty. Women's organizations like the Centre d'information et de documentation sur les droits de l'enfant et de la femme (CIDDEF) had provided training for women candidates prior to the elections on how to give a speech, approach voters, organize public events, and other such campaign skills.

The new presence of large numbers of women in the elections had interesting consequences, both positive and negative. In the 2017 legislative elections, there were districts where parties ran all-female lists, like Chlef in western Algeria, where the Algerian National Front, a centrist opposition party, did so with a list headed by lawyer Khaduja Buska. Women in this district were the most active in the party's local structure in this province, according to the head of the party, Moussa Touati, and they included candidates with backgrounds in law, medicine, and public administration (*Daily Sabah Africa* 2017).

While women were extremely active in some districts, in other instances they were sidelined. Five Algerian political parties (out of the sixty-two that contested the 2017 election) displayed blank-faced female candidates wearing the *hijab* alongside photos of male candidates in the 2017 elections. The election authorities gave the parties two days to replace the posters and display photos of women's faces or

Table 5.2 *Gender representation in the Algerian legislature, 1962–2017*

Year	Women	Men	Percentage of women
1962	10	197	5.07
1963	2	136	1.47
1964	2	127	1.57
1976	10	180	5
1980	10	77	12.9
1985	7	87	8.04
1987	7	295	2.37
1990	12	94	12.7
1994	12	178	6.7
1997	12	380	3.68
2002	27	364	10
2007	34	355	11
2012	146	462	31.6
2017	119	462	25.8

Sources: Karbea (2009), 19–20, Inter-Parliamentary Union (2018)

risk being removed from the election. "This kind of encroachment is dangerous; it is not legal and it opposes all laws and traditions," said Hassan Noui of the Independent High Authority for Election Monitoring (HIISE). He continued: "It is every citizen's right to know whom he will vote for" (BBC Monitoring 2017).

It should be noted that the issue of quota adoption proved to be fairly controversial at the time among some women's groups who felt their priorities lay elsewhere. One of the groups pushing for a greater presence of women has been CIDDEF. It is a partner of the Feminist Peace Organization (CDF), an international organization that works in southeast Europe, Israel, Palestine, and the Maghreb on advancing women's rights. In 2006–2007, the CIDDEF carried out a study of the electoral law and the implications of the constitution, provided documentation on the problem, and organized workshops with media activists, parties, and other members of civil society (CIDDEF

Table 5.3 ***Female candidates in Algerian legislative elections, 1977–2017***

Year	Women candidates	Overall candidates	Percentage
1977	39	783	4.98
1982	39	840	4.64
1987	63	855	7.11
1997	322	7749	4.15
2002	694	10052	6.9
2007	609	11434	5.32
2012	7,700	25,800	29.8
2017	3,636	11,315	32.1

Sources: Karbea (2009), 19–20; Inter-Parliamentary Union (2017)

2007). Bouteflika created a commission in 2009 to prepare draft legislation for the Ministry of Justice. Women's rights groups lobbied political parties and their representatives in parliament, the trade unions, universities, and elsewhere. There were protests in May 2012 in which women actively participated. The government seized on this moment to introduce the constitutional Article 31, which requires that "The State shall work for the promotion of political rights of women by increasing their chances of access to representation in elected assemblies."

According to Nadia Aït Zaï, founder of the CIDDEF, the election results of 2012 were a major victory for women:

> The women's associations acted as pressure groups, and this pressure was effective. The information and documentation center of CIDDEF, for example, has been working systematically on this issue since 2003. We participated in a Maghreb-wide study on the subject of women in politics and pushed for changes at the highest level. The President has received our suggestions favorably. (Sabra 2012)

This was similar to other efforts for policy reform. Aït Zaï continued: "At CIDDEF, we work on advocacy: advocacy on inheritance, advocacy on the elimination of reservations and advocacy on the marriage of minors. We are doing research which allows us to tell the public authorities 'here is my research and here are my proposals.'" As a member of the Collectif Maghreb-Égalité 95, the CIDDEF had learned and borrowed from Morocco and Tunisia as well as sharing its own experiences with activists in the region.

Other Legal Reforms

In addition to the constitutional reforms and the quota laws, other women's rights reforms were also introduced in this period. In 2004, Bouteflika supported the passage of Article 341 of the Penal Code, which criminalizes sexual harassment (Kelly and Breslin 2010). Later, a 2016 law on violence against women was passed in a landmark piece of legislation. In 2005, Bouteflika also amended the 1970 Nationality Code in favor of women (UNHCR 2014). Under Article 6, Algerian women have the right to pass their nationality to children whose father is not Algerian. The original language stated that Algerian women had the right to pass down their nationality only if the non-Algerian father was unknown or was stateless (including Palestinians and Saharawis).

In 2014, Bouteflika presented parliament with legislation to establish a fund for widows in order to provide for their children. In 2016, he called for reconsideration of Algeria's reservations to the CEDAW in order to render existing legislation consistent with it (APS 2016). Current debates are focusing on reforming the Family Code and, as in Morocco and Tunisia, there are debates around reforming inheritance laws.

Cultural Wars

While these changes have been seen on the legal front, equally vigorous contestations are taking place on the cultural front. One woman blogger I interviewed talked about how bicycling became a daring act for a woman in her rural neighborhood. Not surprisingly, women swimming in bikinis have evoked considerable public response. Spontaneous protests continue on the beaches of Algeria. Women were finding it harder to wear a bikini at the beach when a few years earlier they might have been in the majority, especially in the Kabyle region (Agerholm 2017). Women in the thousands started going to the beaches in bikinis to protest the harassment they were confronting. In Annaba – also known as Hippo, the ancient home of the early Christian theologian St. Augustine of the fifth century – women organized protests against an online campaign in which men posted photographs of women in bikinis to mock and expose them for contradicting what they believed were Algerian religious values. A closed Facebook group of 3,200 members formed in response to push back against this form of religious conservatism. Women in bikinis swam together alongside others in one-piece swimsuits and burkinis in protest.

"In the past, women's bodies had no place in public spaces," said Yasmina Chouaki, an activist from Algeria's Amazigh-speaking Tharwa Fadhma N'Soumer feminist group. "When women were obliged to leave their private spheres, they were forced to entirely cover their bodies." She continued: "Today women and their bodies seek to win a place in all public spaces. On the beach, there is a kind of bargaining going on between the woman and society through clothing" (Ghanmi 2017).

For most swimmers, there is no issue. But as Algerian sociologist Yasmina Rahou has explained, "Algerian society is finding itself between the hammer of Islamist extremists who want beaches for women under the watch of police squads ... and the anvil of turning women's bodies into market products of some unbridled form of modernization by Westerners' wants" (Ghanmi 2017).

Another example of this kind of protest was mentioned in the Introduction. It involved a woman, Ryma, who was verbally assaulted and beaten for jogging before *iftar* (sunset meal) during the Ramadan fast in Algiers. A man said to her, "Pourquoi tu cours? Ta place est dans la cuisine à cette heure-ci!" (Why are you running? Your place is in the kitchen at this time of day!). After the assault, she went to the police to complain, but they asked her why she was jogging and did nothing to pursue her aggressor. Ryma then took to social media (Géopolis 2018). The next day, June 9, 2018, over 300 women and men of all ages, including members of some NGOs, came out to jog with her in protest (Rahmouni 2018). They carried slogans like, "Ma place est où je veux, pas dans la cuisine" (My place is where I want to be, not in the kitchen) at the Sablettes beach in Algiers to defend their right to occupy and run in a public space (*Algérie Monde Infos* 2018b). This incident occurred in a context where over 7,500 cases of violence against women were reported to the police during the first nine months of 2017 in Algeria. The lack of response from the police in this case and others does not bode well for the legislation that has been passed around violence against women.

Other such battles have been fought around women's clothing. In one case, on May 9, 2015, a law student was denied access to her exam room at the University of Algiers because her skirt, which was just above her knee, was deemed too short by the supervisor of the exam, who insisted that she buy some trousers to be able to take the exam. The university's vice-chancellor supported the supervisor's decision on the grounds that students must "dress decently" and described this as little more than a trivial incident. However, another woman launched a Facebook page entitled "Ma dignité n'est pas dans la longueur de ma jupe" (My dignity is not in the length of my skirt), on which men and women published photos of their legs in support of the student (Bouziri 2015).[4]

These kinds of protest infuse the daily life of Algerian society. They reflect an important part of the women's movement and an unwillingness, as during the Black Decade, to cave into intimidation and be forced out of the public space and into submission. Young women, particularly in urban areas, are social media savvy and, unlike the 1990s, today they are more aware of international trends. Young women are also more educated than in the past. The percentage of women in Algerian universities today exceeds that of men by 12 percent, with a female to male ratio of 1.46. Already in the high schools, girls are surpassing boys. In 2018, 65 percent of girls (compared with 35 percent of boys) graduated with a *baccalauréat*, the diploma that allows students to go to university (Benfodil 2018). This has resulted in boys going into the business world in greater numbers, while women pursue university degrees in larger numbers. "For girls, it is clear that studies have emerged as the royal road to a form of emancipation from the patriarchal shackles, an instrument of social liberation, in short," as one feminist put it (A16.10.11.16). The number of women graduates in STEM fields is almost the same as men (49 percent women, 51 percent men). Women made up 47 percent of all doctors in 2018 compared with 38 percent in 2007 (*La Croix* 2017). There are a relatively large number of women lawyers and doctors. Women are moving into areas

[4] www.facebook.com/groups/728956213879776/.

that were traditionally the exclusive domain of men, such as driving buses and taxicabs, pumping gas, and waiting tables.

Women are marrying later and starting families later. About 60 percent of women use contraception, that is 3 million women out of a total of 5.3 million married women of childbearing age. As a result, they have more time to gain an education. Young women travel, they watch films from abroad, and they congregate in groups in restaurants and coffeehouses, which in the past were the province of men. At the same time, younger women activists are less keen about legislative reforms and associational membership than older women activists, and instead focus more on daily battles to change the culture by fighting for the right to wear what they want to wear and to occupy spaces dominated by men.

I asked a leading feminist about what feminism meant in Algeria today. She replied:

> Feminism is international feminism, that is, equal rights. However, for the new generation it is also other things. The new generation is not very interested in associations [that fight for legislative reform]. Perhaps because there are many [women's rights] laws have been fought for and passed, they feel they do not have need to talk about them. But we still have major problems such as the Family Code and family relations, and discrimination still exists. Feminism for us is equal rights, equality of access to resources, equality of dignity, equality in everything. (A16.10.11.16)

Decline of Islamist Influence

One of the reasons young women may find it easier to push back against pressures to conform to Islamist ideals is that the Islamist political influence has declined considerably. Since 1990, the Algerian government has sought to keep extremist imams out of the mosques. It has carried out extensive de-radicalization programs to ensure that former extremists are integrated back into society. The government formed a national union of imams in 2013 to ensure that they were sheltered from imported religious ideas. There are also plans underway to start a program to train imams (Gustafsson 2016).

The former FIS leaders cannot run in elections and no Islamist parties have been successful in tapping into the base that the FIS once had when it won the 1991 election with 3 million votes. Since 2006, former FIS leader Ali Benhadj has delivered anti-governmental sermons in Algiers in violation of a ban on such sermons. Another FIS leader, Madani Mezrag, tried to form an Islamist party in 2015 but was prevented from doing so. For the most part, Salafism today is quiescent and divorced from politics. A strand of what is called "scientific Salafism" has expanded, but its rejection of politics means that it is tolerated by the regime (Fabiani 2017). In 2018 the Algerian authorities banned the *niqab*, the full-face veil, in the workplace. The *niqab* is not commonly worn by women in Algeria, but as it is found among Salafists, the ban was seen as a further attempt to suppress them.

In the 2012 legislative elections, the two main secular parties won the majority of seats, significantly increasing their presence in the assembly with 62 percent of the votes: the ruling FLN claimed 221 seats, while the military-backed National Rally for Democracy won seventy out of 462 seats. The Islamist Green Algeria Alliance[5] claimed only forty-seven or 6.2 percent of the seats. This came as something of a shock to the Islamists, who had expected to claim the majority of parliamentary seats (Ottaway 2012). They had coalesced to give some semblance of cohesion to the movement, which up until that time had been plagued by fragmentation. Inspired by the successes of the PJD in Morocco and Ennahda in Tunisia, they thought they could claim at least a quarter of the vote in the 2012 elections. Their predictions were wildly off as they were instead crushed. The Islamist Green Alliance accused the government of manipulating the results, which the government denied, calling upon the Alliance to provide evidence of election tampering. The Movement of Society for Peace (MSP) boycotted the 2014 presidential election because its leadership did not see any point in participating in an election whose outcome they felt was predetermined.

In 2017, the Islamist Green Alliance collapsed. The MSP, the largest of its three parties, formed an alliance with Front for Change but they won only 6 percent of the seats in that year's legislative election. The other Islamist parties, Ennahda and the

[5] The Alliance was a coalition of Islamist parties, the Movement of Society for Peace (MSP, formerly Hamas, which is close to the ideology of the Muslim Brotherhood), the Islamist Renaissance Movement (Ennahda), and the Movement for National Reform (Islah).

Justice and Development Party, formed their own alliance and won 3.7 percent of the seats. In contrast, the ruling secular FLN won 26 percent of the seats in parliament, followed by the National Rally for Democracy (15 percent), whose president is former Prime Minister Ahmed Ouyahia, who stepped down in March 2019. Today, the Islamist parties are regarded as irrelevant, divided, and lacking in consensus around clear objectives (Fabiani 2017, Ghanem-Yazbeck 2014). The Islamist leadership and demands associated with Islamists were all but absent in the 2019 anti-governmental uprisings, a measure of their weakened influence.

It should be pointed out that although religious extremists are in retreat, there have still been occasional incidents. Although the Salafis have little political influence, they have started attacking imams on a daily basis, trying to take control of their mosques in the countryside. The minister of religious affairs filed a complaint with the courts in July 2018 about one such attack in which two people died and dozens were injured, reminiscent of the attacks in the early 1990s. As before, women have been attacked in inflammatory speeches, as have Sufis and Ibadis (a small Muslim group found primarily in Oman, but also in East Africa, Tunisia, and Algeria). There was an escalation of such attacks and calls for the "supreme punishment" to infidels on the Internet in 2018 (Bekkat 2018).

Conclusions

Of the three Maghrebi countries, women's rights in Algeria have been the weakest, no doubt because the political space for women's mobilization has been much smaller. Women activists took advantage of the brief moments of political opening in the late 1980s, and then again after 2011, and in the 2019 uprisings to advance their rights. They were less successful in bringing about change during the critical juncture after independence, but in the post-civil conflict period they have made important gains with legislative changes (e.g., the 2005 Family Code and quota laws). President Bouteflika and the political elite supported the expansion of women's rights as a means of curtailing Islamists, but only after his second term in office. All Algerian leaders to one degree or another cut deals with the Islamists and overlooked their activities at different times because they felt they could not stay in power without the support of Islamists. This strategy became unsustainable after the

1991 elections with the rise of the FIS, as it became clear that the FLN would lose its grip on Algerian politics. Although Bouteflika signed the Charter with the Islamists in 2005, unlike his predecessors, he took aggressive measures to curtail the Islamist expansion and succeeded in crushing them politically. The expansion of women's rights was part of this military, negotiated, and legal strategy. It became crucial to gaining the votes and political support of women. The women's movement in Algeria was bolstered by its ties with the UN Women and other Maghrebian women's organizations.

The accommodations between Islamists and feminists are weaker than one finds in Morocco and Tunisia, no doubt because of the country's recent history of civil war involving the Islamists. Nevertheless, the new accommodations are evident in the quota laws and efforts around violence against women legislation. The Family Code reforms in 2005 indicated some level of compromise between secularists and Islamists, which suggested just how far the tide had turned on women's rights.

Although feminists and Islamist women's rights activists collaborate around particular issues, they have different ideological orientations. As one activist explained:

> There are also women who are Islamists who are deeply in favor of "equality." But we do not have the same definition of feminism. We function together and do not discuss the theoretical issues. We focus on our purpose, our objectives, which have to do with women, dignity, equality, and legal reform. (A16.10.11.16)

When I asked if she worked and collaborated with the Islamists she said yes and gave an example of one of the young lawyers in her secular feminist association.

Another activist explained the feminists' and Islamists' different positions regarding violence against women:

> Recently, they [the Islamists] began campaigning against violence [toward women]. And what is interesting to note is that even violence is not addressed directly as violence against women but as violence within the family. We talk about violence against children and women, but they talk about protecting the woman because she is a mother, not because she is a woman. The woman is constantly brought back to her status as a mother, as one who raises children, and so on. But not as a human being. (A25.10.9.16)

Algeria's experience with prolonged and deadly civil war had many of the same effects we have seen in other parts of Africa, where major conflict disrupted gender relations in ways that resulted in significantly higher rates of women's political representation than in countries that had not experienced civil war. After 2012, Algeria had the highest rates of female representation in the MENA region in its legislature and in local assemblies, and, after 2000, in the cabinet. It had the highest number of female generals (four) in the region as well. It also had made more legislative and constitutional reforms than many other countries in the Middle East. These changes in Algeria and in other postconflict countries are evident in the context of changing international norms regarding women's rights, as well as in places where one finds active women's movements and disruptions in gender relations (Tripp 2015).

Finally, the Algerian process of reform not only follows patterns evident in other Maghreb countries, it also is reflected in the symbolic struggles that were heightened as a result of the Black Decade. Women, women's bodies, and women's sexuality were focal points of the Black Decade as women became key targets of the Islamists. Women had been elevated as fighters in the struggle for independence from France and used this as leverage when they came together with feminists to demand an egalitarian Family Code in 1984. However, at that time the authorities were too intent on placating the Islamists, and the Code that was passed was a disaster in terms of women's rights. It was not until 2005 that one saw some egalitarian reforms in the Family Code, however problematic they appeared to the feminists. Legal reforms have continued, as have new cultural struggles over women's clothing and the right to occupy public space. These struggles culminated in the massive engagement and leadership of women in the 2019 uprising, where the demands for gender equality were incorporated into demands for democracy, freedom, dignity, and transparency.

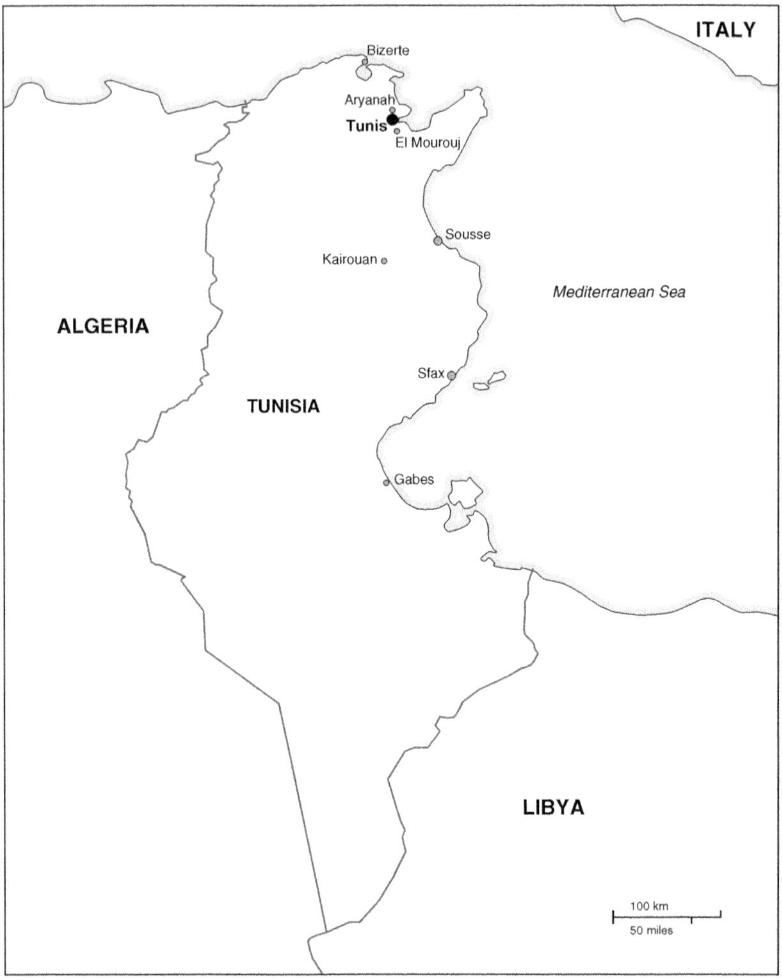

Map 6.1 Map of Tunisia
Credit: Eva Swantz

6 *Tunisia*

After the revolution in Tunisia in 2011, many political prisoners were released, including Salafis, who freely demonstrated with their black flags and verses from the Qur'an (Coelho n.d.). One such flag was placed on the top of the University of Manouba in 2012. In response, Khaoula Rachidi, a twenty-five-year-old student climbed to the top of the university building, removed the Salafi flag, and replaced it with the Tunisian flag, drawing national attention to her act of defiance. She was later honored in a ceremony by Minister of Interior Ali Laarayedh of the Islamist Ennahda Party, who called her "a symbol of the Tunisian woman" and praised her patriotism, suggesting that the Salafi flag represented a foreign influence external to Tunisia (Khalil 2015).

Another equally passionate female student at the same university did not receive such accolades. Emam, a twenty-one-year-old history student, had been expelled for wearing a *niqab* (نقاب, full-face veil), which is banned in educational institutions. "I did it for the sake of God. He will reward me in other ways," she lamented in an interview with journalist Ursula Lindsey (2013). She wore gloves and a brown and beige polyester *niqab* with a second transparent veil over her eyes. The University of Manouba had been the site of a long drawn-out controversy around the wearing of the *niqab* among students, resulting in a sit-in by Islamist students that led to a total shut down of the faculty for several months. The case ended in a court ruling in favor of the university policy of insisting that female students keep their faces uncovered. The dean, who had been at the center of the lawsuit, was convinced that students like this woman were not there to learn, but rather to spread their religious beliefs. Salafis had occasionally violently attacked individuals in institutions of higher learning in Tunisia, including professors. The largely secular faculty was deeply suspicious of them because they feared that the *niqab* would spread the religious influence further. As a professor of literature and media at Manouba, Nabil Charni, explained:

Table 6.1 *Tunisia's postindependence leaders*

President	Terms in office	Party affiliation	Prime ministers
Habib Bourguiba	1957–1959 1959–1964 1964–1969 1969–1974 1974–1987	Neo-Destour (1957–1964) Socialist Destourian Party (1964–1987)	Bahi Ladgham (1969–1970) SDP Hedi Amara Nuira (1970–1980) SDP Mohammed Mzali (1980–1986) SDP Rachid Sfar (1986–1987) SDP Zine El Abidine Ben Ali SDP (Oct.–Nov. 1987)
Zine El Abidine Ben Ali	1987–1989 1989–1994 1994–1999 1999–2004 2004–2009 2009–2011	Socialist Destourian Party (until 1988) Democratic Constitutional Rally (until 2011) Independent after 2011	Hédi Baccouche (1987–1989) SDP Hamed Karoui (1989–1999) SDP Mohamed Ghannouchi (1999–2011) SDP until 1988, DCR after 1988
Fouad Mebazaa	Jan.–Mar. 2011 Mar.–Dec. 2011	Democratic Constitutional Rally (Jan.–Mar. 2011) Non-partisan (Mar.–Dec. 2011)	Mohamed Ghannouchi (1999–2011) Independent Beji Caid Essebsi (Feb.–Dec. 2011) Independent
Moncef Marzouki	2011–2014	Congress for the Republic	Hamadi Jebali (2011–2013) Ennahda Ali Laarayedh (2013–2014) Ennahda Mehdi Jomaa (2014–2015) Independent
Beji Caid Essebsi	2014–	Nidaa Tounes	Habib Essid (2015–2016) Independent Youssef Chahed (2016–) Nidaa Tounes

> If it wasn't the symptom of a bigger project, I wouldn't really have a problem with the *niqab* in class. But there's a tendency to push things further, because it's not a matter of rights, but a matter of changing society, starting with state institutions. Behind the *niqab* there are other demands. One way or another it's an Islamization of the university. We can see it coming. (Lindsey 2013)

The university thus had become an ideological battleground and women's bodies and clothing were symbolically at the center of the dispute. The Arab Spring and its aftermath were replete with such symbolic battles. Often the Tunisian flag represented a central symbol of nationalism which women protesters carried and sometimes draped around themselves. Some researchers, like Andrea Khalil (2014), have discussed the ways in which women and women's bodies were used to advance a nationalist cause in Tunisia and elsewhere during the Arab Spring and in its aftermath. However, in the first vignette, it seems that the flag was used by women themselves as a symbolic protest of the threat Islamists posed to a nation that allows for diverse views, and one that allows women's autonomy and women's rights. Even the Personal Status Code (PSC) of 1956 became a symbol of this secular vision in the post-Arab Spring period, as women took to the streets to defend it, often holding placards with phrases like, "Ne touche pas à mes acquis" (Do not touch the rights I have won). The second vignette highlights how women's Islamist clothing similarly had its own significance of upholding a Salafi vision of society, as this chapter will explore more fully.

At each critical juncture, starting with Tunisia's independence in 1956, after Ben Ali ousted Bourguiba in 1987, and again after the Arab Spring when the Islamist party Ennahda called for a referendum on the PSC, women's rights became a source of contention. At each defining moment, women's organizations pressed for their rights. Feminists felt at each crisis that their gains were quite fragile and could be easily dispensed with (T24.3.0.18). Leading feminist and political leader Maya Jribi,[1] who was one of the fiercest opponents of

[1] Starting in 2006, Jribi led the Progressive Democratic Party (PDP), which merged into the Republican Party in 2012, until her resignation in 2017. She fought to raise awareness around women's rights and was one of the few women visible in leading demonstrations against Ben Ali's regime. Her party was elected to the Tunisian National Constituent Assembly and she was elected a member of the Council, where she played an important role in drafting the new Tunisian constitution. She died in 2018 (Al-Ghanmi 2018).

the Ben Ali regime, explained why moments of change were so dangerous for women:

> I consider extremism as the real threat. Being Islamist, thinking that Islam is a "solution," wearing the veil, and having an Islamist lifestyle are not threats ... But extremism in the name of Islam, the absence of democracy, and dictatorship really are threats. In every time of social change, women are the most threatened ... Women's achievements after the revolution are more threatened, but women are also more visible now ... But to me the most visible aspects of this period are women's activism and combativeness. (Marks 2013)

Mounira Charrad argues that there have been two waves of legislative reform. The first, which occurred after Bourguiba took over, had to do with the legal construction of gender roles within the family. The second wave followed Ben Ali's takeover in 1987 and was focused on the conditions of Tunisian citizenship (Charrad 2011). A third wave of legislative and constitutional reform following the Arab Spring filled in the gaps within the projects of the first two waves.

This chapter looks at these three waves of legislative reform to show how women participated in them. It reveals how Tunisia's authoritarian leaders used women's rights as a means of creating an international image of the country as a modernizer and at the same time to isolate Islamists, particularly extremists. The chapter describes the conflictual nature of the relationship between the secularists/feminists and Islamists and how it has evolved. It shows how Ennahda has changed its position in order to maintain credibility and in response to pushback from women's organizations and internal disputes.

Habib Bourguiba and Women's Rights

Historically, Tunisia has been regarded as the country that made the greatest advances for women in the MENA region (Charrad 2001, 2011). Habib Bourguiba, the country's first president (1956–1987), famously attempted to secularize and modernize Tunisia, using women's rights as a way to drive a wedge between the state and the Islamists, both of whom fought to win women's loyalty. He created a unified legal system and adopted some of the most far-reaching women's rights reforms. When he came to power, he found a tribal system made up of villages that lived traditionally. He demolished this structure and introduced the PSC in 1956, which was highly revolutionary for that time (T2.3.16.17).

The PSC determined that family structures should be based on the legal equality of men and women. Drawing on liberal interpretations of Islam, Bourguiba abolished polygamy and legalized divorce for both men and women, thus abolishing the practice of *khul'*, found elsewhere in the region, which allowed women to divorce their husbands by returning their dowry. Bourguiba set a legal age for marriage and granted women the right to work and to obtain an education. Women gained the right to vote and run for office in 1957 with independence. The 1959 constitution further enshrined these rights and other laws expanded women's rights. Women gained the right to contraception in 1961. As a point of comparison, in the United States the Supreme Court gave married couples the right to use birth control in 1965, but it was not until 1972 that birth control was legalized for all citizens irrespective of marital status. Tunisian women gained the right to abortion in 1973, the same year as their counterparts in the United States. Tunisian family planning was twenty years ahead of Algeria and Morocco and the rest of the Middle East. Modern contraception was introduced in Algeria as late as the 1980s. Bourguiba also promoted women's education. All of these reforms had implications for women's empowerment.

Bourguiba is often given sole credit for the early introduction of women's rights in Tunisia and there is a sentiment that he handed rights to women "on a platter." Activists are quick to point out that these changes were the result of pressures from women's rights activists and other reformists of the day (T24.3.00.17, T23.3.00.17). Since the end of the nineteenth century, there had been a reformist movement in Tunisia composed mainly of men who had asked for the right for women to be educated so that they might play a better role as educators within their families. One of these reformists was Tahar Al Haddad, who was a feminist. In 1930, he published a book *Our Women in Islamic Law and Society*, which called for the emancipation of women (Labidi 1998). Al Haddad drew on Islamic thought, Islamic law, and the Qur'an to argue that women should be equal to men even in terms of inheritance, drawing on the Quranic principle of *al-kiyas*. Even though he had the support of many intellectuals, poets, and journalists, he was nevertheless shunned by the religious establishment. Bourguiba, who was young when Al Haddad was writing, had not supported his ideas at the time, although his views changed later on.

A nascent women's movement took inspiration from Egyptian women like Huda Sha'arawi, who was a feminist, nationalist, and founder of the Egyptian Feminist Union in 1923. Sha'arawi visited Tunis and spoke at a Berrachik House of Culture event that Bourguiba attended. The future president did not really appreciate Tunisian women talking about unveiling at the time because when he was a young student, he had considered the veil a symbol of Tunisian identity in the face of colonization and thought that it was not necessary for women to get rid of it. His views gradually evolved from that time. The Union nationale de femmes tunisiennes (UNFT, National Women's Union of Tunisia) was formed in 1956 by members of the Neo-Destour Party and Bourguiba seized on this organization, strengthened it, and made it an instrument of the state in his efforts to monopolize the struggle for women's rights. He did not allow associations to mobilize independently, which posed serious problems for women's organizations (T7.3.28.17). Many women had sought a larger role in leadership in the postindependence period. As in Algeria, they had participated in the anti-colonial movement and they strongly resented the fact that they were ignored after independence when it came to granting political positions (Goulding 2011).

Bourguiba created several state-sponsored institutions to promote state feminism in addition to the UNFT, including a research center called the Centre de recherche, d'études, de documentation et d'information sur la femme (CREDIF, The Center for Research, Studies, Documentation, and Information About Women), and a ministry for women (Voorhoeven 2013). A few non-state women's groups slowly emerged. But independent women's organizations had great difficulty operating under Bourguiba. They required permission to function and experienced their share of violence, arrests, convictions, and imprisonment. They also had difficulty accessing donor funds. When they planned events or activities, the police harassed them and forbade them from organizing some events (T1.3.16.17).

Nevertheless, some organizations managed to operate within these constraints. Club Tahar El Haddad d'études de la condition de la femme (CECF, Tahar El Haddad Club for the Study of Women's Status) was a cultural organization formed in 1978 by students to study women's conditions. It gradually incorporated women academics, lawyers, journalists, and other professionals and eventually they formed a group called "The daughters of Tahar al Haddad." The Women at Work Commission, otherwise known as the women's section of the main trade union, the Union générale de travailleurs tunisiens (General Union of Tunisian Workers) was formed in 1983 (Charrad 2011).

In spite of his earlier reticence regarding women's rights, Bourguiba may have taken the bold move of promulgating the PSC because of political competition. His main goal was to undercut religious courts and leaders as well as tribal leaders and to create a unified legal system, thereby strengthening a secular state with complete authority. This was a state-building ploy, but it had other purposes.

Bourguiba adopted the PSC as a key element of his efforts to modernize society and the state. The family was reduced to the nuclear family. He saw the modernization of the family as fundamental to the modernization of the state, which is why the PSC was adopted three years prior to the constitution in 1959, to lay the groundwork for his vision of the state. No doubt he was also motivated by a desire to give recognition to women's role in the independence movement, even though he failed to give them political positions, and to ensure women's votes. He established a model that stood out among Arab, African, and Mediterranean countries at the time. He wanted to make Tunisia an example to follow in the Arab region (T7.3.28.17).

As mentioned in Chapter 3, the PSC most notably abolished polygamy, the practice of guardianship, and unilateral repudiation, and it set the legal age of marriage at twenty for men and seventeen for women. The dowry became largely symbolic. The family law was based on the mutual respect and cooperation of the couple rather than the submission of the woman to the man. With time, the PSC was amended to further elaborate on the nature of the cooperation of the husband and wife in managing the affairs of the family (Article 23). The married couple could hold joint property, and women were not obligated to contribute monetarily to the maintenance of the family. In the event of the death of one spouse, the remaining parent would take custody of the children (Grami 2008).

Thus, women's rights often became associated with a top-down strategy that became part of a modernist developmental project typical of many first-generation postindependence African leaders. This somewhat divisive legacy of women's rights being associated with patriarchal authoritarianism was hard to shake later on when independent organizations were established. The association of state feminism with women's issues forced independent women's associations that emerged later on to distance themselves from the state (Moghadam 2017).

At the time, Bourguiba relied on his mouthpiece, the UNFT, to promote his policies. He insulted religious women by calling the veil a "miserable rag" and a "dreadful shroud" (Bessis 1999, 2). By the same token, he was deaf to the demands of secular feminists, who had challenged Bourguiba from the outset. He gave lip service to the idea of equality, while the feminists talked about discrimination. He talked about the achievements of women in the family, while feminists argued that the husband remained head of the family in the PSC, which meant women did not have equal rights in the family or in matters of guardianship and custody. They also highlighted the inequality of inheritance laws. Even the constitution did not embody equality. The Convention on the Elimination of All Forms of Discrimination Against Women (CEDAW) was ratified, but with reservations.

In response to Islamist protests in the late 1970s, Bourguiba launched a repressive campaign against those wearing the veil and began to prevent the further expansion of religious movements (Larif Béatrix 1991). In September 1981, the regime enacted Circular 108, which prohibited those wearing "sectarian dress" (i.e., الحجاب, the *hijab* or veil) from public administration and educational institutions. Veiled women lost out on educational and professional opportunities, affecting women from all social, professional, and educational backgrounds. Although the circular was aimed at curtailing Islamists, the policy ended up also affecting women who had no connection to Islamist movements and wore the veil primarily for personal and cultural reasons (El Gantri 2016). Women shouldered the full weight of religious symbolism, having to decide whether or not they were going to veil and then bear the consequences of their decision.

In this period, the Islamists were deeply unhappy with what they perceived as the secularization of Tunisian society. For this reason, it was in Tunisia that the Islamists first became politically active in the Maghreb. They saw the measures taken under Bourguiba and, in particular, the PSC as a symbol of a broad attack on Islam because it challenged Islamic family law, which was seen as the last bastion of the *shari'a* (Islamic law) in the modern Arab state (Brand 1998). Because Islamists saw the expansion of women's rights as a threat to their values and way of life, women often became the first line of defense of secularism, but also the first victims of Islamist challenges to the state as they began to assert their influence (Brand 1998, 181).

As time wore on, Bourguiba caved in to pressure from Islamists, perhaps feeling that his political future could be in jeopardy. In a 1973 circular he prohibited the registration of marriages between Muslims and non-Muslims. He backed away from his efforts to change the inheritance laws in 1974 and from his support for women entering the workforce. By the 1980s, any efforts to advance women's rights had become paralyzed by the rise of the Islamist influence. The Islamist movements grew in the region in the 1980s and the Maghrebi governments tried to stem the opposition by liberalizing their political systems. Bourguiba attempted to repress the Islamic Tendency Movement (Mouvement de la tendance islamique, MTI) leaders, but he was instead removed from office by Ben Ali's constitutional coup.

Ben Ali and Women's Rights

When Zine El Abidine Ben Ali took over from Bourguiba in a coup d'état in 1987, this was another moment of uncertainty for women as they were being warned that the end of the Bourguiba era marked the end of women's rights. At the start of his rule, Ben Ali moved cautiously in attempting to integrate Islamists into the political process. Feminists and progressives waited anxiously to find out what the orientation of the new government would be with regard to the PSC. They reminded Ben Ali of the absolute necessity of preserving the gains of women and the PSC. Women activists organized petitions and held street marches. On the anniversary of the independence of the country, March 20, 1988, the president gave a speech in which he finally confirmed that there would be no revision of the PSC (T24.3.00.16). Later, at an event at the palace of Carthage on August 13, 1989, Ben Ali officially recognized the women who had played a role in the independence movement between 1930 and 1955, although he did not make the status of women a priority (Bessis 1999, Labidi 1998).

After 1987, more space emerged for independent women's organizations to mobilize, reversing the government policy of abolishing them and elevating state-sponsored organizations in their place (Brand 1998, Charrad 2011). Nevertheless, if organizations did not support the government agenda, their members found themselves attacked, harassed, imprisoned, and even tortured. Women parliamentarians, leaders, and academics were sent abroad to defend the regime against accusations of human rights abuses and authoritarianism (Bessis 1999, Lindsey 2017). Thus, women's rights appeared to be part of a "democratic" gloss to an autocratic regime which supported women's rights only when it served its interests. Some call this "state feminism," but it appears too generous a term for a regime that divided and repressed women of all persuasions.

At the start of Ben Ali's rule, the Islamists were released from prison. Ben Ali made some initial concessions to the MTI but later clamped down on its successor, Harakat Ennahda (Renaissance Movement), particularly after a number of violent incidents in which its members were implicated. In the 1989 legislative elections, Ennahda won 30 percent of the seats (marked as independents), but Ben Ali manipulated the outcome and as a result the party was assigned only 12 percent of the votes. This was followed by increased repression of Ennahda leaders, forcing its head, Rached Ghannouchi, to flee into exile in the United Kingdom. Tens of thousands of Islamists were imprisoned or forced into exile as Ennahda was banned between 1992 and 2011 (Ayari 2015). Ben Ali justified his repression on the grounds that Ennahda did not support women's rights (Coleman 2011). He was particularly tough on women who veiled.

Islamist women continued to forge ties quietly among themselves in those years, which explains why Ennahda was able to reemerge so quickly after the Revolution. They supported one another and maintained lines of communication at a time when the male members of Ennahda had their phones tapped, were imprisoned, and were prevented from gathering. Many of the Ennahda women found it difficult to find employment or access educational institutions because they were veiled (Gray 2012). Thousands of women later lodged complaints with the Truth and Dignity Commission to describe their experiences of sexual violence, rape, torture, and cruelty. They suffered waterboarding, electrocution, and beatings, provoking miscarriages and internal injuries. However, women experienced the additional stigma of rape and sexual assault, which they suffered to a greater extent than men (Gall 2015). Nisa' Tounsiat (نساء تونسيات, Tunisian Women), an

NGO that helps female torture victims, documented these cases, which were mainly from the Islamist opposition.

After Ben Ali broke with the Islamists during 1990–1991, he started promoting women's rights. Ben Ali established the Secretariat of State for Women and Family in 1992, which shortly thereafter became the Ministry of Women's Affairs, the Family and Children, and the Elderly (MAFFEPA). Its job was to coordinate and develop policies relating to women. The ministry had branches in all seven of Tunisia's districts, to encourage women to participate in public and economic life (Norbakk 2016). Ben Ali also enlisted his wife, Leila Ben Ali, in his strategy of promoting women's rights. The first lady often spoke internationally on behalf of Tunisian women, and became president of the Arab Women's Organization. She was active in international NGOs like the human rights organization El Karama. She was often a focal point of anger directed at the regime because of her excesses and those of President Ben Ali with respect to corruption, money laundering, and embezzlement.

Ben Ali's promotion of women's rights was woven into his new discourse on modernity. The idea of Tunisia as a moderate country with a multi-faith identity was revived and women turned out to be a cornerstone of this new orientation (Bessis 1999). In a speech delivered on August 13, 1992, Ben Ali laid out his views on women's rights and linked his agenda to that of Bourguiba's ideals of modernity. He linked his takeover in 1987 to the proclamation of the Republic and the promulgation of the PSC as pivotal moments in Tunisia's history: "The rehabilitation of women, the recognition of their legacy and the consecration of their rights in the context of religious and civil values to which our people are proud to adhere" is an integral part of this glorious legacy, he stated.[2] The nod to Islam in his speech is evocative of French *laïcité* (secularism) or the pre-Erdogan Turkish view that valued religion but limited it to the private realm. Thus, the development of state institutions was delinked from the religious realm (Hawkins 2011). In his speech, Ben Ali focused on modernity, the transition from the extended to the nuclear family, and the need to pass laws. He called on women to participate in the construction of modernity and to assume the highest positions "within the state and society." He said that he expected women to show that they were

[2] www.wikiwand.com/en/Code_of_Personal_Status_in_Tunisia.

worthy of his “solicitude” by participating in all areas of life and activity. He emphasized that they were not to transgress the limits of this emancipation and that they were to become full participants in his anti-Islamist crusade (Bessis 1999). Tunisia no longer stood out in the region as an example of modernity and so he drew on women as one area where he could show that Tunisia was exemplary.

The Ben Ali government thus responded to renewed Islamist challenges by appealing to women and by promoting women as leaders. Ben Ali earmarked 25 percent of his Democratic Constitutional Party (Rassemblement constitutionnel démocratique) seats to women in the 2004 elections and 30 percent in the 2007 election. However, when the party was disbanded in 2011 after the Arab Spring, the quotas disappeared with the party.

Part of Ben Ali’s strategy to combat the growth of Islamist influences was to pass women’s rights legislation (Murphy 2003, 193). The Civil Code provided for equality in work-related matters for the first time (1993). After 2000, women no longer needed their husband’s permission in order to accept work. Ben Ali’s legislative strategy included passing a 1993 law that required the consent of the mother for the marriage of a minor girl, a nationality law of 2010 that allowed women to pass their nationality to their children, as well as rules concerning the custody of children. The PSC had required that the husband pay alimony to the wife in the event of a divorce. Because of a lack of implementation, Ben Ali created a state fund to ensure that divorced women and their children received support (1993). The minimum age for marriage had been fifteen for girls and seventeen for boys in 2007. It was raised to eighteen for both sexes. A 2008 law permitted divorced mothers who had child custody to stay in the marital home, even if it belonged to the father. Only a judge could grant a divorce. A severe penalty was to be imposed for domestic violence and sexual harassment. Women gained the right to manage household finances.

In the 1990s, Ben Ali not only launched a campaign against Islamist leaders but also against Islamist women militants, many of whom were imprisoned for long periods. In response, Ben Ali imprisoned and exiled numerous Islamist leaders, justifying his repression on the grounds that they did not support women’s rights (Coleman 2011). In 2006, Ben Ali reinforced Bourguiba’s 1981 decree prohibiting women from wearing Islamic headscarves in public places because veiled women were seen as political opponents of the regime. They were often treated as second-class citizens as a result. The police started stopping women in the streets and asking them to remove their headscarves. Notably, veiling had increased in Tunisia with the rise in popularity of Arab satellite channels.

As in other parts of the Maghreb, studies have found that for most Tunisian women themselves, veiling was above all an individual choice. Some did so in the face of opposition from parents who felt it was linked to the rise of the Islamists. For other women, assaults on public transport, in the street, at the university, and elsewhere accounted for this need for protection. The respectability granted by the veil was also important to some women. They believed themselves to be valued for their moral, spiritual, and intellectual qualities and not for their physique. As one sixteen-year-old high school student put it, "Before I did not speak with the boys of my class, but, since my veil, I find it easier to communicate. I feel that they respect me and that they cannot have unhealthy thoughts about me" (Ben Salem 2010).

While Ben Ali and Bourguiba had opposed veiling as a political strategy to curb the spread of Islamic extremism, feminists had their own objections and reasoning. As one Tunisian feminist explained in an interview:

> I am against it as a feminist because for me any form of veil is not a manifestation of faith, it is a sign of oppression and submission. We feminists, we say we are against the veil but we are not against veiled women because there are plenty of reasons why they wear the veil . . . I am not for the prohibition of the veil in the street, because it is not possible to ban the veil in the street. I am against the wearing of the veil at school and in administrative [buildings]. I do not like the burkinis but I think it's a very bad policy to ban them. (T2.3.16.17)

There are different feminist positions on the veil. Some argue that veiling is simply a statement about one's faith, while others see it as a phenomenon related to the political rise of the Islamists. The differences regarding the symbolic nature of the veil reveal one of the major casualties of the Ben Ali period, in which the president exacerbated fissures between the Islamist and secular women. Ennahda leaders like Meherzia Labidi, who was elected vice president of the Constituent Assembly, said that some members of the Tunisian elite didn't know much about their struggles and they just decided to write them off. She said that the Tunisian elite said to themselves, "okay, these women were victims – they couldn't finish their studies, they couldn't work.

They are not relevant. We can forget about them" (Marks 2013). Islamist women leaders felt that they had been excluded and that the post-revolution status quo was not sufficiently pluralistic to encompass Islamist perspectives. Labidi added:

> I will never claim to be the symbol of Tunisian women because we made a revolution against having one specific symbol and model – we are diverse, and we are strong. I was exiled for twenty-five years in France because Tunisia stood against the concept of plurality – true social and political plurality. I am one face in Tunisia, one of many others. But I do ask for my due place, and for respect as being one part of this mosaic. (Marks 2013)

Ben Ali attempted to present an image of openness when he took over in 1987. More space emerged for independent women's movements to exist legally, reversing the government policy of abolishing all independent women's associations and elevating state-sponsored organizations in their place. It was during this period that associations like Association des femmes tunisiennes pour la recherche sur le développement (AFTURD, the Association of Tunisian Women for Research and Development) and Association tunisienne des femmes démocrates (ATFD, the Tunisian Association of Democratic Women), were created and gained legal recognition in 1989. The Ligue tunisienne des droits de l'homme (LTDH, Tunisian League for Human Rights) had been legally recognized in 1977 and a women's commission of the LTDH was formed in 1985. They were among the few real independent women's organizations until 2011. However, organizations like the ATFD found it was almost impossible to work during this period because they were advocating for women's equal status with men. Every time they tried to organize an event, they were sabotaged (T4.3.23.17). Thus, the main women's associations during Ben Ali's rule were co-opted organizations.

Like Bourguiba, Ben Ali used women's rights and literacy to project an image of modernity and democracy. As Sophie Bessis explained, "Tunisian modernist circles have understood that the condition of women was fundamental to the project of modernizing society" (T2.3.16.17).

However, it was also a way to hide the repression of women, particularly Islamist women and supporters of the Ennahda movement, as well as those belonging to the Tunisian Workers Communist Party. Both Islamists and feminists were interrogated, intimidated, and threatened with prosecution and rape at police stations and the Ministry of Interior (Labidi 2010). Women journalists, academics, lawyers, doctors, and students were harassed for signing petitions or holding meetings with associations. As such, women's rights were part of a democratic gloss over an autocratic regime, which supported women's rights only when it served its interests. The Ben Ali regime promoted women's rights to avoid talking about its human rights abuses.

Ben Ali's adoption of quotas in his own party was widely regarded as part of a long history of attempts to secularize Tunisia, in part through the advancement of women's rights. His paternalism and top-down autocratic imposition of rights meant that after he was deposed in 2011, women activists sought to clarify that they were not supporters of Ben Ali, but rather had been targeted by his regime in the same way as other Islamist and civil society actors. The few who had participated in the government of Ben Ali were tainted by that affiliation and sidelined. The Union nationale de la femme tunisienne, which had been headed by the president's wife, fell into disarray when she left the country after the ousting of her husband (Goulding 2011).

The Arab Spring

Women were active participants in the Arab Spring that had its beginning in December 2010 and led to the downfall of President Ben Ali in January 2011 after twenty-three years in power. During the revolution women became a visible presence. The real force behind the revolution were the bloggers, rappers, artists, women's rights activists, trade unionists, and students. Women participated *en masse* in demonstrations, using social media and the news media. The Arab Spring brought together a large number of issues, including nationalism, corruption, unemployment, and women's rights. But this all changed with the growing presence of Islamists after the revolution. Ennahda did not participate in the revolution but became more visible in its aftermath.

Ben Ali was ousted in the Arab Spring in 2011 and soon after his departure, Ennahda leader Rached Ghannouchi returned to Tunisia from twenty-two years of exile in Britain and regalvanized the Ennahda movement as a moderate democratic party. A series of prime ministers held power in quick succession and a Troika government was formed after the 2011 Constituent Assembly election, made up of an alliance between three parties, the Islamist Ennahda Party, the social democratic party Ettakatol, and the secular left party Congress for the Republic.

In the Ben Ali period, Rached Ghannouchi had testified that neither he nor his party would endorse any changes to the PSC. As soon as Ben Ali left office, feminists felt that the Islamists were trying to question women's rights. Women demonstrated on January 29, 2011, the eve of Ghannouchi's return to Tunis from exile. Even the first demonstrations organized by women's rights organizations during the Arab Spring were attacked by Islamists who tried to force protestors to go home. The Islamists wanted to hold a referendum on the rights of women, which the feminists felt would jeopardize the progress achieved with the PSC. They believed the Islamists wanted to undermine the PSC and Tunisia's obligation to its international treaties and conventions, and to question the status of the Tunisian woman, arguing that it was complementary to that of the man. Complementarity was a view that claimed equality for men and women, but each in their own spheres of competence, thus relegating women to the home and to traditional roles (T1.3.16.17, T4.3.23.17).

Ennahda's spokesperson Samir Dilou tried to reassure nervous voters, saying, "We are not an Islamist party, we are an Islamic party that also gets its bearing from the principles of the Qur'an" (Ayari 2015). Ennahda won the largest proportion of votes in the 2011 election and formed a government. However, they never fully gained the trust of the secularists, who accused them of being Janus-faced. They gave one face of moderation to the media and displayed another more radical face to other less educated constituencies to whom they called for *jihad* and the imposition of *shari'a* law. They had close ties to the Salafi jihadist group Ansar Al Shari'a, which was connected to Al Qaeda. After the revolution, there were a number of incidents in which Salafis attacked art exhibitions, alcohol vendors, and Sufi shrines. They occupied a university campus where there was a dispute over wearing the *niqab* in class. Despite Ghannouchi's efforts to pacify secularists, their suspicions were confirmed when a secret recording of him was made public in 2012, in which he was seen telling Salafi leaders that they needed to take a long-term approach because the secularists were in control of the economy, the media, and administration, and perhaps even the army and police (Ayari 2015).

Women activists took to the streets frequently between February 2011 and the adoption of the new constitution in January 2014. As one woman explained, "The first women's demonstration was in 2011 and we wanted to say to the Islamists: 'Be careful, we are here!' Because we understood that there was a return of extremists and the Muslim Brotherhood. It is therefore Tunisian women who sounded the alarm" (T21.3.20.17).

A civil society began to emerge after 2011 and there was a proliferation of independent women's organizations, like the Association of Tunisian Women Lawyers, formed in 2011 to improve women's legal status, as well as Nisa' Tounsyat (the Association of Tunisian Women), which was formed in the same year to represent the interests of Muslim Tunisian women, along with the Association des femmes nahdaouis (Association of Ennahda Women) (Honwana 2013).

Feminists, who wanted to improve the PSC, worried that Ennahda was going to question women's gains and say that it was necessary to revise the PSC (T4.3.23.17). Until 2011, although there had been no significant conflict between Islamists and women's rights activists in Tunisia, there had been tensions. But with the political rise of Ennahda, feminists feared that they would be the ones attacked first.

When two leftist politicians were killed by Islamists in 2013, this created a political crisis in which Ennahda was forced to step down. A quartet coalition government involving the trade union federation the Tunisian General Labour Union (UGTT), along with The Tunisian Union for Industry, Business, and Handicrafts (UTICA), the Tunisian League for Human Rights, and the Bar Association, eased the way for the Ennahda government to step down, placing the government in the hands of a technocrat, and allowing a neutral cabinet to oversee new elections, which were held in 2014. The secular Nidaa Tounes Party won the 2014 elections and formed a coalition government with Ennahda, who had not put forward their own presidential candidates but supported the Nidaa Tounes candidate, Beji Caid Essebsi, who became president.

Constitutional Debates

One of the most important outcomes of the Arab Spring for women was the embedding of women's rights in the constitution. Women leaders were convinced that without women's rights, little would have come of the Arab Spring in Tunisia. One woman activist who had sat on the

Constitutional Council of Tunisia explained: "If the revolution succeeds, it will be thanks to women, not to men. This is because we are all motivated. The protests in the Constituent Assembly came mainly from women because women were threatened in every way" (T18.3.29.17).

Women took to the streets once again on August 13, 2013, the day on which the PSC had been promulgated fifty-five years earlier, along with tens of thousands of others. They advocated women's rights and denounced Ennahda. "Our joy will be complete only with the departure of this government and the ANC [Assemblée nationale constituante tunisienne or National Constituent Assembly] and the Tunisian woman will be at the forefront of militancy," Besma Khalfaoui told the demonstrators. Khalfaoui was the widow of Chokri Belaid, one of the two politicians murdered in February 2013. Ennahda had not expected such a pushback (T2.3.16.17).

Women had seen what had happened in Algeria during the Black Decade and in countries like Sudan, Iran, and Afghanistan, where Islamists had called for a reversal of women's rights almost immediately after assuming power. Women activists were determined this would not happen in Tunisia. The political space had opened up and Islamists had taken advantage of it. Women's rights organizations felt that the rise of the Islamists threatened the gains of overthrowing a dictator. Bearded men began to appear in public spaces and large numbers of women suddenly emerged wearing the *niqab* as the Salafis grew in influence. Women's rights activists were concerned that the secularists would lose ground as young people were being influenced by the religious media. As one activist put it, "I felt that there was a problem. We had started wondering why in Tunisia girls were veiled regardless of the revolution." She said the Tunisian revolution was not religious but rather it was about republicanism, modernity, secular freedom, liberty, equality between the sexes, and justice. At no time was there any reference to the Qur'an during this revolution (T20.3.30.17). Another feminist activist explained that "After the Arab Spring women's rights were on the line once again. Ennahda was the most popular political party and to many women it seemed like they were going backward instead of going forward" (T18.3.29.17).

Women's rights activists plunged into activities to reform the constitution. They sought to preserve the historic gains of the PSC and used them to demand more rights for women. Women won 27 percent of the seats in the National Constituent Assembly and of those, 69 percent belonged to Ennahda. Women's rights activists participated in and lobbied the Constituent Assembly and political parties. They prepared texts for transmission to the deputies and strategized with them. Women marched against key clauses in the draft constitution, especially the complementarity clause. They followed the evolution of the constitution very closely (T1.3.16.17).

Women and Leadership, the ATFD, AFTURD, LTDH, and several other organizations formed part of a broader coalition of women's organizations and political parties including the center-left secular party El Massar (Democratic Social Path), the Communist Party, and other progressives and democrats. They sought to lobby for changes and to educate young people (twenty- to thirty-year-olds) because two-thirds of the youth had not voted in the 2011 elections. Women activists went to universities and ran workshops explaining in simple terms what is a constitution, a political regime, their rights and civic duties, and other basic civic concepts (Fatoorehchi 2013).

The struggle over the 2014 Tunisian constitution following the revolution of 2011 highlights the tensions between Islamists and secularists over the notion of complementarity and other concerns. The 2014 constitution, which includes gender-sensitive language, ended up being the most progressive for women's rights in the region. But this outcome was not apparent at the outset of the deliberations.

Ennahda leader Meherzia Labidi was appointed first vice president of the assembly, and three out of the seven members of the bureau supporting the president of the assembly were also women. A woman, Farida Laabidi of Ennahda, was president of the committee in charge of sensitive rights and freedoms, which dealt with women's rights. In these debates two issues related to gender became contentious. Ennahda dominated the assembly numerically and tensions between Islamists and secularists ran deep, the former being put on the defensive around questions of the principle of equality.

The most controversial clause was advanced by Ennahda, stating that the "woman is the complement of man." This complementarity clause, in a country with a long history of gender equality and secularist influences, was regarded as a conservative Islamist influence. The secularists feared it would dramatically set back women's rights (T18.3.29.17, T2.3.16.17). Ennahda's also proposed a change that stated: "The State guarantees the protection of women's rights and the promotion of their gains, as a real partner of men in the mission of the homeland building, and the roles of both should complement each other within the household" (McNeill 2012). Women would be relegated to the domestic sphere and men to the public sphere (T2.3.16.17). Thousands of women protested this clause through demonstrations in the streets of Tunis in August 2012, with the slogan "Equality all the way – no complementarity in the constitution." Ennahda felt that the idea of *mukammil* (مكمل, or complementarity) valued women's roles as wives and mothers, while the secularists and feminists felt that it threatened the achievements of women, reinforcing a patriarchal system that gave power to men and denied women their full citizenship and rights, making them dependents of men. They protested the clause but they also held events to discuss the meanings and the costs and benefits of complementarity and equality. As one feminist activist put it, in the view of Ennahda:

> The woman completes the man but is not equal to the man. The woman is not taken as an independent individual who has obligations ... has rights. The woman exists only through her family, through her children and her husband. Outside the family, she does not exist. There are no rights for single mothers, for example. The woman as such is neglected. (T22.3.15.17)

Another women's rights activist explained that women's opposition to complementarity "does not mean that we are not Muslims. We are all Muslims. I made the pilgrimage to Mecca. But ... I do not see why I should let a man without education interpret the Qur'an for me ... I understand literary Arabic, and so I want to be left to interpret the Qur'an" (Fatoorehchi 2013). In the end, the complementarity clause was removed.

In response to the pushback against complementarity, Prime Minister Ali Laarayedh of Ennahda made a speech in which he announced that he was giving up on complementarity and that equality would remain in the constitution (T1.3.16.17). The complementarity clause was replaced with a strong commitment on the part of the state to protecting women's rights in Article 46:

> The state commits to protect women's accrued rights and work to strengthen and develop those rights. The state guarantees the equality of opportunities between women and men to have access to all levels of responsibility in all domains. The state works to attain parity between women and men in elected

Assemblies. The state shall take all necessary measures in order to eradicate violence against women. (Constitute Project 2014)

Feminist activists won another major victory when they were able to introduce Article 21, which states that "all male and female citizens are equal in rights and duties." They also were able to obtain a non-discrimination clause (Article 21): "All citizens, male and female ... are equal before the law without any discrimination" (Constitute Project 2014). However, women's rights organizations would have liked to see more specificity in Article 21, ensuring the principle of equality and adding the phrase "in all its dimensions." They were concerned that equality would not be extended to the home without such a clause. Women lawyers were also concerned that the idea that "equality before the law" only ensured equality before a judge and not equality in the law (Auffray 2014).

Some of the women in Ennahda who helped draft the constitution were of two minds on some of the clauses, according to the feminists on the committee. They wanted the equality clause but they also wanted to leave the inheritance laws untouched. Thus, they helped draft Article 46, but did so in a way that left out language about total equality because for them the issue of inheritance was a red line they could not cross. They were keen to ensure that the words "equality in inheritance" not be stated explicitly.

Another conflict emerged over a clause having to do with the state protecting the gains made by women. Feminists felt this could include gains made by Islamists. This controversy resulted in compromise language: "The state works to attain parity between women and men in elected Assemblies" and the provision that "The State engages in protecting achievements in the field of women's rights and in reinforcing them."

Ennahda had never expressed support for the PSC although at times their leaders said they would not touch it. Recognizing that there was broad support in Tunisia, not only among women but also among political parties and human rights organizations and a good part of society who thought that they should absolutely not touch the rights of women, they backed down as a tactical move (T24.3.00.17).

The Islamists had wanted to include a reference to the "values of Islam" and the "respect for the sacred" in the preamble of the constitution. Women's rights activists were concerned that if the term "sacred" was not defined, they could be opening themselves up to a reversal of the PSC and laws regarding adoption, abortion, and polygamy that were quite advanced in Tunisia. In place of these clauses, a compromise was reached so that the reference to the sacred was removed from the preamble. The constitution decrees that the state is the guardian of religion and protects freedom of religion:

> The state undertakes to disseminate the values of moderation and tolerance and the protection of the sacred, and the prohibition of all violations thereof. It undertakes equally to prohibit and fight against calls for *takfir* [declaring another Muslim a non-believer (*kafir*)] and the incitement of violence and hatred. (Article 6, Constitute Project 2014)

The preamble references "our people's commitment to the teachings of Islam," but qualifies the latter as being "characterized by openness and moderation, and to the human values and the highest principles of universal human rights."

According to an expert who reviewed the constitution as part of a consensus committee, the notion of universality was also highly contested in their deliberations. Women's rights activists and others argued against Ennahda's desire to talk about cultural specificity rather than the principle of universal rights of all peoples and all religions.

Yet another debate was over the first article, which states that "Tunisia is a free, independent, sovereign state; its religion is Islam, its language Arabic, and its system is republican." Ennahda had wanted to include reference to the *shari'a* as the source of law but there was such a strong reaction in the streets and so much pressure from women, but also from international NGOs and other external actors, that they were obliged to withdraw this provision. Ennahda also wanted to say that "Tunisia is an independent and sovereign state whose religion is Islam. This article cannot be amended." This formulation was struck because secular feminists argued that it was too permanent and that Islam belonged to Tunisia and therefore to the people and not to the state. The state should be neutral as the guarantor of freedom of belief, of worship and freedom of conscience (T1.3.16.17).

Another concern was Ennahda's desire to recognize the child only as a member of the family, which would be a rollback of the 1958 adoption law, which recognized children born out of wedlock. The secularists were able to change this so that Article 47 of the constitution now reads: "The state must provide all types of protection to all children without discrimination and in accordance with their best interest" (T18.3.29.17).

A final key debate was over the status of international treaties to which Tunisia was party. The Islamists wanted to make the treaties subordinate to the constitution, which would mean that the CEDAW might no longer be fully respected (T18.3.29.17). The Islamists were unsuccessful in this pursuit. The end of the constitution drafting process marked a shift in Ennahda's position on women's rights as it no doubt crystallized the limits of how far they could push their agenda when it came to women's rights. Tunisia had too long a history with women's rights to relinquish them so easily. Whether the shift represented a change of heart among party leaders is debatable, but a change in rhetoric did occur.

Ennahda's Reversal in the Post-Constitution Period

In 2011, Ennahda was sending mixed messages regarding its position on women's rights. The party had adopted a program that protected women's rights to work, opposed violence against women, and opposed a compulsory dress code among women. In the same year, Ghannouchi and Meherzia Labidi, vice president of the Constituent Assembly, both spoke at the March 8 International Women's Day celebrations. Ennahda had begun to celebrate March 8, which in the past had been exclusively a concern of leftists and feminists (T24.3.00.17). In Tunisia, Women's Day had previously been commemorated on August 13, the day that Bourguiba's PSC was enacted. Because the Ennahda women were persecuted by Bourguiba, they refused to celebrate August 13.

However, at this time Ennahda's leaders were delivering contradictory messages, which worried secularists and feminists. Spokesperson Samir Dilou stated that Ennahda was determined to include polygamy in the constitution, a comment he was forced to roll back amidst a fierce outcry. Labidi claims that Ennahda never supported such a law, that they never even discussed it, believing the people who raised the specter of such a move on the part of Ennahda were simply trying to create an atmosphere of panic (Marks 2013). Another Ennahda member of parliament called for the repeal of a law protecting single mothers. This was followed by Ennahda statements to the contrary, suggesting that Ennahda's position was evolving as they struggled to distinguish themselves from the Salafis (Abdo-Katsipis 2017).

Ennahda not only changed their positions, they took up ambivalent positions, and even contradictory positions, depending on the skills and knowledge of their spokespeople, their audience, and the pressures they felt they were facing. This may have been a function of the fact that Ennahda's leadership is more moderate than its base, which can be quite conservative and sometimes even radically so. It may have also been a result of differences within the party itself. As a result, many feminists were skeptical that Ennahda had really changed their basic positions (T15.4.10.17). This meant the feminists were not going to take any chances. As one activist put it, "We must always campaign because if tomorrow the Islamists regain power, they will begin to question some women's rights, so we must always campaign and always be vigilant" (T1.3.16.17). Nevertheless, it is unlikely that Ennahda, which in 2019 had the most seats in parliament, will try to roll back women's rights in the near future because of the strength of popular support for these rights, particularly the PSC. One activist explained: "Today, the Tunisian constitution establishes equal rights for citizens; Ennahda has therefore yielded on this point" (T2.3.16.170).

Several new women's organizations emerged to bridge the divide between secular and Islamist groups, who were extremely polarized between 2012 and 2015. For example, Aswat Nisaa (Voices of Women) was formed across political party lines to bring women together to gain skills to run for election and encourage women to vote. It is a secular NGO that supports full equality between the genders but sees a need to work with Islamist women, who make up a large percentage of society. It is creating a safe space to talk across differences.

Ennahda stepped down from the government after the constitution was passed in January 2014. In the 2014 parliamentary elections, it came in second with 28 percent of the vote and did not put forward a presidential candidate. Rory McCarthy (2018) suggests that there were huge struggles within the party over whether it was a movement focused on changing society or a political party with the goal of reforming the state. In 2016, the party separated its religious movement from its political functions as a party, much as the Islamist Party of Justice and Development had done in Morocco. Ghannouchi said that

Ennahda wanted religious activity to be completely independent from political activity: "This is good for politicians because they would no longer be accused of manipulating religion for political means and good for religion because it would not be held hostage to politics" (Middle East Eye 2016). He added that "We are leaving political Islam and entering democratic Islam. We are Muslim democrats who no longer claim to represent political Islam." This shows the extent to which both parties were able to adapt to new circumstances through a form of what McCarthy calls "strategic pragmatism." It also helps explain, in part, the waffling and eventual changes in Ennahda's position regarding women's rights.

During the constitution drafting process Ghannouchi began to openly support democracy, women's rights, and human rights more generally (Cavatorta and Merone 2013, Gorman 2017). Further evidence of this shift came with legislative reforms around women's rights.

Legal Reform

By 2018, Ennahda once again held the majority of seats in the parliament because of attrition from the secular Nidaa Tounes Party. It is important to point out that, despite the feminists' skepticism regarding Ennahda, the party supported an agenda of legislative reforms regarding women's rights. Moreover, they have not tried to undo any of the existing legislation or international treaties.

The issue of legislative quotas is a case in point. The first gender issue that came onto the table after the Arab Spring in 2011 was parity (T9.4.6.17). Women had been poorly represented in the 1999 parliamentary elections, in which women won twenty-one of the total 182 seats in the government (Table 6.2).

A quota law was passed in April 2011 that required parity in party lists, alternating between men and women throughout the list. Parties with any other arrangement would not be allowed to contest. Political parties of all persuasions courted women to become part of their lists (Goulding 2011). During the election cycle, the government also undertook a major campaign to urge women to vote and register to vote. Prior to the election, the United Nations Development Programme (UNDP) helped train women candidates in electoral and communications strategies and campaign management. In the interim, other measures were also adopted.

Table 6.2 *Representation of women in the Tunisian parliament, 1956–2019*

Year	Number of parliamentarians	Number of women in parliament	Percentage of women in parliament
1956	98	0	0
1959	90	1	1.1
1969	108	4	3.7
1979	126	4	3.2
1989	141	6	4.3
1999	182	21	12
2009	214	59	27.6
2019	217	78	35.9

Sources: Inter-Parliamentary Union (1995, 2019)

Despite the quota law, overall women claimed only 26.70 percent of the seats in the 2011 election for the Constituent Assembly, a 1 percent drop from the previous election. Two-thirds of the fifty-seven women elected to the Constituent Assembly belonged to Ennahda, which claimed 41 percent of the seats overall (Abdo-Katsipis 2017). Over 4,000 women ran in the elections, but headed only seven percent of the more than 1,500 candidate lists. This is because there was no requirement for the number of women to head the lists.

Because of such inadequacies in the law, a new quota law was passed in May 2014 which resulted from the new 2014 constitution. The new electoral law required parity, which meant alternation between men and women on the candidate lists. Members of the parliament were to be elected by a proportional representation (PR) system in which party lists that did not follow gender parity would not be admitted. However, women headed up only 11 percent of the party lists, resulting in women winning 31.3 percent of the seats in the 2014 elections but still not reaching parity. Subsequently, the proportion of women in parliament has risen to 36 percent.

The electoral law was further revised in 2017 to require that women head at least half the party lists in regional and municipal elections but not in national elections. Male and female names were to alternate on the party lists. As a result of this law, women made up 47 percent of the local council positions in Tunisia after the May 2018 elections. Mayoral contests did not require a quota and as a result, only a fifth of the seats were won by women.

There were other efforts to bring the laws in line with the gains made in the constitution, particularly around the issue of inheritance (T2.3.16.17). In addition to the quota laws, far-reaching legislation was passed in 2017 to combat domestic violence against women. It forbade physical, economic, and psychological abuse against women and banned sexual harassment in public. It also eliminated a loophole that allowed rapists to avoid jail by marrying their victims. Another law was passed lifting the prohibition on women from marrying non-Muslims.

Finally, it is significant that Ennahda supported the Organic Law that established Tunisia's Truth and Dignity Commission. This law is unique as far as such commissions go in that it mandates that the Commission investigate not only gross human rights violations, including rape and all forms of sexual violence, but also systematic infringements of any human rights committed by the previous regime (Article 3). This is important because women suffered not only gross human rights violations but also daily hardships caused by the *pointage* system, which forced the wives of incarcerated political prisoners to go to the police station up to five times a day, making it impossible for them to work. They suffered from economic abuse at the hands of the state, as they found it difficult to study at the university, or gain or maintain employment, particularly government positions, given the time-consuming *pointage* system. The South African Truth and Reconciliation Commission (TRC) is often held up as a model for such processes because women were involved in its design, they submitted 56.5 percent of the testimonies presented to it, and were provided special structures in which to testify about sexual violence in a way that validated them. However, even the South African TRC focused almost exclusively on extrajudicial killings, torture, and forced disappearances, rather than on the harmful quotidian abuse women often faced, which was recognized by the Tunisian Commission (Gray and Coonan 2016).

President Essebsi discovered in the 2014 election that put him in office that promoting women's rights in a country where women make up the majority of the voting electorate brings votes. Women overwhelmingly supported Beji Caid Essebsi in the election: of the 1.7 million people who voted for him, 1 million were women, representing 60 percent of his supporters. Like his predecessors, he has argued that Tunisia needed to fight gender discrimination and modernize. However, Essebsi dropped a bombshell in the region when in 2018 he called for reform of the inheritance law so that it would not discriminate against women. He also called for the abolition of the dowry and for a law allowing the father and mother to share responsibilities as head of the household. The legislation was adopted by the cabinet in 2018 and is to be debated in the parliament.

While Ennahda has not given any indication of supporting changes in inheritance laws, the fact that most of a legislative agenda regarding women's rights has continued unimpeded with significant Ennahda representation in parliament shows how far they have moved in their position, making important compromises based on careful political calculations. No doubt the ousting of the Muslim Brotherhood in Egypt by General Sisi and the aforementioned assassinations of leftist politicians in 2013 factored into their calculations of how far they could push back against women's rights norms, which have been fairly well established in Tunisia and have been absorbed even by women leaders in Ennahda.

To get a sense of Ennahda's newfound pluralism, the party has on occasion supported women candidates who do not veil (including Souad Abderrahim, who was elected mayor of Tunis in 2018), as well as Jews and some atheists. Other Islamist parties, like the Movement of Society for Peace (MSP), have also supported unveiled women and atheists even if they would have preferred that they pray and observe religious obligations (Boualem 2018b).

Conclusions

Gorman (2017) has argued that the differences between the Islamists and secularists in Tunisia are insignificant when it comes to women's rights, but the measures he uses for women's empowerment pertain only to political representation and not attitudes toward inheritance, veiling, the PSC, or other more controversial measures. Were there no differences between the two groups, there would not have been the fierce battles we have seen over the PSC, over the equality provisions in the constitution, veiling, and, in more recent years, over inheritance laws.

Nevertheless, as a result of pressure from women's movements, the Islamists have retreated considerably from the positions they took when they first reappeared on the scene in 2011, and subsequently accommodated most reforms in women's rights. The process of drafting the constitution revealed the limits of their agenda and the strategic need to compromise on women's rights in order to remain politically relevant. It also helped clarify the boundaries between their political agenda and that of the Salafis. In the first scene in this chapter, it was in fact the Ennahda minister of the interior who gave the female student an award for removing the Salafi flag and replacing it with the Tunisian flag. Had it not been for active and visible pressure from women's movements, Ennahda would not have modified their position. They did so at critical junctures in Tunisia's history, indirectly after independence, but especially after the Ben Ali takeover in 1987, when they had more latitude to mobilize, and then during and after the Arab Spring. The ways in which these battles unfolded, laden with symbolic significance, shows how Ennahda and the women's movement were locked in battles over the future of the state and nation. As Rory McCarthy has pointed out, it is such struggles between the Islamists and other social actors over the state and the "interpretation of symbols and the control of the institutions, both formal and informal, that produce and sustain them" (2018, 6).

While many of the strategies women used in these earlier periods focused on legal reform, today younger women's rights activists are drawing on a much deeper reservoir of tactics that involve daily struggles by civil society to repeal laws, policies, and regressive practices. As blogger Aya Chebbi explained, "After the attacks in Bardo and Sousse,[3] the reaction of people was not to hide at home in the fear of the unknown. On the contrary, they immediately mobilized to go to the scene of the attacks and say 'no' to terrorism" (Jaber 2015). As in Morocco and Algeria, younger women have found new battlefields: patronizing coffeehouses, which in the past were the domain of men; taking self-defense courses to protect themselves; blogging, participating in writing workshops, poetry readings at coffeehouses, and other cultural forms of expression. The range of issues is also expanding. In Tunisia, a country where gays can face up to three years in prison, a queer film festival was launched in 2018. Organizations like the

[3] In 2015 a terrorist bombing in the Bardo National Museum in Tunis killed twenty-one people, mostly European tourists, and injured fifty. The same year, thirty-eight tourists were killed by a gunman at a tourist resort near Sousse.

Tunisian Association of Democratic Women have been advocating to repeal the Penal Code provision (Article 230) for the imprisonment of gays. Shams Association was formed as Tunisia's first LGBT rights organization and received official recognition by the government in 2015. The organization owns an LGBT radio station, which remains open despite continued threats.

Conclusions

Perhaps the most memorable image of the Egyptian revolution in 2011 was the young woman who was stripped of her *abaya*[1] down to her blue bra, beaten, and dragged by soldiers across a street. This scene became emblematic of the repression of protestors, resulting in a protest of 10,000 people of all political and religious persuasions against the violence perpetrated by the army. They chanted, "Egypt's women are a red line" (Shukrallah 2011). The protestors demanded an end to the rule of the Supreme Council of the Armed Forces (SCAF), which had taken over in February 2011, and the creation of a civil state. The slogan "Egyptian women are a red line" was resuscitated two years later as a rallying cry by the Muslim Brotherhood and an alliance of parties and movements that supported Mohamed Morsi after he was ousted as president in a military coup, highlighting the centrality of women in moments of political tumult (Kadry 2013).

As during key turning points in the history of the Maghreb, women's rights have been center stage in watershed moments in the Middle East too. However, unlike the three primary cases in this book, the outcomes for women have been less favorable in Egypt, and in most other Middle Eastern countries. This book has explored the reasons for these different outcomes. The book started with a question, asking why authoritarian regimes adopt women's rights, and sought to answer this by examining the experience of three Maghreb countries – Algeria, Tunisia, and Morocco – since independence. These three countries are compared with one another to show that there has been a convergence in women's rights legal reform between them and that Morocco and Algeria have all but caught up with Tunisia in this regard, even though the latter had taken measures as early as 1956 to improve the status of women.

[1] Black full-body covering worn by Muslim women in parts of North Africa and the Arabian Peninsula.

The book has also explored why these three countries adopted women's rights reforms faster and in more far-reaching ways than the Middle Eastern countries. They have consistently outperformed the Middle Eastern countries when it comes to constitutional reform, legislative reform, and the representation of women in legislatures and local government positions. The Maghreb countries have made advances with constitutional provisions regarding women and work, political representation, gender equality, discrimination against women, and gender-based violence. Their constitutions also stand out in what they do *not* say when compared with other constitutions in the Middle East. They do not mention Islamic jurisprudence as the major source of law, which has implications for women's rights, particularly family law, and reflects the unified character of their legal systems. They do not focus on women in terms of their roles as mothers and the need to protect mothers and motherhood. They do not infantilize women by placing their needs in the same context of dependence and vulnerability as children.

The three Maghreb countries also passed more legislation, and earlier, than most Middle Eastern countries regarding quotas both at the national and municipal/regional levels, sexual harassment, the prohibition of the marriage of victims to their rapist, nationality issues, violence against women, abortion, contraception, polygyny, and family law more generally.

The book argues that in order to explain the variance between the two regions, we are better served by looking at the political strategies of political leaders and women's movements than simply arguments relating to attitudes toward religiosity, which dominate discussions of women's rights in the region. Certainly religion plays a role, but as part of a political contestation. Leaders in the Maghreb countries used women's rights internally to drive a wedge between themselves and Islamist extremists and externally to paint an image of their countries as modernizing. Ruling political parties used these tactics especially at times when their rule was threatened and they needed political support to remain in power. Women's movements, often in the face of a perceived threat of losing gains, heightened their activities during critical junctures, such as changes in power or moments of societal unrest, to expand their influence and advocate for change. They networked within the region and beyond and used these ties to build their strategies at home.

The book shows how much of the communication between the various key actors, including the king (in Morocco), the presidents (in Tunisia and Algeria), the ruling parties, the Salafis and Islamists, and the women's movements has been at a symbolic level, often through positions taken on the veil, or on women's rights legislation like the Moudawana in Morocco, or on whether women can occupy a certain public space. Both symbols and the ritual enactment of symbolic meanings reveal the often conflicting and changing positions people held toward women's rights. But women's rights and the symbols that accompanied them stood for and represented other goals in society beyond those rights themselves: they had to do with modernity, progress, democracy, human rights, secularism, a post-Islamist disposition, and even nationalism. The ambiguity of symbols meant that people could interpret them in a variety of ways to suit their own purposes.

Because the idea of women's rights has been so loaded in so many different ways, it was central to virtually every key political transition experienced in the postindependence period of the Maghreb. Yet the gender dimension has rarely been given its due because observers have employed an all-too-conventional political lens. The adoption of a unified legal system after independence was a central element in the break from France and the repositioning of family law in this system rather than under the jurisdiction of Islamic courts was a major break with colonial legal practice. The advancement of women's rights was a key feature of Bourguiba's state building and consolidation of power in Tunisia after independence, and one of the most crucial pieces of legislation in this period was the Personal Status Code, which was passed even prior to the constitution. Women played major roles in the Arab Spring and in its aftermath, as they pushed back against Islamist efforts to pull back women's rights, particularly in the context of the constitution drafting process, in which the most important struggles focused on women's rights. Women and women's bodies were key targets of the Islamists during the Black Decade in Algeria because the control of women's behavior was one of their central goals in this period. Women sought to reclaim their bodies and lives in the aftermath of this dark period in Algeria's history. Women played a central role in the 2019 uprisings in Algeria, linking demands for democracy and women's rights. In Morocco, the struggles over the Family Code in 2014 led to pivotal confrontations between Islamists and feminists. The Vingt février movement similarly led to constitutional changes of which some of the most important reforms included expansion of women's rights.

Among the most interesting developments in all three countries is the way in which Islamist parties dramatically changed their stated positions on women's rights, particularly Ennahda in Tunisia and the Justice and Development Party in Morocco. While they are far from being feminist, the two parties continued to uphold existing laws and international treaties and supported continued reform in this area. To not continue down this path would have been political suicide. Even some key Salafi leaders began to espouse more flexibility when it came to inheritance laws in a country like Morocco.

Various preexisting conditions supported these dynamics, some more than others. These conditions included aspects of the French legacy and in particular the influence of the elites and women's rights leaders who traveled back and forth between the northern and southern regions of the Mediterranean and resided in both locales. Other conditions that shaped the outcomes included the adoption of unified legal systems after independence in the Maghreb, which had particularly salutary effects on family law. The growing secular Amazigh influence has contributed to an emerging post-Islamist environment. This is also tied to the particular appeal of Sufism to women, which has afforded them religious leadership roles not found in the Middle East. To the extent that there has been political opening and stability in the Maghreb, it has contributed to an environment that makes legislative and constitutional reform more likely. In and of themselves, these background factors cannot explain the changes I am describing because many of them are present in other countries where similar changes have not occurred, or they were present in the Maghreb for a long time prior to the changes seen there. Nevertheless, they helped shape the outcomes I am describing.

By pairing similar countries and taking a snapshot of women's rights legislation adoption, this chapter isolates characteristics that explain some of the differences between the regions (Table 7.1). I contrast the case of Tunisia with Lebanon, Morocco with Jordan, and Algeria with Egypt. This chapter then examines the broader implications of these aforementioned changes for a post-Islamist era in the region. I return in this chapter to the larger questions posed in the book about why autocrats adopt women's rights and what the consequences are for women and women's rights. I also discuss the implications of the

Table 7.1 *Main factors explaining adoption of women's rights reforms in MENA*

	King or head of state		Parties	Women's movement
	Political will of modernizing leader	Neutralized extremists	Political necessity for parties to advance women's rights	Movement advanced at critical junctures
Tunisia	Yes, under Bourguiba, Ben Ali, and Essebsi	Yes	Yes	Yes
Morocco	Yes, under Mohammed VI	Yes	Yes	Yes
Algeria	Yes, under Bouteflika	Yes	No, Islamist parties too weak	Yes
Lebanon	No	No	No	No
Egypt	No*	Yes, but crushed them	No	No
Jordan	No	No	No	No

* Sisi initiated some reforms but his overall record is abysmal.

changes in the Maghreb for understanding other parts of the world with Muslim-majority populations.

Contrasting Lebanon and Tunisia

Tunisia and Lebanon share a common French colonial legacy. The League of Nations gave France the mandate to control Lebanon following the collapse of the Ottoman Empire after World War I. It gained independence before Tunisia, in 1943. The two countries both have populations with attitudes that are more favorable to gender equality than in most countries in the MENA region. Lebanon is even more open to women's rights than Tunisia on most attitudinal measures (Table 7.2). Along some measures (men as better leaders than women, the wearing of the *hijab*, and the question of women's inheritance), the differences in opinion are quite striking, with Lebanese women taking the most liberal positions. No doubt this is related to the fact that Lebanon, which has a population of 6 million, has a large diaspora living outside of the country. These external influences, as in Tunisia, help shape attitudes within the country, which is highly urbanized and has a large educated class.

However, unlike Tunisia, Lebanon has passed very little woman-friendly legislation, least of all in the area of family law. Its multiple court system makes it exceptionally difficult to bring about universal legal reform for all women in this area. The courts are fractured between fifteen different confessional groups, each with their own personal status laws and courts. This makes overall reform of these laws virtually impossible. Each confessional group has exclusive jurisdiction over laws pertaining to engagement and dowry, marriage and divorce, legal and illegal filiation, adoption, parental authority and guardianship of children and minors, and child support (Stephan 2009). All of the personal status laws are discriminatory toward women. Moreover, all efforts to introduce a unified civil status have failed, including the most recent attempt in 2010. Thus, Lebanon does not even have a national minimum age for marriage. Religious courts decide on the age for marriage and some allow girls under the age of fifteen to marry. Most countries in the region have set a minimum age for marriage of eighteen.

Discriminatory laws exist not only in Lebanon's personal status laws, but also nationality laws and the criminal code. In 2014,

Table 7.2 *Attitudes toward gender equality, Tunisia, Lebanon, and the Middle East, 2016 (%)*

Question	Lebanon	Tunisia	Middle East (excluding Lebanon)
Agree/Agree strongly: Married women can work outside home [1]	90.3	87.8	85.3
Disagree/Disagree strongly: Men are better political leaders [2]	47.3	42.8	29.5
Agree/Agree strongly: A woman can become president or prime minister of a Muslim country [3]	76.6	62.6	64.0
Disagree/Strongly disagree: University education more important for males [4]	92.0	88.2	81.6
Agree/Agree strongly: Women should wear modest clothes without needing to wear *hijab* [5]	70.3	89.2	48.7
Agree/Agree strongly: Women and men should have equal inheritance rights [6]	94.6	97.6	96.3
Disagree/Strongly disagree: Inheritance laws should be in accordance with Islamic law [7] 2013	63.6	16.2	6.4
Disagree/Strongly disagree: Husbands should have final say in family [7]	46.1	41.5	37.8

Source: Arab Barometer Database, Wave IV, 2016–2017; www.arabbarometer.org/

Lebanon passed legislation around domestic violence, and in 2017 it passed legislation to eliminate the rape loophole (allowing the rapist to marry the victim to avoid prosecution) as a result of pressure from women's groups. But otherwise it has left its laws on violence against women virtually untouched. There has been no reform of nationality laws, so women cannot confer their nationality to their children. Lebanon does not even comply with the international standard of a minimum fourteen-week maternity leave, providing only seven weeks' paid leave. According to International Social Security Association reports, these benefits are not implemented in practice.

Lebanon has an equality provision in its constitution, which is found in all MENA constitutions except that of Saudi Arabia, but it does not mention gender equality specifically.

Lebanon has no quota laws and as a result, 4.7 percent of its legislative seats are held by women, which means that Lebanon ranks 185th in the world with respect to female legislative representation, ahead only of Kuwait, Oman, and Yemen. Prior to the 2018 elections, the women's ministry together with the United Nations and the European Union ran a campaign to promote parity between the sexes. In the May 2018 election, eighty-six female candidates stood for office, and six won. This was an increase on 2009, when only twelve women ran for parliament, but it hardly represents the kind of numbers we have seen in the Maghreb countries like Tunisia, where 31 percent of the parliamentary seats are held by women (Domat 2018). The proportion of cabinet ministers in Lebanon is 4 percent, which puts it second to last in the MENA region, ahead of Saudi Arabia.

Lebanon's Prime Minister Saad Hariri appointed a man, Jean Ogasapian, as his country's first minister of women's affairs, which drew widespread criticism among women's organizations. KAFA, a prominent women's rights organization, protested the move with the slogan, "No women, no legitimacy."

Unlike Tunisia and the other Maghreb countries that used women's rights to isolate extremists, the leadership of Lebanon has been too entangled with both the Salafis and Hezbollah to be able to advocate for women's rights in a meaningful way. Salafi jihadism has a long history in Lebanon that goes back to the 1940s, gaining traction during the civil war and the Syrian occupation of Lebanon between 1990 and 2005. In 2005, the Prime Minister of Lebanon, Rafik Hariri, was killed and it is widely believed that the Syrian Assad regime and Shi'ite Islamist militia of Hezbollah masterminded the assassination. Salafis and Sunnis more generally saw this as a blow to their power and large sums of external Salafi money flowed into Lebanon during the 2005 elections. The Salafis are based in northern Lebanon and are a divisive power in the country as they have become increasingly militant (Rabil 2015). Saad Hariri, who assumed the mantle of his father Rafik, needs the Salafi votes and money but he also wants to maintain his distance from them.

After Rafik Hariri's death, the Cedar Revolution erupted and forced Syrian troops to withdraw from Lebanon, having been based there since 1975 as part of an Arab League force brought in to the restore calm during the civil war between Christian, Druze, and Muslim militias and the Palestinian Liberation Organization. The Salafis were among the first to support the 2011 rebellion against Bashar al-Assad and helped train fighters from the Al Nusra Front, which was affiliated with Al Qaeda. Lebanon became a target of Islamist militancy after the Syrian conflict started in 2011. Salafi jihadi groups like ISIS and Hay'at Tahrir al-Sham (previously Al Nusra Front and then Jabhat Fatah al-Sham) launched attacks in and around Beirut. Their numbers grew after 2014. The Lebanese government's response has been to arrest suspects and launch a military crackdown, but it has not involved a political strategy of the kind seen in the Maghreb, where incorporating women's rights was a way of isolating the Salafis and Hezbollah, because it has been too closely tied with these groups. By the same token, Hariri has done little to limit the influence of Hezbollah, which has fought alongside the Assad regime and is represented in the Lebanese government.

Lebanon has a fairly active women's movement, but it has not had the impact one would have expected, largely due to a lack of political will on the part of the authorities. Hariri's Future Movement tried to introduce a quota to ensure that 30 percent of parliamentary seats would be held by women, but faced fierce resistance from the other parties, forcing him to abandon the proposition.

Unlike Morocco and Tunisia, the Lebanese political parties have not seen it to be in their existential interest to adopt women's rights platforms and they do not see major negative political consequences for not doing so. Thus, Lebanon provides an example of a country that would be an excellent candidate for gender reform, given the attitudes of its citizens and activism of its women's organizations, but is constrained by instability and a leadership that is too beholden to conservative interests to break away. The Lebanese political parties have not used women's rights in the same way as the Maghreb leaders as part of a strategy to drive a wedge between themselves and jihadist extremists.

Contrasting Algeria and Egypt

Algeria can be compared with Egypt since both are governed by military governments which operate behind a president, although Algeria's president was all but absent, while Egypt's is more than visible. Of the three paired comparisons here, these two countries have the most in common with respect to women's rights but with some important differences. Both cases highlight the difficulties of making significant progress without allowing space for civil society to act and engage the state. In Egypt, women's mobilization and civil society more generally have been silenced and virtually crushed by President Sisi in his bid to remain in power, while in Algeria they exist but with restrictions. The Muslim Brotherhood and other Salafis have been heavily repressed in Egypt, whereas they operate and engage politically today in Algeria, although much subdued relative to their heyday in the early 1990s. In Algeria, women's rights are seen as part of a strategy to keep extremism at bay, while in Egypt women's rights activists are treated almost as enemies of the state.

Egypt has a long history of state-sponsored feminism and of women's activism. Gamal Abdel Nasser, who came into power first as Egypt's prime minister and later as president from 1956 to 1970, promoted various pro-women policies as part of his ideology of modernizing nationalism. Women gained the right to vote and run for office in 1956. Nasser encouraged women to seek employment and promoted laws that made it easier for them to work outside the home. These included paid maternity leave, affordable health care, and child care. At the same time, independent women's organizations were banned or crippled and women leaders were suppressed.

Women's rights activists had become more visible by the time Anwar Sadat came into power in 1970 after the death of Nasser. He initially aligned himself with Islamists and tore up Nasser's 1962 socialist Charter for National Action, which had called for gender equality. Reflecting his desire to appease Islamists, Sadat's 1971 constitution only allowed for gender equality as long as it did not contradict *shari'a* law. *Shari'a* law was further entrenched in the 1976 constitution as the principal source of legislation. At the same time, under Sadat, independent feminist mobilization was harshly suppressed along with other elements of civil society.

Soon after and somewhat paradoxically, President Sadat sought to assert himself on the international scene as a modernizer and promoted gender equality in the areas of education, employment, and political representation. Women had the right to work outside the home and were guaranteed equal salaries (Sika and Khodary 2012). He created the Egyptian Women's Organization and the National Commission for

Women, which focused on family planning, illiteracy, and child welfare.

In 1979, with strong encouragement from his wife Jihan Sadat, the president granted thirty (8 percent) reserved parliamentary seats to women in his National Democratic Party and 20 percent of local council seats were allocated to women. While feminists supported the substance of the gender reforms, they rejected the authoritarian manner in which these laws were enacted. The quota law was eventually abolished in 1986 by the Constitutional Court. As a result, the percentage of women parliamentarians dropped back down to 2.2 percent.

Sadat's wife established welfare organizations. She also successfully encouraged him to reform the Personal Status Law, particularly the right to divorce. He introduced provisions that gave first wives the right to refuse polygamy and stopped the practice of using the police to force wives to return to their husband's home against their will. The law gave divorced women alimony and allowed divorced wives the right to the family home if they had custody of children, which they could be granted automatically if the child was under the age of ten for boys and twelve for girls. Custody could be extended by a court decision (Botman 1999, Keddie 2006). The parliament refused to make these changes to the Personal Status Law and so Sadat unilaterally enacted the law in 1979 by presidential decree. By the time Hosni Mubarak came to power in 1981, he found himself under even greater pressure from the Islamists. His policies became increasingly more conservative when it came to family law and women's political participation (Al-Ali 2000). As a result, his Constitutional Court threw out Sadat's Personal Status Laws in 1985 along with other women's rights reforms implemented under Sadat, on the grounds that they were Western and un-Islamic.

Women's organizations had proliferated in the early 1980s, when Nawal al-Saadawi formed the Arab Women's Solidarity Association (AWSA) and other Islamist women's activist groups were created. The government formed a National Council of Women (NCW) to advance women's status in 2000 but at the same time it passed an NGO law that gave the Ministry of Social Affairs the ability to dissolve NGOs, thus once again putting women's organizations in jeopardy.

Under Hosni Mubarak, a series of women's rights reforms were implemented that were referred to as "Suzanne's Laws" because they had been supported by the first lady Suzanne Mubarak, who was president of the NCW. These included a law on women's alimony rights and the *khul*ʿ law, which gave women the right to ask for a divorce by returning her dowry to the husband. The Convention on the Elimination of All Forms of Discrimination Against Women (CEDAW) was adopted in 1981 and ratified in 1985 with reservations. Female genital mutilation (FGM) was criminalized and a 2005 law allowed for children of divorced parents to remain in their mother's custody until the age of fifteen. The laws were passed as a result of the NCW's ties to the regime, thus leading to the association of women's rights with a dictatorial regime. The NCW lost further credibility during the 2011 revolution because it did not condemn the violence perpetrated against women during the protests. Today the NCW has become an apologist for the Sisi regime, the sexual crimes of its security forces, and the repression of women's rights NGOs.

When Mohamed Morsi took over as president with the victory of the Freedom and Justice Party of the Muslim Brotherhood in the 2011 elections, there were fears that his Brotherhood-led government would further roll back the few gains made under Mubarak, namely to repeal the FGM law and pass legislation that would allow girls as young as thirteen to be married. But Morsi's 2012 constitution did not in fact repeal women's rights legislation. His was the first Egyptian constitution to provide for "equality and equal opportunities for all citizens, men and women." The constitution guaranteed maternal and child services free of charge and guaranteed the reconciliation of a woman's duties toward her family and her work. It sought to eradicate illiteracy of both women and men. It regarded women and men as partners in national gains and responsibility.

Morsi's rule was short-lived as he was ousted militarily by his army chief General Sisi in July 2013. Hundreds of members of the Muslim Brotherhood were killed, thousands were injured, and hundreds more imprisoned, including Morsi and the Muslim Brotherhood's leaders. The Brotherhood was banned along with its associations, and its assets were seized. Morsi was sentence to death in 2015 along with 120 others. Subsequently even more Islamists have been sentenced to death, imprisoned, and tortured.

Sisi tries to give the appearance of supporting women's rights but there is little to cheer about the way women are treated under this regime. The 2014 Egyptian constitution has provisions for women's rights in employment, political representation, gender equality, and gender-based violence. Despite these many provisions regarding women, however, much of it is cast within the framework of motherhood and women's roles in the home.

Women's rights organizations had mobilized to influence the constitution-writing process. In 2011, 16 feminist NGOs met to form the Egyptian Coalition of Feminist Organizations, which had been working together on freedom of association issues and the enforcement of women's rights based on CEDAW since the 1990s. Energized by the Arab Spring, they sought to influence the criteria for membership of the constitution drafting committee, conduct surveys to get Egyptian women's views on their rights, and influence the phrasing of women's rights provisions in the constitution. The coalition, along with other women's organizations, monitored the process very closely. Five women (10 percent) ended up on the Constitutional Committee, including the Chair of the National Council of Women, Chair of the National Council for Motherhood and Childhood, feminist academic Hoda Elsadda and feminist lawyer Mona Zulficar. Women's rights organizations lobbied the Constitutional Committee around five articles and suggested alternate phrasing. It appears that many of their views were incorporated in the final version.

However, in the end feminists were divided over whether or not to support the constitution in the 2014 referendum because even though the constitution had women's rights provisions, it also allowed for military trials for civilians and allowed economic privileges for the military, which contravened human rights. The majority of feminists ended up voting in favor of the constitution – a Faustian bargain – the consequences of which have been disastrous for women's rights, women's mobilization and human rights more generally (Kamal 2015).

Even though General Sisi declared 2017 to be the year of the woman, he has done little beyond rhetoric. He had sat on a panel of the Supreme Council of the Armed Forces (2011–2012) before becoming head of the military and did nothing to stop the massive wave of sexual assaults that occurred at Tahrir Square during the protests, including assaults by the military who beat, tortured, strip-searched women in front of male soldiers, and forced them to undergo so-called "virginity tests." The Nazra Association for Feminist Studies (2014) documented around five hundred cases of sexual assault during the protests from

2012 to 2014. Moreover, Sisi did nothing subsequently to punish the perpetrators of these assaults.

Since the passage of the constitution, Gen. Sisi has overseen a regime that has become extraordinarily repressive, not just of the Muslim Brotherhood and Islamists but of all of civil society. Women activists have been suppressed. The twenty-one-year-old singer Shyma was sentenced to two years in prison for "harming public morality" because her clothing was regarded as too revealing. Doaa Salah, the host of the "Dody Show," was sentenced to three years in prison for talking about pregnancy outside of marriage. There was a massive wave of violence against LGBTQ people in Egypt in October 2017. This has led some feminists to call the Egyptian government "the antithesis of feminism" (Allemandou 2017).

Unlike Algeria, there is no unified family code in Egypt and the principles of *shari'a* dominate family law. There is no quota law at the national level as one finds in Algeria, although a quarter of the local council seats are reserved for women by the 2014 constitution (Article 180). Fifteen percent of the legislative seats are held by women. In 2017, the constitutional court ruled unconstitutional a law that prohibited the official registration of marriages for children under eighteen. Up until then, Egypt had been the only country in the MENA region that did not allow exceptions to the legal age for marriage, which is eighteen for both men and women. Since 2000 it has been possible for women to initiate divorce through *khul'*, but these cases are difficult to get approved throughout the courts. Abortion is prohibited altogether, not even to save the life of the mother, whereas it is permitted in Algeria. Unlike Algeria, Egypt has passed few laws regarding violence against women, however, it did abolish the rape loophole for rapists in 1999. Also in 2014, Egyptian feminist activists were able to get an amendment to Article 306 of the penal code passed that criminalizes sexual harassment, making it punishable by a fine up to \$2,755 and a prison sentence of six months to five years. According to a 2013 study by the United Nations, over 99 percent of Egyptian women have been the victim of harassment (Amnesty International 2015).

In spite of some constitutional reforms and a few legislative reforms, there are considerable differences between Algeria and Egypt when it comes to the legal status of women. Much of the difference between the Sisi and Bouteflika regimes is captured by the level of repression of civil society, especially of Islamists. Sisi overthrew the Muslim Brotherhood leader Mohamed Morsi in 2013 and became president in 2014. He won the 2018 election with 97 percent of the vote after harassing and intimidating other potential candidates. Fourteen international and regional rights organizations stated that the elections did not meet the minimum requirement to qualify as free and fair. Sisi's regime has been characterized by heavy repression of independent organizations, prosecutions, and repressive legislation. Torture is pervasive (HRW 2018).

Leaders of independent women's organizations like Nazra that work to provide legal, medical, and therapeutic assistance to victims of sexual violence are labeled whores and are maligned by the pro-government media (Langer 2018a). Leaders of the Center for Egyptian Women's Legal Assistance (CEWLA), which has long been campaigning for judicial reform, have experienced travel bans, they have had their assets frozen, and were forced to close their offices. These restrictions make it near-impossible for women's rights activists to influence policy. The CEWLA's director, Azza Soliman, said, "We live in a dictatorship," adding that "nobody trusts the judiciary, the police or the courts." She herself witnessed a fatal shooting of a female acquaintance who was involved in a demonstration in Cairo in 2015. The woman was allegedly shot by a member of the security forces. Soliman went to the police to report the incident and ended up arrested and charged with disrupting the public order even though she did not participate in the protest. Eventually she was acquitted (Langer 2018b).

Sisi has not used women's rights instrumentally in the same way as other Maghreb governments have done, mainly because he has completely suppressed the Muslim Brotherhood and other Islamists. His repressive government and use of the military have given him almost complete control with little room for opposition. He tried very hard to appeal to women in his 2014 and 2018 campaigns, and indeed a large number of women (and men) voted for him in 2014 (we do not have the male/female breakdown for the 2018 election yet). However, with the exception of women over sixty, he received less support from women than men in the 2014 elections in which he ran against one candidate and gained 97 percent of the vote. The elections were boycotted by all opposition parties.[2] With a 38 percent turnout, he once again won

2 لجنة الانتخابات الرئاسية 2014 https://pres2014.elections.eg/results-and-stats?id=81:demogragpic-stats&catid=2:uncategorised.

97 percent of the votes in the 2018 election, which was widely regarded as a sham (USAID 2019). After this victory, he appointed six women to the cabinet, bringing the number of females to 18 percent of the cabinet. Although he targeted women voters in both elections he did not need to appeal to them because he had other corrupt means at his disposal to ensure a near-100 percent score (*The National* 2018). Moreover, he did not use women's rights or representation as a means of isolating his political opponents and extremists because he had simply crushed them. Thus, even though Algeria and Egypt share many similarities in their governance structures, the lack of political space afforded civil society, women's rights activists, and Islamists, combined with the lack of any real commitment by the head of state in Egypt, has resulted in divergent outcomes between the two countries.

Contrasting Jordan and Morocco

Jordan's King Abdullah II is much like the Moroccan King Mohammed VI, regarding himself as a modernizer within a traditional monarchy and society. In Jordan, the monarch has much the same stance as Mohammed VI when it comes to women's rights, but he has not pushed for reforms of women's rights in a way that would neutralize Islamist elements as Mohammed VI did. King Abdullah and the Jordanian state have been more ambivalent about challenging Islamist extremists and take a noncommittal stance in a society that equates secularism with being anti-Islamic. As a result, Jordan has made some gains in women's rights, but it has moved at a glacial pace compared with Morocco, and some argue that it is going backwards.

Like his Moroccan counterpart, the Jordanian king has control of all key political institutions. The king appoints the prime minister and upper house of the legislature. He can dissolve the parliament at his discretion. He controls the internal security service, the Mukhabarat intelligence agency, as well as the legal restrictions on party formation, and charitable and social service organizations.

As in Morocco, there was a series of protests by a variety of movements in 2011 against unemployment and corruption, calling for the restoration of stolen public funds, and calling for the privatization of national resources. The protests, which spread from Dhiban to Amman, Karak, and Irbid, called for modern and democratic elections and constitutional reform. Like the Moroccan king, the Jordanian King

Abdullah announced a series of limited reforms that were aimed at transforming the Jordanian parliament and making it more engaged in governance and, as in Morocco, these reforms stopped far short of fundamentally democratizing the political system.

Gender equality has been backsliding in Jordan, according to data from the World Economic Forum Global Gender Gap Report (2018), which tracks a variety of indicators related to education, health, economic opportunity, and political participation. Only Yemen and Syria, two war-torn countries, ranked lower than Jordan when it came to economic participation and opportunity. Jordan, for example, does not have legislation prohibiting gender discrimination in the workplace. Maternity leave and day care provisions are nonexistent for many private-sector employees. Moreover, women are finding it difficult to claim their portion of their inheritance as male relatives take advantage of them and claim their portions.

One hundred of the 130 seats in the Jordanian lower house are held by independents who are tribal figures or businessmen. Fifteen seats are reserved for women who fail to win district seats and twelve are reserved for religious and ethnic minorities. Five women won seats outside of reserved seats and three of them were Islamists. The opposition Islamic Action Front (IAF) has ten seats in all and other smaller parties have one to five seats. In 2016, over 150 women from around the country, led by the Jordanian National Commission for Women, demonstrated inside the Jordanian parliament, demanding that at least one seat for women be provided in each of the twenty-three constituencies. This would have increased the minimum number from fifteen to twenty-three. The bill to this effect was voted down by legislators in 2016 (Staton 2016).

Because the bulk of parliamentary representatives are not organized into political parties, it is difficult to lobby them around particular issues since decisions are made based on tribal or personal loyalties. The parliamentary system is fragmented and individualist and does not encourage programmatic parties or blocs. Women in the only substantial party with a block of votes, the IAF, are not keen on promoting women's issues, nor is the male leadership of the IAF. The IAF is the legal political wing of the core Muslim Brotherhood, which was banned in 2015. Three IAF women won seats in the parliament (Husseini 2016).

Thus, the fragmentation of parliamentary interests and the lack of a coalescence of interests into a party formation makes it almost impossible to negotiate programmatic concerns in Jordan. The largest single party represented is an Islamist formation with no incentive or interest in advancing women's rights. Moreover, unlike Morocco, there is little pressure from the king to incentivize political parties and actors to take up these concerns. Unlike the PJD in Morocco, which has had to change its position on women's rights out of necessity, there is no political consequence for political parties or individual MPs in Jordan for not adopting women's rights. And finally, the women's movement has not seized upon key moments of transition to push for major reforms. Thus, all the elements one found in Morocco are absent in Jordan.

Final Word

The three paired comparisons above are quite different from each other, but all three point to the factors that have made it possible for leaders in the Maghreb to advocate for women's rights. Each takes us back to the question of why authoritarian countries adopt women's rights. Each comparison shows that there is no reason why one might expect authoritarian regimes to do so when there is an absence of political will at the top to see such reforms carried out, as one finds in Jordan, Lebanon, and Egypt.

The fractured legal system for family law across fifteen confessional groups makes women's rights reforms exceptionally challenging in Lebanon. But the dependence of the prime minister on extremist groups makes reform unlikely even though Lebanon has some of the most liberal attitudes toward women's rights in the region. In Egypt, the suppression of women's associations and civil society more generally, including Islamist organizations and parties, makes the evolution of a meaningful women's rights agenda virtually impossible even though this country has a long history of women's rights activism. Its constitutional reforms thus become little more than window dressing. In Jordan, the fractured nature of the parliament, the lack of a developed party system, coupled with a lack of political will, makes gender reform unlikely. This makes it all the more interesting to understand why the Maghreb countries have progressed with a series of constitutional and legislative reforms.

The idea of states adopting female-friendly policies, sometimes known as "state feminism," was first developed primarily within the context of scholarship on Europe, North America, and Australia. Such policies have been promoted globally by the United Nations, the European Union, the African Union, and other such regional and international bodies since the mid 1970s with the formation of women's national machineries globally, but most consistently since the 1995 United Nations Conference on Women held in Beijing. State feminist policies have not only been adopted by democracies, but increasingly by nondemocratic states as well throughout the world (Barrig 1999, Fischler 2001, Gilmartin 1995, Hatem 1994a, Racioppi and O'Sullivan See 1995).

In looking at some of the reasons for adopting female-friendly policies in nondemocratic contexts, one should keep in mind that woman-friendly policies in democratic contexts have not always been introduced with the primary objective of enhancing women's welfare and status. Even in the United States, the adoption of the Civil Rights Act in 1964, which prohibited discrimination based on race and sex, was not originally intended to improve women's status, only that of African Americans. Howard W. Smith, a Virginia Democratic who chaired the House Rules Committee and opposed the legislation, attempted at the last minute to defeat the bill by inserting a clause that prohibited sex discrimination. He believed that this would sink the bill altogether, particularly among the legislators from the eighteen southern democratic states. He was wrong and the act passed.

While this was an attempt to limit citizenship within a democracy, women's rights have also been adopted as part of an effort to shape democracy within a specific frame. Many gender equality policies in Scandinavia, for example, had their origins in labor market policies and within the broader welfare state ethos of equality for all citizens. Women could gain equality within the dominant egalitarian ideology, but they could not be expressed as special interests like "women's interests" (Hernes 1987). Because of the emphasis on women's rights in the context of the labor market, there was a general reluctance to address issues of domestic violence that fell outside of the labor rights frame (Gelb 1989). Thus, even in democratic contexts, women's rights have not always been defined in terms of what is best for women, but rather they have been seen in the service of other broader goals.

In the Maghrebi cases, the heads of state and other national leaders had two different sets of goals in using women's rights. One was to draw a line between themselves and religious conservatives, particularly extremists. The other was to gain international legitimacy by using women's rights to portray their countries as modernizing, progressive, and democratizing. Tunisia's Ben Ali, like many other autocratic leaders, used this strategy to gain international legitimacy at a time when he was restricting civil rights and political liberties at home through censorship and repression of the opposition (Voorhoeven 2013).

The dangers of such policies are many. Policies in which women's rights are instrumental to other purposes may mark symbolic advances, but they may also run the risk of not directly addressing women's rights concerns, of having problematic unintended consequences, of not including women representatives in the crafting of policies, and of not being developed with the interests of women themselves in mind. If they are used to divert attention from human rights violations, they can work at cross-purposes to women's rights, which are contingent on freedom of association, freedom of speech, free and fair elections, and the right to freely participate in politics. Policies which are enacted for the purposes of expediency and of pleasing an external audience may look good on paper, but they may not be implemented or funded at a level that would bring about real changes for women. And finally, those women's rights activists who are associated with these reforms, however sincere they are in their goals, may find themselves tainted by association with a corrupt and dictatorial government, especially once the country democratizes.

The increase in female political representation as a result of the introduction of a legislative quota or reserved seats may end up benefiting parties and movements that are not interested in women's rights reforms. They may strengthen problematic patronage relations and ties of political obligation between authorities and women's rights organizations and leaders. And finally, if the reformists fail, they may result in pitting groups against one another, namely feminists and religious extremists, in ways that can create backlashes and hostilities.

At the same time, the adoption of women's rights reforms by leaders in a top-down fashion may bring about an awareness of a particular problem affecting women. They may raise the bar of expectations regarding how women should be treated. They may result in real policy reforms, as we have seen with the quota laws. They may indeed help isolate religious extremists and create new norms around which society is mobilized. In Morocco, the changes within the leading Islamist party, the PJD, regarding its stated positions on women's rights over the past two decades are among the most interesting outcomes of the top-down policies of the king.

Morocco and Tunisia have seen both top-down and bottom-up pressures for gender reform. In Morocco, the king was influenced by women's rights activists who pushed for change at critical moments. In Tunisia, top-down pressures came during the Bourguiba, Ben Ali, and Essebsi governments, while societal pressures were most evident at critical moments of transition, including the 2011 Arab Spring. As in Morocco, the stated position of the Tunisian Islamist party Ennahda evolved toward adopting a stronger women's rights platform, especially when confronted with opposition during the 2014 constitution drafting process. This was made possible in no small measure by the political opening that took place after Ben Ali was ousted. In Algeria, the Black Decade's confrontation between secularists and Islamists (1991–2002) created a somewhat different dynamic with similar outcomes to Morocco and Tunisia. Because women were targeted so brutally and directly during the civil war, the need to address their circumstances became more urgent in its aftermath.

In all three countries, women, women's bodies, and women's rights became the frontline of the struggle between feminists and secularists on the one hand and Islamists and Salafis on the other. In the process, the line moved with respect to laws, constitutions, and treaties. Whether these legal gains can be translated more fully into gains for women in their daily lives remains a question.

References

20 Minutes. 2015. "Algérie: la campagne 'ne laisse pas tes femmes sortir avec une tenue osée' fait fureur sur le Web." May 26. www.20minutes.fr/monde/1616211-20150526-algerie-campagne-laisse-femmes-sortir-tenue-osee-fait-fureur-web.

Abdennebi, Zakia. 2011. "Morocco's PM-elect: no Islamic dress code for women." *Reuters*, December 10. https://af.reuters.com/article/topNews/idAFJOE7B901J20111210.

2018. "Morocco struggles to curb rise in number of girls married underage." *Reuters*. April 26. www.reuters.com/article/us-morocco-women/morocco-struggles-to-curb-rise-in-number-of-girls-married-underage-idUSKBN1HX22T.

Abdo-Katsipis, Carla. 2017. "Islamists in power and women's rights: the case of Tunisia." *Middle East Brief* 112. www.brandeis.edu/crown/publications/meb/meb112.html.

Abdulrazak, Fawzi. 1982. "Arabization in Algeria." *MELA Notes* 28: 22–43.

Abou-Zeid, Gihan. 2006. "The Arab Region: women's access to the decision-making process across the Arab nation." In *Women, Quotas and Politics*, edited by Drude Dahlerup, 168–193. New York: Routledge.

Abounaï, A. 2012. "Les femmes marocaines et 'le printemps arabe'." *Tumultes* 1–2 (38–39): 115–132.

Adorno, Theodor et al. 1950. *The Authoritarian Personality*. New York: Harper & Brothers.

Agerholm, Harriet. 2017. "Algerian women in their thousands are defying conservative Islamists by wearing bikinis." *Independent*. August 7. www.independent.co.uk/news/world/africa/algeria-women-bikinis-conservative-islamists-muslim-cover-up-skin-beach-a7880371.html.

Ahmed, Dawood I., and Moamen Gouda. 2015. "Measuring constitutional Islamization: the Islamic Constitutions Index." *Hastings International and Comparative Law Review* 38 (1): 1–74.

Ahmed, Leila. 1982. "Feminism and feminist movements in the Middle East, a preliminary exploration: Turkey, Egypt, Algeria, People's Democratic

Republic of Yemen." *Women's Studies International Forum* 5 (2): 153–168.

Ahmed, Sumayya. 2016. "Learned women: three generations of female Islamic scholarship in Morocco." *Journal of North African Studies* 21 (3): 470–484.

Ait Dada, Abdessamad, and Richard van Schaik. 2012. "Political Islam and the Moroccan Arab Spring." Final research report, January 23. Rabat: Nederlands Institut Marokko.

Alami, Aida. 2014. "Leader's words about women jolt Morocco." *New York Times*. June 18. www.nytimes.com/2014/06/19/world/middleeast/prime-minister-told-parliament-women-better-off-at-home-than-in-workplace .html.

Alexander Amy. 2015. "Big jumps in women's presence in parliaments: are these sufficient for improving beliefs in women's ability to govern?" *Advancing Women in Leadership* 35: 82–89.

Alexander, Amy C., and Christian Welzel. 2011. "Islam and patriarchy: how robust is Muslim support for patriarchal values?" *International Review of Sociology* 21 (2): 249–276.

Algérie: Constitution du 28 novembre 1996. http://mjp.univ-perp.fr/constit/ dz2008v.htm.

Algérie Monde Infos. 2018a. "Salafistes en France: ils sont passés de 5 000 à 50 000 en moins de 15 ans." May 28. www.algeriemondeinfos.com/sa lafistes-france-passes-de-5-000-a-50-000-de-15-ans/.

2018b. "Afin de protester contre l'agression de Ryma: un 'footing citoyen' organisé hier à Alger." June 10. www.algeriemondeinfos.com/afin-de-protester-contre-lagression-de-ryma-footing-citoyen-organise-hier-a-al ger/.

2018c. "Appels à l'agression des femmes non voilées: Tayeb Louh confirme l'arrestation d'un des auteurs." June 19. www.algeriemondein fos.com/appels-a-lagression-femmes-non-voilees-tayeb-louh-confirme-l arrestation-dun-auteurs/.

2018d. "Maroc: les femmes ripostent à ceux qui veulent les voiler." July 23. www.algeriemondeinfos.com/maroc-femmes-ripostent-a-veu lent-voiler/.

Al-Ali, Nadje Sadig. 2000. *Secularism, Gender and the State in the Middle East*. New York: Cambridge University Press.

Ali, Zahra. 2017. "Women's rights are under threat in Iraq." *Washington Post*. November 20. www.washingtonpost.com/news/monkey-cage/w p/2017/11/20/womens-rights-are-under-threat-in-iraq/.

Al Jazeera. 2018. "Morocco criminalises violence against women and sexual harassment." September 12. www.aljazeera.com/news/2018/09/mor occo-violence-women-law-effect-180912061837132.html.

Allalou, Samia. 2009. "Algeria: women's movement still going strong." *Common Ground News*. April 27.

Allemandou, Ségolène. 2017. "Female emancipation in Egypt 'can only come from Egyptian women'." *France24*. December 18. www.france24.com/en/20171218-women-rights-egypt-emancipation-egyptian-feminists-sisi.

Allison, Simon. 2012. "Amina Filali: a story of rape, suicide and the society searching for its soul." *Daily Maverick*. March 20. www.dailymaverick.co.za/article/2012-03-20-amina-filali-a-story-of-rape-suicide-and-the-society-searching-for-its-soul/.

Amnesty International. 2015. "'Circles of Hell': domestic, public and state violence against women in Egypt." January 20. www.amnestyusa.org/reports/circles-of-hell-domestic-public-and-state-violence-against-women-in-egypt/.

Angrist, M. 2012. "War, resting the west, and women's labor: toward an understanding of Arab exceptionalism." *Politics & Gender* 8: 51–82.

APS. 2016. "Algeria: President Bouteflika calls for reconsidering reservations on convention against discrimination toward women." March 8.

2017. "ALGERIA: promotion of women's political rights, fundamental for Algerian state." February 23.

2018a. "Women's rights promotion: Algeria committed to UN resolutions." March 14. www.aps.dz/en/algeria/23282-women-s-rights-promotion-algeria-committed-to-un-resolutions.

2018b. "Algerian women remain 'guarantor of our country's stability,' says President Bouteflika." March 8. www.aps.dz/en/algeria/23202-algerian-women-remain-guarantor-of-our-country-s-stability-says-president-bouteflika.

2018c. "Conference on women's involvement in politics: Algeria to implement recommendations." March 19. www.aps.dz/en/algeria/23351-women-s-involvement-in-politics-algerian-state-to-work-for-implementation-of-recommendations.

Arab Barometer. 2013. "Arab barometer." www.arabbarometer.org/.

Article19.ma. 2018. "Controversy – the picture of new education minister in unusual prostration before the king provoked tough criticism on the web." January 25.

Asharq Al-Awsat. 2012. "Asharq Al-Awsat interview: Bassima Hakkaoui." June 11. https://eng-archive.aawsat.com/theaawsat/features/asharq-al-awsat-interview-bassima-hakkaoui.

Ashraf, Ajaz. 2018. "As Supreme Court decides on banning polygamy, a look at how Muslim countries deal with the practice." *Scroll.in*. March 30. https://scroll.in/article/873813/as-supreme-court-decides-on-banning-polygamy-a-look-at-how-muslim-countries-deal-with-the-practice.

Auffray, Elodie. 2014. "Droits des femmes: les ambivalences de la constitution tunisienne." *Libération*. January 9. www.liberation.fr/planete/2014/01/09/droits-des-femmes-les-ambivalences-de-la-constitution-tunisienne_971549.

Aujourd'hui Le Maroc. 2017. "Violence contre les femmes: El Othmani évoque l'accélération de l'adoption de la loi." December 27. http://aujourdhui.ma/societe/violence-contre-les-femmes-el-othmani-evoque-lacceleration-de-ladoption-de-la-loi.

2018. "Les femmes représentent 10,83 % à la Chambre des conseillers en 2017." April 10. http://aujourdhui.ma/politique/les-femmes-representent-1083-a-la-chambre-des-conseillers-en-2017.

Ayari, Farida. 2015. "Ennahda movement in power: a long path to democracy." *Contemporary Review of the Middle East* 2 (1–2): 135–142.

Bacha, Roxanne. 2013. "La reconnaissance des droits des femmes dans le contexte du 'printemps arabe': le cas du Maroc." Master diss., Mondialisation et développement international, l'Université d'Ottawa.

Bachleda, Catherine, Nicolas Hamelin, and Oumaima Benachour. 2014. "Does religiosity impact Moroccan Muslim women's clothing choice?" *Journal of Islamic Marketing* 5 (2): 210–226.

Baliamoune-Lutz, Mina. 2013. "The effectiveness of foreign aid to women's equality organizations in the MENA: does aid promote women's political participation?" WIDER Working Paper 2013/074. Helsinki: UNU-WIDER.

Barbouch, Rachid. 2019. "Amina Maelainine s'est fait lyncher pour être apparue sans voile." *Mediapart*. January 14. https://blogs.mediapart.fr/rachid-barbouch/blog/140119/amina-maelainine-sest-fait-lyncher-pour-etre-apparue-sans-voile.

Barrig, Maruja. 1999. "The persistence of memory: feminism and the state in Peru in the 1990s." Working paper Civil Society and Democratic Governance in the Andes and the Southern Cone. Comparative Regional Project, Ford Foundation – Department of Social Sciences, Pontificia Universidad Católica del Perú, Lima.

Batha, Emma. 2015. "Morocco's Islamic women preachers lead social revolution." *Reuters*. May 19. www.reuters.com/article/us-morocco-women-morchidat/moroccos-islamic-women-preachers-lead-social-revolution-idUSKBN0O40MG20150519.

BBC Monitoring. 2017. "Algeria parties ordered to show female faces on posters." April 18. www.bbc.com/news/world-africa-39636548.

BBC News. 2017a. "Jordan MPs vote to scrap rape law loophole." August 1. www.bbc.com/news/world-middle-east-40793049.

2017b. "Lebanon rape law: parliament abolishes marriage loophole." August 16. www.bbc.com/news/world-middle-east-40947448.
Becker, Cynthia. 2015. "The Kahina: the female face of Berber history." *Mizan Project*. October 26. www.mizanproject.org/the-kahina-the-female-face-of-berber-history/.
Begum, Rothna. 2017. "Middle East on a roll to repeal 'marry the rapist' laws." *Al Jazeera*. August 24. www.aljazeera.com/indepth/opinion/2017/08/middle-east-roll-repeal-marry-rapist-laws-170822095605552.html.
Bekkat, Réda. 2018. "Menaces sur les mosquées." *El Watan*. July 9. www.elwatan.com/chroniques/edito/menaces-sur-les-mosquees-09-07-2018.
Belabd, Houda. 2012. "Bassima Hakkaoui: l'abrogation de l'article 475 ne se fera pas sous la pression." *Yabiladi*. March 21. www.yabiladi.com/articles/details/9537/bassima-hakkaoui-l-abrogation-l-article-fera.html.
Belarbi, Aïcha. 2012. *Égalité-parité: histoire inachevée*. Casablanca: Le Fennec.
Ben Saga, Ahlam. 2018. "Social media users launch 'be a man' campaign against women swimwear." *Morocco World News*. July 17. www.moroccoworldnews.com/2018/07/250663/morocco-be-a-man-campaign-against-women-swimwear/.
Ben Salem, Maryam. 2010. "Le voile en Tunisie. De la réalisation de soi à la résistance passive." *Revue des mondes musulmans et de la Méditerranée* 128. https://journals.openedition.org/remmm/6840.
Bendaoudi, Abdellilah. 2018. "How lessons from Algeria can shape Iraq." *The Washington Institute: Fikra Forum*. August 8. www.washingtoninstitute.org/fikraforum/view/how-lessons-from-algeria-can-shape-iraq.
Benfodil, Mustapha. 2018. "Echec des garçons au bac: pourquoi ça ne les fait plus rêver." *El Watan*. July 23. www.elwatan.com/edition/actualite/echec-des-garcons-au-bac-pourquoi-ca-ne-les-fait-plus-rever-23-07-2018.
Bennoune, Karima. 2013. *Your Fatwa Does Not Apply Here: Untold Stories from the Fight Against Muslim Fundamentalism*. New York and London: W. W. Norton.
Benrabah, Mohamed. 2013. *Language Conflict in Algeria: From Colonialism to Post-Independence*. Bristol: Multilingual Matters.
Benzenine, Belkacem. 2013. "Les femmes algériennes au Parlement: la question des quotas à l'épreuve des réformes politiques." *Égypte/Monde Arabe* 10. http://journals.openedition.org/ema/3196.
Berriane, Yassmine. 2013. *Femmes, associations et politique à Casablanca*. Rabat, Morocco: Centre Jacques-Berque.
Bessis, Sophie. 1999. "Le féminisme institutionnel en Tunisie." *Clio. Histoire, femmes et sociétés* 9. https://journals.openedition.org/clio/286.

Bessis, Sophie, and Souhayr Belhassen. 1992. *Femmes du Maghreb: l'enjeu*. Paris: J. C. Lattès.

Bilgili, Özge, and Silja Weyel. 2009. *Migration in Morocco: History, Current Trends and Future Prospects*. Migration and Development Country Profiles. Maastricht: Maastricht Graduate School of Governance.

Bordo, Susan. 1993. *Unbearable Weight: Feminism, Western Culture, and the Body*. Berkeley, CA: University of California Press.

Botman, Selma. 1999. *Engendering Citizenship in Egypt*. New York: Columbia University Press.

Boualem, M. 2018a. "Fermeture des sièges de FARD et AFEPEC: neuf associations fustigent les décisions liberticides du wali d'Oran." *Algérie Monde Infos*, March 2. www.algeriemondeinfos.com/fermeture-sieges-de-fard-afepec-neuf-associations-fustigent-decisions-liberticides-wali-doran/.

2018b. "Candidates non-voilées et des non-croyants en 2022: Makri sur les trâces de Ghannouchi." *Algérie Monde Infos*, May 15. www.algeriemondeinfos.com/candidates-non-voilees-non-croyants-2022-makri-traces-de-ghannouchi/.

Bouteflika, Abdelaziz. 2018. "Message de Bouteflika à l'occasion du 8 Mars: le texte intégral." *TSA*. March 8. www.tsa-algerie.com/message-de-bouteflika-a-loccasion-du-8-mars-le-texte-integral/.

Bouziri, Amira. 2015. "'Trop courte ma jupe?' L'Algérie montre ses jambes." *France24*, May 14. https://observers.france24.com/fr/20150514-trop-courte-jupe-algerie-montrer-jambes-polemique.

Brand, Laurie A. 1998. *Women, the State, and Political Liberalization: Middle Eastern and North African Experiences*. New York: Columbia University Press.

Bras, Jean-Philippe. 2007. "La Réforme du code de la famille au Maroc et en Algérie: quelles avancées pour la démocratie?" *Critique Internationale* 37 (4): 93–125.

Bremmer, Ian. 2017. "The top 5 countries where ISIS gets its foreign recruits." *Time*. April 14. http://time.com/4739488/isis-iraq-syria-tunisia-saudi-arabia-russia/.

Brown, Nathan J. 2001. "Arab judicial structures." A study presented to the United Nations development Program: Programme of Governance in the Arab Region (POGAR). http://web.dubaichamber.ae/LibPublic/Arab%20judicial%20structures.pdf.

Brownlee, Jason, Tarek Masoud, and Andrew Reynolds. 2015. *The Arab Spring: Pathways of Repression and Reform* Oxford: Oxford University Press.

Brumberg, Daniel. 2013. "Transforming the Arab world's protection-racket politics." *Journal of Democracy* 24 (3): 88–103.

Bruneau, Caroline. 2012. "Le Maroc choqué après le suicide d'une jeune fille violée." *Le Figaro*. March 17. www.lefigaro.fr/international/2012/03/15/

01003-20120315ARTFIG00733-le-maroc-choque-apres-le-suicide-d-une-jeune-fille-violee.php.

Bush, Sarah Sunn. 2011. "International politics and the spread of quotas for women in legislatures." *International Organization* 65 (1): 103–137.

Bush, Sarah Sunn, and Amaney A. Jamal. 2015. "Anti-Americanism, authoritarian politics, and attitudes about women's representation: evidence from a survey experiment in Jordan." *International Studies Quarterly* 59: 34–45.

Business News. 2018. "Représentativité des femmes dans les conseils municipaux: la Tunisie bat la France et l'Allemagne!" May 10. www.businessnews.com.tn/representativite-des-femmes-dans-les-conseils-municipaux–la-tunisie-bat-la-france-et-lallemagne-,520,79939,3.

Butler, Judith. 1990. *Gender Trouble: Feminism and the Subversion of Identity*. New York: Routledge.

Caris, Tobias, and Bernd Hayo. 2012. "Female labour force participation in Arab countries: the role of identity." MAGKS Joint Discussion Paper Series in Economics No. 41-2012.

Cavatorta, Francesco, and Emanuela Dalmasso. 2009. "Liberal outcomes through undemocratic means: the reform of the Code de statut personnel in Morocco." *Journal of Modern African Studies* 47 (4): 487–506.

Cavatorta, Francesco, and Fabio Merone. 2013. "Moderation through exclusion? The journey of the Tunisian Ennahda from fundamentalist to conservative party." *Democratization* 20 (5): 857–875.

Celis, Karen, Sarah Childs, Johanna Kantola, and Mona Lena Krook. 2008. "Rethinking women's substantive representation." *Representation* 44 (2): 99–110.

Cesari, Jocelyne. 2017. "Introduction." In *Islam, Gender and Democracy in Comparative Perspective*, edited by Jocelyne Cesari and José Casanova, 1–10. Oxford: Oxford University Press.

Chaarani, Ahmed. 2004. *La Mouvance islamiste au Maroc: du 11 septembre 2001 aux attentats de Casablanca du 16 Mai 2003*. Paris: Éditions Karthala.

Charef, Abed. 2017. "La Tunisie et le Maroc entrent dans l'ère post-islamiste." *Middle East Eye*. June 18. www.middleeasteye.net/fr/opinion/la-tunisie-et-le-maroc-entrent-dans-lere-post-islamiste.

Charrad, Mounira. 2001. *States and Women's Rights: The Making of Postcolonial Tunisia, Algeria, and Morocco*. Berkeley, CA: University of California Press.

2011. "Tunisia at the forefront of the Arab world." In *Women in the Middle East and North Africa: Agents of Change*, edited by Fatima Sadiqi and Moha Ennaji, 107–113. New York: Routledge.

Cheref, Abdelkader. 2006. "Engendering or endangering politics in Algeria? Salima Ghezali, Louisa Hanoune and Khalida Messaoudi." *Journal of Middle East Women's Studies* 2 (2): 60–85.

CIDDEF. 2007. "Projet CIDDEF-MEPI année 2006–2007: femmes et politique en Algérie." www.ciddef-dz.com/pdf/revues/revue-15/femmes-et-politique-en-algerie.pdf.

Clark, Janine A., and Amy E. Young. 2008. "Islamism and family law reform in Morocco and Jordan." *Mediterranean Politics* 13 (3): 333–352.

Coelho, Nuno. n.d. "The Arab Spring in Tunisia – a semiotic perspective." Unpublished document, University of Coimbra.

Coleman, Isobel. 2011. "Is the Arab Spring bad for women?" *Foreign Policy*. December 20. https://foreignpolicy.com/2011/12/20/is-the-arab-spring-bad-for-women/.

Collectif Egalité-Maghreb 95. 1995. "Cent mesures et dispositions pour une codification égalitaire des relations familiales au Maghreb." French version edited by Women Living under Muslim Laws, Grabels, France.

Comaroff, John L., and Jean Comaroff. 1992. *Ethnography and the Historical Imagination*. Studies in the Ethnographic Imagination. Boulder, CO: Westview Press.

Commission of the European Communities. 2000. Communication on "Reinvigorating the Barcelona Process." 6 September

Constitute Project. 2014. Tunisia's constitution of 2014. www.constituteproject.org/constitution/Tunisia_2014.pdf.

Crawford, R. 1984. "A cultural account of 'health': control, release, and the social body." *Issues in the Political Economy of Health Care*, edited by J. B. McKinlay, 60–103. New York: Tavistock.

La Croix. 2017. "La démographie médicale 2017 en chiffres." www.la-croix.com/Monde/demographie-medicale-2017-chiffres-2017-10-12-1300883681.

Daadaoui, Mohamed. 2016. "Islamism and the state in Morocco." *Hudson Institute*. April 29. www.hudson.org/research/12286-islamism-and-the-state-in-morocco.

Dahlerup, Drude. 2006. *Women, Quotas and Politics*. Philadelphia, PA: Taylor & Francis.

Daily Sabah Africa. 2017. "Algeria unveils first ever electoral list composed entirely of women." April 21. www.dailysabah.com/africa/2017/04/21/algeria-unveils-first-ever-electoral-list-composed-entirely-of-women.

Daoud, Kamel. 2016. "La misère sexuelle du monde arabe." *New York Times*. February 12. www.nytimes.com/2016/02/14/opinion/sunday/la-misere-sexuelle-du-monde-arabe.html.

Daoud, Zakya. 1996. *Feminisme et politique au Maghreb: sept décennies de lutte*. Casablanca: Eddifi Maroc.

Darhour, Hanane. 2016. "Engendering political representation in the aftermath of the Arab Spring." The Second International Conference on Women's Political Participation and Leadership, March 7–8, 2016, New York University in Abu Dhabi.

Darhour, Hanane, and Drude Dahlerup. 2013. "Sustainable representation of women through gender quotas: a decade's experience in Morocco." *Women's Studies International Forum* 41 (2): 132–142.

Debbagh, Souad. 2011. "Aïcha Qandicha, une femme comme les autres." *Qandisha*. November 14.

Dennerlein, Bettina. 2012. "Remembering violence, negotiating change: the Moroccan Equity and Reconciliation Commission and the politics of gender." *Journal of Middle East Women's Studies* 8 (1): 10–36.

Dernières Infos d'Algérie. 2018. "Réouverture des bureaux des associations FARD et AFEPEC à Oran." March 6. http://dia-algerie.com/reouverture-bureaux-associations-fard-afepec-a-oran/.

Desrues, Thierry. 2012. "Le mouvement du 20 février et le régime Marocain: contestation, révision constitutionnelle et élections." *L'Année du Maghreb* VII: 359–389.

Devisch, Renaat. 1985. "Approaches to symbol and symptom in bodily space-time." *International Journal of Psychology* 20: 389–415.

Dieste, Josep Lluîs Mateo. 2009. "'Demonstrating Islam': the conflict of text and the Mudawwana reform in Morocco." *The Muslim World* 99 (January): 134–154.

Dilday, Ka. 2007. "Nadia Yassine's journey." *Open Democracy*. August 2. www.opendemocracy.net/globalization-village/nadia_yassine_journey.

Dirèche, Karima. 2010. "Les *Murchidât* au Maroc. Entre islam d'État et islam au féminin." *Revue des mondes musulmans et de la Méditerranée* 128 (December): 99–111.

Domat, Chloé. 2018. "Women in Lebanon: how election dashed their political hopes." *Middle East Eye*. May 10. www.middleeasteye.net/news/women-lebanon-how-election-dashed-their-political-hopes.

Donno, Daniela, and Bruce Russett. 2004. "Islam, authoritarianism, and female empowerment: what are the linkages?" *World Politics* 56 (4): 582–607.

Douglas, Mary. 1970. *Natural Symbols*. London: Barrie & Rockliff, Cresset Press.

Dris-Aït-Hamadouchea, Louisa, and Yahia Zoubir. 2007. "The Maghreb: social, political, and economic developments." *Perspectives on Global Development and Technology* 6: 261–290.

Dwyer, D. H. 1978. "Women, Sufism, and decision-making in Moroccan Islam." In *Women in the Muslim World*, edited by L. Beck and N. Keddie, 585–598. Cambridge, MA: Harvard University Press.

Economic and social Commission for Western Asia. 2016. "Against wind and tides: a review of the status of women and gender equality in the Arab region 20 years after the adoption of the Beijing declaration and platform for action." January 7. https://sustainabledevelopment.un.org/content/documents/2283ESCWA_Women%20and%20Gender%20Equality%20in%20the%20Arab%20Region_Beijing20.pdf.

Eddouada, Souad, and Renata Pepicelli. 2010. "Maroc: vers un 'féminisme islamique d'État'." *Critique Internationale* 46: 87–100.

Edelman, Murray. 1964. *The Symbolic Uses of Politics*. Champaign, IL: University of Illinois Press.

1971. *Politics as Symbolic Action: Mass Arousal and Quiescence*. Cambridge, MA: Academic Press.

1988. *Constructing the Political Spectacle*. Chicago, IL: University of Chicago.

ElBoudrari, Hassan, ed. 1993. *Modes de transmission de la culture religieuse en Islam*. Cairo: Institut français d'archéologie orientale (IFAO).

Elhassani, Ihsane Elidrissi. 2018. "Women *adoul* in Morocco: the not so modern legal dilemma." *Morocco World News*. September 30. www.moroccoworldnews.com/2018/09/254339/women-adoul-morocco-public-notary/.

Engelcke, Dörthe. 2014. "Processes of family law reform: legal and societal change and continuity in Morocco and Jordan." DPhil thesis, Oriental Studies, St Antony's College, Oxford University, Oxford.

Esping-Andersen, Gösta et al. 2002. *Why We Need a New Welfare State*. Oxford: Oxford University Press.

Fabiani, Riccardo. 2017. "Algerian Islamists, fragmented and irrelevant." *Carnegie Middle East Center*. April 14. https://carnegie-mec.org/sada/68679.

Fakih, Lama, and Amy Braunschweiger. 2015. "Interview: women unequal under Lebanon's law." *Human Rights Watch*. January 19. www.hrw.org/news/2015/01/19/interview-women-unequal-under-lebanons-law.

Fakir, Intissar. 2017. "Morocco's Islamist party: redefining politics under pressure." *Carnegie Endowment for International Peace*. December 28. https://carnegieendowment.org/2017/12/28/morocco-s-islamist-party-redefining-politics-under-pressure-pub-75121.

Farris, Sara R. 2017. *In the Name of Women's Rights: The Rise of Femonationalism*. Durham, NC: Duke University Press.

Fatoorehchi, Cléo. 2013. "Les femmes en Tunisie – Partie 2: Jaouida Guiga: 'si la révolution tunisienne réussit, ce sera grâce aux femmes'." *Opinion*

Internationale. May 22. www.opinion-internationale.com/2013/05/22/les-femmes-en-tunisie-partie-2-jaouida-guiga-si-la-revolution-tunisienne-reussit-ce-sera-grace-aux-femmes_17699.html.

Fernea, Robert A., and James M. Malarkey. 1975. "Anthropology of the Middle East and North Africa: a critical assessment." *Annual Review of Anthropology* 4: 183–206.

Fischler, Lisa. 2001. "Women at the margin: challenging boundaries of the political in Hong Kong, 1982–1997." Unpublished PhD thesis, Political Science, University of Wisconsin, Madison.

Fish, Steven. 2011. *Are Muslims Distinctive? A Look at the Evidence*. New York: Oxford University Press.

France24. 2014. "Au Maroc, le Premier ministre Benkirane s'attire les foudres des femmes." June 25. www.france24.com/fr/20142506-maroc-egalite-hommes-femmes-foyer-benkirane-polemique-lustre-anamachitria-pjd.

Franceschet, Susan, and Jennifer M. Piscopo. 2008. "Gender quotas and women's substantive representation: lessons from Argentina." *Politics & Gender* 4 (3): 393–425.

Gall, Cavorta. 2015. "Women in Tunisia tell of decades of police cruelty, violence and rape." *New York Times*. May 28. www.nytimes.com/2015/05/29/world/africa/women-in-tunisia-tell-of-decades-of-police-cruelty-violence-and-rape.html.

El Gantri, Salwa. 2016. "Our voices will not be silenced: charting women's struggle for justice in Tunisia." *ICTJ*. June 21. www.ictj.org/news/women-struggle-justice-tunisia.

Gaouane, Zineb, and Madeleine Elie. n.d. "Analyse et perspective d'un parti islamique au Maroc: Lahcen Daoudi." *Institute for Research and Debate on Governance*. www.institut-gouvernance.org/en/entretien/fiche-entretien-55.html.

Gattioui, J. 2018. "Bassima Hakkaoui: 'il reste encore des efforts à déployer pour atteindre la parité'." *LesEco.ma*. March 8. www.leseco.ma/supplements/548-8mars-journee-de-la-femme/64285-bassima-hakkaoui-il-reste-encore-des-efforts-a-deployer-pour-atteindre-la-parite.html.

Geertz, Clifford. 1973. *The Interpretation of Cultures*. New York: Basic Books Classics.

Geiger, Susan. 1987. *TANU Women: Gender and Culture in the Making of Tanganyikan Nationalism, 1955-1965*. Social History of Africa Series. Portsmouth, NH, Oxford, Nairobi, Dar es Salaam: Heinemann; James Currey; East African Educational Publishers; Mkuki Na Nyota.

Gelb, Joyce. 1989. *Feminism and Politics: A Comparative Perspective*. Berkeley, CA Los Angeles, CA and London: University of California Press.

Géopolis, Par. 2018. "Agression d'une joggeuse: 300 Algériennes ont couru à Alger pour leur liberté." *Franceinfo*. June 11. www.francetvinfo.fr/monde/afrique/societe-africaine/agression-dune-joggeuse-300-algeriennes-ont-couru-a-alger-pour-leur-liberte_3054319.html.

Ghanem-Yazbeck, Dalia. 2014. "The decline of Islamist parties in Algeria." *Carnegie Endowment for International Peace*. February 13. https://carnegieendowment.org/sada/54510.

2018. "Specter of jihadism continues to haunt Maghreb." *Middle East Institute of the Carnegie Middle East Center*. September 18. https://carnegie-mec.org/2018/09/18/specter-of-jihadism-continues-to-haunt-maghreb-pub-77312.

Ghanmi, Lamine. 2017. "Algerian 'bikini rebellion' may be hype but harassment isn't." *The Arab Weekly*. August 20. https://thearabweekly.com/algerian-bikini-rebellion-may-be-hype-harassment-isnt.

Al-Ghanmi, Monia. 2018. "Obituary: Maya Jribi, Tunisia's first woman party leader, dies." *Al Arabiya*. May 20. http://english.alarabiya.net/en/features/2018/05/20/Obituary-Maya-Jribi-Tunisia-s-first-woman-party-leader-Maya-dies.html.

Ghorbani, Mégane. 2012. "Mobilisations pour les droits des femmes: capacités d'influence féministe dans la transition politique tunisienne." Master diss., Coopération internationale, action humanitaire et politiques de développement, Université Paris 1 Panthéon-Sorbonne, Paris.

Gilmartin, Christina K. 1995. *Engendering the Chinese Revolution: Radical Women, Communist Politics, and Mass Movements in the 1920s*. Berkeley, CA: University of California Press.

Goldstein, Eric. 2006. "Algeria's amnesia decree." *Open Democracy*. April 9. www.opendemocracy.net/en/algeria_3435jsp/.

Gorman, Brandon. 2017. "The myth of the secular-Islamist divide in Muslim politics: evidence from Tunisia." *Current Sociology* 66 (1): 145–164.

Goulding, Kristine. 2011. "Tunisia: women's winter of discontent." *OpenDemocracy 50.50*. October 25. www.opendemocracy.net/en/5050/tunisia-womens-winter-of-discontent/.

Grami, Amel. 2008. "Gender equality in Tunisia." *British Journal of Middle Eastern Studies* 35 (3): 349–361.

Gray, Doris H. 2012. "Tunisia after the uprising: Islamist and secular quests for women's rights." *Mediterranean Politics* 17 (3): 285–302.

2013. *Beyond Feminism and Islamism: Gender and Equality in North Africa, International Library of African Studies*. London and New York: I. B. Tauris.

Gray, Doris H. and Terry Coonan. 2016. "Reframing Gender Narrative through Transitional Justice in Tunisia." In *Transitional Justice in the*

Middle East and North Africa, edited by Chandra Sriram, 103–122. London: Hurst.

Guenfoudi, Mohammed. 2018. "Where do the Moroccan jihadists come from and who do they affiliate with?" *Moroccan Institute for Policy Analysis*. June 29. https://mipa.institute/5748.

Guerraoui, Saad. 2016. "Sufism in Morocco 'a powerful weapon' against extremism." *The Arab Weekly*. April 1. https://thearabweekly.com/sufism-morocco-powerful-weapon-against-extremism.

Gustafsson, Jenny. 2016. "Has Algeria taken an anti-IS vaccine?" *IRIN*. September 28. www.thenewhumanitarian.org/analysis/2016/09/28/has-algeria-taken-anti-vaccine.

El Hachimi, Mohamed. 2015. "Democratisation as a learning process: the case of Morocco." *The Journal of North African Studies* 20 (5): 754–769.

El Haitami, Meriem. 2012. "Restructuring female religious authority: state-sponsored women religious guides (*murshidat*) and scholars (*ʿalimat*) in contemporary Morocco." *Mediterranean Studies* 20 (2): 227–240.

2014. "Women and Sufism: religious expression and the political sphere in contemporary Morocco." *Mediterranean Studies* 22 (2): 190–212.

Hanafi, Leila, and Danielle Hites. 2017. "Women's rights in Morocco: balancing domestic and international law." *Atlantic Council*. October 12. www.atlanticcouncil.org/blogs/menasource/women-s-rights-in-morocco-balancing-domestic-and-international-law.

Hatem, Mervat Fayez. 1994a. *Privatization and the Demise of State Feminism in Egypt* London: Zed Books.

1994b. "Egyptian gender discourages and political liberalization: do secular and Islamist views really differ?" *Middle East Journal* 48 (4): 661–676.

Hawkins, Simon. 2011. "Who wears *hijab* with the president: constructing a modern Islam in Tunisia." *Journal of Religion in Africa* 41: 35–58.

Hernes, Helga Maria. 1987. *Welfare State and Woman Power: Essays in State Feminism*. Oslo: Norwegian University Press.

Himmelstrand, Ulf. 1960. *Social Pressures, Attitudes and Democratic Processes*. Stockholm: Almqvist & Wiksell.

Honwana, Alcinda Manuel. 2013. *Youth and Revolution in Tunisia*. London and New York: Zed Books.

Htun, Mala, and S. Laurel Weldon. 2018. *The Logics of Gender Justice: State Action on Women's Rights Around the World*. New York: Cambridge University Press.

Huffpost Maroc. 2016. "Abouzaid El Mokrie El Idrissi appelle à une réforme de l'héritage en faveur des femmes." March 21. www.huffpostmaghreb.com/2016/03/21/heritage-maroc-pdj-abouzaid_n_9514726.html.

Hughes, Melanie, and Aili Mari Tripp. 2015. "Civil war and trajectories of change in women's political representation in Africa, 1985–2010." *Social Forces* 93 (4): 1513–1540.

Human Rights Watch (HRW). 2014. "Algeria: bureaucratic ploys used to stifle associations." March 30. www.hrw.org/news/2014/03/30/algeria-bureaucratic-ploys-used-stifle-associations.

2018. "Morocco: new violence against women law." www.hrw.org/news/2018/02/26/morocco-new-violence-against-women-law.

Husseini, Rana. 2016. "Women's rights groups hesitant to celebrate election results." *The Jordan Times*. September 22. http://jordantimes.com/news/local/women%E2%80%99s-rights-groups-hesitant-celebrate-election-results.

Ibnouzahir, Zineb. 2016. "Lalla Salma: plus qu'une femme de style, un symbole d'ouverture du Maroc." *Le Maroc des Femmes*. April 21.

IDEA. 2018. "Gender quotas database: Morocco." Edited by International Institute for Democracy and Electoral Assistance, Stockholm. www.idea.int/data-tools/data/gender-quotas/country-view/200/35.

Inglehart, Ronald, and Pippa Norris. 2003. "The true clash of civilizations." *Foreign Policy* 135: 62–70.

Inter-Parliamentary Union. 1995. "Women in parliaments, 1945–1995." Worldwide Statistical Survey. Geneva: Inter-Parliamentary Union.

Inter-Parliamentary Union. 1997. "Democracy still in the making: a world comparative study." Reports and Documents No. 28. Geneva: Inter-Parliamentary Union.

Inter-Parliamentary Union. 2017. "Algeria – National People's Assembly." https://data.ipu.org/node/3/elections?chamber_id=13314.

Inter-Parliamentary Union. 2018. "Women in national parliaments." http://archive.ipu.org/wmn-e/classif.htm.

Jaber, May Abu. 2015. "Aya Chebbi: redefining feminist narratives in Tunisia." *AWID*. October 23. www.awid.org/news-and-analysis/aya-chebbi-redefining-feminist-narratives-tunisia.

Al Jazeera. 2017. "Morocco bans sale of full-face veil." January 10. www.aljazeera.com/news/2017/01/reports-morocco-bans-production-sale-burqa-170110140716164.html.

Jung, C. G. 1980. *The Archetypes and the Collective Unconscious*, edited by G. Adler and R. F. C. Hull. 2nd ed. Princeton, NJ: Princeton University Press.

Kabbadj, Omar. 2019. "Les tartuferies islamistes du PJD." *Telquel*. January 18. https://telquel.ma/2019/01/18/tartuferies-islamistes_1625769/?utm_source=tq&utm_medium=paid_post.

Kadiri, Mohamed. 2017. *The Evolution of Morocco's Human Rights Movement*. Paris: Arab Reform Initiative.

Kadry, Ahmed. 2013. "The Morsi alliance and the red line drawn for Egypt's women." *Atlantic Council*. November 22. www.atlanticcouncil.org/blogs/menasource/the-morsi-alliance-and-the-red-line-drawn-for-egypt-s-women.

Kamal, Hala. 2015. "Inserting women's rights in the Egyptian constitution: personal reflections." *Journal for Cultural Research* 19 (2): 150–161.

Kang, Alice. 2015. *Bargaining for Women's Rights: Women's Mobilization and Politics in an Aspiring Muslim Democracy*. Minneapolis, MN: University of Minnesota Press.

Karbea, Bothayna. 2009. *Esteqra Alwdea Alrahen Lemosharaket Almarafe Alhayat Alsayasya fe Aljazair wa Almagreb wa Tunis [Induction of Current Status of Women's Participation in Political Life in Algeria, Morocco, and Tunisia]*. Tunis: Manshourat Markez Almara Alarabia Leltadreebwa Albohoth.

Kasraoui, Safaa. 2018. "Inheritance debate and the call for gender equality persist in Morocco." *Morocco World News*. April 8. www.moroccoworldnews.com/2018/04/244028/inheritance-debate-call-gender-equality-persist-morocco/.

Keddie, Nikki R. 2006. *Women in the Middle East: Past and Present*. Princeton, NJ: Princeton University Press.

Kelly, Sanja, and Julia Breslin, eds. 2010. *Women's Rights in the Middle East and North Africa: Progress and Resistance*. New York: Freedom House.

Kenworthy, L., and M. Malami. 1999. "Gender inequality in political representation: a worldwide comparative analysis." *Social Forces* 78 (1): 235–268.

Khalil, Andrea. 2014. *Gender, Women and the Arab Spring*. London: Routledge.

Klatch, Rebecca E. 1988. "Of meanings & masters: political symbolism & symbolic action." *Polity* 21 (1): 137–154.

Koundouno, Tamba François. 2018a. "Study finds a growing trend of single women in Morocco." *Morocco World News*. April 14. www.moroccoworldnews.com/2018/04/244492/study-finds-growing-trend-single-women-morocco/.

2018b. "Morocco's educated women challenge society's norms about sexuality and marriage." *Morocco World News*. June 7. www.moroccoworldnews.com/2018/06/248097/moroccos-educated-women-challenge-societys-norms-sexuality-marriage/.

2019. "Moroccans should focus on MP Maelainine's politics, not her clothes." *Morocco World News*. January 7. www.moroccoworldnews.com/2019/01/262586/morocco-maelainine-politics-pjd/.

Kowalewski, David. 1980. "The protest uses of symbolic politics: the mobilization functions of protestor symbolic resources." *Social Science Quarterly* 61: 93–113.

Labidi, Kamel. 2010. "Tunisia is backtracking on women's rights." *Guardian*. August 25. www.theguardian.com/commentisfree/libertycentral/2010/aug/25/tunisia-backtracking-womens-rights.

Labidi, Lilia. 1998. "Discours féministe et fait islamiste en Tunisie." *Confluences méditerranée* 27: 67–78. www.revues-plurielles.org/_uploads/pdf/9_27_8.pdf.

2017. "Tunisian women's literature of denunciation." In *Women's Activism in Africa: Struggles over Rights and Representation*, edited by Balghis Badri and Aili Mari Tripp, 61–96. Oxford: Zed Books.

Lalami, Feriel. 2012. *Les Algériennes contre le code de la famille. La lutte pour l'égalité*. Paris: Presses de Sciences Po.

2014. "Algérie, pause dans les mobilisations féministes?" *Nouvelles Questions Féministes* 33 (2): 34–42.

Lamlili, Nadia. 2018. "Maroc: Jamila El Moussali, la 'féministe islamiste' du PJD." *Jeune Afrique*. May 7. www.jeuneafrique.com/558087/politique/maroc-jamila-el-moussali-la-feministe-islamiste-du-pjd/.

Langer, Annette. 2018a. "Women in Egypt: harassed, mutilated and disenfranchised. Part 1: violence against women." *Spiegel Online*. March 23. www.spiegel.de/international/tomorrow/almost-every-egyptian-woman-is-subjected-to-sexual-harassment-a-1198328.html.

2018b. "Women in Egypt: harassed, mutilated and disenfranchised. Part III: women's rights in Egypt." *Spiegel Online*. March 23. www.spiegel.de/international/tomorrow/rampant-miscarriages-of-justice-against-women-in-egypt-a-1199327.html.

Larif Béatrix, Asma. 1991. "Changement dans la symbolique du pouvoir en Tunisie." *Annuaire de l'Afrique du Nord* 28: 141–151.

Liebesny, Herbert J. 1972. *The Law of the Near & Middle East: Readings, Cases, & Materials*. Albany, NY: State University of New York Press.

Lindsey, Ursula. 2013. "Islamist movement challenges universities." *Chronicle of Higher Education*. April 1. www.chronicle.com/article/Islamic-Fundamentalists/138183.

2017. "Some gains, many sacrifices: women's rights in Tunisia." *Al-Fanar Media*. July 10. www.al-fanarmedia.org/2017/07/scholars-debate-legacy-state-feminism-chances-overcoming-islamist-secularist-divide/.

Liu, Shan-Jan Sarah. 2018. "Are female political leaders role models? Lessons from Asia." *Political Research Quarterly* 71 (2): 255–269.

Lombardo, Emanuela, and Petra Meier. 2014. *The Symbolic Representation of Gender: A Discursive Approach*. Farnham: Ashgate.

Lukes, Steven. 1975. "Political ritual and social integration." *Sociology* 19 (May): 289–308.

Lynch, Marc. 2013. *The Arab Uprising: The Unfinished Revolutions of the New Middle East*. New York: Public Affair.

ed. 2014. *The Arab Uprisings Explained: New Contentious Politics in the Middle East*. New York: Columbia University Press.

Maktabi, Rania. 2012. "The *politicization* of the *demos* in the Middle East: *citizenship* between *membership* and *participation* in the *state*." Unpublished PhD thesis, Political Science, University of Oslo.

Marks, Monica. 2013. "Women in Tunisian politics: two contrasting perspectives: interviews by Monica Marks with Mehrezia Labidi and Maya Jeribi." *Heinrich Böll Foundation*. May 27. http://tn.boell.org/fr/2014/05/27/women-tunisian-politics-two-contrasting-perspectives-publications.

Maroc Leaks. 2018. "Maroc: #Koun_Rajel, une nouvelle campagne 'anti-nudité'." July 20.

Marzouki, Nadia. 2010. "Algeria." In *Women's Rights in the Middle East and North Africa: Progress Amid Resistance*, edited by Sanja Kelly and Julia Breslin, 29–57. New York and Lanham, MD: Freedom House and Rowman & Littlefield.

Masbah, Mohammed. 2013. "The moderation of Moroccan Salafis since the beginning of the Arab Spring." *SWP Comments* 1. swp-berlin.org/fileadmin/contents/products/comments/2013C01_msb.pdf.

2015. "His majesty's Islamists: the Moroccan experience." *Carnegie Middle East Center*. March 23. carnegie-mec.org/2015/03/23/his-majesty-s-islamists-moroccan-experience-pub-59442.

2016. ردكلة الجهاديين: أقلمة الجهاد والعالمي المحلي وجدلية بالمغرب. PhD thesis, Université Mohammed V, Rabat.

2017. "Morocco's Salafi ex-jihadis: co-optation, engagement, and the limits of inclusion." *Middle East Brief* 108. www.brandeis.edu/crown/publications/meb/meb108.html.

2018a. "Between preaching and activism: how politics divided Morocco's Salafis." *Moroccan Institute for Policy Analysis (MIPA)*. May 13. https://mipa.institute/5615.

2018b. "Rise and endurance: moderate Islamists and electoral politics in the 'Moroccan Spring'." In *Islamists and the Politics of the Arab Uprisings: Governance, Pluralisation and Contention*, edited by Paola Rivetti and Hendrik Kraetzschmar, 127–148. Edinburgh: Edinburgh University Press.

Le Matin. 2018. "Plan gouvernemental de l'égalité." July 22. https://lematin.ma/journal/2018/ad-eddine-el-othmani-plan-ikram-2-meilleur-cadre-convergence-toutes-initiatives-visant-renforcement-droits-femme/297616.html.

Mayer, Ann Elizabeth 1995. "Reform of personal status laws in North Africa: a problem of Islamic or Mediterranean laws?" *Middle East Journal* 49 (3): 432–446.

McCarthy, Rory. 2018. *Inside Tunisia's al-Nahda: Between Politics and Preaching*, Cambridge Middle East Studies. Cambridge: Cambridge University Press.

McNeill, S. T. 2012. "Wording on women sparks protest in Tunisia." *Al-Jazeera*. August 19. www.aljazeera.com/indepth/features/2012/08/201281981854620325.html.

Media Line News Agency. 2009. "Algerian woman becomes country's first female general." *Media Line News Agency*. July 9.

Medias24. 2018. "Condition de la femme: Lalla Meryem suggère d'adresser un mémorandum au Roi Mohammed VI." March 8. www.medias24.com/MAROC/SOCIETE/181033-Vers-un-memorandum-sur-la-situation-de-la-femme-et-de-l-enfant-au-Maroc.html.

Meddi, Adiène. 2015. "Is impunity the cost of peace in Algeria?" *Middle East Eye*. October 5. www.middleeasteye.net/news/impunity-cost-peace-algeria.

Meko, Tim. 2018. "Now that the Islamic State has fallen in Iraq and Syria, where are all its fighters going?" *Washington Post*. February 22. www.washingtonpost.com/graphics/2018/world/isis-returning-fighters/.

Mekouar, Hamza. 2017. "Moroccan cleric defies taboo on women's inheritance." *Arab News*. May 6. www.arabnews.pk/node/1095266/middle-east.

Merolla, Daniela. 2001. "Questioning gender, nationalism and ethnicity in the Maghreb: voices of women in the Kabyle literary space." *Race, Gender & Class* 8 (3): 70–101.

Mersch, Sarah. 2014. "Tunisia's compromise constitution." *Cairo Review of Global Affairs*. January 27. www.thecairoreview.com/tahrir-forum/tunisias-compromise-constitution/.

Messahel, Abdelkader. 2018. "What the world can learn from Algeria's anti-extremism strategy." *The Local*. May 16.

Messaoudi, Khalida. 1995. *Une algérienne debout: entretiens avec Elisabeth Schemla*. Paris: Flammarion.

Middle East Eye. 2016. "Ennahda leader Ghannouchi: 'we are Muslim democrats, not Islamists'." May 19. www.middleeasteye.net/news/ennahda-leader-ghannouchi-we-are-muslim-democrats-not-islamists.

Ministère de la Culture et de la Communication, Royaume de Maroc. 2014. "Mme Hakkaoui: le Maroc est un pays pionnier dans le monde arabe en matière de promotion des droits de la femme." March 3. www.maroc.ma/fr/actualites/mme-hakkaoui-le-maroc-est-un-pays-pionnier-dans-le-monde-arabe-en-matiere-de-promotion.

2016. "HM the king chairs first religious lecture of Ramadan." June 9. www.maroc.ma/en/royal-activities/hm-king-chairs-first-religious-lecture-ramadan.

Moghadam, Valentine M. 2017. "Feminist movements in the Maghreb." In *Women's Movements in the Global Era: The Power of Local Feminisms*, edited by Amrita Basu, 333–360. Boulder, CO: Westview Press.

Mohsen-Finan, Khadija. 2013. "Changement de cap et transition politique au Maroc et en Tunisie." *Pouvoirs* 145: 105–121.

Monjib, Maâti. 2011. "The 'democratization' process in Morocco: progress, obstacles, and the impact of the Islamist-secularist divide." Saban Center Working Paper. Washington, DC: Brookings Institution.

Montenegro, Robert. 2014. "Algeria promotes more female military officials than any other Arab country." *Big Think*. July 14. https://bigthink.com/ideafeed/algeria-female-generals.

Moroccan American Center for Policy. 2013. "Morocco fights radicalism: raising a new generation of Islamic scholars, advocates." *Morocco on the Move*. June 28. https://moroccoonthemove.com/2013/06/28/moroccos-fight-against-radicalism-raising-a-new-generation-of-islamic-scholars-advocates-macp/.

Moussaoui, Abderrahmane. 2004. "La politique de l'injure. Une décennie meurtrière en Algérie." *Revue des mondes musulmans de la Méditerranée* 103–104: 165–179.

Murphy, Emma C. 2003. "Women in Tunisia: between state feminism and economic reform." In *Women and Globalization in the Arab Middle East: Gender, Economy, and Society*, edited by E. A. Doumato and M. P. Posusney, 169–193. Boulder, CO: Lynne Rienner.

Naaim, El Houssaine. 2015. "Amazigh civilization: a lesson in how to treat women." *Morocco World News*. February 2. www.moroccoworldnews.com/2015/02/149995/amazigh-civilization-lesson-treat-women/.

Naciri, Rabéa. 1998. "The women's movement and political discourse in Morocco." UNRIS Occasional Paper 8. Geneva, Switzerland: United Nations Research Institute for Social Development, United Nations Development Programme.

The National. 2018. "Egypt's Sisi targets women's vote in presidential re-election campaign." March 3. www.thenational.ae/world/mena/egypt-s-sisi-targets-women-s-vote-in-presidential-re-election-campaign-1.709597.

Nazra for Feminist Studies. 2014. "First verdict in cases of mob-sexual assault and gang rape in Tahrir Square is no end to the story; all previous crimes of sexual violence must be investigated: Joint Statement." July 19. https://nazra.org/en/2014/07/first-verdict-cases-mob-sexual-assault-and-gang-rape-tahrir-square-no-end-story.

The New Arab. 2017. "Feminising the Ma'zoon: Morocco allows women to officiate marriages." September 6. www.alaraby.co.uk/english/society/2017/9/6/feminising-the-mazoon-morocco-allows-women-to-officiate-marriages.

Norbakk, Mari. 2016. "The women's rights champion. Tunisia's potential for furthering women's rights." *CMI*. www.cmi.no/publications/5973-the-womens-rights-champion.

Oldfield, Sophie, Elaine Salo, and Ann Schlyter. 2009. "Body politics and the gendered crafting of citizenship." *Feminist Africa* 13: special issue "Body Politics and Citizenship": 1–10.

Olimat, Muhamad S., ed. 2013. *Arab Spring and Arab Women: Challenges and Opportunities*. New York: Routledge.

Osman, Hibaaq. 2017. "Laws that allow rapists to marry their victims come from colonialism, not Islam." *Independent*. August 2. www.independent.co.uk/voices/rape-conviction-laws-marry-rapist-jordan-egypt-morocco-tunisia-came-from-french-colonial-times-a7872556.html.

Ottaway, David. 2012. "Algeria's Islamists Crushed in First Arab Spring Elections." Woodrow Wilson International Center for Scholars, Washington, DC: Middle East Program. Viewpoints No. 3.

Oulahbib, Lucien-Samir. 2016. "Nationalisme arabe et islamisme, les deux faces d'une même médaille." *Mondesfrancophone.com: revue mondiale des francophonies*. https://mondesfrancophones.com/espaces/politiques/nationalisme-arabe-et-islamisme-les-deux-faces-d%e2%80%99une-meme-medaille/.

Patai, Raphael. 1965. "The structure of endogamous unilineal descent groups." *Southwestern Journal of Anthropology* 21 (Winter): 325–350.

Pew Research Center. 2013. *The World's Muslims: Religion, Politics and Society*. Washington, DC: Pew Research Center.

Popenoe, Rebecca. 2004. *Feeding Desire: Fatness, Beauty, and Sexuality Among a Saharan People*. London: Routledge.

Rabil, Robert. 2015. "Salafism in Lebanon." *The Washington Institute*. February 20. www.washingtoninstitute.org/policy-analysis/view/salafism-in-lebanon.

Rachidi, Ilhem. 2007. "New law leaves divorced Algerian women homeless." *Women's E-News*. November 7. https://womensenews.org/2007/03/new-law-leaves-divorced-algerian-women-homeless/.

Racioppi, Linda, and Katherine O'Sullivan See. 1995. "The 'woman question' and national identity: Soviet and post-Soviet Russia." In *The Women and International Development Annual*, edited by R. S. Gallin, A. Ferguson, and J. Harper, 73–202. Boulder, CO: Westview Press.

Rahmouni, Zahra. 2018. "Algérie: elle voulait faire son footing, il la frappe et lui dit que « sa place est dans une cuisine." *Jeune Afrique*. June 11. www.jeuneafrique.com/575731/societe/algerie-elle-voulait-faire-son-footing-il-la-frappe-et-lui-dit-que-sa-place-est-dans-une-cuisine/.

Rausch, Margaret. 2006. "Ishelhin women transmitters of Islamic knowledge and culture in southwestern Morocco." *Journal of North African Studies* 11: 173–192.

Reischer, Erica, and Kathryn S. Koo. 2004. "The body beautiful: symbolism and agency in the social world." *Annual Review of Anthropology* 33: 297–317.

Rizzo, Helen, Abdel-Hamid Abdel-Latif, and Katherine Meyer. 2007. "The relationship between gender equality and democracy: a comparison of Arab versus non-Arab Muslim societies." *Sociology* 41 (6): 1151–1170.

Roberts, Adam, Michael J. Willis, Rory McCarthy, and Timothy Garton Ash, eds. 2016. *Civil Resistance in the Arab Spring: Triumphs and Disasters*. Oxford: Oxford University Press.

Roberts, Hugh. 1988. "Radical Islamism and the dilemma of Algerian nationalism: the embattled Arians of Algiers." *Third World Quarterly* 10 (2): 556–589.

Rosen, Jennifer. 2012. "Effects of political institutions on women's political representation: a comparative analysis of 168 countries from 1992 to 2010." *Political Research Quarterly* 66 (2): 306–321.

Ross, Michael. 2008. "Oil, Islam, and women." *American Political Science Review* 102 (1): 107–123.

Sabra, Martina. 2012. "Interview with the Algerian women's rights activist Nadia Ait Zai: 'We need to completely change the system of government'." *Qantara.de*. June 14. https://en.qantara.de/content/interview-with-the-algerian-womens-rights-activist-nadia-ait-zai-we-need-to-completely.

Sadiqi, Fatima. 2017. "The Moroccan feminist movement (1946–2014)." In *Women's Activism in Africa: Struggles over Rights and Representation*, edited by Balghis Badri and Aili Mari Tripp, 97–120. Oxford: Zed Publishers.

Sadiqi, Fatima, and Moha Ennaji. 2006. "The feminization of public space: women's activism, the family law, and social change in Morocco." *Journal of Middle East Women's Studies* 2 (2): 86–114.

2011. *Women in the Middle East and North Africa: Agents of Change*. New York: Routledge.

Salhi, Zahia Smail. 2010. "The Algerian feminist movement between nationalism, patriarchy and Islamism." *Women's Studies International Forum* 33: 113–124.

2011. "Gender and violence in Algeria: women's resistance against the Islamist femicide." Public lecture, University of Leeds, 31 January.

Salime, Zakia. 2011. *Between Feminism and Islam: Human Rights and Sharia Law in Morocco*. Minneapolis, MN: University of Minnesota Press.

2012. "A new feminism? Gender dynamics in Morocco's February 20th movement." *Journal of International Women's Studies* 13 (5): 101–114.

Sandberg, Eve Nan, and Kenza Aqertit. 2014. *Moroccan Women, Activists, and Gender Politics: An Institutional Analysis*. Lanham, MD: Lexington Books.

Sater, James. 2012. "Reserved seats, patriarchy, and patronage in Morocco." In *The Impact of Gender Quotas*, edited by Susan Franceschet, Mona Lena Krook, and Jennifer Piscopo, 72–86. New York: Oxford University Press.

Sengupta, Somini. 2017. "On Europe's far right, female leaders look to female voters." *New York Times*. March 2. www.nytimes.com/2017/03/02/world/europe/political-strategy-for-europes-far-right-female-leaders-wooing-female-voters.html.

Sharia Source. 2016. "The dissolution of Sharīʿa in the 1965 Moroccan court unification law." December 16. https://shariasource.blog/2016/12/16/the-dissolution-of-shari%ca%bfa-in-the-1965-moroccan-court-unification-law/.

Sharkey, Heather J. 2014. "Review: Benrabah Mohamed's *Language Conflict in Algeria: From Colonialism to Post-Independence*." *Journal of French Language Studies* 24 (2): 317–318.

Shukrallah, Salma. 2011. "10,000 Egyptian women march against military violence and rule." *Ahram Online*. December 20. http://english.ahram.org.eg/NewsContent/1/64/29824/Egypt/Politics-/,-Egyptian-women-march-against-military-violence-a.aspx.

Sika, Nadine, and Yasmin Khodary. 2012. "One step forward, two steps back? Egyptian women within the confines of authoritarianism." *Journal of International Women's Studies* 13 (5): 91–100.

Singh, Susheela, Lisa Remez, Gilda Sedgh, Lorraine Kwokand, and Tsuyoshi Onda. 2017. "Abortion worldwide 2017: uneven progress and unequal access." Guttmacher Institute. www.guttmacher.org/report/abortion-worldwide-2017.

Le Site Info. 2018. "Maroc: la riposte a la campagne contre la nudité des femmes." July 20. www.lesiteinfo.com/maroc/maroc-la-riposte-a-la-campagne-contre-la-nudite-des-femmes/.

Slimani, Leïla. 2017. *Sexe et mensonges: la vie sexuelle au Maroc*. Paris: Les Arènes.

Sonneveld, Nadia. 2012. *Khulʿ Divorce in Egypt: Public Debates, Judicial Practices, and Everyday Life*. Cairo and New York: The American University in Cairo Press.

Spiegel, Avi. 2015. *Young Islam: The New Politics of Religion in Morocco and the Arab World*. Princeton Studies in Muslim Politics. Princeton, NJ: Princeton University Press.

Staton, Bethan. 2016. "Jordan's women fight for political representation." *Al Jazeera*. March 8. www.aljazeera.com/news/2016/03/jordan-women-fight-political-representation-160306101829565.html.

Stephan, Rita. 2009. "The family and the making of women's rights activism in Lebanon." Unpublished PhD thesis, Sociology, University of Texas, Austin.

Stephan, Rita, and Mounira M. Charrad. forthcoming. *Women Rising: Resistance, Revolution and Reform in the Arab Spring and Beyond*. New York: New York University Press.

Stora, Benjamin. 1991. *La gangrène et l'oubli: la mémoire de la guerre d'Algérie*. Paris: La Découverte.

Storm, Lise. 2007. *Democratization in Morocco: The Political Elite and Struggles for Power in the Post-Independence State*. Oxford: Routledge.

Tabet, Marie-Christine. 2017. "Religion, famille, société: qui sont vraiment les musulmans de France." *Le Journal du Dimanche*. June 21. www.lejdd.fr/Societe/Religion/Religion-famille-societe-qui-sont-vraiment-les-musulmans-de-France-810217.

Tahri, Rachida. 2003. "Women's political participation: the case of Morocco." Paper presented at the International Institute for Democracy and Electoral Assistance (IDEA)/Electoral Institute of Southern Africa (EISA)/Southern African Development Community (SADC) Parliamentary Forum Conference The Implementation of Quotas: African Experiences Pretoria, South Africa, November 11–12.

Tchaïcha, Jane. D., and Khedija Arfaoui. 2012. "Tunisian women in the twenty-first century: past achievements and present uncertainties in the wake of the Jasmine Revolution." *The Journal of North African Studies* 17 (2): 215–238.

Terem, Etty. 2014. *Old Texts, New Practices: Islamic Reform in Modern Morocco*. Stanford, CA: Stanford University Press.

Tillion, Germaine. 1966. *Le Harem et les cousins*. Paris: Éditions du Seuil.

Toumi, Habib. 2018. "Saudi Arabia could soon appoint women as judges." *Gulf News*. August 6. https://gulfnews.com/world/gulf/saudi/saudi-arabia-could-soon-appoint-women-as-judges-1.2262252.

Tripp, Aili Mari. 2013. "Regime type and gender." In *Oxford Handbook on Gender and Politics*, edited by Georgina Waylen, Karen Celis,

Johanna Kantola, and Laurel Weldon, 514–535. Oxford: Oxford University Press.

2015. *Women and Power in Postconflict Africa*. Cambridge Studies in Gender and Politics. New York: Cambridge University Press.

Tripp, Aili Mari, and Alice Kang. 2008. "The global impact of quotas: on the fast track to increased female legislative representation." *Comparative Political Studies* 41 (3): 338–361.

Turner, Victor. 1982. *From Ritual to Theatre: The Human Seriousness of Play*. New York: Performing Arts Journal Publications.

United Nations High Commissioner for Refugees (UNHCR). 2014. "Background note on gender equality, nationality laws and statelessness." www.unhcr.org/protection/statelessness/4f5886306/background-note-gender-equality-nationality-laws-statelessness-2014.html.

United Nations Population Fund (UNFPA). 2017. "Worlds apart: reproductive health and rights in an age of inequality: state of world population report 2017." https://esaro.unfpa.org/en/publications/worlds-apart-reproductive-health-and-rights-age-inequality.

UN Women. 2017. "Tunisia passes historic law to end violence against women and girls." August 10. www.unwomen.org/en/news/stories/2017/8/news-tunisia-law-on-ending-violence-against-women.

2018. "Land rights at last for Sulaliyyate women in Morocco." August 29. www.unwomen.org/en/news/stories/2018/8/feature-land-rights-at-last-for-sulaliyyate-women-in-morocco.

USAID. 2019. "Election guide: democracy assistance and elections news." www.electionguide.org/elections/id/3047/.

US Department of State. 2018. "2017 country reports on human rights practices." April 20. www.state.gov/j/drl/rls/hrrpt/2017/nea/277249.htm.

Verduzier, Pauline. 2015. "En Algérie, une campagne incite les hommes à voiler leur femme pour être plus virils." *Le Figaro*. May 26. http://madame.lefigaro.fr/societe/sois-un-homme-la-campagne-anti-jupe-qui-agace-lalgerie-260515-96699.

Voorhoeven, Maaike. 2013. "Tunisia: protecting Ben Ali's feminist legacy." *Think Africa Press*. January 31. https://thinkafricapress.com/future-state-feminism/.

Wadowiec, Jamie. 2013. "Muslim Algerian women and the rights of man: Islam and gendered citizenship in French Algeria at the end of empire." *French Historical Studies* 36 (4): 649–674.

Wainscott, Ann Marie. 2018. *Bureaucratizing Islam: Morocco and the War on Terror*. New York: Cambridge University Press.

Warrick, Catherine. 2009. *Law in the Service of Legitimacy: Gender and Politics in Jordan*. Abingdon-on-Thames: Routledge.

Wegner, Eva, and Miquel Pellicer. 2009. "Islamist moderation without democratization: the coming of age of the Moroccan Party of Justice and Development?" *Democratization* 16 (1): 157–175.

Welborne, Bozena Chrisina. 2010. "The strategic use of gender quotas in the Arab world." William and Kathy Hybl Democracy Studies Fellowship Paper, IFES Fellowship in Democracy Studies. Washington, DC: IFES.

Willis, Michael. 1996. *The Islamist Challenge in Algeria: A Political History*. Washington Square, NY: New York University Press.

Willis, Michael J. 1999. "Between alternance and the Makhzen: At-Tawhid wa Al-Islah's entry into Moroccan politics." *The Journal of North African Studies* 4 (3): 45–80.

2002. "Political parties in the Maghrib: ideology and identification. A suggested typology." *Journal of North African Studies* 7 (3): 1–28.

2014. *Politics and Power in the Maghreb: Algeria, Tunisia and Morocco from Independence to the Arab Spring*. New York: Columbia University Press.

World Bank. 2015. "Morocco – mind the gap: empowering women for a more open, inclusive and prosperous society." https://doi.org/10.1596/24004.

2018. "Women, business and the law 2018." March 29. www.worldbank.org/en/news/video/2018/03/29/women-business-and-the-law-2018.

World Economic Forum. 2018. "Global gender gap report 2018." December 17. www.weforum.org/reports/the-global-gender-gap-report-2018.

Zeghal, Malika. 2005. *Les Islamistes marocains le défi au monarchie* Paris: Éditions La Découverte.

Ziou Ziou, Aziza. 2015. "Le personnage de Châaibia, un féminisme new âge." *Qandisha*. March 8.

Zunqat 20. 2018. "Video 'Amzazi' the new Minister of Education entangled in the first exam before the king!" January 22.

Index